Comparative & International Library Science

edited by

JOHN F. HARVEY

The Scarecrow Press, Inc.
Metuchen, N.J. & London
1977

Library of Congress Cataloging in Publication Data
Main entry under title:

Comparative and international library science.

   Includes index.
   1. Comparative librarianship--Addresses, essays,
lectures. 2. International librarianship--Addresses,
essays, lectures. I. Harvey, John Fredrick, 1921-
Z665.C7455   020'.8   77-8923
ISBN 0-8108-1060-3

CONTENTS

iii

INTRODUCTION

John F. Harvey

Interest and thought in comparative and international library science seem to have increased in recent years. Some evidence, at least, exists to suggest that this is so. I attempted to trace the growth of interest in these fields in several ways. In their recent and well-known volumes, both Danton and Simsova commented on the rise of interest in these fields. [1,2] Danton carefully traced librarians' interest in international activities as it has developed during several decades of the twentieth century. In citing the sharp increase in the number of library school courses taught in these fields, the Boaz paper in this book provides strong evidence of change.

An increase also seems to have occurred in the number of theses relating to the comparative and international areas which are being produced in American library schools. A rough count in Library Literature indicated limited interest in the 1960s but a surprising increase in interest in the 1970s. Presumably, this reflected the increase in the course work offered in these fields. It must be pointed out, however, that many of these internationally related theses were bibliographies or histories, likely to have relatively modest impact on the policies or practices of library service.

Library Literature's international subject entries were examined for papers published on these subjects in the last decade and a half. The assumption was made that an increase in interest in these fields could be measured quantitatively in the number of papers published and indexed therein. Of course, Library Literature covers primarily the English-speaking library world and leaves other worlds to other indexing services. Since 1967, the number of articles indexed in these two fields in Library Literature has been approximately constant. However, if we compare the late 1960s and 1970s to 1963, then yes, there is a considerable increase in indexed publications by the late 1960s.

In the past decade, several new journals have come on the scene to make significant contributions in these fields. They in-

---

[1] Danton, J. Periam. The Dimensions of Comparative Librarianship. Chicago: American Library Association, 1973, pp. 1-6.

[2] Simsova, Silva and MacKee, M. A Handbook of Comparative Librarianship. Hamden, Conn.: The Shoe String Press, 1975, pp. 8, 11-13.

clude such titles as International Library Review, Focus on International and Comparative Librarianship, and the IFLA Journal. Other new journals, such as International Cataloging, INSPEL, and the Journal of the International Agricultural Librarians, cover more specialized fields but should make useful contributions, also. The number of overseas and international journals indexed in Library Literature has increased in recent years.

Several other evidences of increased interest must be recognized. Undoubtedly, an increase in travel and communication in the past two decades has brought the world library community closer together. Some of this travel has involved visits to local libraries of other countries. There is no shortage of articles which reflect these tours. In addition, the library and information activities of UNESCO, FID, IFLA and other information organizations has increased, and such organizations are now the center of much attention in the international library world. Council on Library Resources subsidies for the International Federation of Library Associations have greatly augmented the activities of that organization. Its current journal, constitutional revision, and increasing conference attendance suggest its current upswing. Though the American Library Association's International Relations Round Table seems to have reached a membership plateau, the membership of The British Library Association's International and Comparative Librarianship Section has grown recently.

Apparently, an increase has occurred in the number of nations with a strong interest in well developed libraries. In certain developing countries, library science has moved ahead strongly in the last two decades, to the point where it is of sufficient breadth and quality to be interesting to librarians in other countries. Some of this activity can be seen in connection with UNISIST and IFLA.

A final bit of evidence can be presented. All persons interested in comparative and international library science should take heart at the need for a second edition of the Simsova and MacKee volume. For a library science book to go into a second edition is still relatively unusual, so it is heartening to know that these fields are of sufficient interest to students and librarians that Simsova and MacKee is required in a second edition only five years after the first was published.

The growth described above has occurred primarily in the field of international library science; progress in the field of comparative library science has not kept pace. The useful literature of the latter research field remains extremely sparse, and, as Danton points out, much that passes for comparative library literature is not! We have a number of volumes in which both comparative and international library science are treated; for instance, Simsova and MacKee, but very few volumes which are devoted primarily to comparative library science.

As a matter of fact, there seems to be very little research

in either comparative or international library science. Much jour-
nalistic writing exists about international library matters, but very
little that can be called research. Of course, this is true of many
other library science fields as well. While there is some indication
of rising interest in comparative and international library science,
both fields are in their infancy. Research and mature thought have
hardly begun.

The two subjects, comparative library science and international library science, have been combined in the present book because they are very closely related in the minds of librarians
throughout the world. The phrase is normally tripped off the tongue
as a whole, "comparative and international library science," although, clearly, the "and" in the middle shows two discrete subjects
to be covered here. Not enough literature is available in comparative library science to warrant a collection of papers such as appear
in this volume. A vast majority of this book's material relates
primarily to international rather than to comparative library science.

The purpose of this collection of papers is to describe and
assess significant recent progress in comparative and international
library science. To a considerable extent, this is a set of state-
of-the-art papers in two fields which are just beginning to develop
and be recognized. This book should form an early and relatively
comprehensive description and assessment of these fields. It is intended to emphasize significant and scholarly work, not the bulk of
available material. It emphasizes assessment, not mere description,
of the significant literature.

The book attempts to cover all of the major subject fields of
library science--e. g. , children's library science--and closely related fields, such as audio-visual media. It is limited by the lack
of intellectual development of the field, lack of useful and significant
research, and lack of understanding and comparison of the library
science in other countries.

The book's parameters are limited by the editor's failure to
obtain papers in the six areas of Library Literature, Special Library
Science, Archives Studies, Law Library Science, University Library
Science, and an Introduction to the International Dispersion of Library Science Ideas. In certain cases, no author could be located,
even after much correspondence, and in other cases, the authors
chosen failed to complete their manuscripts.

This introduction will not attempt to duplicate Danton's chapter on definitions, merely to support it. I agree with Danton's
statements. It should be pointed out that I regard the words <u>library</u>
<u>science</u> and <u>librarianship</u> as meaning the same thing. To some li-
brarians, however, library science seems to refer to the field as
a scholarly discipline while librarianship refers to its practice. Because of this popular distinction, I prefer to use library science to
librarianship in this book, but a few of the authors herein insisted

on the more traditional word, librarianship. Otherwise, the definitions used here are those which are standard in library science generally.

Each author received a letter from the editor which asked him
or her to write the paper, stressed the difference between comparative
and international library science, and enclosed a detailed and suggested
outline of the paper. Each author was asked that the paper be pitched
at a high level of professional sophistication. In certain cases, there
was some correspondence about the paper and modification of it. The
authors were chosen for their knowledge of specific chapter subject
fields, and I feel very fortunate to have been able to persuade such a
group of leading scholars to become contributors. A revised and edited
draft was sent to each chapter author for final approval before publication. The editor prepared the index at the end of the book.

Anthony Thompson's paper was not included in the original
book outline. Thompson was asked to write a paper on another subject, but declined and asked if he could write one on the language
problems of these fields.

Why should anyone encourage use of the comparative research
technique in library science? Why should anyone study international
library science? Several arguments may be presented, but regrettably, few writers have sought to argue persuasively on these subjects, although both Simsova and Danton have mentioned these questions.

Similarities and differences between the libraries being
studied will highlight comparison. No other research method can
stress comparisons as well. It provides an alternate technique for
analyzing library policies and practices, one now seldom used. It
can be used successfully in conjunction with other research methods,
indeed, should be used in this way to achieve greater understanding
of the subject. This method enables the researcher to manipulate
the evidence in different ways to reveal facets of it which would not
otherwise be seen and understood.

When comparison of two sets of ideas or facts is needed, the
comparative research technique which Simsova describes is well
adapted to that task. Such a comparison enables the researcher to
assess his primary set of data in a larger framework. Such inten-
sive comparisons are not now possible with other research methods.
While library science is generally much under-researched, the comparative analysis research technique has been used very seldom and
yet gives promise of helpfulness.

Arguments for the study of international library science are
different. Many ideas are being used elsewhere in the world which
can be useful to other local librarians, and providing them with information about these ideas is a useful service. Such ideas are
helpful primarily to persons working in the same subject field. For
example, the person who will profit most from knowing about work
elsewhere in the art library field will be the local art librarian.

New international efforts are increasingly influential on local activities as knowledge of them becomes more widespread. Spreading such knowledge is a useful function. As library science improves in developing countries, librarians in developed countries are enriched. At the present time, however, international library science may often be of greater usefulness to developing nations since some of them still have more to learn about ideas and techniques than is true of the developed countries. To the extent that each nation presents unique ideas in developing service patterns, these ideas are useful for all to know.

A segment of the library world not previously covered well in national and local library literature is being referred to here. Just as British public library science needs to be described and studied carefully for British librarians, so we need to learn and understand the ways in which British and Brazilian public libraries, for example, are alike and different, so that each one can gain ideas and perspective from the information made available. The relationship of libraries in different countries, such as Canadian National Library use of a West German computer program, is relevant here. The same generalization is true for all other kinds of libraries and nations. Providing this information is a useful and desirable function which needs to be enlarged and extended.

An aspect of international library science deals with the activities of international libraries and organizations, such as the U.N. and the UNESCO libraries in New York, Geneva, and Paris, and IFLA and FID in The Hague. These are not national but international library activities and naturally should be studied in international library science. The study of these ideas and policies is just as desirable as is the study of British and Brazilian libraries. Development of the literature dealing with these libraries, associations and relationships is necessary to make their activities better known. Development of research on these activities is essential if they are to be better understood.

Acknowledgments. --The editor would like to thank each one of the chapter authors individually and collectively for their important contributions to this work. The editor's secretaries, Betty Warta and Carolyn Camputaro, as well as Hofstra University and Lyndon State College, must be thanked for significant contributions.

PART I

DEFINITIONS AND RESEARCH

DEFINITIONS OF COMPARATIVE AND INTERNATIONAL LIBRARY SCIENCE

J. Periam Danton

The audience to which this volume is primarily addressed no doubt requires little if any justification for a paper on definitions and terminology. Nonetheless, a few brief comments by way of introduction may be useful.

It is commonly recognized that great confusion has existed as to what comparative and international librarianship are and what the difference between them is. * It is well-known that numerous conflicting, and often internally self-contradictory views and definitions have appeared in print. 1 It seems reasonable to infer that one of the deterrents, though hardly the most crucial one, to the advancement of comparative, if not of international librarianship, has been this confusion and conflict. Finally, it is worth noting that the phrase "comparative librarianship" is included in none of the more than twenty glossaries and dictionaries of library terms, although "international librarianship" appears in several.

A volume published in 1973 undertook, among other topics, a comprehensive discussion and critique of all definitions and discussions of comparative and international librarianship published up to fall, 1972. A large number of representative views regarding comparative and international work in related disciplines, such as education, sociology, and political science, was included. 2 As that work is widely available, it seems wholly unnecessary to review the literature published before 1972, or to reproduce the argumentation that resulted in proposed definitions of comparative and international librarianship. The conclusions and definitions, however, are given here for reference and as a basis for discussion of later publications. **

A study in comparative librarianship must include: 1) a cross-societal, or cross-cultural element, which does <u>not</u> neces-

---

*Dislike of the phrase "library science" leads the writer to use the synonym "librarianship" throughout this paper, except, of course, in the case of direct quotations.

**It happens that a number of relevant publications appeared between late 1972 and early 1974. Presumably they were written at approximately the same time, since their authors were not familiar with each other's work. These publications are included here.

sarily mean a cross-country/cross-national element; 2) actual comparisons, which are more than simply the juxtaposition of like data
from the two or more societies being studied; and 3) explanation, or
at least discussion, of the observed similarities and differences. A
work on the public libraries of Denmark, no matter by whom, or
how well prosecuted, is not a comparative study so long as the public libraries of no other society are included. On the other hand,
a study of the cantonal libraries of Switzerland may be comparative
inasmuch as these libraries have been influenced by the quite differing French, German, and Italian elements and cultures of the country.

        Points 2 and 3 above are also so cardinal as to suggest
elaboration.   The goal of the comparativist is analysis of the phenomena he observes in order to try to determine not how things
are, but why.   His task, therefore, is not the making of descriptive
studies, however useful or necessary they may be as steps toward
the end product.   So even though the data from descriptive, case,
area, or other studies are placed in juxtaposition, the result falls
short of being a comparative study until or unless the patterns, the
similarities and differences that the two sets of data are made to
reveal are analyzed and their probable causes determined.   Thus a
work on the university libraries of Belgium, Germany and Holland,
describing seriatim and tabulating their services and resources, is
not a comparative study so long as no comparisons are made.   Noah
and Eckstein make the point thus:

          The scholar who collects data on, say, teacher training
          practices for European secondary education, arranges them
          in convenient categories, discusses the validity of the cate-
          gories and the reliability of the information, and goes no
          further, is stopping just at the point where comparative
          investigation begins. [3]

        Studies in comparative librarianship are defined as: "analy-
ses of libraries, library systems, some aspect of librarianship, or
library problems in two or more national, cultural, or societal environments, in terms of socio-political, economic, cultural, ideological, and historical contexts.   These analyses are made for the
purpose of understanding the underlying similarities and differences
and for determining explanations of the differences, with the ultimate aim of trying to arrive at valid generalizations and principles. "[4]

        Kaser has suggested the possibility "of substituting 'or' for
'and' as the antepenultimate word in the first sentence. "[5] As the
historical context can seldom be ignored, the substitution of "or/
and" seems preferable.

        It is essential to make a distinction between the subject or
field of comparative librarianship as a total complex, on the one
hand, and comparative studies in librarianship on the other.   The
subject embraces the teaching of comparative librarianship; area and

case studies of different societies; the collection and use of data about libraries or aspects of libraries in other countries; and the study of library development, practices, problems and the like in different countries. In short, it includes many publications which are potentially capable of contributing to comparative studies, but which are not, themselves, such studies.

The word "international," like the word "comparative," is well-known in other fields, as shown by the common phrases "international education," "international government," and "international law." Like librarianship, until quite recently some disciplines often used the terms "comparative" and "international" synonymously. There is a difference between the two, however, and it is important that that difference be understood and recognized. The difference is pointed up if one considers the activities and responsibilities of the American Library Association's International Relations Committee, International Relations Office, and International Relations Round Table, on the one hand, and on the other, the study by Jean Hassenforder, Développement Comparé des Bibliothèques Publiques en France, Grande-Bretagne et aux Etats-Unis dans la Seconde Moitié du XIXe Siècle (1850-1914) (Paris: Cercle de la Librairie, 1967), or Frank M. Gardner's Public Library Legislation: A Comparative Study (Paris: UNESCO, 1971).

The three ALA groups referred to above are engaged in a large number of activities related to various aspects of librarianship in foreign countries, but they are not engaged in any work that is comparative. Hassenforder's and Gardner's studies are comparative works.

Paraphrasing and modifying somewhat a definition of international education suggested by Fraser and Brickman, the following definition was offered:

> International librarianship connotes the various kinds of relationships--intellectual, cultural, and educational-- among individuals and groups from two or more nations. It is a dynamic concept in that it involves a movement across frontiers, whether by a person, book, or idea. International librarianship refers to the various methods and practices of international cooperation, understanding, and exchange. Thus, the exchange of teachers and students, aid to underdeveloped countries, and teaching about foreign library systems all fall within the scope of this term. [6]

Comparative librarianship, and occasionally international librarianship as well, occupy an intellectual territory where certain other disciplines--chiefly those of the social sciences, but also sometimes the humanities, librarianship itself, and a cross-societal or cross-national dimension--intersect.

Attention may now be paid to the most recent definitional and

terminological statements, proposals, and arguments.   Some of them
attest to the continuing ambiguity and confusion regarding "comparative" and "international" librarianship.   Chandler, for example,
makes this comment: "H. C. Campbell is an excellent example [of
comparative librarianship] in his international studies of metropolitan library systems.   Yet Danton would not consider these to be
comparative.   Similarly he rejects K. C. Harrison's book on Scandinavian Libraries. "[7,8,9] Considerable pains were taken to under-
score the fact that the deservedly praised works by Harrison and
Campbell were important and useful contributions in areas that had
not previously been treated. [10] Neither, however is a comparative
study, simply because hardly any of the data and findings are directly compared, country with country.   Campbell, in fact, notes in his
Introduction that "most of the material in this book is descriptive"
and that "attempts have been made only occasionally to compare one
metropolitan area with another. "[11]

     If we are to achieve a common understanding in discussing
our problems, programs, and publications, it is important, indeed
it is essential, that we use concepts and terminology with precision.
It is, then, a serious disservice if we describe something as "comparative" when it is not comparative at all, but purely descriptive.
Later in his "Editorial" Chandler says, "surely ... comparative librarianship must include all studies which involve two cultures...."[12]
This is unarguably true if the statement means that all studies involving two cultures belong to the subject of comparative librarianship, but it is incorrect if it means that all publications belonging to
the subject are comparative studies.   The difference is crucially important.

     Confusion of a different sort was displayed in a statement is-
sued by the Policy Review Sub-Committee of the International and
Comparative Librarianship Group (ICLG) of the British Library Association.   The Sub-Committee reported:

          It was agreed that, whilst cross-national comparative li-
          brarianship was an important part of international librarian-
          ship, the term 'comparative librarianship' could also be
          applied to comparative studies within one country and to
          that extent would fall outside the scope of the Group.   This
          led to agreement on a recommendation that the name of the
          Group be changed to 'International Librarianship Group, '
          on the understanding that the term 'international' was taken
          to include cross-national comparative studies. [13]

     The first sentence in the statement not only robs international
librarianship of its separate and important position, but also implies
the synonymity of "cross-national" with cross-cultural, thus impos-
ing an incorrect, as well as an undesirable limitation.   It is gratify-
ing to report that the Group's Annual General Meeting did not accept
the recommendation of the Sub-Committee that the ICLG's name be
changed. [14]

Much of the discussion in an article by Jayakuru concerns an attempt to distinguish between "international comparison" and "comparative librarianship."[15]

Of the first, she suggests that it "could be viewed as a supporting factor directed toward and encouraging a truly international perspective in librarianship or in terms of sponsored research," that it is "accepted in librarianship as a specialized method of research," and that it "is linked in terms of subject content and research method to other dimensions of research."[16]

Comparative librarianship, on the other hand, concentrates on research "and is particularly interested in scientifically acceptable comparisons which will provide concrete information for librarianship." Further,

> comparative librarianship, whose distinguishing element is international and cross-cultural comparison, defines itself as a distinct and unique field of study ... with ... emphasis upon scientific method and having an implied primary affiliation away from librarianship toward other comparative studies. International comparison is seen as a 'special focus' of an enquiry, set apart from other library studies, and looking forward to comparative studies in other disciplines (such as education) for direction and pedigree.[17]

There seems to be an overlapping here and a lack of clear-cut distinction. In any case, Mrs. Jayakuru's assertion, early in her article, that "international comparison is already an accepted dimension of library research, quite independent of comparative librarianship, having been successfully used for research purposes by Danton, Hassenforder, Withers and IFLA," is far off the mark.[18] International comparison, far from being "quite independent" of comparative librarianship, is the heart of it; at least two of the works she cites are indubitably examples of comparative studies.

A major area of confusion, evident in a number of publications, results from an unwillingness to accept traditional, widely held views of the bounds of the "cross-cultural" element in comparative studies. These views hold that a "cross-cultural" comparison, when not cross-national, is a comparative study only when two different societies are present within a single national boundary. Writing on this point, Simsova says, "this leaves out a whole area of cross-cultural comparisons such as Sikh and Hindu Londoners, or working-class and middle-class readers."[19] So it does. Simsova concludes her comment here by adding, "It could be argued that comparative research within a national boundary is just plain research in librarianship...."[20] To this, the only response can be, Amen.

A study of "working-class and middle-class readers" is obviously not merely a legitimate but a highly worthwhile enterprise. And it is obviously "comparative" in one of the dictionary meanings

of that word. But it is not a comparative study in librarianship,
any more than an inquiry into the education of working-class and
middle-class Londoners would be considered a comparative study in
education.

The reason lies in the fact that the activities of these readers have not in any fundamental way affected the libraries they use;
the institution is not basically altered, because the social history
from which it arose and the social milieu in which it exists remain
unchanged. The branch public library in one part of London or Chicago or Oslo is ideologically and conceptually the same as the branch
public library in another part of those cities. To be sure, book collections, the subject and language competencies of staff, and the nature of the information disseminated may and should differ depending
upon differences in the libraries' clientele. But differences of this
kind exist in libraries of all kinds everywhere. Such differences do
not affect the basic nature of the institution. And it is changes in
the institution, produced by changes in the society in which it exists,
that chiefly concern us. Thus, French-speaking and English-speaking Canada and the French, German, and Italian parts of Switzerland
have each produced different kinds of public libraries because of the
cultural and ideological differences of the different societies. In
fact, if we were to make the mistake of calling an enquiry into the
reading of working-class and middle-class library patrons a comparative study in librarianship, we should have, in logic, to admit
studies of the reading of businessmen and housewives, of elementary
and secondary school children, of, in short, any two elements or
groups imaginable; in this case the phrase "comparative study" in librarianship would become quite meaningless.

To quote just one statement from the several score that might
be cited from other disciplines, Marsh notes that "comparative sociology ... is concerned with the systematic and explicit comparison
of social phenomena in two or more societies[21] (emphasis added).
The "social phenomena" in which we are primarily interested are libraries and librarianship, and our overriding concern is the changes
in the phenomena which the differences in "two or more societies"
have produced.

This is not the place to comment on points other than terminological in Simsova's article. It is not irrelevant, however, to
point out that her implication that Wood considers area studies to be
comparative ones if the "areas" consist of a single culture or society, is incorrect.[22]

Simsova repeats her view in a later article.[23] In this, however, she provides part of the argument against acceptance of cross-
cultural comparisons within a national boundary when such comparisons are not cross-societal: "The emphasis in comparative librarianship should be on the understanding of the dependence of institutions
within librarianship on the local culture and on the investigation of
the systems of values which constitute the various cultures."[24]

In an interesting and instructive article, Simsova presents the results of a survey of opinion on a large number of aspects of comparative librarianship, using the Delphi technique. [25] She queried ninety-four "experts," of whom seventy-nine were from Britain and fifteen from elsewhere. From the first circularization, forty-five returns were received. The second, however, produced only twelve full replies--a response, as the author notes, that provides too small a sample.

Two of the questions Simsova asked involved the terminological question just discussed. To the question, "Do comparative studies have to cross a national boundary?", ten respondents, or twenty-six per cent said "yes," and twenty-eight, or seventy-two per cent said "no." As asked, the question must be answered "no." But the more meaningful question would be, "Do comparative studies have to be cross-cultural or cross-societal when not cross-national?" Two of the comments to Simsova's question, not reported in the article but in the mimeograph summary of the first stage of the Delphi survey, pinpointed the distinction. One comment was, "Logically they should, but in a nation with vast cultural and socio-economic differences, a comparison could be made within one nation." The second comment was, "Geographical boundaries are unimportant, national ones not essential consideration. But a comparative study must be defensibly cross-societal."

The other question Simsova asked was, "Do area studies belong to comparative librarianship?" Unfortunately, no definition of area studies was given. Twenty-nine, or seventy-four per cent of the respondents said "yes," and four, or ten per cent said "no." Clearly, if an area covers two or more societies or cultures, as many do, a study within the area may be comparative. On the other hand, if the area constitutes a single society or culture only--Denmark, for example--a study of it is not comparative.

In her article, "Comparative Librarianship as an Academic Subject," Simsova offers "a simple definition" which she suggests as the "common denominator" of the definitions published at the time of her writing, presumably no later than early summer 1973. The definition is: "Comparative librarianship is a subject which deals with things in librarianship that can be compared." To this she adds: "Comparative method is an essential part of comparative librarianship." [26] This is certainly a least common denominator, but it is at the same time both too broad and too limited to be of much assistance. It is too broad in that, for example, a comparison of the furniture supplied by two different manufacturers is not a comparative study in the sense understood elsewhere in the academic world. And it is too limited in that it does not speak to the essentiality of the cross-cultural element, actual comparisons, and explanation of differences. It is only fair to add that, later on, in a section entitled "What Can Be Investigated?" the author greatly narrows the "things" that can be compared to libraries and their environments and cultures. [27] However, if the six relationships in librarianship that she lists are taken at face value they are too restrictive. They provide no place, for example, for a comparative study of library education in two societies.

Inasmuch as Simsova and MacKee's A Handbook of Comparative Librarianship is so well known, it should probably be noted that the second edition (London, Clive Bingley, 1975) includes no definitions or terminological considerations that were not covered in the first edition of 1970, or that have not been covered in one or another of the publications already cited above. Simsova does not attempt to reconcile the definitions she considers, nor does she suggest ones of her own.

Havard-Williams has defined international librarianship "as cooperative activity in the field of librarianship done for the benefit of the individual librarian in the whole of the world...."[28] Is this not much too restrictive, too limiting? In the first place, cooperation is often not at all or only to a small extent involved, as in the case of the work of consultants and teachers. In the second place, the benefit is frequently not to an individual librarian, but rather to a government, a library, or a library school. And in the third place, international library activities are seldom of such scope and significance as to result in benefit for librarians "in the whole of the world."

Parker, in a thoughtful and analytical article, discusses the concept and role of international librarianship.[29] He identifies three main functional areas under which "the activities carried out under the heading of international librarianship" may be subsumed.[30] These areas are, first, Service Provision; that is, the provision, through international action, of common or mutual library, documentation, and allied services operating across national boundaries or at the international level. In "common ... library services" he includes such items or activities as the libraries of international organizations, international bibliographical services, regional schools of librarianship, international programs and institutions for the provision of library and related services, international interlibrary loan and the international exchange of publications. Parker calls his second main functional area Service Promotion. Here fall aid and technical assistance of various kinds, propaganda, planning, consultant and advisory work. The third area, Information Transfer, includes conferences, meetings, publications, study tours, staff exchanges, and research and evaluation. Needless to say, the areas frequently merge or overlap, and a particular activity or event may foster or pertain to more than one area. Parker's analysis leads him to the following definition:

> International librarianship consists of activities carried out
> among or between governmental or non-governmental insti-
> tutions, organizations, groups or individuals of two or more
> nations, to promote, establish, develop, maintain and eval-
> uate library, documentation and allied services, and librar-
> ianship and the library profession generally, in any part
> of the world.[31]

This definition, prepared for the Policy Review Sub-Committee of
the ICLG was approved by it, by the parent committee, and finally
also by the Group's Annual General Meeting in June, 1974.

The definition seems the best that has yet been proposed, and
a better one than that quoted earlier in this paper.   The definition
has the advantages of conciseness, precision and inclusiveness.   It
also has the considerable advantage of having been formally adopted
by the largest group of its kind in the world.

It is most unfortunate that a considerable number of recent
publications about comparative and international librarianship were
written and/or went to press at such times that the authors were un-
aware of what their colleagues were thinking.   To be specific on
this point, the statement applies to the articles already cited by
Chandler, Jayakuru, Parker, and to Simsova's first two articles and
the second edition of A Handbook....   The statement applies also to
an extensive article by Harvey. 32 Further, neither Harvey's article
nor the second edition of Simsova's A Handbook..., despite its 1975
publication date, could take account of the work cited on the first
page of this paper.

After discussing and generally criticizing a number of the
definitions extant at the time he wrote, Harvey underscores two of
the points made earlier in this paper, namely that a comparative
study must be cross-geographical or cross-societal, and that it must
compare, and not merely list or describe. 33

The heart of Harvey's paper, so far as our interests here
are concerned, lies in a series of four definitions, as follows:

(a) International library science, a comprehensive term,
an umbrella phrase, covers the entire field of library international relations and its studies of non-national library
science.   As sub-categories, it includes the three major
and four minor fields listed below.   Every paper in the
field fits into this general concept.

(b) Foreign library science is the description of any aspect of library operation in one or more countries other
than the author's own country.   It specifically omits both
comparative and international institutional library science.
A Harvey paper on the Iranian Documentation Centre would
be an example of foreign library science.   All foreign area
library studies as well as foreign case library studies, systematic library studies, and topical approach library studies
are mutually exclusive subdivisions of foreign library science.

(c) International institutional library science refers to the
librarianship of international libraries, organizations, institutions, and associations.   A paper on the library-con-
nected International Children's Film Festival held annually
in Tehran would be an example.

> (d) Comparative library science is a separate and exact-
> ing field, and few first-rate examples of it exist. It is
> the objective and systematic comparison and contrast of
> libraries in two or more countries on a specific topic in
> order to reach conclusions useful in understanding
> them.... [34]

It seems to this writer, as it does to Parker and others,
most unwise to consider international librarianship as an umbrella,
overall concept, if for no other reason than that there is, as Parker well points out, a quite clear-cut group of activities which justify its separateness and abundantly distinguish it from comparative
librarianship.

What Harvey includes under "foreign library science" belongs,
rather, in this view, under the rubric "international library science,"
or international librarianship. Further, as discussed elsewhere in
detail, the word "foreign" is coinage of very questionable utility,
simply because what is "foreign" to the Englishman writing about
France is not "foreign" to the Frenchman; knowledge of the national
origin of the author is therefore indispensable in understanding the
use of the word. [35]

Harvey justifies a separate category and definition for "international institutional library science," rather than its inclusion under
"foreign library science," on the grounds that "it should be realized
that the definition of foreign library science is violated by international institutional library science's frequent inclusion of the author's
own country in its considerations, when the local agency has international concerns. "[36] This is quite true provided one grants the
validity of the separate area, "foreign library science." Not grant-
ing this, there is no reason that what Harvey includes in "international institutional library science" cannot be placed, as Parker
places it, in "international library science."

Finally, the definition of "comparative library science" has
several faults. In the first place, it speaks of "two or more countries," whereas it is societies and cultures, wherever found, that
concern us. In the second place, the definition confines itself to
"comparison ... of libraries" only. A comparative study, might,
however, be of library education, international exchanges of personnel, or several other aspects of librarianship that are not "libraries."
Lastly, and no less important, though less easily correctable, Harvey's definition of "comparative library science" assumes that this
category includes "objective and systematic" studies only. There is,
then, no place here for the subject of comparative librarianship as
discussed earlier in this paper, no place, for example, for the library school course, or discussion and writing on terminology, definition, scope, purpose, or value. The definition of "comparative library science" as a whole is both less precise and less comprehensive than the one quoted earlier in this paper. There has, in fact,
been no objection raised against it, or improvement suggested of it,
except the small one by Kaser noted earlier.

In the light of all the foregoing this paper proposes that the profession adopt, use, and adhere to the definitions of comparative library studies and comparative librarianship mentioned at the beginning of this paper, and the Parker-ICLG definition of international librarianship.

A final proposal is offered. There has been a steadily increasing volume of writing about comparative and international librarianship during the past two decades. The volume has accelerated greatly since 1970. While a great deal of important activity has been and is constantly taking place in international librarianship and in the field of comparative librarianship, the number of comparative studies is most distressingly small. Let us call a moratorium on writing about the subject and devote our energies to doing comparative work.

Grateful acknowledgment is made of the sterling reference and bibliographical assistance rendered by Miss Patiala Khoury in the preparation of this paper.

NOTES

1. J. Periam Danton. The Dimensions of Comparative Librarianship. Chicago: American Library Association, 1973, pp. 27-46.
2. Ibid., and pp. 47-62.
3. Harold J. Noah and Max A. Eckstein. Toward a Science of Comparative Education. New York: Macmillan, 1969, p. 140.
4. Danton, op. cit., p. 52.
5. College and Research Libraries XXXV (May, 1974), p. 215.
6. Stewart E. Fraser and William W. Brickman, eds. A History of International and Comparative Education. Glenview, Ill.: Scott, Foresman, 1968, p. 1.
7. George Chandler, "Editorial Commentary," International Library Review VI (January, 1974), p. 1.
8. K. C. Harrison. Libraries in Scandinavia. London: Deutsch, 1961.
9. H. C. Campbell. Metropolitan Public Library Planning Throughout the World. Oxford: Pergamon Press, 1967.
10. Danton, op. cit., pp. 90-91.
11. Op. cit., p. x.
12. Chandler, op. cit., p. 1.
13. Focus on International and Comparative Librarianship V (June, 1974), p. 15.
14. "Editorial," Focus on International and Comparative Librarianship V (September, 1974), p. 18.
15. Mrs. K. S. Jayakuru, "Comparative Librarianship--Subject or Research Methods?" Library Association Record LXXVI (May, 1974), pp. 91-92.
16. Ibid., p. 91.
17. Ibid.

18. Ibid.
19. S. Simsova, "A Scholarly Study," Library Review XXIV (Winter, 1973-74), p. 163.
20. Ibid.
21. Robert M. Marsh, "Comparative Sociology, 1950-1963. A Trend Report and Bibliography," Current Sociology XIV (1966), p. 5.
22. Bryce Wood, "Area Studies," in International Encyclopedia of the Social Sciences, Vol. 1, 1968, pp. 401-407.
23. S. Simsova, "Comparative Librarianship as an Academic Subject," Journal of Librarianship VI (April, 1974), pp. 115-125.
24. Ibid. , p. 117.
25. S. Simsova, "A Delphi Survey of Comparative Librarianship," International Library Review VII (October, 1975), pp. 417-426.
26. Simsova, "Comparative Librarianship...," op. cit. , p. 116.
27. Ibid. , p. 118.
28. Peter Havard-Williams, "International Librarianship," UNESCO Bulletin for Libraries XXVI (March-April, 1972), p. 64.
29. J. Stephen Parker, "International Librarianship--A Reconnaissance," Journal of Librarianship VI (October, 1974), pp. 219-232.
30. Ibid. , p. 221.
31. Ibid. , p. 221.
32. John F. Harvey, "Toward a Definition of International and Comparative Library Science," International Library Review V (July, 1973), pp. 289-319.
33. Ibid. , p. 295.
34. Ibid. , p. 301.
35. Danton, op. cit. , p. 43.
36. Harvey, op. cit. , p. 301.

RECENT COMPARATIVE AND INTERNATIONAL
STUDIES IN NON-LIBRARY FIELDS

D. J. Foskett

Any investigation of natural or social phenomena seeks a deeper understanding of the world in order to master, and not be mastered by, the environment. That environment is but a small part of the total cosmos, yet it may be affected by any event, even in remote parts of the cosmos. Man alone, among the animal species, has evolved a brain capable of making abstractions from experience, speculating, forming hypotheses about how things work, and testing them by experiment. We could not do this without the ability to identify, classify, and compare. These are the basic mental operations by which we understand, explain and control our daily lives. Even in the most exact sciences, where observation accuracy has become highly refined through developments in instrumentation, the method of comparison--matching the new with the already known --is fundamental. J. P. Scott stresses this, and adds, "We are so used to the system of standard units of measure that we are apt to forget that the essential process of any measurement is comparison."[1] S. R. Ranganathan described the scientific method as an "endless spiral":

1. From individual experiences, through generalisation, to empirical laws derived from them, with the aid of induction and normal equations;
2. Through their reduction to a few normative principles, with the aid of imagination and/or intuition;
3. Through deductive laws or canons derived from the normative principles with the aid of methods of inference and semantics;
4. Through fresh individual experiences not conforming to them;
5. Back again, through another cycle; and
6. So on, without end.[2]

Brian Holmes, a physicist who has made a considerable contribution to comparative education as a scientific study, draws a clear distinction between two methods of investigation, the inductive and the hypothetico-deductive. Further, he maintains that there is a unity of method in the sciences, both social and physical sciences. The mere statement of facts about experience, though it constitutes an essential element in any scientific investigation, does not advance understanding unless set into a pattern of other facts which together make up a "system." Here, I believe, lies the justification for the view that one can indeed find a methodology with unity of form applied to diversity of content.

The theory of systems has made an important contribution to the philosophy of science. The central feature is the concept of whole entities, whose parts are linked by a specific pattern of relations; the system as a whole is greater than the mere sum of its parts by virtue of this pattern. Each part may be considered a system, and the whole entity may in its turn be part of a supra-system. This series extends from the ultimate small entities, fundamental particles, up to the ultimate large entities such as the universe or the United Nations. The concept that a system comprises both internal and external relations excludes reductionism, that is, the claim that any entity can be explained entirely in terms of the properties of its parts, which can then be explained in terms of the properties of their parts, and so on. The higher order entities exist through the relationships between the parts, and these form a qualitatively new feature which disappears if the entity is broken up into its parts. It disintegrates in the literal sense, and all we are left with is a heap of parts.

A social science such as library science presents problems, however, both in assembling the data and in codifying them, and some social scientists have questioned the existence of any normative principles or deductive laws. In dealing with people, we lack the freedom to manipulate experiments which we have with laboratory materials. Yet, to understand social phenomena, we must have access to a method of investigation which will give reliable results; the comparative method is one such. It involves the systematic study of all types of institution, that is, the analysis of each social phenomenon as a system, so that its internal dynamics--the role of each element and its relation to the other system elements--are clearly revealed. As Feibleman shows, such an analysis can be applied to all types of human institutions, from those which derive from basic "tissue needs," through social groups and organizations, up to whole cultures and what Toynbee calls "civilisations." The dynamics of a single system cannot be fully understood by examining that system in isolation, however, for the way it functions depends on its reaction with its environment as much as on the interactions between its own parts. Human society consists of a series of systems of an increasing organizational complexity, and any one level can be analyzed only by a systematic comparison between different instances of the same level. The main problem, as Bottomore points out in relation to identifying the "units of comparison," is that "there are formidable problems in comparing whole societies with each other, and a common procedure has been to compare a particular social institution, or the relationship between two institutions, in different societies."[3]

This situation has resulted in a common error in comparative library science work, a confusion between comparative and international studies. Of course, in order to find different societies we usually must look in different countries. However, the comparative method does not depend on this, as a review of other comparative study fields will show. If we look at some of the earliest developments, Linnaeus in botany and Cuvier in biology secured the foundations of comparative anatomy by examining large numbers of structures and noting their differences and similarities in order to predict the relations between those specimens and others yet to be found. Cuvier's deduction of the form of a prehistoric animal from a single fossilized bone is well known, and Linnaean classification is used to this day. In T. H. Huxley's great work supporting Darwinian evolutionary theory, <u>Man's Place in Nature</u>, he showed side by side the skeletons of several apes and compared their structure and physical features with those of man in order to show the extent and the limit of the "family" relationship. These studies did not depend on examining specimens from different countries; there was an "international" element, to be sure, but it had no fundamental significance, since many of the specimens came from the same country, even the same small area. This principle can be applied in library science. One might study the working of a special library and a public library in the same town, or the effectiveness of a dictionary catalogue and a classified catalogue in the same library.

If we consider that biological comparisons show us the different qualities that separate man from the apes, we have next to investigate how these qualities emerge, by what mechanisms, and in what ways they influence man's behavior. Therefore, we arrive at the study of human society; first, the primitive societies which have been observed by anthropologists. By looking at the forms of institutions such as kinship systems, marriage, child rearing, "rites de passage," tribal conflicts, found in such societies, estimates can be made of the role and relative importance of each one in establishing and safeguarding the society's stability. From this, generalizations are derived which may then be applied to modern societies, in order to explain the forces which shape them and influence their development. Radcliffe-Brown, for example, used the term "opposition," which does not mean enmity but the way in which two elements may interact and lead to certain visible results, such as prohibitions like marriage taboos. As a structural principle, "opposition" is a force which separates but also unites, like the male-female opposition by which the very existence of any species is secured and continued. Evans-Pritchard, on the other hand, expressed doubts about the existence of sociological "laws" in the sense of generalizations comparable to physical laws, on the grounds that societies are far too complex for any codified statement to have general validity. He pointed out that use of the comparative method, from the nineteenth century onwards, had been applied in an evolutionary sense, emulating Darwin in the search for hypotheses about historical origins which can never be proved or disproved. Yet the search for regularities must go on, based on a proper understanding of ethnographic data, the collection of which has sometimes diverted attention from the quest for generalizations. If we do not arrive at social "laws," at least we shall come to a better understanding of our own social behavior.

While the main emphasis in the nineteenth century lay on fact-finding, influenced by political expansion and the need for knowledge about foreign areas for trade and empire, the characteristic feature of our time has been the wider-ranging search for more general ideas, both in relation to method and the formulation of theories of social activity and development. A typical instance is the treatment of "totemism" by Claude Levi-Strauss, who subjects the assumptions of previous scholars to a fundamental re-appraisal and shows that they had limited their vision to this problem in isolation from other phenomena characteristic of social, as distinct from biological, levels of life. This analysis represents a landmark in the development of "structuralism," that is, the linking of a range of disciplines by identifying similarities of form, or structure. The content of each discipline will be characteristic of itself, but the elements react with each other to produce an integrated discipline which has clear and recognizable features. As Piaget shows, the basic notions of structuralism can be seen in the exact sciences and the social sciences, and there is a clear resemblance to general systems theory: "the idea of wholeness, the idea of transformation, and the idea of self-regulation," says Piaget, "comprise the three key ideas in the notion of structure."[4] Compare this with Ervin Laszlo's statement of the four basic concepts of systems philosophy: ordered wholeness, system stability in the face of environmental disturbance, system reorganization capability, inter-systemic hierarchy consisting of sub-system, system, and supra-system. In his preface, Laszlo criticizes two features of contemporary thought: "that the majority of philosophers continue to offer highly refined but factually anaemic theories; and that scientists, in their increasingly frequent excursions into general philosophical problems continue to be shackled by the optic of their particular specialities."[5]

Structuralism stems from the Swiss linguist, Ferdinand de Saussure, who, in the early twentieth century, broke away from the traditions of comparative philology, the gathering of masses of facts about language forms, and drew the distinction between synchronic, or static, and diachronic, or evolutionary, linguistics. He maintained that the signs making up language have a real existence: "signs and their relations are what linguistics studies; they are the concrete entities of our science."[6]

This new approach was developed by others, notably by the Prague School of Linguistics, and by J. R. Firth, first holder of the Chair of General Linguistics, University of London, who introduced the additional idea of the context of situation, meaning an approach to linguistics "based on an acceptance of the whole man in his pattern of living."[7] While the comparative philologists had directed their main search towards the discovery of a hypothetical "parent language" such as Indo-European or Indo-Germanic, Firth advanced beyond Saussure, whose theory he regarded as static mechanical structuralism. He treated linguistics as a group of related techniques--phonetics, grammar, lexicography, semantics--used for the analysis and explanation of what he called "language events." An example of this kind of contextual approach in a related field can be seen in Allardyce

Nicoll's study of one particular form of language use, the drama.
He relates the historical characteristics of the drama in various
ages and the styles of individual dramatists to external factors such
as theatre construction, the nature of audiences, and the general
character of the society of the time.

A similar movement has occurred in other branches of the
social sciences, which from Comte to Durkheim had concentrated on
the collection and classification of social facts, in the manner of the
natural sciences.   This has not lessened in importance; indeed, the
computer has brought a new dimension into the compilation and use
of data inventories.   In particular, the work of Unesco and the International Social Science Council has given a powerful impetus through
the extension of survey research and the collection of national data
archives.   A new level of approach has developed, as in linguistics,
which is directed towards qualitative assessment of the criteria needed for making social judgments which continue to be founded on empirical, usually quantitative, data.   This widening of the horizon has
increased what McKee calls the self-consciousness of sociologists:
"By becoming comparative, sociology has enriched the materials of
analysis and broken through an American parochialism, but the implications of this for theory and methodology are yet to come. "[8]

Some firm strides in this direction have already been taken.
One need only recall Toynbee's Study of History to see how far he
has moved from the assembly and classification of data into a vast
imaginative reconstruction of the great civilizations.   Stein Rokkan's
report on the 1965 Conference of the ISSC and Unesco points to the
emergence of new themes which are centered on qualitative alternatives and may be summarized as: 1) methods of cross-cultural analysis; 2) comparative analysis of historical change; 3) comparative
analysis of processes of modernization in societies.   An interesting
example of multum in parvo, the use of a highly specific phenomenon
to make qualitative deductions, is Sebald's analysis of the contents of
the song books used in German and American schools during the Hit-
ler regime, from which he identified the attitudes inculcated towards
"universal dimensions," that is concepts related to 1) the relation of
individuals to authority; 2) the concept of the self; 3) areas of primary conflict.

Such a qualitative approach has long been evident in two of
the oldest and major institutions of society, Religion and Law.   Both
Anderson and Horton stress the difficulty of an objective approach to
religion, since most religion students base their interest on convic-
tion and faith in one particular creed.   A comparative approach, by
contrast, aims at discovering what factors in society account for the
origins and development of a particular religion--its deity, code of
belief, forms of ritual--and, as Horton remarks, often such an approach is regarded with suspicion by practicing worshippers.   Yet he
shows that certain roles are plainly integral to all religions: 1) as
instruments in relation to human needs, explanations of events; 2) as
morality, guidance; and 3) as ends in themselves, corresponding to
a basic facet of the human personality, the search for faith in an

ideal towards which we may aspire. In spite of his title, Werblowsky's entertaining article stresses the need for philosophical understanding in a spirit of detachment: "We might say that concern with
methodology should be an occasional pastime, in which we may in-
dulge at moments when we take an occasional respite from our substantive labours, but with plenty of bacon, as it were, in the lard-
er. "[9] While rejecting reductionism, he relates all forms of human
experience, including social existence and religion, to certain basic
anthropological ("in the philosophical sense") structures, and cate-
gorizes religions as systems of meaning.

    In politics and law we find the clearest distinction between
the international and the comparative. In both, the international aspect concerns the establishment and regulation of relations between
different countries; indeed, in the arena of politics this is usually
given the name of International Relations, of which the foreign policy
of each country is its contributory element. In comparative politics,
on the other hand, attention focuses on the home policies. Similarly, in law, the aim is to examine the rules that each country has
established to deal with its internal situation. Gutteridge suggests
that there are three forms of comparative law, the descriptive, the
applied, and the speculative; of these, applied comparative law usually aims at reform, and it is this form "which is the most vigorous
and fertile in output. "[10]

    There are many parallels between library science and educa-
tion, and international and comparative education studies have produced a massive literature. From Marc-Antoine Jullien onwards,
the nineteenth century saw many travelers reporting on systems in
foreign countries; Henry Barnard in America, Matthew Arnold and
Michael Sadler in the UK, are famous names among those who laid
the foundations for the great advances of recent decades. Jullien's
own method was essentially classificatory, but the historical-cultural
approach of Kandel, Schneider and Hans dominated the inter-war
years. The two Yearbooks of Education published by Teachers College, Columbia, and the University of London Institute of Education
recorded a series of descriptive accounts from over the world, and
the assembly of statistical data began in earnest with the foundation
of Unesco. Already in 1950, Unesco circulated a questionnaire to
member states, which resulted in the publication of the World Handbook of Educational Organizations and Statistics in 1952. This was
later supplemented by the five-volume World Survey of Education,
published between 1955 and 1971, which, though not always up-to-
date, provides scholars with a wealth of basic data probably unsur-
passed in any other research fields. From the international point of
view, it has also meant that there is no longer the same need for
individuals to spend their time recording and classifying such data,
apart from the much smaller task of bringing certain sections up-to-
date.

    Attention has therefore turned away somewhat from the purely
historical and descriptive, towards the more analytical, philosophical
and sociological aspects of comparative studies. The physicist

Holmes has applied current trends of thought in the philosophy of
science and acknowledged a particular debt to John Dewey and Karl
Popper. He has been a pioneer of the "problem approach" to education, that is, the depth analysis of specific problems arising in
educational systems, in the light of theories of social change based
on ideas concerning the nature of man and society, the inter-connec-
tions between social institutions, and the contemporary state of society itself in any given country. Both Holmes and King, though in
different ways, relate the structure of an educational system to the
needs of society, and King has paid particular attention to the influence of technological change and development on requirements placed
on schools in respect of curricula, vocational training, and the
matching of qualifications to job opportunities.

Detailed studies of methodology applied to the use of sources
and the processing of data have been made, for example, by Bereday and by Eckstein and Noah, who have not only described and advocated the correct application of scientific methods, but have supported their views by a selection of contributions from Aristotle onwards. These writers have helped to clarify a number of issues
concerning the classification of data according to level of relevance,
psychological, sociological, administrative, and so on; Bereday has
put all comparativists in his debt by the way in which he has settled
the confusion between juxtaposition and comparison.

Education reveals the same type of international and comparative progress as most other fields. We find first a curiosity stimulated by differences in practice between one society and another;
closer examination shows up similarities as well as differences, and
this leads, in fields like anthropology, philology and religion, to
speculations about possible origins, whether each system has passed
through the same pre-historical and historical epochs, and whether
or not they have a common ancestor.

Improved facilities for data-gathering, better means of travel
and correspondence, lead to a more systematic appraisal of the
causes of various features and the function of various elements, such
as symbols and ritual in religion, systems of control and punishment
in law and social custom, the curriculum and examinations in schools.
Relating these causes and functions to the economic and technological
development of society, identified by Marx as the base on which all
social and ideological superstructures are founded, brings us to the
point where new understanding makes possible planning for change
and reform. As many writers emphasize, comparative studies are
a method of work rather than a branch of the subject, but this in no
way lessens their significance. On the contrary, they provide us
with a means of exercising control over our own lives, for once we
understand cause and effect, and the inter-relations between the several areas of social practice, we are on the way to conscious deci-
sion-making about the way in which we wish societies to develop.
By studying what people in other societies have decided to do, we
may arrive at a more sympathetic understanding of their needs and
aspirations, and so contribute, not only to our own satisfaction with

life, but to greater harmony between the many different cultures across the world.

International Associations

We have long been accustomed to the work of international professional associations. International recognition of scholarship goes back to the most ancient times. As Sarton remarks, "Primitive people could move as fast as Napoleon's soldiers; sometimes they moved much faster," and they took their knowledge with them. Thales of Miletos studied in Egypt, Plato traveled widely in his youth, and in middle age was called to Syracuse to train the tyrants Dionysius I and Dionysius II to become his "philosopher-kings." In medieval times, the Wandering Scholars achieved both fame and notoriety, and in 1813 Sir Humphry Davy and Michael Faraday visited Paris, although England was at war with France; Napoleon agreed to the visit because science, unlike politics, is international.

Many international science associations were founded in the nineteenth century, and this practice still continues. Indeed, we now have an organization of organizations, the International Council of Scientific Unions, which has made substantial contributions to science documentation through the ICSU/Abstracting Board. Recently, in collaboration with Unesco, ICSU has sponsored establishment of the World Science Information Centre known as UNISIST. The story of UNISIST and of many other organizations involved with international documentation has been well told by Coblans, whose own life makes him the paradigm of the international scholar of today.

As was expected, the UN and its specialized agencies have been the major agents of international cooperation since World War II, and not the least part of their activities has been devoted to documentation. Unesco founded the International Committee for Social Sciences Documentation, and it has prospered under the enthusiastic and capable hands of Stein Rokkan, its first Chairman, and Jean Meyriat, the present General Secretary. Among its most notable achievements are the four series of the International Bibliography of the Social Sciences: Anthropology, Economics, Political Science, Sociology. Anyone making comparative studies in these fields will find easy access to the literature through their indexes. ICSSD represents a large number of international associations covering the whole of the social sciences, including IFLA and FID, so its work not only contributes to bibliographical organizations, but brings together specialists from many countries and disciplines. Being worldwide in scope, the UN and its specialized agencies act as a bridge between countries with different, sometimes opposing, political systems and ideologies.

There are many regional groupings on an inter-governmental as well as a professional basis. Among the best known are the Council of Europe, the European Economic Community, the Organization of American States, and the Council for Mutual Economic Assist-

ance. Of these regional groupings, the Organization for Economic
Cooperation and Development (OECD), based in Paris and originally
confined to Western Europe, has broadened its base to include countries outside Europe. It is of particular interest because the Director of the Department for Scientific Affairs is Alexander King, a
former FID President. It illustrates a somewhat less fortunate aspect of international activities in that an occasional lack of cooperation occurs between OECD and its near neighbor Unesco.

The field of Education is particularly blessed with both international and comparative associations. Unesco has a special responsibility in this field, and the reputation of its International Bureau
of Education in Geneva stands very high. The names of its directors,
Jean Piaget, Pedro Rossello, Leo Fernig, suffice to guarantee international recognition of the quality of its work. Cooperation between
the IBE, the EUDISED (European Documentation and Information System in Education) project of the Council of Europe, and ERIC (Educational Resources Information Center) in the USA was already begun
when the Institute of Educational Information in Prague organized the
"First International Colloquium on Designing Information Systems in
the Field of Education" (EDICO) in Prague, November 1974. At this
colloquium, representatives of information systems at national and
international levels, mostly from East and West Europe, gathered to
explore the ways in which wider-ranging international cooperation
might develop. A second EDICO is planned for 1977 or 1978.

These are international activities, but Comparative Education
has its own international bodies such as the Comparative Education
Society and the Comparative Education Society in Europe. Both of
them hold regular meetings and conferences, and the Comparative
Education Review acts as the official journal in the USA, Comparative Education in Europe.

Apart from coordinating activities through the establishment of
central committees, holding conferences, even setting up specialized
research institutions such as the International Atomic Energy Agency
and the European Centre for Nuclear Research (CERN), several international bodies have undertaken specific tasks in order to facilitate
cooperation. The well known work of Barbara Kyle in the 1950s and
1960s on a classification scheme for the social sciences was undertaken for the ICSSD and helped to improve the arrangement and indexing systems of their international bibliographies. At the International Labour Organization, G. K. Thompson has collaborated with the
OECD to produce the Macrothesaurus, and this in turn is closely related to the Thesaurus for Information Processing in Sociology, compiled by Jean Viet of the Maison des Sciences de l'Homme in Paris,
who is Assistant General Secretary of the ICSSD. A similar effort
towards standardizing terminology in a field which is notoriously
shaky has been made by the International Political Science Association, which has set up a Committee on Conceptual and Terminological
Analysis (COCTA), with Giovanni Sartori of the University of Florence as its Chairman, and Fred W. Riggs of the University of
Hawaii as its Secretary.

Such a brief account can do no more than highlight a few of
a considerable number of significant activities of an international
and comparative character, through various types of associations of
professional people. As indicated above with reference to Religion
and Law, they serve two related but distinct functions: firstly, to
inform each individual group of the work and results of its colleagues
in other parts of the world, so that each may learn from the others;
and secondly, to establish international links on matters of common
concern, so that the different nations may act together in harmony
and avoid conflicting over issues which could well be resolved on the
basis of agreed concepts, objectives and standards.

Lessons for Comparative and International Library Science

The fact that scholars in other fields continue to argue about
the comparative method should not deter librarians and information
scientists from taking advantage of systematic analysis and comparisons in our own field. It is clear that valid explanations in the social sciences are possible, provided we are aware of what we are
attempting and do not allow ourselves to be led astray into a search
for absolutes, which are now regarded with some suspicion even in
the so-called "exact" sciences. The infinite complexity of human
beings and their inter-relations does not mean that we have no hope
of understanding, sometimes in considerable depth, the role of various social and psychological factors in determining the course of
events. What is essential is the rejection of the metaphysical mode
of thought, isolating the specific factors under investigation from the
larger context in which they operate. In comparative studies, this
requires knowing the structure and dynamics of the communities
served by library and information services, and the relationship between the objectives of those communities on the one hand, and on
the other the technical processes which provide the internal dynamics
of the library services. In international studies, it requires an understanding of the role of a different type of system, namely those
organizations such as Unesco, IFLA or FID, which have an international basis for their activities. This area includes much of the
work of certain national bodies like the Ford Foundation and the
British Council, which have a very large international role and responsibility.

This idea applies with particular force to studies of technical
processes. Recently, we have enjoyed the widely ranging powers of
revaluation made possible by modern techniques of quantitative analysis, to the point where some of our colleagues have committed themselves to the view of Lord Kelvin, that the only knowledge worth the
name is that which is expressible in quantitative terms. Comparative studies in fields like anthropology, history and religion prove
that this extreme view no more holds water than its opposite, that
the only real knowledge comes from introspection. Subjects like linguistics and education exhibit a judicious mixture of the statistical,
the observational, and the speculative. Let us profit by such examples; let us have no more, for example, of studies of indexing

systems, however meticulous, which purport to draw "general" conclusions without once mentioning the psychology of the user's approach.

Meticulous attention to detail can easily pass as depth study,
especially since we still lie to some extent under the domination of
the fact--the total preoccupation with the details of the parts of a
system, while ignoring the system itself with its own characteristic
mode of existence. Such preoccupation is merely pedantry and, as
Radcliffe-Brown stressed, leads to the danger of mistaking what are
actually superficial appearances for the fundamental realities, which
may well remain obscure. The most painstaking examination of in-
numerable single trees will not tell us much about the nature of a
forest. Of course, we have to know about the trees, and I have
often emphasized that for valid comparisons we need first-hand
knowledge whenever possible. Nevertheless, we may on occasion
speculate with some confidence on the basis of second-hand information. In two such different fields as philology and anatomy, prehistoric forms of which no one has direct knowledge have been deduced
from fragmentary remains like the Gothic Bible and fossilized skeletons.

This type of deduction may look into the future as well as
the past, but must be handled with care, for while the past is over,
the future is yet to come. The labor of implementing long-range
plans may be saddled on others. This consideration lays stress on
"neutrality," more often labeled "objectivity." While our views must
be colored by our personal history, when assessing the character of
a social institution we should stand away from our own preconcep-
tions and predilections and view the matter from a detached perspective. The pained tone of Toynbee's replies to some of his critics
showed his distress that they sometimes allowed themselves to judge
various elements of his work by their opinions of his whole theory
of "civilization" and not by the intrinsic worth of the elements themselves.

No one would expect to find this sort of "neutrality" in anyone's conclusions, which are sure to be the expression of an individual personality. Neutrality consists of an impartial presentation of
evidence, uncolored by personal opinion, and this in turn depends on
the ability to collect and assess data.

This overview has demonstrated the vast range of information
amenable to comparative analysis. A library and information service
exhibits most of the types investigated, either directly or by analogy.
As an institution of society, it deals with relations between people,
not the biological, perhaps, but certainly the psychological, in relations with users. As a social institution based on a particular community, the library depends on structures of authority and government, like other organs of public responsibility. As a communication channel, it has links with many forms of knowledge, their roles,
means of transmission, and function in preserving and advancing society. As an institution concerned with its own effectiveness, it
uses statistical and other management techniques.

These different types of data require different methods of handling in detail, but all exhibit one basic feature or principle of organization. The empirical data, of whatever class, must be assembled into a pattern with a recognizable structure; they must be classified. The forms of classification may vary, even within the same field and with the same data, but unless we have a systematic structure, or classification which relates to the purpose of the investigation, we shall not know whether or not our sets of data are comparable. We could enumerate the characteristics of a library and information service network alongside of the League of the Iroquois Indians, but such a juxtaposition would tell us little about either organization.

We may learn a great deal from comparative and international studies in other fields, but mere imitation will never guarantee success. We can learn about method; we cannot learn to the same extent about specific content. While these studies prove that we can speak of "the comparative method" as a technique of investigation, they prove that each field must apply that method to its own situation in its own way. They do not tell us about library and information services; they do not explain the internal systemic relations of our own field.

The lines along which advances could be made include, first, a precise distinction between international and comparative library science. There are encouraging signs that this is under way, and I have tried to clear the ground in the "Introduction" to the Reader in Comparative Librarianship. The International Library Review, for example, has provided excellent instances of both international and comparative studies, but it is sometimes difficult to tell which is which.

I do not think we need worry about data collection. Librarians are articulate, and we have an abundance of material. What we lack is recognition of the role of pattern, or structure. This may change, more than once, during a particular research, since a flexible approach naturally follows from the pursuit of neutrality in presentation and assessment. The value lies in the fact that such changes of direction are planned and deliberate and come from the character of the material under study and not from the student's own prejudices.

Problems of identifying and validating sources have received little attention. Even in well established fields of comparative study one often finds a ready acceptance where one would prefer a critical caution. There must be scope for a full-scale philosophical as well as methodological study of the forms and functions of primary and secondary sources. This study would benefit comparativists and throw a searching light on our professional media and communication channels.

Finally, we come to the basic questions which ought to lie somewhere near the surface of all our minds. Toynbee claims that

comparative studies of a number of specimens are made "with a
view to discovering whether or not there is a standard type to which
they conform, notwithstanding their individual pecularities."[12] For
many years, lacking a comparative approach, the librarians of a
few advanced countries were very prone to assume that their systems were the best in the world and should be imitated by everyone.
Several experts tried to transplant their own systems and found the
new ground inhospitable. In due course, the lesson was noted, and
the pendulum swung. But does this mean that every country has to
search for its own pattern absolutely de novo? Surely not. We can
search for standards, or models, provided that we recognize them
for what they are: indications of desirable performance levels ad-
justable to different circumstances, though derived from a set of
principles which are public knowledge, subject to scrutiny, criticism,
and modification.

These, then, are the results I look for in comparative and
international library science: a systematic analysis of professional
practice in all its forms, which leads to a recognition of unity in
diversity, identifying and elaborating our social role in precise relation to the many social contexts in which library and information
services may operate. Such a development will not only enable the
field to plan its future more wisely, it will make a fundamental contribution to the establishment of a true science of library and information service.

NOTES

1. Scott, John Paul. Animal Behaviour. Chicago: University of
   Chicago Press, 1958.
2. Ranganathan, S. R. Classified Catalogue Code. London: Asia
   Publishing House, 1964, p. 20.
3. Bottomore, T. B. Sociology: A Guide to Problems and Literature. London: Unwin University Books, 1962.
4. Piaget, Jean. Structuralism. London: Routledge and Kegan
   Paul, 1971.
5. Laszlo, Ervin. Introduction to Systems Philosophy; Toward a
   New Paradigm of Contemporary Thought. New York: Gordon
   and Breach, 1972.
6. Saussure, Ferdinand de. Course in General Linguistics. New
   York: Philosophical Library, 1959.
7. Firth, J. R. Papers in Linguistics, 1934-1951. Oxford: University Press, 1957.
8. McKee, James B. "Some Observations on the Self-consciousness of Sociologists," in: The Sociology of Knowledge, ed.
   by J. E. Curtis and J. W. Petras, vide infra, pp. 531-544.
9. Werblowsky, R. J. Zwi. "On Studying Comparative Religion:
   Some Naive Reflections of a Simple-minded Non-philosopher,"
   Religious Studies XI (June, 1975), pp. 145-156.
10. Gutteridge, H. C. Comparative Law: An Introduction to the
   Comparative Method of Legal Study and Research. 2nd ed.
   Cambridge: University Press, 1949.

11. Sarton, George. A History of Science. 2 vols. Cambridge,
    Mass.: Harvard University Press, 1959.
12. Toynbee, Arnold J. A Study of History. Vol. XII. Reconsid-
    erations. London: Oxford University Press, 1961.

BIBLIOGRAPHY

Allen, W. Sidney, "Relationship in Comparative Linguistics," Trans.
    Philol. Soc. (1953), pp. 52-108.
Anderson, J. N. D. Christianity and Comparative Religion. Lon-
    don: Inter-Varsity Press, 1970.
Andrews, W. G., ed. European Political Institutions: A Compara-
    tive Government Reader. Princeton, N. J.: Van Nostrand,
    1962.
Bereday, G. Z. F. Comparative Method in Education. New York:
    Holt, Rinehart and Winston, 1964.
Bottomore, T. B. Sociology: A Guide to Problems and Literature.
    London: Unwin University Books, 1962.
Brislin, Richard W., Lonner, Walter J., and Thorndike, R. M.
    Cross-Cultural Research Methods. New York: Wiley, 1973.
Bristow, Thelma and Holmes, Brian. Comparative Education
    Through the Literature. London: Butterworths, 1968.
Coblans, Herbert. Librarianship and Documentation: An Internation-
    al Perspective. London: Andre Deutsch, 1974.
Curtis, James E. and Petras, John W. The Sociology of Knowledge:
    A Reader. London: Duckworth, 1970.
De Reuck, Anthony and Knight, Julie. Communication in Science:
    Documentation and Automation. London: Churchill, 1967.
Eckstein, Max A. and Noah, Harold J. Scientific Investigation in
    Comparative Education: An Anthology Illustrating the Strategy
    and Tactics of Comparative Education. London: Macmillan,
    1969.
Eisenstadt, Shmuel N., "Social Institutions: Comparative Study," in:
    Encyclopedia of the Social Sciences. New York: Crowell,
    Collier and Macmillan, 1968.
_____, ed. Comparative Perspectives on Social Change. Boston:
    Little, Brown, 1968.
Evans-Pritchard, E. E. The Comparative Method in Social Anthro-
    pology. London: Athlone Press, 1963.
Feibleman, James K. The Institutions of Society. London: George
    Allen and Unwin, 1956.
Firth, J. R. Papers in Linguistics, 1934-1951. Oxford: Univer-
    sity Press, 1957.
Foskett, D. J., ed. Reader in Comparative Librarianship. Wash-
    ington, D. C.: Microcard Editions Books, 1976.
Gutteridge, H. C. Comparative Law: An Introduction to the Com-
    parative Method of Legal Study and Research. 2nd ed. Cam-
    bridge: University Press, 1949.
Hans, Nicholas. Comparative Education: A Study of Educational
    Factors and Traditions. 3rd ed. London: Routledge and
    Kegan Paul, 1964.
Holmes, Brian, "Comparative Education as a Scientific Study,"

British Journal of Educational Studies XX (June, 1972), pp. 205-219.

————. Problems in Education: A Comparative Approach. London: Routledge and Kegan Paul, 1965.

Horton, Robin, "Men and Their Gods," in: Man in Society, ed. by Mary Douglas. London: Macdonald, 1964, pp. 104-125.

Huxley, T. M., "On the Relations of Man to the Lower Animals," in: Man's Place in Nature. London: Macmillan, 1910.

Jones, P. E. Comparative Education: Purpose and Method. Queensland: University Press, 1971.

Judge, P. M., "The User-system Interface Today: National and International Information Systems," in: Communication in Science, ed. by DeReuck and Knight, vide supra, 1967, pp. 37-51.

King, E. J., "Analytical Frameworks in Comparative Studies in Education," Comparative Education XI (March 1975), pp. 85-103.

Lafferty, William M., "Contexts, Levels, and the Language of Comparison: Alternative Research," Social Science Information XI (1972), pp. 63-91.

Laszlo, Ervin. Introduction to Systems Philosophy; Toward a New Paradigm of Contemporary Thought. New York: Gordon and Breach, 1972.

Levi-Strauss, Claude. Totemism. London: Penguin University Books, 1973.

McClellan, A. W., "Comparative Reading: A Librarian's View," in: Proceedings of the ICLG Conference Scotland 1974, ed. by Allan Whatley, vide infra.

McKee, James B., "Some Observations on the Self-consciousness of Sociologists," in: The Sociology of Knowledge, ed. by J. E. Curtis and J. W. Petras, vide supra, pp. 531-544.

Macridis, Roy C. and Brown, Bernard E. Comparative Politics: Notes and Readings. 2nd ed. Homewood, Ill.: The Dorsey Press, 1964. "Their study of politics (as for Aristotle) becomes the study of a 'system' linked organically with social structure, traditions and ideologies, culture, and the environment within which it operates. It may then be possible to discern significant similarities and differences which mere description of the legal forms of a state does not suggest."

Mikhailov, A. E., Chernyi, A. I. and Gilyarevskii, R. S. International Forum on Informatics. 2 vols. Moscow: VINITI, 1969.

Nicoll, Allardyce. World Drama: From Aeschylus to Anouilh. London: Harrap, 1949.

Noah, H. J. and Eckstein, Max A. Towards a Science of Comparative Education. New York: Macmillan, 1969.

Pei, Mario. Invitation to Linguistics. London: George Allen and Unwin, 1965. "Comparison may be said to lead to reconstruction, which is in itself a technique and a method."

Piaget, Jean. Structuralism. London: Routledge and Kegan Paul, 1971.

Radcliffe-Brown, A. R., "The Comparative Method in Social Anthropology," Journal of the Royal Anthropol. Inst. LXXXI (1951), pp. 15-23.

Ranganathan, S. R. Classified Catalogue Code. London: Asia

Publishing House, 1964.
Roberts, G. K. What Is Comparative Politics? London: Macmillan, 1972.
Rokkan, Stein, "The Development of Cross-national Comparative Research: A Review of Current Problems and Possibilities," Social Science Information I (October, 1962), pp. 21-38.
_____, ed. Comparative Research Across Cultures and Nations. Paris-The Hague: Mouton, 1968.
Sarton, George. A History of Science. 2 vols. Cambridge, Mass. : Harvard University Press, 1959.
Sartori, Giovanni, "Concept Misinformation in Comparative Politics," American Political Science Review LXIV (December, 1970), pp. 1033-1053.
Saussure, Ferdinand de. Course in General Linguistics. New York: Philosophical Library, 1959.
Scott, John Paul. Animal Behaviour. Chicago: University of Chicago Press, 1958.
Sebald, H. , "Studying National Character Through Comparative Content Analysis," Social Forces XI (May, 1962), pp. 318-322.
Smelser, Neil J. , "The Methodology of Comparative Analysis," in: Comparative Research Methods, ed. by Warwick and Osherson, vide infra. , pp. 42-86.
Toynbee, Arnold J. A Study of History. Vol. XII. Reconsiderations. London: Oxford University Press, 1961. "A comparative study of a number of specimens means noting their likenesses and differences with a view to discovering whether or not there is a standard type to which they conform, notwithstanding their individual peculiarities. "
Warwick, Donald P. and Osherson, Samuel, eds. Comparative Research Methods. Englewood Cliffs, N. J. : Prentice-Hall, 1973.
Werblowsky, R. J. Zwi, "On Studying Comparative Religion: Some Naive Reflections of a Simple-minded Non-philosopher," Religious Studies XI (June, 1975), pp. 145-156.
Whatley, Allan, ed. Proceedings of the ICLG Conference Scotland 1974. London: The Library Association, International and Comparative Librarianship Group, 1974.

PROBLEMS OF RESEARCH IN COMPARATIVE AND
INTERNATIONAL LIBRARY SCIENCE

Frank L. Schick

The field of international and comparative library science requires research because the study of one's profession in other countries presents information, provides insights and leads to conclusions
which are not otherwise obtainable. Comparative and international library science and its study of practices and performance are invalu-
able tools of research which frequently contribute to a better com-
prehension of one's own country's problems by indicating adaptations
and possible solutions. Studies which UNESCO initiated during the
last half-dozen years demonstrate that nearly all member states have
libraries; a large number have library associations[1] and a surprising-
ly extensive number have library schools and offer other related
training facilities. [2]

Problems of Research

Research can be based on existing sources or conducted by
personal investigation. Original research in international library science is essential for the discovery of new concepts and information.
This approach adds the cost of foreign travel and underlines the advantage of knowing foreign languages and familiarity with other customs and cultures.

All research projects gain by exposure to discussions and
criticisms as well as comments and advice from colleagues at home
and abroad. Comparative, even more than institutional or national,
research concepts have to be brought before international audiences
to be exposed to discussion and review, before actual research is
started. The organizations which provide forums for exposure and
evaluation, including estimates of feasibility of execution and general
merit, are the International Federation of Library Associations
(IFLA), the Fédération International de Documentation (FID) and the
International Organization for Standardization, Technical Committee
46 (ISO/TC46), among others. [3] These organizations are roughly
comparable to the American Library Association (ALA), the Special
Libraries Association (SLA) and the American Standards Institute,
Standards Committee Z39 (ANSI/Z39).

International organizations differ from national ones in most
respects, including their research attitudes. In the U.S., library
research is usually initiated by a librarian who sees a problem he

needs to solve or by a library school faculty member; sometimes
projects are started by committees of state or national associations.
In order to be recognized, international projects should originate at
international conferences, should be sponsored by committees and
be put on the programs of the relevant international organizations.

Limitations of International Research Activities

Compared to national projects, international research efforts
are small in number, limited in scope, and usually more of a descriptive than analytical nature.   Among the reasons for these conditions, the following may be considered:

a) Cultural, educational and technological differences of researcher and research country create barriers.

b) After international discussion, projects can get so complicated and impractical that few researchers are sufficiently challenged
to continue.

c) The lapse of time before receiving agreement for a research project may discourage potential researchers.

d) It is difficult to secure funds for extensive research studies which include travel and per diem expenses.   Due to the general
economic slump in the mid-1970s, most countries reduced or discon-
tinued funding for library studies.   Iran for its own purposes and
UNESCO for other parts of the world remain among the few viable
sources.   During recent years UNESCO has given increasing emphasis to research related to developing countries.

e) The limited number of completed international research
projects is related to the different research emphases and to the different backgrounds of librarians and their professional needs.

To overcome these obstacles, to understand how international
projects can gain support or how they get sidetracked, requires participation in international library conferences.   The close observer
will learn who controls committee action, what motivates certain
committees, which parts of the program receive attention, and how
far projects can be advanced through a specific committee or organization.   As a member of a task force or a committee, it is easier
to advance proposals and get involved in their execution.   When considering these problems in initiating action, it is useful to remember
that one is usually not only looked upon as a member of the committee, but also as a national of a country.

Possibilities for Research Comparability and Coordination

Comparability of research results can only be obtained if research efforts are directed from a central office or agency.   UNESCO,

IFLA, ISO, FID and possibly other organizations provide such coordination. The policies and goals of these agencies and organizations depend on their memberships and differ considerably. UNESCO deals primarily with member states (governments) and secondarily with international organizations. UNESCO, which aims to develop an integrated and international library development program, is guided by its member countries and their research needs. ISO concerns itself only with standardization and research which lends itself to this aim. IFLA's research arm is the UBC (Office of Universal Bibliographic Control).

International Library Data Collections,
Their Scope and Dissemination

        Demands for international library statistics have been traced to 1853 but no data were actually collected until UNESCO published the first set of library data in 1952. [4]   Due to the impact of IFLA and ISO/TC46, improvements were made during the 1960s and early 1970s. [5]

        Considering this century-long period of gestation, the last dozen years have been quite successful because the statistics committees of IFLA and ISO/TC46 have insured that UNESCO provide the data which were required by the international library community. The 1970 UNESCO Library Statistics Conference, which wrote the present standards on which the current data collection forms are based, was attended by over 70 countries from all parts of the world. To accomplish this program, the statistics committees of IFLA and ISO/TC46 met frequently from 1964 to 1970 and drafted the basic suggestions. In 1970, UNESCO called a Conference to finalize the document produced by these committees and submit it to the review of member states. Their "recommendation" was accepted by the UNESCO member states and formally adopted the same year. [6] ISO/TC46 issued the same document as an international standard. [7] Attached to the UNESCO document is the survey instrument which has been used to collect library data from all national governments every three years.

        The data UNESCO collects in these surveys are primarily administrative. They provide numerical information regarding the number and different types of libraries and their resources, professional and support staff components. They also describe the physical facilities and certain of the activities in which these libraries engage.

        There are problems concerning the collection of these data. They are collected only every three years; they are based on national library surveys which are then adjusted to respond to UNESCO's prescribed format. As has to be expected, not all countries respond equally well, and not every country is in a position to provide all requested data. While this method of data collection is not the fastest or the most efficient, it is the least expensive and one which all countries can afford and support. Since UNESCO's forms have to

fit all types of libraries in all countries, they have the advantage of
collecting data which are truly comparable. The results of these
surveys are published regularly in the UNESCO Statistical Yearbook.
There is the assurance that this data service will continue and from
time to time improve and be updated, also. The most encouraging
aspect of the UNESCO statistical survey is the cooperative spirit in
which it was developed. UNESCO has the function and staff to collect library statistics; ISO/TC46 has the responsibility to review existing standards every five years; IFLA, with its active membership,
uses the data and sees to it that new ideas are incorporated into the
current standard.

The Standardization of Library Information--
Yardsticks for Evaluation

The functions of library standards have been summarized at
various times but never more capably than in 1968:

> Library standards may be defined as the criteria by
> which ... library services may be measured and assessed.
> They are determined by professional librarians in order to
> attain and maintain the objectives they have set themselves.
> Standards may be interpreted variously as the pattern of
> an ideal, a model procedure, a measure for appraisal, a
> stimulus for future development and improvement and as an
> instrument to assist decision and action not only by librari-
> ans themselves, but by laymen concerned indirectly with
> the institution, planning, and administration of ... library
> service. [9]

Standards are needed and used nationally and internationally
as a means of comparison and evaluation. The work of standardization is announced in the U.S. by the American National Standards Institute, Technical Committee Z39 (ANSI/Z39), and internationally by
its affiliate, the International Department for Standardization and its
Technical Committee 46 (ISO/TC46). In both cases, Z39 and TC46
represent subcommittees which deal with libraries, documentation
and related publishing practices; the PH5 subcommittee deals with
photographic reproduction and X3 with computers and information
processing.

Frequently ANSI standards are transmitted to ISO/TC46 and
become internationalized; at times an international standard is made
more specific for national use. In the absence of an international
standard, American researchers have found it useful to adapt a U.S.
standard for another country which is being studied. A list of currently adopted U.S. and international standards is given in the ALA
Yearbook. [10] The scope of the international standards covers a wide
range of subjects, such as "International Information Exchange on
Magnetic Tape," "Bibliographic References--Abbreviations of Typical
Words," "Title Leaves of a Book," "International Standard Serial
Numbers," "International List of Periodical Title Word Abbreviations,"

"Codes for the Representation of Names of Countries," and "Guidelines for the Establishment and Development of Monolingual Thesauri."

In summarizing the current status of standards, Jerrold Orne
wrote recently that "the need for a dynamic program of standardization has been thoroughly documented; it may be second only to the
difficulty of obtaining consensus and adoption of any specific standard.
Despite these complications, increasing numbers of our colleagues
are giving more time and effort to the production of new and revised
standards." Among the reasons for the slow production of standards
are the need to draft definitions, the need usually also to develop a
new terminology, and finally the necessity of going through an adoption procedure.

Progress in standardization during the last two decades has
been sufficiently encouraging to lead to the hope that standards, along
with library statistics, can become basic tools for the international
library research community. Work related to statistics and standards will continue to occupy programs of international library associations.

Conclusion

There seems to be an intrinsic relationship between the political, economic and cultural state of the world and international research studies, including those relating to library science. Reviewing the recent past, most students of research will agree that during
the 1970s these activities diminished in comparison to the work carried on during the 1950s and 1960s. The increased emphasis during
these decades can be explained as an attempt to overcome the isolation, alienation and economic preoccupations during World War II.
The reduction of international research is undoubtedly influenced by
the economic recession of the 1970s. A similar expansion and con-
traction can be traced to World War I and the period between the
two wars.

Seen in this light of the pendular movements of cultural history, international library science research can be compared to the
building of bridges to our colleagues around the globe, and can be
considered a testimony to our professional concern for the free flow
of information and the sharing of data in our area of competence.

NOTES

1. Fang, Josephine R., and Songe, Alice B. International Guide to
    Library, Archival, and Information Science Associations.
    New York: R. R. Bowker Co., 1976.
2. UNESCO. World Guide to Library Schools and Training Courses
    in Documentation. Paris: UNESCO, 1973.
3. "International Library Associations," Bowker Manual of Library

and Book Trade Information.   21st edition, 1976.   New York:
R. R. Bowker Co. , 1976, pp. 333-41.
4.   Schick, Frank L.   "Library Statistics," Encyclopedia of Library
and Information Science.   New York: Marcel Dekker, 1975,
Vol. 16, pp. 63-74.
5.   Op. cit. , pp. 69-70.
6.   Recommendation Concerning the International Standardization of
Library Statistics.   Paris: UNESCO, Nov. 13, 1970.*
7.   Draft International Standards ISO/DIS 2789, International Library
Statistics.   Berlin: ISO/TC46 Secretariat, July 3, 1972.
8.   Recommendation Concerning the International Standardization of
Book Production and Periodicals.   Paris: UNESCO, Nov. 19,
1964.*
9.   Standards for South African Public Libraries.   2nd ed.   Potchef-
stroom, Republic of South Africa, 1968.
10. Orne, J.   "Standards," ALA Yearbook.   1976 Centennial Edition.
Chicago: American Library Association, 1976, pp. 331-33.
11. Op. cit. , p. 331.

---

*A "recommendation" is an international document which has to be
signed by the Secretary of State to be binding on the signatory.   A
treaty is a similar document which has to be ratified by Congress
to oblige a country to cooperate.

PART II

RECENT PROGRESS IN INTERNATIONAL
AND COMPARATIVE LIBRARY SCIENCE

INTERNATIONAL ORGANIZATIONS

David Kaser

It is the purpose of this paper to comment upon the relationship between progress in international library science and the work
of selected international organizations which embrace some kind of
library aspiration within their primary or secondary objectives.   It
will pursue this aim by reviewing a few basic characteristics and
some recent activities programs of several such international organizations, generalizing about the relative effectiveness of some of
their programs and about the strengths and weaknesses of some of
their efforts, and suggesting some reasonable expectations as to future progress in international library science likely to result from
the continuing work of such organizations.   There appears to have
been little written upon these relationships in the past, and the field
seems particularly to need more research.

That research, however, cannot be attempted here.   The nar-
row compass allowed for discussion of the subject in this volume dic-
tates that only a few accomplishments of a few selected organizations
be noted.   The selection of organizations, although somewhat personal and arbitrary, has attempted to take into account the following
three criteria: 1) the likelihood of their continued viability; 2) the
diversity of their organizational or functional profiles; and 3) their
greater appropriateness to this essay than to coverage elsewhere in
this volume.

The following nine international organizations, all with some
kind of primary or subordinate library objective, were chosen as
fitting these three criteria: the Association of International Libraries, the Central Treaty Organization, the International Council of
Scientific Unions, the International Federation of Library Associations,
the International Organization for Standardization, the International
Youth Library, the Seminar on the Acquisition of Latin American Library Materials, the United Nations, and the United Nations Educational Scientific and Cultural Organization.   The diversity at least of
these nine organizations is immediately apparent, yet they have also
some commonality of concern in that they are all interested in libraries.   Some of the basic characteristics of each of these organizations will be brought out in the ensuing paragraphs.

The Association of International Libraries (AIL) was established in 1963 with the promotion of cooperation among international
libraries as its stated purpose.   Membership is available to libraries
of international organizations and to persons prepared to support

AIL's purpose. Its funds are derived from membership dues. AIL
has devoted most of its attention to providing a forum for discussion
of problems common to its members and to such projects as indexing publications of international organizations. AIL is a member of
IFLA. It keeps its members informed of its work through publication of a Newsletter.

The Central Treaty Organization (CENTO) was established in
1955 to achieve collective security through cooperation among Turkey,
Iran, Pakistan, the UK, and the USA in matters of military and political defense, and the promotion of the economic and cultural progress of the regional countries. CENTO maintains a small photographic laboratory and archives; it issues reports, many of which
are restricted in distribution; and it disseminates literature and information needed for its purposes (e. g. , medicine, agriculture, industry, etc). Its costs are borne by its member states.

The International Council of Scientific Unions (ICSU) was
founded in 1919 to facilitate and coordinate activities of the international scientific unions, each of which has the exchange of scientific
knowledge among its primary objectives. In addition to the work of
its member unions in determining international standards, units, and
nomenclature to facilitate communication, ICSU established in 1952
its Abstracting Board to organize and promote international exchange
and publication of primary and secondary publications. ICSU receives funds from its member unions, both national and non-governmental; from UNESCO; and from other sources.

The International Federation of Library Associations (IFLA)
dates from 1927. Its object is to promote cooperation in the field
of librarianship and bibliography, and particularly to carry out investigations and make relevant propositions. A non-governmental
organization, IFLA welcomes library associations to its membership
and libraries to its associate membership. Its budget is based upon
membership dues as well as contracts and grants from such organizations as UNESCO, the Council on Library Resources, and the
Dutch government. During its first thirty years of existence IFLA
was basically a forum for the discussion of librarianship in Western
Europe, but in the last decade especially it has broadened its area
of interest to the entire world and has initiated a number of far-
reaching action programs. It works closely with UNESCO and the
International Federation for Documentation (FID) on projects of common interest. It issues a quarterly Journal.

The International Organization for Standardization (ISO), founded in 1926, has as its purpose to work to develop common industrial,
commercial, engineering, and safety standards throughout the world.
Its Technical Committee 46 handles standards for documentation, and
its work in developing basic rules for such things as bibliographies,
periodicals, and transliteration has facilitated international communication. ISO's membership comprises national committees--one for
each nation--of representatives from scientific and technical organizations which deal with standards. It derives its income from

membership dues and has consultative status within UNESCO.   It issues a monthly Journal.

The International Youth Library (IYL) in Munich dates from
1949.   Intended originally to diminish through books national preju-
dice in the minds of young people, the IYL now continues that purpose as well as serving as a world-wide reference center for information about children's literature.   Although it has received grants
from the Rockefeller Foundation and UNESCO, the IYL derives its
operating budget from the West German government, the Bavarian
state government, and the municipality of Munich.   Its collections
comprise children's books primarily donated by their publishers.

The Seminar on the Acquisition of Latin American Library
Materials (SALALM) came into being in 1956.   SALALM's original
purpose was to provide a forum and clearinghouse of information for
persons charged with the development of Latin American collections
in libraries of the United States.   Its revised constitution, however,
which was adopted in 1968, contains a statement of purpose, some
sixteen paragraphs in length, touching upon many aspects of library
service, education and development in the Western Hemisphere that
relates to Latin America.   Claiming 207 individual members and 89
institutional members in 1974, the Seminar functions on income from
membership dues and registration fees.   Reports of the Seminars
are published.

The United Nations (UN) in 1949 promulgated a statement of
purpose for its libraries; it is to enable the delegations, Secretariat
and other official groups of the Organization to obtain the library
material and information needed in the execution of their duties and
to serve others as possible.   Virtually the entire library mission of
the UN therefore, with the exception of UNESCO, which is discussed
next, is accomplished through the many libraries it operates throughout the world.   In addition to its two major general libraries at the
UN and in Geneva, this organization maintains such special libraries
as those of the International Atomic Energy Agency in Vienna, the
Food and Agriculture Organization in Rome, the Economic Commissions for Africa in Addis Ababa and for Asia in Bangkok, and of the
International Labour Office and World Health Organization, both in
Geneva.

The United Nations Educational, Scientific and Cultural Organization (UNESCO) was established in 1946 for purposes of diffusing
knowledge and culture.   Its efforts to fulfill this broad mandate have
brought it into many library activities, carried on for the most part
through its Division of Libraries, Documentation and Archives.
UNESCO's work on libraries has fallen into three categories: development of libraries; bibliography and documentation; and the international exchange of publications.   A specialized agency of the United Nations, UNESCO is funded by assessments against its member states.
UNESCO has provided subventions to, and supported the work of, a
number of other organizations discussed here, such as ISO, ICSU,
and IFLA, when their work has converged with its own purposes.   It

TABLE I. SELECTED CHARACTERISTICS OF ORGANIZATIONS DISCUSSED

	AIL	CENTO	ICSU	IFLA	ISO	IYL	SALALM	UN	UNESCO
World-Wide	X		X	X	X	X		X	X
Primarily Library	X			X		X	X		
Open Membership	X		X	X	X		X		
Governmental		X				X		X	X
Special Library	X	X	X			X		X	
Multi-Purpose	X			X		X	X		X

TABLE II. LIBRARY ACTIVITIES OF ORGANIZATIONS DISCUSSED

	AIL	CENTO	ICSU	IFLA	ISO	IYL	SALALM	UN	UNESCO
Nat'l/Internat'l Planning				X					X
Bibliog/Coll'n Development	X			X		X	X		X
Delivery of Information		X		X		X		X	X
Standardization			X	X	X				X
Provision of Forums	X			X			X		X

has published the UNESCO Bulletin for Libraries since its inception
and has produced a large number of other manuals, reports, and
compendia of concern to librarianship.

There are few if any common characteristics among these
nine organizations beyond the simple facts that all are international,
all have demonstrated some permanence, and all, in one way or another, embrace some kind of library or library-related purpose.
Some of them are governmental; some are non-governmental.   Some
are world-wide; some are regional.   Some have libraries as their
primary concern; some have libraries as a subordinate concern.
Some are oriented to general libraries, some to special libraries.
Some have a single library purpose; some have many such purposes.
Some have open membership; others have closed membership.   Table I charts some of these diverse characteristics.

Since the nine organizations here under discussion were selected in part because of their diversity, it should not be surprising
that no identifiable patterns of characteristics show up in Table I.
If all international organizations with library objectives were being
considered instead of a selected few, it would doubtless be possible
to propose some kind of reasonable taxonomy or classification for
them.   There are some similarities, for example, between IFLA
and the International Federation for Documentation (FID) and the International Council on Archives (ICA).   AIL shares obvious common
traits with the International Association of Metropolitan City Libraries (INTAMEL) and the International Association of Technological
University Libraries (IATUL).   There are some similarities (as well
as some obvious differences) between SALALM and the Ligue des
bibliothèques européennes de recherche (LIBER).   It would be a useful exercise to make such a classification, but the task is beyond
the scope of the present assignment.   Many of these other organizations are, of course, discussed elsewhere in this collection of essays.

It is a bit easier to group the main library activities of these
several organizations.   With some understandable overlapping and obvious interlocking almost all of them can be gathered under one or
more of five headings: national and international planning; bibliography and collection development; the delivery of information; standardization; and the provision of forums for the discussion of common
problems.   These groupings, although somewhat simplistic, are
shown in Table II.

When Table II is superimposed as a template over Table I, a
few rudimentary correlations seem to emerge.   As one would expect,
the two world-wide organizations with multi-purposes--IFLA and
UNESCO--turn up in all five activities groups.   These two, moreover,
are the only organizations with aims sufficiently all-embracing to pre-
sume to engage in the complex work of national and international planning.   Only the five organizations with multifarious library interests
--AIL, IFLA, IYL, SALALM, and UNESCO--are engaged extensively
in bibliographic and collection development work.   Joining IFLA and
UNESCO in their concern for the delivery of information are the

three governmental organizations serving specialized clienteles--
CENTO, IYL, and the UN.   The two organizations with major concern for special scientific communication--ICSU and ISO--share
IFLA's and UNESCO's interest and activity in standardization.   IFLA
and UNESCO, together with the two open-membership library organizations with multi-purposes--AIL and SALALM--actively provide
forums for the discussion of common problems.

     It is important to note that any apparent pattern of interrela-
tionships between these organizational profiles and activities must be
perceived here solely as observations with neither generalizations
nor claims for causality ascribed to them.   They are much too
sketchy to reveal more.   They may be wholly coincidental.   They
deserve to be examined in greater detail in hopes that further observation might indeed permit of some meaningful generalizations as
well as allow some evaluation of program effectiveness of certain organizational profiles.

     Such research into program effectiveness should of course
take also into account questions of program significance.   The recent
omnibus program of UNESCO to develop "national information systems" (NATIS), for example, brings together under a single rubric
many of its own traditional concerns as well as representing a con-
vergence of many of the long-established programs and aspirations
of IFLA, FID, and ICA.   Certainly if NATIS does not let itself be
overwhelmed by its own sheer grandeur, and if it can sustain the
good will of all relevant parties, its significance may well prove
paramount among all of the programs here under discussion.

     Program effectiveness clearly derives also from strengths
and weaknesses of the promulgating organizations, and these also
would benefit from careful investigation.   A cursory review of the
nine organizations being examined in this paper appears to permit a
few trial generalizations on this matter.

     The following, for example, seem rather obviously to be
sources of strength in international organizations claiming library
purposes:

     1) Sound continuing objectives.   Those appear to serve best
that strike a balance: they should be broad enough to allow the completion of some projects and programs and the initiation of others
without revising an organization's statement of purpose; they should
also be specific enough to sustain the interest and enthusiasm of a
constituency.   This is not an easy balance to find.   A primary objective of "providing a forum" seldom proves to be of lasting satisfaction.   AIL, IFLA, and SALALM, for example, have all found it
necessary to broaden their interest to embrace action programs.

     2) Assurance of continuous funding.   With the exception of the
IYL and SALALM, all of these organizations have operated from the
beginning with assurance of continuous funding, and this funding has
proved essential to their viability.   There appears to be a common

tendency, on the other hand, for international organizations to dissi-
pate energy from time to time wrangling over the distribution of assessments among member states. It would perhaps seem reasonable
to base assessments upon value received, but such calculations have
been difficult to agree upon.

3) Human resources. Most of the nine organizations have
been able to draw heavily upon the volunteer efforts of their individual members or delegates. In fact, most of their programs have
been conducted by volunteers with the benefit of only limited financial support. For the organizations other than CENTO, IYL, and
UN to buy and pay for fulfillment of their programs would simply be
beyond their means.

4) Prestige. High prestige has been essential to program effectiveness among the nine organizations under discussion here. The
ability of the prestigious among them to bring moral suasion upon
nations to support decisions taken at the supra-national level has
proved very useful. For this reason, the recent coalition in support
of common goals of UNESCO, with its influence upon the governments of its member states, and IFLA/FID/ICA, with their influence upon non-governmental professional communities, seems particularly felicitous.

The aggregate experiences of these nine international organizations, on the other hand, seem also to permit the following generalizations to be proposed as to sources of weakness:

1) Finding common problems. Lacking as they do the force
of law, international organizations must identify their goals through
consensus, a commodity difficult to attain among nations with widely
diverse traditions; educational, technical, and economic problems;
levels of industrial development; and resulting concepts of priority
need.

2) Representative participation. A problem common to all organizations, the "representativeness" of international bodies is doubly
difficult to attain--first at the national level and then, from within
that constituency, at the international level. Except in states with
central authority, the problem of unrepresentative participation in
some of these organizations has sometimes resulted in slowness of
national approbation for international actions or in ill-considered international decisions which may not be perceived locally as being in
the best interests of the member states.

3) Duplication of effort. There has been some duplication of
effort among a number of these organizations, but with each discrete
effort manifesting an emphasis somewhat different from the others,
as with UNISIST/INIS/AGRIS and IFLA's "Universal Bibliographical
Control." Such conflicting emphases can be counter-productive if they
are not consciously resolved through inter-organizational cooperation,
as these particular conflicts have recently been. An ameliorating
factor in some such situations in the past has been the fact that

sometimes the key individuals active in one organization have also
been active in other seemingly duplicative organizations.

4) Growing pains.   This ailment is as endemic to international organizations as to any other fast-growing organisms.   The faster
the development, the greater is the portion of an organization's energy that must go to non-productive sustenance of its infrastructure.
From among the nine groups here being reviewed, SALALM and
IFLA especially have recently suffered from this problem.

There are certainly other strengths and other weaknesses in
these nine organizations, some perhaps of even greater moment than
the ones noted here.   Some of these strengths and weaknesses may
be structural while others may be ascribable to other causes.   Investigation in greater depth may help to identify ways in which their
strengths can be ultimately enhanced and their weaknesses diminished,
or the ratio of the former to the latter improved, in support of program effectiveness.

Even such a superficial recounting as this one of the landmark issues and accomplishments in international library science
through international organizations reveals a couple of apparent long-
term trends on the basis of which future expectations may probably
be warranted.   Primary among these trends is the inexorable movement throughout this century toward increasing international library
cooperation.   This trend has been largely promoted by international
organizations which, interestingly, have increased considerably their
own interorganizational cooperation in the process, resulting in less
duplication of effort among them.   A second notable long-term trend
resulting from the work of all nine of these organizations, whether
in fulfillment of stated objectives or not, has been increased standardization in a wide range of library-related matters--bibliographical
description, technical terminology, professional practice, transliteration, educational method, and a host of other specific areas.

Thus far there appear to be few if any counter-tendencies
which might in the coming decades reverse or seriously impede progress in these two important areas of international library science.
Here again, however, it seems reasonable to expect that research
into the work of international library-oriented organizations would
help not only to clarify what is happening in the field but to sharpen
expectations as to likely developments as well.

REFERENCES

American Library Association.   International Relations Office.   Who
        Is Doing What in International Book and Library Programs.
        Washington: The Office, 1967.
Bowker Annual of Library and Book Trade Information.   20th ed.
        New York: R. R. Bowker, 1975.
Encyclopedia of Library and Information Science.   New York:
        Marcel Dekker, 1968-

International Federation of Library Associations.   IFLA Journal.   1,
    1975-
Landau, Thomas, ed.   Encyclopaedia of Librarianship.   3d ed.
    New York: Hafner, 1966.
Ligue des Bibliothèques Européennes de Recherche.   Acquisitions
    from Around the World.   London: Mansell, 1975.
Seminar on the Acquisition of Latin American Library Materials.
    Final Report and Working Papers.   1, 1956-
UNESCO Bulletin for Libraries.   1, 1947-
U. S. Library of Congress.   International Scientific Organizations.
    Washington, D. C. : The Library, 1962.

NATIONAL ORGANIZATIONS

Norman Horrocks

Other chapters have shown the involvement of various national
library associations in the work of such international bodies as
UNESCO, NATIS, IFLA, and FID. This chapter will look at some
of the ways in which national associations have handled their international concerns internally, i. e. , as part of their domestically based
programs. Major emphasis will be placed on the associations in
North America and Great Britain. From the very earliest days of
library associations there have been transatlantic links. James
Yates of the Free Library of Leeds, England, was present at the inaugural conference of the American Library Association in Philadelphia, 1876. A party of twelve U. S. librarians returned the compli-
ment by sailing the Atlantic to attend the inaugural meeting of the
Library Association in London in 1877. It is a pleasing coincidence
that in 1977, the President of the American Library Association will
be a librarian, born and educated in England, who, after a brief
spell in Canada, has now settled in the United States.

American Library Association

The history of the international activities of the American Library Association has been well documented in the literature. Not
only have there been many articles on various aspects of ALA's work,
but, in addition, the monthly newsletter, Libraries in International
Development, was a regular source for information during the years
of its publication, 1968-72. A good starting point for our present
purpose is the survey by Peggy Sullivan in the January 1972 Library
Trends. [1] This frank and entertaining essay was written at the time
when ALA was in the process, for the second time, of phasing out
its International Relations Office. It was somewhat ironic that this
closure came in 1972, designated as International Book Year.

The International Relations Office drew its rationale from the
section of the ALA charter which gave as one of the Association's
purposes, "promoting library interests throughout the world. "

To fulfill this obligation the International Relations Office had
responsibility for:

(1) helping foundations and government agencies to identify,
develop, administer, and evaluate projects and plans involving libraries or library materials abroad and the interna-

tional aspects of library programs in the United States--
thereby giving professional assistance and counsel to other
agencies, institutions, and individuals; (2) assisting in promoting the exchange of librarians; (3) offering assistance
in promoting library education and training programs
abroad, and training librarians from overseas in the United
States; (4) disseminating pertinent information abroad about
the state of librarianship in the United States and information about the international activities of ALA to all interested parties in the United States and abroad. [2]

The small staff, headed at this time by David G. Donovan, operated
from the ALA International Relations Office in Washington, D. C.

The late 1960s and early 1970s was a time of great ferment
within ALA as the Association sought to re-establish its priorities
against the background of political turmoil within the United States
itself.   In 1970, the Association's Activities Committee on New Directions recommended that international programs be carried forward
in an Office for Social Responsibility.   The later ANACONDA report
was more direct and specific in recommending that the ALA Council
"reaffirm the Association's commitment to activities and programs
in the area of international relations including the International Relations Office. "

Despite these sentiments, financial stringency led to the closure of the International Relations Office, which had been dependent
on outside funding.   When this was withdrawn, the Association was
unwilling to find replacement funds from within its own budget.   The
responsibility for international activities within ALA fell to the International Relations Committee, which had hitherto been an advisory
body to the Office.   The International Relations Committee, a standing committee of the ALA Council, has as its mandate:

To promote the exchange of librarians between this and
other countries; to encourage and facilitate the use of library and bibliographic techniques and knowledge throughout the world; to assist in the exchange of professional information, ideas, and literature between this and other
countries; to coordinate the activities of other units of the
association within this field. [3]

The eight-member Committee, meeting twice a year--at the Midwinter and Summer ALA meetings--did what it could to respond to matters referred to it.   Headquarters staff support was provided by Executive Director Robert Wedgeworth with assistance from divisional
executive secretaries.   Lacking was the full-time attention to international activities formerly given by the Director of the International
Relations Office.

The International Relations Committee felt the need for focus-
ing attention on the diminished importance within the Association of
international matters.   At the January 1973 Midwinter meeting of the

Association, the International Relations Committee asked for and
gained Council approval for the appointment of an ad hoc committee
to study the international dimension of ALA's responsibilities, with
the following directions:

> ... to review broadly this area of activity and the funding
> thereof within the Association, to confer with the Interna-
> tional Relations Committee at Las Vegas (site of the 1973
> Summer Conference) and to report its decision no later
> than the 1974 Midwinter meeting. [4]

This ad hoc Committee was chaired by Keith Doms, director of the
Free Library of Philadelphia.   It held open hearings, received written testimony and had several meetings before presenting its final
report at the 1974 Summer Conference in New York, after having
given a progress report at Midwinter. [5]

The major recommendation of the Committee's report called
for the establishment of the position of international relations coordinator at ALA headquarters.   The duties of the coordinator were to
be a liaison for international relations within ALA and with other national, regional and local library associations.   It was expected that
the person to be appointed would be knowledgeable enough to respond
to overseas experience, also.   The adoption of the ad hoc committee's report by the ALA Council did not guarantee funding of this
position.   In accordance with ALA procedures, the Committee on
Program Evaluation and Support (COPES) had to include funding in
its 1975-76 fiscal year budget which Council then had to approve.
It was thus necessary to obtain both Council and COPES support.
At the January 1975 Midwinter meeting Council Orientation Session,
Esther J. Walls, who had chaired the International Relations Committee in 1973-74, presented an Issue Paper to Councilors which explained to them the importance and significance of the international
dimension of ALA's programs. [6]   This writer, who chaired the International Relations Committee in 1974-75, presented the Committee's
case to COPES.   Executive Director Wedgeworth lent his strong support to the cause and the position of International Relations Coordinator was duly funded.

In January 1976, Jane Wilson was appointed to this position
at the ALA headquarters in Chicago.   A graduate of the University
of California at Berkeley School of Librarianship, Ms. Wilson had
had experience as Librarian for the Asia Foundation in San Francisco, had traveled extensively and worked in Europe, Asia and South
America, and had been active in ALA international affairs.   In
this position, Ms. Wilson serves as staff liaison to both the International Relations Committee and the International Relations Round
Table.

The International Library Education Committee serves also
as a Committee of the Library Education Division of ALA.   The
International Library Education Committee is

Responsible for projects relating to both basic and continuing library education outside the United States, gathering
and disseminating information about library education in
other countries, promoting the exchange of library educators between this and other countries, promoting the exchange of information on curriculum and teaching methods
between library education programs in this and other countries, facilitating aid to library education programs in
emerging nations. [7]

Until 1974 the Library Education Division had an Equivalencies and
Reciprocity Committee, which was concerned with reconciling foreign
library qualifications with those awarded in North America. Finding
this task impossible, the Committee voted itself out of existence but,
in doing so, transferred to the International Library Education Committee responsibility for the maintenance of a Directory of Country
Resource Panels. This Directory, edited by Nasser Sharify,
lists for a number of countries and regions the names of three experts who can give advice on the educational level of library qualifications there. [8] One of the three is a resident of the country or
region concerned. The International Library Education Committee
has also produced two statements for distribution from ALA headquarters in response to frequent inquiries received there. One reviews the requirements for employment in libraries in the United
States and the other the requirements for admission to U.S. library
schools.

A sub-committee of the International Relations Committee
is designated as advisory and is for Liaison with Japanese Libraries.
It is concerned with arranging meetings from time to time in Japan
and the United States which bring together librarians of higher education and research institutions. Members of the International Relations Committee and the International Library Education Committee are normally appointed for the standard two-year term. Membership of the Liaison with Japanese Libraries sub-committee appears to be virtually self-perpetuating.

The other major ALA unit with international concerns is the
International Relations Round Table. A Round Table can be formed,
with the approval of Council, on the petition "of not less than 100
members of the Association who are interested in the same field of
librarianship not within the scope of any division. ... " (A Division
represents a type of library or type of library activity.) The IRRT
was established in 1949 as the Round Table for Library Work Abroad.
Its primary objectives then were:

(1) To investigate the current situation regarding library
work in its international aspects; and (2) to explore the
possibilities of implementing existing programs and developing others to improve international library relations and
library services throughout the world. [9]

Not only has the title of the Round Table been changed but
also its terms of reference, which now read:

To develop the interests of libraries in activities and problems in the field of international library relations; to serve
as a channel of communication and counsel between the International Relations Committee and the members of the
Association; and to provide hospitality and information to
visitors from abroad.   The I.R.R.T. arranges programs
and business meetings and appoints representatives to attend meetings of the other professional groups. [10]

Membership in IRRT is open to any member of ALA interested in its
activities, upon payment of a modest annual subscription.   In addition to receiving free of charge the quarterly newsletter, Leads, now
edited by Edward Moffat, Round Table members are eligible to
vote for members of the Round Table's Executive Committee.   This
Committee comprises the Chair, Vice-Chair, Secretary-Treasurer,
Past Chair and two members-at-large.   The Round Table has two
standing committees: membership and nominating.   In addition, it
has area chairpersons who have interest in and responsibility for
certain designated areas in the world.

The IRRT Executive Committee meets at the Midwinter and
Summer meetings of ALA.   At the Summer meeting, traditionally it
holds a general business meeting linked with a program meeting and
sponsors a reception for foreign visitors. [11]   At this reception, held
in a prominent library or cultural institution in the host city, all
foreign visitors are invited as guests of the Round Table.   Generally
members of the ALA Executive Board attend also to greet foreign
visitors in what is regarded as one of the most pleasant occasions
of the annual conference.

Although the International Relations Committee and the International Relations Round Table and their various subcommittees are
directly concerned with ALA's international activities, there are
other bodies both within and outside the Association working in this
area.   Joint committees operate with ALA representation often determined by one of the Association's units.   The 1975-76 ALA Handbook on Organization[12] shows the following joint committees with international concerns: 1) the ad hoc Joint Steering Committee for Revision of the Anglo-American Cataloging Rules (AACR) which has
representatives from ALA, the Library Association (of the United
Kingdom), the Canadian Library Association, and the Library of Congress; 2) the Association for Childhood Education International and
American Association of School Librarians joint committee, which is
concerned with the paperback field; 3) the ALA Resources and Technical Services Division Joint Advisory Committee on Nonbook Materials with the Canadian Library Association, Educational Media Association of Canada, Music Library Association of Canada and Association of Educational Communication and Technology, which is concerned with rules for organizing nonbook materials in libraries and
revisions of the AACR.

ALA appoints representatives to outside agencies and holds
membership in organizations outside the United States.   As in some

instances given above, these include links with Canadian bodies
and a special relationship between the American Library Association and the Canadian Library Association. This is exemplified by
the arrangement whereby the ALA Committee on Accreditation is
recognized by the Canadian Library Association as the agency to ac-
credit first professional degrees in Canadian library schools. In addition to this, ALA has representatives to and/or membership in the
Association for Asian Studies, the Association of American Library
Schools, the Association of International Libraries, the International
Association of Law Libraries, the International Association of School
Librarianship, the International Board on Books for Young People,
the International Federation for Documentation, the International Federation of Library Associations, the International Personnel Management Association, the Library Association of the United Kingdom,
the Library Association of the United Kingdom's Hospital Libraries
and Handicapped Readers Group, the Middle East Librarians' Association, the United Nations--its U.S. Mission and Non-Governmental
Organizations/Public Information Office, U.S. Department of State,
Bureau of Economic Affairs; its Advisory Panel on Copyright Matters, and its Government Advisory Committee on International Book
and Library Programs--and the U.S. National Commission for
UNESCO. [13]

The international concerns of ALA are by no means exhausted
by the above listings and descriptions. Some Divisions and Round
Tables have committees with international programs. These include
the American Association of School Librarians International Relations
Committee, the Association of College and Research Libraries Asian
and African Section, the ACRL Slavic and East European Section, the
ACRL Western European Language Specialists Discussion Group, the
ACRL affiliate--the Ukrainian Librarians' Association of America,
the Children's Services Division International Relations Committee,
the Health and Rehabilitative Library Services Division International
Relations Committee, and the Government Documents Round Table International Documents Task Force. Other units, e.g., the Resources
and Technical Services Division, which may not have a specifically
designated international committee, are also involved with international matters.

Technically, all international activities of the units mentioned
above should be coordinated by the International Relations Committee,
according to its mandate. To achieve this, representatives from
these units meet with the IRC at the Midwinter and Summer meetings
of the Association. However, in many instances in recent years the
Committee was reacting to matters brought to it rather than initiating
or even coordinating activities. At the 1975 Summer Conference of
ALA, the Committee organized a program meeting entitled "The International Dimensions of A. L. A." At this session, those present
heard a brief introduction to ALA's international programs and reports from representatives of a number of ALA units. Brief sum-
maries of these presentations in the October/November 1975 issue of
the IRRT's Leads give a useful if selective overview of ALA's international concerns.

At the conclusion of the meeting, Executive Director Wedgeworth spoke and

> challenged the IRC and members of the audience to develop
> a coherent and well-focused ALA international relations
> policy. He reminded his listeners that one of the under-
> lying reasons behind the closing of the ALA International
> Relations Office in 1972 was the lack of commitment on
> the part of the general ALA membership to an internation-
> al relations program. For this reason, it was imperative
> that the IRC, with help from concerned ALA members, de-
> velop a cohesive ALA international relations policy that
> focuses on specific commitments that can be supported
> throughout the Association--a general 'concern' with inter-
> national activities will not be enough. [14]

It was clear that Wedgeworth, having given his strong support to the
recommendations of the ad hoc committee leading to the appointment
of an International Relations Coordinator, did not wish to see another
setback to the Association's international program. In effect, he
was putting the International Relations Committee on notice that it
could not take its existence for granted; it had not only to formulate a
policy for the Association but also to see that this policy is explained,
interpreted and "sold" to the membership at large.   The Committee
has before it the usual dilemma of responding to immediate matters
--e. g. , nominating representatives to the Bookweek U.S.A. program
in Ibadan, Nigeria, a joint project of ALA and the Association of
American Publishers, or advising on possible ALA assistance to a
proposed library school in Tanzania--and looking at medium-range
problems such as developing a statement of responsibility for ALA
representatives to international meetings and events, while also developing a long-term strategy for the international relations policy
as envisaged by Wedgeworth.

It will not be an easy task but it is an essential one for reasons given elsewhere:

> First, the entire world of librarianship, of which the U.S.
> is a part, is going forward and if the U.S. wants to have
> any influence on the nature and direction of this progress,
> then it has to make known its views. Second, to do this
> effectively, it has to know what is happening in other parts
> of the world. ...   Third, there is still a tremendous reser-
> voir of library expertise in this country which could profit-
> ably be made available to other countries. ... [15]

In purely tactical terms, the International Relations Committee
might study the means by which another standing committee of Council, the Intellectual Freedom Committee, has been successful in cop-
ing with both the short-term and long-range problems in its area
while at the same time mobilizing Council support for its operations.
Somewhat ironically perhaps, the two Committees were brought together in 1973-74 when they were directed by Council to develop a

policy for dealing with cases in the intellectual freedom area affecting foreign nationals. The resulting statement, largely drafted by
Kathleen Molz, was adopted as Council policy at the Summer 1974
meeting. [15,16] Its implementation soon followed when at the Midwinter 1975 meeting a jointly sponsored resolution was brought to Council, and carried, protesting the exclusion of Israel from certain regional affiliations in UNESCO. [17] There have since been other matters considered by the two committees in the light of this policy, not
always with agreement between the two. Despite its being Council
policy, drawn up with the full cooperation of the International Relations Committee, not all members of the Association who have international interests look with favor on these almost always tendentious
matters coming before the Committee.

Other North American Library Associations

The American Library Association is not the only national association in the United States which has international programs.
Other associations have appropriate committee structures; e. g. , the
Medical Library Association has its International Cooperation Committee with the following terms of reference:

> The Committee consists of as many members as deemed
> necessary, each member serving at least two years. The
> membership has international representation. The Interna-
> tional Editor of the Bulletin and MLA News is an ex officio
> member, as is the MLA representative to the Bridging
> Committee for the International Congress on Medical Li-
> brarianship.

> The Committee serves as a clearing house on medical li-
> brarianship for foreign librarians, libraries and related
> organizations. It collects information on international edu-
> cational, scholarship, and fellowship opportunities and on
> exchange programs. It awards and administers the annual
> Cunningham fellowships. The Committee members coordi-
> nate itineraries and other plans for visiting foreign librari-
> ans. [18]

Others, such as the Special Libraries Association, have affiliations with other organizations in the international field; e. g. , with
the Association of American Library Schools, Canadian Library Association, International Federation of Library Associations, and the
United Nations Office of Public Information, Non-Governmental Organizations. In addition, SLA has European, Montreal and Toronto chapters. There is Canadian involvement with other chapters, most no-
ticeably that of the Pacific Northwest; just as the Medical Library
Association has a Canadian group and strong involvement with the Pacific Northwest Regional Group, and the Upstate New York and Ontario Regional Groups.

The Canadian Library Association has an International Relations Committee with these terms of reference:

> To collect information of interest to Canadian libraries
> and librarians about international meetings and activities
> and to distribute it to the members. To seek ways in
> which Canadian librarians can be better informed of and
> can more actively participate in international library activ-
> ities. [19]

At the 1975 annual conference in Toronto, this Committee heard reports from the various international organizations to which CLA belongs: the International Association of School Libraries, the Commonwealth Library Association, the International Federation of Library Associations, UNESCO, the Special Libraries Association and
the International Board on Books for Young People. Despite some
recent procedural reorganizations, this Committee does not seem to
have made any great impact on the CLA membership. Its budget for
1975-76 was modest--$250, and it is difficult to see what major im-
pact it can have at this level of support. This is not to say that
Canadian librarianship cannot influence the international scene in ways
which will be examined below.

The Library Association

The Library Association of the United Kingdom has a long
history of involvement in the international arena although it is only
in comparatively recent years that this has shown in the organizational chart. The International and Comparative Librarianship Group was
formed in 1967. [20] In the organizational structure of the LA, a
Group is formed upon receipt of a request in writing from not less
than fifty members of the Association. The Council shall have power
to create a Group notwithstanding that no such request has been received. [21] The International and Comparative Librarianship Group has
officers and area representatives in a manner somewhat akin to that
of the ALA's International Relations Round Table.

At its 1971 meeting, the Group passed the following resolution:

> that the Council of the Library Association be asked to re-
> consider as a matter of urgency the decision not to investi-
> gate the establishment of an International Relations Office
> and that the Association should immediately establish a
> Standing Committee on International Relations to advise on
> and coordinate the already considerable international com-
> munications and documentation of the Association and its
> membership. [22]

This view was supported in the Report of the Working Party on (Library) Association Services and by the head of the School of Librarianship at the Polytechnic of North London, Edward Dudley. [23]

As seen in the above resolution, the International and Comparative Librarianship Group has been seeking the establishment of
an International Relations Office for the Library Association. It has

based its case in large part on the Dudley paper, which made three major points:

> 1. The LA should recognize that it is virtually the only body which could coordinate the work of international collaboration in this country and speak for librarians in this matter.

> 2. The Association must decide on its priorities and, thus, the deployment of finance, and, if it was decided not to establish an IRO, this must be done in the full knowledge that a significant international role has been lost.

> 3. The least the LA could do at present is to constitute a proper policy and a deliberative body which could advise Council and Officers on matters of international library affairs. [24]

Harold Lancour, speaking to the ICLG, gave additional support to the cause by explaining the achievements of ALA's International Relations Office. [25]

For reasons which would be familiar to those close to the American Library Association scene--namely, finance--there is not yet an International Relations Office at LA headquarters in London. There is now an International Relations Sub-Committee of the General Purposes Committee of the LA which might be regarded as approximating to the International Relations Committee of ALA. The Deputy Secretary of the Library Association, Dan Haslam, served as International Relations Officer until his retirement in April 1976. The new Deputy Secretary of the Association will be Russell Bowden, now a member of the International Relations Sub-Committee and an active participant in the work of the Group.

In an interview in the Library Association Record at the time his new appointment was announced, Bowden is quoted as saying that "He sees continued progress in relationships with ... organs like IFLA and COMLA (the Commonwealth Library Association), which contribute to international harmony and peace. "[26]

We might accept the parallel between the LA's International Relations Sub-Committee and the ALA's International Relations Committee, or that of the International and Comparative Librarianship Group and the International Relations Round Table (even to the extent that both issue newsletters, Focus and Leads; the ICLG issues an Occasional Papers series for which neither IRRT nor IRC can offer any parallel). However, there is another body in the Library Association which has no parallel in ALA, the Association of Assistant Librarians. The AAL has its own International Relations Officer, a volunteer, who has been very active in recent years in arranging for international tours of foreign librarians to the U.K. and of British librarians abroad.

One of the early major concerns of the ICLG was "the problem of the international reciprocity and equivalency of library qualifications." As noted above, the ALA has given up on this task--at least for the time being--as has the Canadian Library Association, but organizations other than the LA still regard it as a matter of concern, as is shown by the recent activities in Australia, in the Commonwealth Library Association and potentially in the European Economic Community. [27,28,29] For many years, the Library Association was a major influence on the education of librarians in many parts of the world. This was achieved through its system of holding examinations in overseas centers; by this means successful candidates could prepare themselves for admission to the Register as Chartered, i. e., professionally qualified, Librarians. With the growth of library schools in overseas countries and for other educational reasons, the Association is phasing out the overseas examination centers. However, it is still accepting overseas candidates for the Fellowship by thesis.

Other Organizations

As mentioned above, national library associations are not the only bodies concerned with international library developments. Many national organizations of a governmental or quasi-governmental nature are involved. In the United States, the United States International Agency (USIA) operating overseas as the United States Information Service (USIS) and a branch of the State Department, is the best known. Through it, U. S. librarianship is made known in regions throughout the world, not only by example but also by the provision of in-service training facilities to librarians in the host countries.

Foundations, very much a feature of United States life, have supported librarianship overseas either directly--e. g., the Carnegie Corporation of New York and the Rockefeller Foundation--or through other agencies, e. g., the Ford Foundation through the Council of Library Resources. The Asia Foundation has for some years funded Asian students of librarianship in the United States to attend the annual conference of the American Library Association. The State Department has operated a program whereby promising middle-rank librarians from overseas countries are brought to the United States for several weeks to attend formal instruction at the Graduate School of Library and Information Sciences at the University of Pittsburgh, followed by practical work at libraries in various parts of the country.

In Canada, agencies such as the Canadian International Development Agency and the International Development and Research Centre have supported projects in the field of librarianship. In Britain, the British Council has been a major factor in supporting librarianship not only abroad--in a manner akin to but different from the USIS--but also by bringing many overseas librarians to the United Kingdom for formal study and study tours. [30] One of the centers for which the British Council has sponsored overseas visitors is the annual International Graduate Summer School in Librarianship and Informa-

tion Science, held at the College of Librarianship, Wales in conjunction with that institution and the Graduate School of Library and Information Sciences of the University of Pittsburgh.

Given the straitened circumstances of the American, British
and Canadian Library Associations, the comparatively liberal financial support of the various governmental and quasi-governmental
agencies has led to their playing an increasingly important role in
international library developments. It is a possible area for research to determine whether more significant progress has been
achieved under library association auspices or by others. What
might be studied, also, is the influence of library schools on international library developments. A recent tabulation in Leads shows
the number of North American schools which have faculty who have
an interest in international and comparative library science. [31] Certain schools have made significant contributions not only by their programs for students from overseas countries--e. g. , Dalhousie,[32]
Denver,[33] Pittsburgh[34]--but also by their provision of faculty members to teach in overseas schools--e. g. , Dalhousie, Kent State, Illinois, Western Ontario. Pittsburgh's International Library Information Centre was developed at first by Nasser Sharify, and has been
continued by William V. Jackson and now by Richard Krzys. [35] Other
schools have provided consultancies for overseas countries; one of
the most recent and ambitious has been that coordinated by Nasser
Sharify at Pratt Institute for the national library service of Iran. [36]

In Britain there is room for improvement in the degree of library schools' concern for studies in international and comparative
library science. [37] There are obvious exceptions to this generalization.
The College of Librarianship, Wales with its International Summer
School has been mentioned already.   The Liverpool School of Librarianship offers each summer a program on European library science
and other schools offer occasional international courses or tours. The
work of Mme. Simsova at the Polytechnic of North London is known
throughout the library world by her Handbook of Comparative Librarianship, now in its second edition (1975). [38] The University of Sheffield
School of Librarianship has made many international contributions
through the work of its Director, W. L. Saunders, and his staff. One of
the features of library education in different parts of the world is still
the presence of international faculty members, e. g. , United States faculty in Iran, such as Alice Lohrer, John F. Harvey and Beverley Brewster;
American, British and Canadian faculty in the West Indies, such as Dorothy Collings, J. Clement Harrison, Frank Hogg and Janette White; Ronald Benge from Britain in Ghana; Larry Amey from Canada at both Ibadan
and Ahmadu Bello in Nigeria; and the many American and British educators in Australia--John Dean, A. C. Foskett, Nancy Lane, Ann Painter,
Michael Ramsden, Edward Reid-Smith, and Melvin Weinstock, among
others. Co-incidentally with all of this importation by Australia the International Library Review is now edited from that country since George
Chandler went to the National Library of Australia.

What of the future? --As has been shown above, the national
library associations and their involvement with international programs

are at something of a crossroads. The American Library Association, with its recently appointed staff officer, is seeking to reestab-
lish its international role in a manner not yet determined by its International Relations Committee. The Canadian Library Association,
in its present financial difficulties, can do little on the operating
budget it has granted to its International Relations Committee. Both
ALA and CLA have established top-level review committees this
year, designed to recommend possible changes in organizational
structure. It will be interesting to see how these review committees regard their international programs.

"In Britain, by the recent reorganization of its committee
structure, the Library Association Council now has the opportunity
to re-examine the place of international activities in its overall program. "39 When looking at the British scene, it is always necessary
to remember the strength represented in the Register of Chartered
Librarians, i. e. , those who are regarded as professionally qualified
by virtue of being Associates or Fellows of the Association. Reten-
tion of this qualification is dependent upon the payment of annual
dues. Failure to pay means the withdrawal of the credential, not
something that is taken lightly by its holders. As a result, there
is still a considerable membership in the Library Association of
British librarians who are working overseas and of librarians from
outside Britain who have qualified in the British system. The withdrawal of the overseas examination centers will affect this situation
although it will be some years before the impact is felt. The recently established Commonwealth Library Association may develop
into a unifying force in the manner of the Library Association at
present.

There is, then, still considerable activity in the international
aspects of librarianship outside the national associations--through library schools, foundations, and government agencies. Yet the associations remain the obvious focal point for bringing together all interested parties. It will be the challenge of the next few years to
these associations to see that their role is clearly delineated and
supported by their members.

NOTES

1. Sullivan, Peggy, "International Relations Program of the Ameri-
    can Library Association," Library Trends XX (January 1972),
    pp. 577-591.
2. Donovan, David G. , "International Relations Activities of the
    American Library Association in 1970," Bowker Annual ...
    1971. New York: R. R. Bowker Co. , 1971, p. 454.
3. American Library Association. Handbook of Organization. Chi-
    cago: ALA, 1975-1976, p. 9.
4. "Information Report to Council of Ad Hoc Committee to Study In-
    ternational Responsibilities, Jan. 25, 1974. " 1973-74 ALA
    Council Document # 23, p. 1.
5. Ibid.

6. "ALA's Role in International Relations: issue paper for Council
    Orientation at Midwinter meeting, January 1975; submitted by
    Esther J. Walls."
7. ALA Handbook, op. cit., p. 40.
8. American Library Association. International Education Commit-
    tee. Directory of Country Resource Panels, 1975.
9. ALA Bulletin XLIII (June 1949), p. 215.
10. ALA Handbook, op. cit., pp. 57-58.
11. However, see Norman Horrocks "What's Ahead for the Interna-
    tional Relations Round Table," Leads XVI (March 1973), pp.
    1-5.
12. ALA Handbook ... passim.
13. ALA Handbook ... passim.
14. "The International Dimensions of ALA," Leads XVII (October/
    November 1975), p. 6.
15. Norman Horrocks. "The U.S. In World Librarianship," Library
    Journal CI (January 1, 1976), p. 223.
16. "Policy on the Abridgement of the Rights of Freedom of Expres-
    sion of Foreign Nationals." ALA Policy Statement 103, 12.
    Approved July 1974.
17. See the account in Wilson Library Bulletin XLIX (March 1975),
    "ALA Midwinter 1975," p. 486.
18. Medical Library Association. Directory, 1975-76. Chicago:
    MLA, 1976, p. 14.
19. Canadian Library Association. Directory of Committees, 1975/
    76, p. 27.
20. See Marigold Cleeve, "International and Comparative Librarian-
    ship, 1967/68," International Library Review I (January 1969),
    pp. 93-96; and Colin Norris, "The International and Compara-
    tive Librarianship Group of the Library Association, 1970-
    1972," International Library Review V (October 1973), pp. 381-
    385.
21. The Library Association. Year Book, 1975. London: LA, p.
    41.
22. Quoted in M. Dewe and G. E. Gleave, "An International Rela-
    tions Office for the Library Association," Library Association
    Record LXXV (April 1973), p. 73.
23. E. P. Dudley. "Internationalism, Public Libraries and Library
    Associations," in Proceedings, Library Association Public Li-
    braries Conference, 1971, London, pp. 41-51.
24. Dewe and Gleave, op. cit.
25. Quoted in M. Dewe, "A British International Relations Office:
    A Report," Focus III (April 1972), pp. 5-14.
26. "Serving the Profession as a Whole," Library Association Record
    LXXVIII (April 1976), p. 143.
27. "Foreign Librarians and the Committee on Overseas Professional
    Qualifications," Australian Library Journal XXIII (October
    1974), pp. 313-315.
28. COMLA Newsletter, passim.
29. Herbert Schur. "The European Communities and the Harmoniza-
    tion of Educational and Professional Qualifications," Journal
    of Librarianship VII (January 1975), pp. 49-65.
30. Although dated, the thrust remains as shown in Henry James,

Jr., "To Win Friends," Library Journal LXXXI (March 1, 1956), pp. 589-595.

31. Norman Horrocks, "Schools Offering Courses in International Librarianship," Leads VI (June 1975), p. 13.

32. Through links with EMPRAPA--Empresa Brasileira de Pesquisa Agropecuaria in Brasilia.

33. Through its program for Latin American students.

34. Through its hosting for the U.S. Department of State of the program for Multi-National Librarians.

35. "International Library Center Established by the University of Pittsburgh," Library Journal XC (April 15, 1965), p. 1854.

36. "Planning on Unprecedented Scale Shaping New National Library," American Libraries VI (November 1975), p. 587.

37. See Minutes of meeting of the Library Association. International and Comparative Librarianship Group, 5 February 1976, item 4.3.

38. S. Simsova and M. MacKee. A Handbook of Comparative Librarianship. 2nd ed. rev. London: Clive Bingley, 1975.

39. D. D. Haslam, "The Association's Work: I. International Relations Activities," Library Association Record LXXVII (March 1975), p. 54.

NATIONAL LIBRARY SERVICES

John G. Lorenz

Many national leaders have become newly aware recently of
the need to initiate or upgrade national library and information services. Governments now recognize that efficient access to information is an essential tool of national development, economic and industrial, as well as of educational and cultural development. The
library is recognized as a necessary component of any effective in-
formation-dependent system. It is society's most experienced, widely accepted, and flexible agency for information delivery from a variety of sources and formats to the eventual user--whether to an individual or a group. [1]

UNESCO has given strength, encouragement, and resources
to promote the development of some of these efforts. As Carlos
Penna, former Director of the UNESCO Division for the Development
of Documentation, Library, and Archives Services, so aptly put it:

> A number of recent developments have emphasized the need
> to focus more attention on the planning, at national and in-
> ternational levels, of library and documentation services.
> In many less-developed countries there is the sombre chal-
> lenge of growing populations still without access to the
> printed word. Conversely, the more developed countries
> are finding that the twin challenges of the growth of re-
> search and the improvement of educational standards and
> the equally striking growth in the number of publications
> to which access is required call for a more systematic and
> planned approach to the provision of library and documenta-
> tion services. Meanwhile, both developed and developing
> countries are constantly subject to economic pressures and
> have been awakened to the necessity of reaching their ob-
> jectives with a minimum of fragmentation and waste. [2]

Penna's UNESCO booklet includes planning techniques for various
types of library service, including national library service. In 1966
UNESCO sponsored a meeting of experts on national planning for library services in Latin America which resulted in a list of national
library functions:

> To collect and ensure the conservation of national book pro-
> duction, for which, in addition to other resources, it will
> receive copies of publications deposited under the copyright
> laws; it should, furthermore, ensure that copyright laws are
> enforced.

To provide national and foreign readers and research workers with an adequate and efficient information service, for
which it will assemble the necessary general collections
and collections of reference works, prepare a union catalogue of all the country's libraries and compile the national bibliography and any other bibliographies necessary for
the performance of its functions.

To organize the national or international exchange of publications.

To centralize inter-library loans with libraries abroad.

To rationalize the acquisition of publications, including
periodicals, among the libraries covered by the plan for
the development of library services.

To centralize the cataloguing and classification of publications and ensure the distribution of catalogue cards or catalogues published by certain categories of libraries.

To co-operate, whenever its own organization and the development of planning render it advisable, in the extension
and improvement of school and public library service.[3]

This list of duties and functions for national libraries followed closely the one compiled at the 1958 Symposium on National Libraries in
Europe, organized by UNESCO in Vienna. Some national libraries
provided services beyond this basic list, and some were still attempting to develop even the most basic functions.

UNESCO Concern

Under IFLA auspices, an International Symposium on European Library Systems was organized at Prague, November 27-Decem-
ber 2, 1972, with financial assistance from UNESCO. Forty-seven
participants from Czechoslovakia and thirty-five from sixteen other
European countries attended. The symposium promoted closer cooperation between European library systems through division of labor
and exchange of experiences, ideas, and results. National library
systems, functions and tasks of national libraries, problems of library and information services, legislation, and education of librarians were discussed. The group adopted the following resolution
unanimously:

The discussions of the Symposium have shown that, for the
rational acquisition and utilization of literature and information, in the interests of the social, economic and cultural development of each country, and in order to make them
accessible to the entire population, it is necessary to organize library services into large systems, effectively in-
terlinked, highly co-ordinated and co-operating on a

national scale. An important part in the organization and
functioning of such a system is played by national and central state libraries.

As not even well-organized and efficient national library
systems can exist independently, it is necessary to create
and develop effective international co-operation and to aim
for the greatest possible compatibility and convertibility of
the technical bases of the library services.

National library systems should be formed in such a way
as to enable them to carry out their tasks both in the
sphere of education, training and culture and in connection
with the increasing demands and needs of scientific and
technical progress and applied research.

Close co-operation between libraries and information centres is called for in order to meet most effectively scientific information requirements.

In order to ensure the formation of efficient library systems on a national scale, it is necessary to create an appropriate framework of library legislation and other legal
norms and rules.

We feel that the experience and opinions which were discussed can, while taking into account local conditions,
serve to a great extent also in the setting up of library
systems in the developing countries. [4]

Move to Establish a National Library Association, In or Out of IFLA

National librarians have been exchanging ideas for many years.
The meetings of such organizations as the International Federation of
Library Associations (IFLA) have been well attended by national library representatives. One of the principal IFLA units has been the
Section on National and University Libraries. Because no existing
organization had sole relevance to national library and national information system concerns, in November 1974, the National Library of
Canada called together a group of national library directors and IFLA
representatives to discuss the feasibility of forming an international
association of national libraries. Discussions included whether or
not the group should be a part of IFLA. [5]

An informal follow-up meeting of national librarians was organized during the 41st IFLA meeting in Oslo, at which 64 countries
were represented. A working paper, "The Role of National Libraries
in National and International Information Systems," the principles of
which were unanimously adopted, stressed national library concerns
to improve world arrangements for: 1) recording and exchanging information concerning library materials; 2) making library materials

available by loan or photocopy; and 3) retrieval of information on library materials, including indexing, abstracting, subject cataloging,
classifying, and translating.   A separate meeting of national librarians interested in exchanging machine-readable records was planned
for October 1975 in Paris.   While national libraries agree on the
need to discuss their problems, their relationship to existing organizations remains an unsettled problem.   Meanwhile, the group planned
to meet during the 1976 IFLA meeting in Lausanne, and a major discussion topic was to be interlibrary lending. [6]   At that meeting,
IFLA was scheduled to act on new statutes and organization patterns
including a major division for General Research Libraries, under
which national libraries could logically organize an important section.
National library directors seemed to feel a need for organization,
communication and coordination among themselves within the IFLA
structure in order to take advantage of the strength and effectiveness
of an international organization which promotes development for all
library and information services.

UNISIST

        The vital role of information in national development caused
UNESCO's seventeenth General Conference to launch the UNISIST program to achieve a World Science Information System.   This system
planned to cultivate information as a resource and an instrument for
shaping governmental policies, scientific and technical development,
and for guiding social evolution.   The 1972 General Conference recognized the need of Member States to create national focal points and
UNISIST National Committees to ensure maximum program participation.   With regard to national focal points, the feasibility study adopted by the 1971 UNISIST Inter-governmental Conference recommended
a national governmental or government-chartered agency to guide,
stimulate and coordinate information resources and services development in the perspective of national, regional and mondial cooperation. [7]   The UNISIST program's long-range goal was to develop international information service networks in the various science sectors.
National libraries which supported programs for generating, organizing, and disseminating scientific information were involved through
exchanging published information for scientists' use and through assistance in reducing administrative and legal barriers to the international flow of scientific information.

        Research libraries have long demonstrated information-sharing.
They share the costs of acquisition by accepting specialization.   The
Federal Republic of Germany developed a plan by which several national libraries share responsibilities for servicing scientific research;
the national libraries of Denmark, Finland, Norway and Sweden
agreed on a comparable plan for sharing collecting responsibilities
for scientific fields.   They developed regional and national networks
linked by telecommunications systems to share resources through inter-library loans and photocopies.   They are now computerizing the
regional and national union lists of scientific literature used in international borrowing.   Increasingly libraries have sought cooperative
means of sharing both resources and workloads.

MARC

Another important development has been the U.S. Library of Congress achievement in producing a standardized machine-readable catalog record which can be manipulated and reformatted by other libraries to meet particular needs. Known as MARC (Machine-Readable Cataloging), this project became international through coordinated programs in the United Kingdom (the British National Bibliography) and Canada. This format is becoming the basis for the international standard for communicating bibliographic information. These developments strengthened the technologies which national library and information systems could employ and demonstrated trends towards interdependence and cooperation.[8]

NATIS

Following UNISIST, a program of even more far-reaching significance for national libraries emerged. Again as a result of UNESCO sponsorship, an Intergovernmental Conference on Planning of National Documentation, Library and Archives Infrastructures was held in Paris, September 23-27, 1974. The purpose of the conference was to provide a framework for governments of Member States to exchange views and experiences on coordinated planning for national documentation, library and archives policies, methods and services in the humanities, culture, sociology, economics, law, administration, and pure and applied science. A further aim was to recommend guidelines for creating and developing national library and information infrastructures and their links with the sectors of national development plans. The infrastructure was concerned with those persons who want information, where it was to be found, those persons who organized it and the manner in which it was to be organized.[9]

The principal objective of NATIS (National Information Systems) was to establish strong information policies in each country as bases for national plans for the well-balanced growth of documentation, libraries and archives. Many countries had bodies which were in charge of such over-all planning. The conference working document called attention to areas of possible cooperative action while recognizing international agreements, accepted standards and guidelines.[10]

NATIS stressed Universal Bibliographic Control as a long-term international program based on national action. UBC was concerned with national bibliographic production, formats and manipulation of bibliographic data, both manually and computer-aided, with the ultimate goal of achieving a world-wide system for controlling and exchanging bibliographic information through an International Centre for UBC. Each country needed a national bibliographic agency, for legal deposit law, for accepting international standards of bibliographic description, etc.[11]

Plans for national information systems must recognize the

newer technologies and the possibilities of using them.   Under the
UNISIST program, work was proceeding to resolve the question of
bibliographic control and information retrieval.   A need existed for
minimum agreement on standards, both technical and intellectual. [12]

The recommendations of the 1974 Intergovernmental Conference on Planning National Documentation, Library and Archives Infrastructures were fully endorsed at the eighteenth UNESCO General
Conference.   There, the Director-General was invited

> to promote the general concept of over-all planning of na-
> tional infrastructures of documentation, libraries and ar-
> chives and to invite Member States to take appropriate
> steps to create or improve their national information sys-
> tems; to assist Member States, especially the developing
> countries, to plan and develop their national infrastructures
> or national information systems (NATIS) in such a way as
> to ensure co-ordination at the national level and to prepare
> the bases for active participation in world information sys-
> tems. [13]

Columbia and Venezuela have already created national information systems.   Including a library component in the Second Indonesian Five-Year Plan signaled a new era for the professions of archives, documentation and library science there.   Accepting the
NATIS national information system proposed by UNESCO makes Indo-
nesia one of the first developing countries to view its information
processes as a whole and to consider appropriate planning and funding. [14]

The Romanian government made an in-depth analysis of information and documentation services and passed a presidential decree
ordaining a national information and documentation system based on
NATIS principles.   The National Council for Science and Technology
was given responsibility for planning, organizing and developing the
system and for assuring its efficient functioning.   Under the National
Council, the National Institute for Information Documentation (INID)
was created to provide information services for government departments and other official bodies and to ensure education facilities and
methodological coordination for all system elements.   INID worked
closely with the Romanian National Library, which benefited from
legal deposit and carried out national bibliographic control and UBC
participation. [15]

UNESCO will hold an intergovernmental conference in 1978 to
review progress achieved within the framework of the NATIS, UNISIST
and UBC programs as well as to make recommendations for implementing national and international action.   The conference will enable
both governmental and nongovernmental bodies to evaluate the multi-
faceted NATIS, UNISIST and UBC program and to plan for the future. [16]

UBC

     At the 1974 UNESCO Intergovernmental Conference, IFLA
presented a working document, "Universal Bibliographic Control: a
Long Term Policy, a Plan for Action." This document presented
the basis of the UBC concept in relation to past bibliographic activities and a detailed program of projects and recommendations which
should lead to UBC system establishment.

     The UBC concept depended on creating a network of compo-
nent national units, covering various publishing, library and bibliographic activities within each country, integrated to form a total
international system. For each component national unit to become
part of the international network, a record must be made of each
publication on issue, and the machinery necessary for making the
bibliographic record must be available. A national agency must be
established for bibliographic control, and it may be a national library division. The national bibliographic agency should receive and
distribute intra-nationally records similar to those received from
other national bibliographic agencies. Normally, this agency should
be established in the national library which receives all types of published material by legal deposit, the complete national collection. [17]
Eventually, this agency may create and publish the retrospective national bibliography.

     The UBC concept was the result of UNESCO's bibliographic
work and the Library of Congress' Shared Cataloging Program in
which it established book procurement centers in nations with inadequate bibliographic control. Much of the UBC effort was undertaken
through IFLA sections and committees which benefited from national
and research library representation:

> Bibliography--compiling information on existing national
>   bibliographies
> Cataloging--through its work in establishing international
>   standards
> Mechanization--through studies directed toward achieving
>   machine system compatability
> Serial Publications--in establishing, jointly with the Com-
>   mittee on Cataloging, standards for serial cataloging
>   and description
> Statistics and Standards--in coordinating IFLA standards
>   work and maintaining liaison with the International
>   Standards Organization.

     A world-wide UBC system will benefit national library and in-
formation system operation. In presenting the UBC program, IFLA
noted that many of its component parts already existed but that the
entire integrated communications system called for long-term planning and a sustained action program. IFLA intended to support all
activities assisting in total system creation. An international office
was created at the British Library, London, to coordinate IFLA's
UBC program. Its functions included organization of meetings,

servicing other projects, editing and publishing, information activities, clearinghouse, advising and consulting, and coordinating with
other international bodies. A Steering Committee and an Advisory
Committee, subordinate to the IFLA Executive Board, assisted the
office. The office promoted international cooperation and brought
the UBC goal closer. [18]

ISDS

        Various individuals worked toward developing the International
Serials Data System, within the UNISIST concept. In cooperation
with UNESCO, the French Government offered to support this system, and an International Center (IC) of ISDS was established in
Paris. The IC/ISDS administered International Standard Serial Number (ISSN) assignments to national and regional centers to develop
and maintain a uniform international control system over serial publications. [19] Argentina, Australia, Canada, the Federal Republic of
Germany, Finland, the United Kingdom, and the United States established national centers, and twenty-three other countries designated
centers which were not yet operational. IC authorized a national
center to use ISSN solely for those publications emanating from that
nation.

        The ISDS sought to provide a comprehensive and reliable reg-
istry of serial publications in all languages and covering all subject
areas. The system was responsible for assigning to each serial
published under a given title a unique and unambiguous numeric code
identifier, the ISSN.

        The National Serials Data Program (NSDP) at the Library of
Congress served as the U.S. national ISSN center and had the dual
responsibility of registering U.S. publications and obtaining ISSNs
for imprints from other ISDS centers as needed by United States institutions. Since early 1973, currently cataloged serials processed
by the three national libraries, Library of Congress, National Agricultural Library, and National Library of Medicine, have been regis-
tered by the ISDS.

        A group of research libraries began in 1974 the Cooperative
Conversion of Serials Project (CONSER) to establish a relatively comprehensive serial bibliographic data base quickly enough to avoid continuing redundant and expensive local, regional, and national conversion efforts. CONSER was housed at the Ohio College Library Center (OCLC), Columbus, which had a proven capability to produce
workable network software and support. With the CONSER development, NSDP extended its national coverage to include responsibility
for assigning ISSNs to the U.S. imprints input by CONSER participants, 14 U.S. libraries. [20]

        National ISDS centers were responsible for promoting ISSN
use within their own countries. They were charged to communicate
with serials publishers and obtain their participation.

An additional ISDS national center responsibility was to disseminate information from the national file. Duplicate files or sub-
sets of the international file may be maintained in order to serve
user communities. A registry of all serials in the NSDP files to
which numbers had been assigned through March 1975 was being prepared for publication. After March 1975 all ISSNs assigned were
added on-line to the CONSER system and were available immediately
through OCLC and LC's MARC Distribution Service.

The International Standard Serial Number (ISSN) is an eight-
digit number providing a universally accepted brief, unique and unambiguous serial identification code. An ISSN consists of seven
digits plus a check digit (an essential part of the number) and is
written in the form: ISSN 1234-5679. The check digit is always
located in the right-most (low order) position and is calculated on a
modulus 11 basis, using the weighting factors 8 to 2. The check
digit's purpose is to avoid errors generated by incorrect number
transcription.

One of the greatest benefits of the ISSN system is its ability
to provide a brief and unambiguous means of identifying a serial,
regardless of the type or form of citation used. The number serves
as a common denominator linking the varying identification conven-
tions of libraries, abstracting and indexing services, subscription
agents, publishers, and distributors.

The ISDS record provides the basis for documenting ISSN registration and provides an internationally acceptable "building block"
upon which national cataloging agencies and others can base a complete bibliographic record suitable to their constituent needs and requirements. [21]

Recent Organizational Changes in National Libraries

The British Library. --In 1971 the British Government issued
a White Paper announcing a new national library organization. The
British Library Act followed in 1972, and the new library organization was established in July 1973.

The British Library combines the formerly separate British
Museum library departments, the National Central Library, the Na-
tional Lending Library of Science and Technology, the British Nation-
al Bibliography, and the National Reference Library of Science and
Invention. The new organization is divided into three main divisions:
Reference (London), Bibliographic Services (London), and Lending
(Boston Spa, Yorkshire). [22]

According to the British Library Act, the national library is
to consist of a comprehensive collection of books, manuscripts, periodicals, films and other recorded matter, whether printed or otherwise; therefore, the Library is concerned with the whole range of
book and non-book material. The Act provides for the Library to

be a national center for reference, study, bibliographical and other
information service in both science and technology and the humanities.   The Library's activities cover all kinds of information services in all subject fields.   The British Library should be well
equipped to provide central services for other British libraries and
has the legal power to act as a Government agent in promoting more
efficient and cost-effective library and information systems.   The
new Library is the principal national depository for British copyright
publications, produces the national bibliography, serves as the central loan library, the main source of support for library and information science, research, and as a major developer and operator of
computer-based bibliographic and other information services.   It is
expected to be the hub of the nation's library services.

     The Library's Reference Division was formed from former
library departments, and the National Reference Library of Science
and Invention of the British Museum.   Its activities are planned to
provide the essential central reference services around which other
British libraries can develop their own collections and services.

     Interlibrary lending in Britain had become a very large opera-
tion.   The British Library's Lending Division, formed from the former National Lending Library for Science and Technology and the
National Central Library, was planned to improve and extend this
activity.   About three million loans are made every year, of which
two million are sent to the British Library system.   The nine regional library bureaus account for a half-million requests and another
half-million requests are directed to other libraries without going
through either the national or the regional interlending networks.   Demand on the British Library is growing at the rate of 15 per cent
per annum.   The main factors accounting for the growth of demand
on the central facilities are the Lending Division's acquisition pro-
gram--which seeks to acquire all significant serials and reports in
all languages, together with English language monographs--and the
speed with which loan requests are met.   The main burden of inter
library lending has been lifted from individual libraries which are
free to adapt their acquisitions and stock-holding procedures accordingly.   From the national viewpoint, the interlending process has become not only quicker and more efficient, but cheaper.

     The Library's Bibliographic Services Division was established
because an effective and economic bibliographic network was essential if libraries were to function at optimum efficiency.   The high
cost of providing bibliographic access to material prompted the development of cooperative and centralized arrangements for the services required.   Computer-based services were attractive in this context because they permitted the Library to process much larger
quantities of information than could be processed manually.   This
Division comprises the former functions of the British National Bibliography, the Copyright Receipt Office and certain other functions of
former British Museum library departments.   These operations were
already computer-based, and the Copyright Receipt Office listed all
legal deposit material at the library.

The central services provided now and for the future by The British Library were planned to develop British computer-based networks rapidly. The Library's MARC tape service can provide current cataloging, bibliographic listing, catalog cards and machine-readable cataloging input. The British National Bibliography was converted in MARC format back to its 1950 beginning. All regions operate a system for recording accessions in numerical form by International Standard Book Number with coded library locations and computer sorting. The machine-based current cataloging activities are being extended to all British Library accessions. Soon, a range of new services will cover the areas of British Library accessions which are not now part of MARC services.

The British Library assisted in supporting the IFLA UBC office and adopted the Anglo-American cataloging rules and the MARC format. A Bibliographic Standards Office was established to focus national discussion on appropriate internal and external standards. [23]

The British Library's new building will bring under one roof many separate units, greatly relieve space pressure in the British Museum, and provide a worthy home for the Reference Division, now scattered around London. [24]

Canada. --The Canadian National Library emerged late. Although established in 1953, until it moved into the new National Library and Archives Building in Ottawa in 1967, it was more a bibliographic center than a true library. For fifteen years, staff concentrated on compiling and publishing the national bibliography, Canadiana, and building and maintaining a national union catalog. In the sixties, the Library started to publish an annual list of Canadian Theses Accepted by Canadian Universities and to reduce them on microfilm, now microfiche, and to publish a union list of serials. The Library offered limited lending and reference service. When the new building opened in 1967, new services were offered. At the outset, the limited funds available were used to establish strong collections only in Canadian subjects, bibliography and general reference. There was no attempt to duplicate in the National Library the collections existing in the 30-year-old National Research Council library or the strong collections of the Department of Agriculture or the Geological Survey of Canada. The National Library planned to build collections in the humanities, the arts and the social sciences.

In 1969, Parliament adopted a new National Library Act which confirmed the Library's original mission, provided for all existing functions to continue, and strengthened considerably the National Librarian's powers and duties, both at the federal and the national levels. The Act provided:

> Subject to the direction of the Governor in Council, the National Librarian may coordinate the library services of departments, branches and agencies of the Government of Canada including (a) the acquisition and cataloging of books;

(b) the supply of professional advice, supervision and personnel; and (c) the provision of modern information storage and retrieval services including photocopying and microfilming services, electronic and other automated data processing services and facsimile or other communication of information services. [25]

Coordinating all aspects of library services at the federal government level is now the statutory responsibility of the National Librarian. The Act provides further that: "The National Librarian may ... enter into agreements with libraries and library and educational associations and institutions in and outside Canada."[26] This provision was prerequisite to developing cooperative schemes for a decentralized national library network. The Government increased the National Librarian's duties and the personnel and financial resources required for the job. In the past six years, the library staff has grown from 200 to 500 and the budget from $1,600,000 to $7,300,000. These resources have been increased to enable the National Library to initiate and develop an ambitious and diversified program and to exercise national leadership in many ways. All library parts were considerably strengthened, existing branches reorganized, new offices created, and active cooperation with other libraries and librarians obtained to meet the challenge of the seventies. [27]

Late in 1972, the National Library took a major step by appointing a Canadian Union Catalogue Task Group. Its long-range goal is to support cooperative library development. Methods for developing a Canadian Union Catalogue in machine-readable form are being studied as well as alternate methods for providing Canadian Union Catalogue service.

National Library automation progress is evident in other areas. A data base of machine-readable bibliographic master records was started with the Canadiana records. They were used to produce cards for the Canadiana proof slip service, replacing the photocopy proof sheets, cards for National Library catalogs, and the text and index of Canadiana itself.

In 1973, a Canadiana MARC office was established at the National Library, charged with implementing recommendations for a Canadian MARC format, and a Canadian MARC distribution service was instituted. The primary difference between Canadian MARC and Library of Congress MARC is that the former can provide bilingual equivalents for all access points to a record. During that year, too, the National Library adopted the International Standard Bibliographic Description for Canadiana, and the MARC format was developed to accommodate the changes. A Canadian MARC format for serials is being implemented, also.

The National Library was designated the Canadian agent for the International Serials Data System and began assigning ISSNs to Canadian serials. An Office of Library Standards was established to coordinate endeavors in developing a Canadian position on library standards for intergovernmental organizations and to facilitate participation with other Canadian libraries in similar endeavors at the national and international levels.

A Retrospective National Bibliography Division was formed. Its first task was to edit Canadiana 1867-1900, a bibliography in the making for 20 years, to be followed by a comprehensive bibliography for 1900-1950. [28]

United States. --In 1966 President Johnson appointed a National Advisory Commission on Libraries in the United States to investigate the problems of the "knowledge explosion" and whether or not traditional library and information services were adequate to modern world needs. A major conclusion of the Advisory Commission was that national library and information needs and developments required continued planning and coordination. Accordingly, it recommended that a National Commission on Libraries and Information Science be established as a permanent agency to advise the President and Congress.

The 91st Congress acted upon this recommendation, and on July 20, 1970, Public Law 91-345 was signed by President Nixon. [29] The Act created the National Commission as an independent agency and gave it the following comprehensive charges and powers:

(1) [to] advise the President and the Congress on the implementation of national policy by such statements, presentations, and reports as it deems appropriate;

(2) conduct studies, surveys, and analyses of the library and informational needs of the Nation, including the special library and informational needs of rural areas and of economically, socially, or culturally deprived persons, and the means by which these needs may be met through information centers, through the libraries of elementary and secondary schools and institutions of higher education, and through public, research, special, and other types of libraries;

(3) appraise the adequacies and deficiencies of current library and information resources and services and evaluate the effectiveness of current library and information science programs;

(4) develop overall plans for meeting national library and informational needs and for the coordination of activities at the Federal, State, and local levels, taking into consideration all of the library and informational resources of the Nation to meet those needs;

(5) be authorized to advise federal, state, local, and private agencies regarding library and information sciences;

(6) promote research and development activities which
will extend and improve the Nation's library and informa-
tion-handling capability as essential links in the national
communications network. [30]

The Commission consists of the Librarian of Congress ex officio
and fourteen appointed members, five of whom shall be professional
librarians or information specialists, and at least one in addition
who shall be knowledgeable about the technological aspects of library
and information science.

At its first meeting in September 1971, the Commission affirmed through a resolution that "equality of access to information
is as important as equality of education. " In order to gain direct
information on the needs and views of user groups throughout the
country it held public hearings, conducted studies, and in 1973 appointed a committee to draft a proposed National Program. Toward
a National Program for Library and Information Services: Goals for
Action was released in 1975 and endorsed by several library organizations. The National Program includes significant recommendations
for the Library of Congress:

1. Expansion of the Library's lending and lending-manage-
   ment function to that of a National Lending Library of
   final resort.
2. Expansion of the National Program for Acquisitions and
   Cataloging (NPAC).
3. Expansion of Machine-Readable Cataloging (MARC) to include cataloging in substantially all languages for current monographic, serial, and other significant library
   and information material being acquired by the Library
   of Congress; distribution of this data base, perhaps to
   state and regional centers and other national network
   nodes for library and information service.
4. Distribution of bibliographic data through on-line communication.
5. Development of an expanded general reference program
   to support the national system for bibliographic service.
6. Operation of a comprehensive National Serials Service
   that will integrate and expand the Library's present
   serials activities and provide an organized set of serial
   services for the nation.
7. Establishment of a technical services center to provide
   training in, and information about, Library of Congress
   techniques and processes, with emphasis on automation.
8. Development of improved access to state and local publications and cooperation with state and local agencies
   to standardize cataloging and other organization techniques.
9. Further implementation of the national preservation program.

In addition, the National Program calls for expanding the important

ongoing national programs in the Division for the Blind and Physically Handicapped. 31

        The Library of Congress in Washington, D.C. celebrated its
175th anniversary in 1975. Since the U.S. bicentennial was celebrated in 1976, the nation took 24 years after independence was
gained to create a national library. The Library of Congress' primary role is to perform research for members and committees of
Congress. Traditionally, Congress shares the Library's collections
and services with the public. The Library has functioned as the
national library of the United States.

        During the last decade, Library of Congress programs ex-
panded tremendously. The principal increase occurred in the National Program for Acquisitions and Cataloging (NPAC), under which the
Library was authorized to acquire all material of research and scholarly significance world-wide, catalog it promptly and distribute cataloging information to libraries. To avoid unnecessary duplication of
cataloging already accomplished in other countries, the Library
adopted "shared cataloging" techniques whenever possible in cooperation with foreign national bibliography producers and uses cataloging
data already prepared in the countries of origin. Information is
transferred to the Library of Congress where cataloging is completed
and cards are printed. Depository sets of NPAC material are distributed to selected research libraries which acquire foreign publications on a large scale; these libraries search their receipts and purchase orders against the sets and supply the Library of Congress
with information on newly published titles for which no LC catalog
card is available. If the titles are not already on order or being
cataloged, the research Library orders them and prepares catalog
copy as soon as possible. All libraries profit from the increased
amount of cataloging performed by the Library of Congress under
NPAC since the cataloging information is available in the form of
printed catalog cards, the Library's printed book catalogs, MARC
tapes, and other specialized services and catalogs. 32 Since the
NPAC program was authorized in 1965, the Library of Congress has

        Doubled the number of titles cataloged per year from about
        100,000 in 1964 to about 250,000 in 1974.

        Increased the cataloging copy available for research libraries
        from about 50% to over 75%.

        Saved libraries many millions of dollars each year in cata-
        loging.

        Speeded up access to cataloging and extended use of standard
        cataloging.

        Another major achievement of national and international sig-
nificance was the MARC development and building a machine-readable
data base of standard cataloging for over 1.2 million monographs,
thereby allowing the addition of about 125,000 titles per year. The

MARC records are used to produce book catalogs, special listings, other printed output, and MARC tapes, which are available to other libraries, library networks, and commercial publishers through the MARC Distribution Service. The tapes can be used to print cards, book catalogs, and duplicate tapes. They follow standards set by the American National Standards Institute for interchanging information on magnetic tape. [33]

CIP, or Cataloging in Publication is the most recent and accessible means by which a book identifies itself. The CIP Program was established in 1971 to provide Library of Congress cataloging information in monographs produced by American book-trade publishers, academic presses and scholarly reprint publishers. Through the cooperative effort of LC and American publishers, LC catalogers process the galley proofs of new books sent by participating publishers and supply those elements of cataloging that require professional decisions, such as main entry, a short title, series statements, bibliographical notes, subject headings, added entries, LC call number, Dewey Decimal classification number, and LC card number. Before the CIP program started, libraries cataloged books themselves or waited to receive printed catalog cards; now, a library receiving a CIP book has sufficient information to make its own catalog cards or to establish preliminary controls and get the book into circulation immediately. Libraries which receive books under the CIP program save the expense of cataloging and processing them. Over 1,050 publishers cooperate in the program. Since CIP inception, more than 60,000 titles have been processed. Several countries have requested program details as background for developing their own similar programs.

In 1972, LC modernized and expanded its preservation workshops and established a research laboratory to investigate paper deterioration problems and develop methods to combat them. The Preservation Office sponsors a continuing program of on-the-job training in preserving and restoring library material for selected students and responds to national and international inquiries.

The national program for the blind has been expanded to include services for the physically handicapped as well. The number of persons served has increased from 94,000 to 422,000 through regional and sub-regional libraries; the program includes braille and talking books and new technology has been applied in using cassette tapes.

The past decade has brought many other significant achievements as well, including editing and publishing the retrospective National Union Catalog. This publication will be the largest bibliographic tool ever created.

The past decade saw the Library of Congress staff grow from 3,300 to 4,600, the collection from 53 million to 70 million, and the annual budget from $36 million to $116 million.

In addition to the Library of Congress, two other United
States libraries provide special national library services--the National Agricultural Library and the National Library of Medicine.

The National Agricultural Library (NAL) is located in a modern, 11-story building in Beltsville, Maryland, a suburb of Washington, D. C.   As an agency of the U. S. Department of Agriculture and
as one component of the United States national library system, the
National Agricultural Library is responsible for collecting and disseminating national and international agricultural information.   Increased emphasis has been placed on expanding capabilities for utilizing information by user groups.   At the same time, attention has
been focused on the need for greater personal services.

NAL celebrated its 110th anniversary on May 16, 1972 when
the Associates NAL, Inc., presented an exhibit to the library on
"Abraham Lincoln and His Legacy to American Agriculture." Among
the historic documents exhibited was a facsimile of the Organic Act
which established the Department of Agriculture with a mandate to
disseminate useful agricultural information. [34]

NAL utilizes new computer technologies to support, extend,
and improve personal library service to its clientele.   The bibliographic data base went on-line in July 1973.   This data base contains agricultural bibliographic information (using the broadest possible definition) and can be searched on many data elements for single
searches or full bibliographies with computer print-out.   Serial titles
owned by the library are included in an automated record which is
useful in expediting serials handling and improving document delivery.

NAL participates with federal and other research libraries in
adding titles to the Ohio College Library Center (OCLC) data bank.
The latter provides direct access to medical literature sources for
agricultural scientists and researchers through an on-line National
Library of Medicine MEDLINE system computer terminal. [35]

The National Library of Medicine, founded in 1836, is the
world's largest research library in a single scientific and professional field.   It is located in Bethesda, Maryland, a suburb of Washington, D. C.   To meet the demand for recent information on biomedical topics, the library maintains a collection of nearly 1.5 million
items in more than 40 languages.   Approximately 13,000 serials are
received.   Material is collected exhaustively in 40 biomedical areas,
and, to a lesser extent, in such related areas as chemistry, physics,
zoology, botany, psychology, and instrumentation. [36]

The Library's computer-based Medical Literature Analysis &
Retrieval System (MEDLARS) began operating in January 1964.   It is
based on the Library's publication, Index Medicus.   The system has
stations in other large medical libraries and provides service to scientists and educators as well as physicians.   Three hundred and fifty
institutions throughout the U. S. have on-line access to its computerized bibliographic data bases. [37]   Through the National Medical Audio-

visual Center in Atlanta, Georgia, the library operates a national program for the development, production, evaluation and distribution of biomedical films and videotapes. [38]

During fiscal year, 1974, NLM and the British Library Lending Division in Boston Spa, Yorkshire, initiated an experimental cooperative project using the British Lending Library as back-up for United States document delivery service.

NLM's involvement with the Library of Congress' Cataloging in Publication Program was expanded considerably during fiscal year 1974, with the preparation of approximately 1,700 biomedical titles. There are plans to continue the increase in NLM's contribution to this program.

As a result of cooperative programs with the Library of Congress, the Council on Library Resources, and major academic libraries, a modification to the standard Library of Congress MARC record format was adopted which enabled NLM and other libraries to make their machine-readable records compatible with the LC MARC records. NLM provides a link with OCLC which makes its cataloging data available to network users. [39]

U.S.S.R. --The State V. I. Lenin Library, founded in 1862, serves as the U.S.S.R. national library. Its functions were described in an exhibition for the 1970 IFLA General Council Meeting held in Moscow. It serves as:

(1) the central library of the U.S.S.R.
(2) a state depository of printed publications and manuscripts
(3) the leading scientific and research institution in the fields of library science, bibliography and the history of printing
(4) a center of recommendatory bibliography
(5) a methodological and consultative center. [40]

It is the main center for international contacts and cooperation. According to 1970 reports, books were exchanged with 3,800 organizations in 96 countries; 270 organizations in 35 countries borrowed books from the State Lenin Library; approximately 100 Library staff had recently toured abroad; 300 librarians from 30 countries had visited the library in 1969. [41]

Early in 1970, the Lenin Library established a development program for the next ten to fifteen years. The Lenin Library, like certain other national libraries, will continue the trend not to acquire certain kinds of publications, primarily ephemeral literature and less frequently used literature of regional or local interest. However, decentralization will not apply to the center stock core which must be kept together for universal, multidisciplinary and interdisciplinary studies. Comprehensive records will be kept of the availability of decentralized material. [42] National special libraries will be responsible for coordinating special services in specific fields. The study pointed to the need for all national libraries to form an entity, but not necessarily an administrative entity.

Coordination and cooperation with the country's other lending libraries and information centers are thought to be major means for optimizing the Lenin Library's activity and for implementing its plans. It handles the jobs of acquisition and better utilization of stock, and checking their increase rate; pursues a policy of purposeful, scientific formation of its readership, scientifically processed printed works by introducing state standards for their description, centralized cataloging, and a computerized storage and retrieval system.[43] Computerization is "proceeding, but somewhat slowly because they had found it would be necessary to have a machine that would perform 12,000 separate commands."[44]

The Lenin Library continues to intensify cooperation and to improve contacts with many libraries and information institutions abroad. Its plan for 1976-1980, which has come to be known as "Place, Role and Functions of the Lenin Library within the Framework of the Library and Information System of the Socialist Communist Countries," includes action on this problem. [45]

In 1970, the Lenin Library established an information center for library science and bibliography with the object of providing abstracts, translations, bibliographies, etc. It cooperates with similar centers in the All Union Library of Foreign Literature and the State Public Scientific and Technical Library. [46]

The Lenin Library is the major U.S.S.R. national library with a collection of more than 26.5 million items and staff of 2,700. A new wing provides additional book space and quarters for a greatly expanded photoduplication center.

The document reproduction service has been expanded as a means of providing information speedily to individuals who could come to the library. A special duplication center provides prompt photocopying service. [47]

The Lenin Library functions as a methodological center which does summary planning of the methodological work of general scientific libraries and provides guidance, analysis and plans for library development on all lines. It plans library network centralization, improvement of public library stock, creation of a unified system for the national library stock, a system of depositories, book publicity, enhancement of the library's role in the system of scientific and technical information, improvement of library service for children and adolescents, training of library personnel, and introduction of a scientific labor organization. [48]

An information center on culture and arts problems is planned by organizing the service of relevant scientific information on culture and arts, through union republic state libraries and other libraries and institutions, through systematic study and information processing of Soviet and foreign literature on culture and arts problems, and rapid and differentiated provision of information from organizations, the Party, government executives, scientists, scholars, and experts.

The Lenin Library publishes union catalogs and a wide range of recommendatory bibliographies, such as a standard catalog of books for children, school libraries and district libraries. The Library is able to give nationwide service through these special lists.[49]

Construction of New National Library Buildings

Egypt. --The new Egyptian National Library building opened a few years ago on a site of outstanding beauty overlooking the Nile. The decision must have been made at a very high level to give the National Library so outstanding a site and so large a permanent accommodation. It indicated a measure of priority not often accorded to libraries.[50]

The staff and processing departments are on the ground floor and the main reading rooms on the higher floors. Behind them are the stacks, conveniently situated with direct access from the specialized reading rooms. On the top level are facilities for meetings, conferences, and receptions.

Ivory Coast. --The foundation stone for the National Library of the Ivory Coast at Abidjan was laid on March 9, 1971, and the fully equipped library was officially opened by the President of the Ivory Coast Republic, Mr. Houphouet-Boigny, on January 9, 1974.

Planning for the Library, which was part of a national plan for systematically developing reading habits, seen as a key social factor in promoting development, dated to 1966 when a UNESCO expert and the Chief of the Libraries and Publications Department, Ivory Coast Directorate for Cultural Affairs entered into close collaboration.

The project's total cost was 648 million CFA francs, more than $2.5 million U.S., for premises, equipment and staff training, two-fifths financed by the Ivory Coast and three-fifths by Canada. The Library covers 6,500 square metres and accommodates 300,000-600,000 volumes.

Since 1969, the National Library has been designated to receive six of the seven copyright deposit copies and can use them for exchanges. Since 1970, it has published the National Bibliography, which brings in revenue.

The National Library is associated with the National Documentation Centre, previously the main repository for ancient publications of national interest, but now one of the library's specialized departments. The other departments or services are: the national publications exchange bureau, working and reading rooms, sales counters, the record library and the film library. A lecture hall seats 250.[51]

Japan. --The National Diet Library was established by law in 1948 by incorporating the tradition of the former Imperial Library and the libraries of the Two Houses of the pre-war Imperial Diet. The National Diet Library moved into its new building located beside the Diet Building in 1961. The building was greatly expanded in 1968. [52] The NDL has three functions: service to the Diet, to government agencies, and to the public.

NDL has a legal deposit system for publications produced in Japan and maintains a large collection of the nation's literature. It collects foreign material, either by purchase or international exchange, and has been designated a depository of several international organizations. Information on current national publications acquired is disseminated weekly and the national bibliography is compiled and published annually. As a national information center, the Library cooperates with UNESCO and other institutions abroad in sending bibliographic data on national publications, and it has been designated the national center for the International Serials Data System. A committee of senior officials coordinates the work involved in NDL's role as the Japanese Center for ISDS. [53]

Since establishment in 1948, the NDL has published many bibliographies, printed cards, an index to Japanese periodicals, subject bibliographies, acquisition lists and a union catalog of foreign books as the tools for national bibliographic control. The rapid increase in the number of documents to be handled, however, has caused delays in publishing these bibliographies. NDL's aim in introducing library automation was to solve this problem and to make the bibliographies themselves more useful. The NDL Preparation Office for Library Automation was established in July, 1969, and the Japanese computer HITAC-8400 and the Kanji-printer JEM 3800, which can print out 6,528 characters in a photocomposition mode, were both installed in January, 1971. [54] Library services computerized were:

1) Automated compiling system for the General Index to the Debates of the National Diet.
2) Listing system for serials in Western languages held by the Library.
3) Processing system for Western books by using LC MARC tapes.
4) Listing system for Japanese serial publications held by the Library.
5) Automated compiling system for the Monthly list of foreign scientific and technical publications.
6) Payroll calculation system for the staff of the Library and the House of Councilors. [55]

Iran. --An American librarian's study of development in library science, information science and bibliography, which compared Iran's status in 1967 and 1972, indicated that the National Library, organized in 1937, was "poor" in almost every way. [56] Plans are now being made for all this to change. Under the high patronage of the Shahanshah of Iran, the Pahlavi National Library at Tehran is planned to become the center of a vast complex of modern library and information services for the whole country. The project falls

within the conceptual framework of NATIS, with which UNESCO is
closely associated. [57]

An international team of nearly 70 experts in library services
and related functions, including many Americans, has prepared reports for a projected national library complex. A final report was
completed in March 1976 for the director general of the library and
the deputy minister of the Imperial Court of Iran for Cultural Affairs.
The ultimate aim of the report is to provide plans for a comprehensive, broadly accessible array of library services for scholars, professionals and the general public at all levels. The immediate aim
was to describe the functions to be covered in architectural planning
and provide the information necessary for a world-wide architectural
competition to be held by the Cultural Affairs Ministry. Because
the projected services will be largely new, they may form the most
advanced system technically in the international library world, according to Nasser Sharify, Iranian-born dean of Pratt Institute's
Graduate School of Library and Information Science, New York, who
is chairman of the consultants. [58]

The Pahlavi Cultural, Scientific and Resource Centre is
planned to contain several components: a National Library with comprehensive national and international collections in all branches of
knowledge, to act as a normative and methodological body to develop
a nationwide network of library services; an International Affairs Library with collections on foreign cultures and civilizations, area
studies, etc.; a Scientific and Technological Information Centre, particularly in areas of interest to national development and industries;
a Centre for Iran Studies, research-oriented, and for which fellowships and resident scholarships can be granted.

In addition to the ambitious plans developing in Iran, national
library construction or planning for future construction is taking place
in Brazil, Libya, Saudi Arabia, Iceland, and Nigeria.

Trends for the Future

The challenge to national libraries is partially based on the
tremendous expansion of world publishing, and partially on the increasing reliance of research and development on rapidly changing
current knowledge. In the past, users of such national libraries as
the Bibliothèque Royale de Belgique in Brussels were mainly readers
in history, literature, religion, and other traditional disciplines.
They entered the reading room and sat for long periods of time reading and taking notes. It was a genteel, orderly, and relatively slow
study method.

Today, users of the Bibliothèque Royale and most other national libraries are scientists, economists, planners, engineers, and
others whose information needs are practical and immediate. They
want the latest research results as soon as they are published. The
information needed is largely in journals and continuations. They

have little interest in or need for dusty collections of historic works. The librarian must turn attention to processing, cataloging, and retrieving information in all forms as rapidly as possible. Acquiring and processing the information is only one side of the problem. Equally difficult is disseminating the required information to users. The scope of scientific publishing is so great that no single library has complete resources. Even the Library of Congress was estimated to acquire, at best, six to eight per cent of the world's publications. This situation has encouraged increasing cooperative efforts among national libraries. Key elements in this exchange are cooperative acquisitions within a country, union catalogs, cooperative cataloging internationally, and automation. Today's national library is more complex than ever. Planning and deliberate steps to meet current demands and anticipate future ones are part of national library thinking today. [59]

The principal trend in the immediate future will almost certainly be toward greater sharing of bibliographic resources and information among libraries, both within a single country and between those of several countries. Utilizing whatever new technologies are applicable for improving national and international bibliographic control and for more rapid delivery of texts, national libraries will move as rapidly as possible toward making available to users the nation's total library resources.

Almost certainly, regional lending libraries will develop so that overlapping of individual collections can be reduced and rapid access to needed materials assured. Processing will be increasingly centralized so that the benefits of national and international standards can be applied. In the more distant future, advanced computer-based information systems, including specialized discipline-oriented systems, should become available. [60]

As more national library systems achieve the objectives and benefits of NATIS and UNISIST, national and international control of the "information explosion" will result and will benefit those who need and use library resources and information.

NOTES

1. Robert Vosper. "National and International Library Planning." Unpublished introductory working document presented at the 40th General Council Meeting of the International Federation of Library Associations, Washington, D. C., November 18, 1974, p. 1.
2. Carlos Victor Penna. The Planning of Library and Documentation Services. 2d ed., rev. and enl. by P. H. Sewell and Herman Liebaers. Paris: United Nations Educational, Scientific and Cultural Organization, 1972, p. 13.
3. Ibid., p. 55.
4. "International Symposium on European Library Systems, 1972," Unesco Bulletin for Libraries XXVII (November-December

1973), p. 358.
5. "Official Summary Report of the Meeting on the Feasibility of an International Association of National Libraries, Ottawa, Canada, November 13-14, 1974," Library of Congress Information Bulletin XXXIII (December 6, 1974), pp. A252-53.
6. Thomas R. Barcus, "National Libraries," Library of Congress Information Bulletin XXXIV (October 10, 1974), p. 403.
7. United Nations Educational, Scientific and Cultural Organization. UNISIST: Information Policy Objectives (UNISIST Proposals) "SC/74/WS/3." Paris, April 1974, p. 1.
8. United Nations Educational, Scientific and Cultural Organization and the International Council of Scientific Unions. UNISIST: Synopsis of the Feasibility Study on a World Science Information System. Paris: United Nations Educational, Scientific and Cultural Organization, 1971, pp. 32-33.
9. United Nations Educational, Scientific and Cultural Organization. National Information Systems (NATIS): Objectives for National and International Actions "COM.74/NATIS/3. COM.74/CONF. 202/COL.8." Paris, 1974, p. 2.
10. Ibid., p. 5.
11. Ibid., p. 6.
12. Ibid., p. 6.
13. "National Information Systems (NATIS)," Unesco Bulletin for Libraries XXIX (March-April 1975), p. 58.
14. Philip Ward. "Indonesian Libraries Today," Unesco Bulletin for Libraries XXIX (July-August 1975), p. 187.
15. "Romanian Decree on a National Information and Documentation System," Unesco Bulletin for Libraries XXIX (September-October 1975), p. 241.
16. UNESCO. National Information Systems (NATIS), op. cit., pp. 31-32.
17. Ibid., p. 24.
10. International Federation of Library Associations. IFLA and the Role of Libraries. The Hague: Netherlands, 1974, pp. 10-12.
19. Paul Vassallo, "The National Serials Data Program," Proceedings of The LARC Institute on Automated Serials Systems, ed. H. William Axford. Tempe, Arizona: LARC Press, Ltd., 1973, pp. 18-19.
20. Lois Upham, "CONSER: Cooperative Conversion of Serials Project," Library of Congress Information Bulletin XXXIII (November 29, 1974), pp. 245-58.
21. Mary Sauer, "National Serials Data Program," Drexel Library Quarterly XI (July, 1975), pp. 40-48.
22. Michael Yelland, "Library Developments in the United Kingdom," The Bowker Annual of Library & Book Trade Information. 19th ed. New York: R. R. Bowker Co., 1974, pp. 353-54.
23. Harry T. Hookway, "National Library Planning in Britain," The Bowker Annual of Library & Book Trade Information. 20th ed. New York: R. R. Bowker Co., 1975, pp. 340-46.
24. Yelland, Bowker Annual, op. cit., pp. 353-54.
25. Canada. National Library Act, 1969. 17-18 Eliz. 2, h 47, Sec. 7(2). Statutes of Canada, 1094-1095.

26. Ibid., pp. 1094-95.
27. Guy Sylvestre, "The National Library of Canada," Minutes of the Eighty-Fourth Meeting (of the Association of Research Libraries), May 9-10, 1974, Toronto, Canada, (1974), pp. 3-13.
28. Katherine H. Packer, "Canadian Library Developments," The Bowker Annual of Library & Book Trade Information. 19th ed. New York: R. R. Bowker Co., 1974, p. 357.
29. U.S. National Commission on Libraries and Information Science. Annual Report, 1971-72. Washington, D.C.: Government Printing Office, January 31, 1974, pp. 19-21.
30. U.S. National Commission on Libraries and Information Science. Annual Report, 1971-72, op. cit., p. 9.
31. U.S. The National Commission on Libraries and Information Science. Toward a National Program for Library and Information Services: Goals for Action. Washington, D.C.: U.S. Government Printing Office, 1975, pp. 66-70.
32. Nancy Robins Mitchell, "The Library of Congress: a Library's Library," Catholic Library World XLVI (April 1975), p. 378.
33. Ibid., p. 378.
34. Leila Moran, "National Agricultural Library," The Bowker Annual of Library & Book Trade Information. 18th ed. New York: R. R. Bowker Co., 1973, p. 80.
35. Leila Moran, "National Agricultural Library, U.S. Department of Agriculture, Beltsville, Md. 20705, 301-655-4000," The Bowker Annual of Library & Book Trade Information. 20th ed. New York: R. R. Bowker Co., 1975, pp. 30-32.
36. F. Kurt Cylke, "Federal Libraries," The Encyclopedia Americana, International ed. (1975), XVII, p. 358.
37. Robert B. Mehnert, "National Library of Medicine, Bethesda, Maryland 20014," The Bowker Annual of Library & Book Trade Information. 20th ed. New York: R. R. Bowker Co., 1975, p. 27.
38. Cylke, op. cit., p. 359.
39. U.S. Department of Health, Education, and Welfare. The National Library of Medicine: Programs and Services, Fiscal Year 1974. "DHEW Publication No. (NIH) 75-256." Washington, 1975.
40. George Chandler, ed., "Three Russian National Libraries: An Analysis of Soviet Studies," International Library Review IV (April 1972), p. 213.
41. Ibid., p. 218.
42. Ibid., p. 219.
43. Nikolai M. Sikorsky, "Library Planning in the Soviet Union" (Paper presented at the Plenary Session of the 40th General Council Meeting of the International Federation of Library Associations, Washington, D.C., November 20, 1974), p. 12.
44. A. Robert Rogers, "Some Impressions of Three Russian Libraries," Ohio Library Association Bulletin XLIII (July 1973), pp. 7-8.
45. Sikorsky, op. cit., p. 13.
46. Chandler, op. cit., p. 221.
47. Ibid., p. 222.

88   Comparative/International

48. Sikorsky, op. cit., p. 13.
49. Chandler, op. cit., p. 224.
50. George Chandler, "Near, Middle and Far Eastern Libraries,"
    International Library Review III (April 1971), pp. 190-92.
51. "National Library of the Ivory Coast," Unesco Bulletin for Li-
    braries XXVIII (July-August 1974), p. 235.
52. The National Diet Library. Tokyo, 1975, p. 1.
53. "Japanese National Centre for ISDS--its Background, Tasks, and
    Problems," National Diet Library Newsletter XXXIX (Novem-
    ber 1974), p. 8.
54. "National Diet Library as a National Library," National Diet Li-
    brary Newsletter XLI (July 1975), p. 7.
55. The National Diet Library. Tokyo, 1975, p. 5.
56. John F. Harvey, "Core Activities for National Library and Bib-
    liographic Development," Unesco Bulletin for Libraries
    XXVIII (March-April 1974), p. 82.
57. "The Pahlavi Cultural, Scientific and Resource Centre of Iran,"
    Unesco Bulletin for Libraries XXIX (July-August 1975), p. 178.
58. Chandler B. Grannis, "International Team Plans National Li-
    brary for Iran," Publishers Weekly CCVIII (October 20, 1975),
    pp. 34-6.
59. Alan Reed, "The Bibliothèque Royale de Belgique as a National
    Library," The Journal of Library History X (January 1975),
    p. 35.
60. William S. Dix, "University Libraries," The Encyclopedia Amer-
    icana, International ed. (1975), XVII, p. 341.

BIBLIOGRAPHY

Barcus, Thomas R. "National Libraries," Library of Congress In-
    formation Bulletin XXXIV (October 10, 1974), p. 403.
Canada. National Library Act, 1969. 17-18 Eliz. 2, Ch. 47, Sec.
    7(2). Statutes of Canada, 1094-95.
Chandler, George. "Near, Middle and Far Eastern Libraries," In-
    ternational Library Review III (April 1971), pp. 187-227.
    _____, ed. "Three Russian National Libraries: An Analysis of
    Soviet Studies," International Library Review IV (April 1972),
    pp. 213-34.
Cylke, F. Kurt. "Federal Libraries," The Encyclopedia Americana,
    International ed. (1975), XVII, pp. 358-59.
Dix, William S. "University Libraries," The Encyclopedia Ameri-
    cana, International ed. (1975), XVII, pp. 339-41.
Grannis, Chandler B. "International Team Plans National Library
    of Iran," Publishers Weekly CCVIII (October 20, 1975), pp.
    34-6.
Harvey, John F. "Core Activities for National Library and Biblio-
    graphic Development," Unesco Bulletin for Libraries (March-
    April 1974), pp. 79-86.
Hookway, Harry T. "National Library Planning in Britain," The
    Bowker Annual of Library & Book Trade Information. 20th
    ed. New York: R. R. Bowker Co., 1975, pp. 340-46.

International Federation of Library Associations. IFLA and the Role
    of Libraries. The Hague, Netherlands, 1974. ("A back-
    ground document for Unesco's Intergovernmental Conference
    on the Planning of National Documentation, Library and Ar-
    chives Infrastructures. Paris, 23-27 September 1974.")
"International Symposium on European Library Systems, 1972,"
    Unesco Bulletin for Libraries XXVII (November-December
    1973), p. 358.
"Japanese National Centre for ISDS--Its Background, Tasks, and
    Problems," National Diet Library Newsletter XXXIX (Novem-
    ber 1974), pp. 8-12.
Mehnert, Robert B. "National Library of Medicine, Bethesda, Mary-
    land 20014," The Bowker Annual of Library & Book Trade In-
    formation. 20th ed. New York: R. R. Bowker Co. , 1975,
    pp. 27-30.
Mitchell, Nancy Robins. "The Library of Congress: A Library's
    Library," Catholic Library World XLVI (April 1975), pp. 375-
    81.
Moran, Leila. "National Agricultural Library," The Bowker Annual
    of Library & Book Trade Information. 18th ed. New York:
    R. R. Bowker Co. , 1973, pp. 80-82.
    _____. "National Agricultural Library, U.S. Department of Agri-
    culture, Beltsville, Md. 20705, 301-655-4000." The Bowker
    Annual of Library & Book Trade Information. 20th ed. New
    York: R. R. Bowker Co. , 1975, pp. 30-32.
The National Diet Library. Tokyo, 1975.
"National Diet Library as a National Library," National Diet Library
    Newsletter XLI (July 1975), pp. 1-15.
"National Information Systems (NATIS)," Unesco Bulletin for Librar-
    ies XXIX (March-April 1975), p. 58.
"National Library of the Ivory Coast," Unesco Bulletin for Libraries
    XXVIII (July-August 1974), p. 235.
"Official Summary Report of the Meeting on the Feasibility of an In-
    ternational Association of National Libraries, Ottawa, Canada,
    November 13-14, 1974," Library of Congress Information Bul-
    letin XXXIII (December 6, 1974), pp. 252-53.
Packer, Katherine H. "Canadian Library Developments," The Bow-
    ker Annual of Library & Book Trade Information. 19th ed.
    New York: R. R. Bowker Co. , 1974, pp. 355-59.
"The Pahlavi Cultural, Scientific and Resource Centre of Iran,"
    Unesco Bulletin for Libraries XXIX (July-August 1975), pp.
    178-79.
Penna, Carlos Victor. The Planning of Library and Documentation
    Services. 2d ed. , rev. and enl. by P. H. Sewell and Her-
    man Liebaers. Paris: United Nations Educational, Scientific
    and Cultural Organization, 1972.
Reed, Alan. "The Bibliothèque Royale de Belgique as a National
    Library," Journal of Library History X (January 1975), pp.
    35-51.
Rogers, A. Robert. "Some Impressions of Three Russian Libraries,"
    Ohio Library Association Bulletin XLIII (July 1973), pp. 4-10.
"Romanian Decree on a National Information and Documentation Sys-
    tem," Unesco Bulletin for Libraries XXIX (September-October

1975), p. 241.

Sauer, Mary. "National Serials Data Program," Drexel Library Quarterly XI (July 1975), pp. 40-48.

Sikorsky, Nikolai M. "Library Planning in the Soviet Union." Paper presented at the Plenary Session of the 40th General Council Meeting of the International Federation of Library Associations, Washington, D. C. , November 20, 1974.

Sylvestre, Guy. "The National Library of Canada," Minutes of the Eighty-fourth Meeting (of the Association of Research Libraries), May 9-10, 1974, Toronto, Canada, (1974), pp. 3-13.

United Nations Educational, Scientific and Cultural Organization. National Information Systems (NATIS): Objectives for National and International Action "COM. 74/NATIS/3. COM. 74/ CONF. 202/COL. 8. " Paris, 1974. (Prepared for Intergovernmental Conference on the Planning of National Documentation, Library and Archives Infrastructures.)
        . UNISIST: Information Policy Objectives (UNISIST Proposals). "SC/74/WS/3. " Paris, April 1974.

United Nations Educational, Scientific and Cultural Organization and the International Council of Scientific Unions. UNISIST: Synopsis of the Feasibility Study on a World Science Information System. Paris: United Nations Educational, Scientific and Cultural Organization, 1971.

U. S. Department of Health, Education, and Welfare. The National Library of Medicine: Programs and Services, Fiscal Year 1974. "DHEW Publication No. (NIH) 75-256. " Washington, 1975.

U. S. National Commission on Libraries and Information Science. Annual Report, 1971-72. Washington, D. C. : Government Printing Office, January 31, 1974.
        . Toward a National Program for Library and Information Services: Goals for Action. Washington, D. C. : U. S. Government Printing Office, 1975.

Upham, Lois. "CONSER: Cooperative Conversion of Serials Project," Library of Congress Information Bulletin XXXIII (November 29, 1974), pp. A245-58.

Vassallo, Paul. "The National Serials Data Program," Proceedings of The LARC Institute on Automated Serials Systems. Ed. H. William Axford. Tempe, Arizona: LARC Press, Ltd. , 1973, pp. 15-25.

Vosper, Robert. "National and International Library Planning." Unpublished introductory working document presented at the 40th General Council Meeting of the International Federation of Library Associations, Washington, D. C. , November 18, 1974.

Ward, Philip. "Indonesian Libraries Today," Unesco Bulletin for Libraries XXIX (July-August 1975), pp. 182-87.

Yelland, Michael. "Library Developments in the United Kingdom," The Bowker Annual of Library & Book Trade Information. 19th ed. New York: R. R. Bowker Co. , 1974, pp. 353-54.

PUBLIC LIBRARIES

H. C. Campbell

Definition and Scope of Public Library Science

It is now common to accept the definition that public libraries exist as systems of libraries to meet user needs and provide the material and service which many people require in all countries. The public library concept has developed from that of a repository of material into one of many outlets of books and information being required for the public within an organized system. In some countries, the entire national library network is considered to provide service to citizens, from national, state and university libraries down to the local factory, trade union and school library. In most countries, however, definite groups of libraries are recognized as public libraries, while others, although often financed wholly by public funds, exist outside the network of public library systems and retain their individual organization.

The definition of public library science adopted here was the broadest one possible. It covered all activities dealing with library services which meet public needs, whether or not considered to be "public libraries." However, this paper concentrates on library systems traditionally recognized as open to the public freely, though it is impossible to speak of public library activities without reference to the larger group, also.

Place of Comparative Studies and Research

Any review of recent progress in comparative and international public library science must account for several basic areas in which study and research has been carried out:

a. Public library system planning and development.
b. Public library system goals and objectives.
c. Public library system organization and management.

These areas will be considered briefly with emphasis on the contrasts between the developed and developing countries and on the role played by international government and non-government agencies. However, it is impossible to consider public library studies in isolation from

a. National economic and social change.

b. National cultural policy, particularly literary culture.
c. Regional and local government re-organization.
d. Reading, media and user studies.

Each one of these areas has produced important data which must be considered in developing concepts about the purposes of public library systems. Such systems may be vitally affected by such reports. In order to describe recent progress, activities in the areas mentioned above will be considered.

National Economic and Social Change. --When a society decides to transform an "elitist" education system into one serving the mass of people, and to use that system as an instrument for national development, the society is beset by many problems. In developing countries these problems have been highlighted by the failure of investment in education in the past two decades to provide the benefits expected. Some useful work has been done to produce methods of systems analysis of national education which provide more meaningful guidance for planning than was provided by traditional studies of education input and results. This analysis resembles what a doctor does when he examines the most complicated system of all--a human being. It is never possible to know completely a human being's system and its functional processes. The strategy of diagnosis is to concentrate on selected critical indicators and their relationships within the educational system and between it and its national background. This analysis of educational services as systems has revealed that they consist not merely of several levels and types of education, but that they include informal systems and programs, also. The latter include literacy education, on-the-job and in-service education, continuing adult education, professional education, special youth programs and the entire public library system.

While considerable amounts are now spent on continuing and informal education, in many countries public library systems receive little support. In certain countries which realize that informal education plays a vital part in national development, considerable emphasis has been placed on the public library system's role. In other countries, where producing educated leaders has been the prime concern, emphasis has been placed on higher education for the few.

The goals established to transform a country economically and socially are of basic concern in appraising public library progress. Improvements in public library science cannot be expected to occur in those countries which lack full realization that the public library system requires major national and social planning support. For this reason, it is difficult to compare countries at differing stages of economic and social development and with differing public library service goals. Where a country has adopted a vigorous national library development policy, public libraries must be integrated with it so that they receive an adequate share of available financial and manpower resources, and so that the resulting services are relevant and contribute usefully to the attainment of national objectives.

National Cultural Policies. --An area of concern which has recently received considerable attention has been the progressive establishment of national cultural policies to support indigenous economic and social change, while keeping the country aware of overseas cultural developments. In certain countries, the phrase "cultural pollution" has been used to describe the receipt through mass media of unwanted material and cultural information unrelated to real population needs. By their overproduction of mass communication media, including books and other material, many larger nations have a decided effect on the national cultures of smaller countries.

Where clearly defined national cultural policies have been developed, normally they include schemes to provide greater resources for national cultural agencies, share and coordinate duties and responsibilities among national, municipal and other organizations in the cultural field, and provide financial support for publishing, literature, music, the arts, etc. In these cultural policies, it is important that the public library systems play a leading part. Cultural policies may not always take responsibility for all cultural services, however, and many examples exist of public library systems having been by-passed and new organizations created to spread books and reading.

Since cultural policy formulation is of particular concern to public library systems, the general aims of national cultural policy adopted in certain countries may be summarized as follows:

a. Cultural policy tries to create a richer social environment and a higher quality of life.
b. Cultural policy measures should improve communication between various social groups and give more individuals the opportunity of sharing cultural activities.
c. Cultural policy should protect freedom of speech and encourage freedom of artistic and cultural expression.
d. Cultural policy should guarantee preservation and promotion of the society's indigenous and cultural heritage, particularly in the face of foreign encroachment.
e. A general requirement exists to reduce the negative effect of commercialism on national cultural development.

In the German Democratic Republic, the U.S.S.R., Czechoslovakia, and Poland, literary culture research plays an important role in shaping the public library model. Reciprocally, public libraries contribute significantly towards spreading creative literature and help varied social groups to participate in national and world culture.

In some cases, coordinating the services of public libraries with those of other cultural agencies has led to initial friction and to the assumption of stiffly competitive roles. All agencies are particularly sensitive to the role played in handling the "new" media. Time appears to change this matter, however. Often this occurs because of constant pressures from library users to undertake new

cultural services and respond to new challenges.   Flexible management of all cultural agencies plays a key role in these instances.
Public libraries have great advantages as cultural change agents.
They can systematically direct activities toward different user groups,
and their services are freely available to all citizens, so they can
provide a base for activities which create new contacts between people and their culture.

Regional and Local Government Reorganization Studies. --All
parts of the world need new government systems to meet local needs.
This matter is caused primarily by continuing population growth and
the influx of people into larger communities, thereby increasing community size and the need for new types of local government structures.   In many developed countries, where regional and local government systems have existed for centuries, the process of change
and adaptation goes on quite slowly.

Change in local government structure is one of the most de-
cisive factors in producing change in public library systems.   The
reverse is not true, however.   Where change is brought about independently in a public library system, if it is not synchronized with
change in other local government services, and if there is no general reorganization of other government services, then the change
may remain unproductive.   Many examples of public library change
can be found in countries where small local government units have
been consolidated into larger units.   There are examples of the reverse happening, also.   As many countries develop and become more
heavily populated, they go through a phase when more--not fewer--
local government units are created, e. g. , in Mines Gerais State,
Brazil, the number of municipalities has more than doubled in the
past 10-20 years.   Both directions emphasize the importance of integrating planning for public library system development with planning
for regional and local government activities.

Public library systems are attempting to deal with the growing change in many countries' populations, their conversion from
agrarian and rural to industrial and urban.   A major result of urban
concentration has been greater benefits for city dwellers in interpersonal communication, goods, services and access to the work
place.   Consequently, the urban public library system must deal with
many problems not apparent to the rural public library system.   Public library development models in one type of area have little relevance for the other type.   At a certain urban growth point, an optimum concentration point is reached where interpersonal communication, the provision of goods and services, and access to the work
place become more difficult than before.   Problems have frequently
risen between the public library system serving the semi-rural area
surrounding an urban center and the system in the urban center.
Who should take responsibility for service in the rural area immediately adjacent to a metropolis?   One of the objectives of English and
Welsh local government reorganization in the 1970s was to bring
town and country together in one government unit so that one could
support the other.   Public library services benefited greatly by this
change.

Many national government policies attempt to provide the same advantages to rural area residents as to urban area residents. To bring this about, the rural public library service area should be better supported; it could then provide many new services.

Efforts in many countries to carry out inter-jurisdictional and interdisciplinary studies of urban and rural problems have resulted in frequent crossing of professional and disciplinary boundaries. Many aspects of economics, geography, engineering, communication, sociology and psychology are being coordinated and focused on urban problems. Public library science must take into account the findings of these interdisciplinary studies, particularly in view of the continuing trend towards growth in large urban centers. Similarly, certain local authorities are studying the concepts of corporate management in relation to library development and planning.

Reading, Media and User Studies. --In the related field of reading and media studies, the effects of communication media are analyzed and the results of user reaction to them made available. These studies are particularly important if public library systems are to find adequate answers to the new problems caused by new media technology. While many libraries have attempted to study the problems of print, telecommunications and electronic systems for conveying information have not been adequately studied. Much work carried out in these fields lies outside the experience of public librarians. For this reason, library systems should gain access to research facilities so that they can examine the implications of work in related fields and develop library applications from such work.

Activities Influencing Change in Public Library Science

Various agencies are attempting to change public library activities. Local, regional, national and international agencies must be consulted for information on the different directions being pursued. Particularly important roles are played by the many methodological centers which plan national public library system development. Such national centers exist in more than thirty countries. Those in the Soviet Union and Eastern Europe are linked with centers for developing standards and methods for library education. In certain national centers, such as that in West Berlin operated by the German Library Association, work is confined to analyzing statistical information, publishing reports and holding meetings. In the United States, with no single national center, a number of separate and competing services are offered by the specialized national library associations and state libraries. The American Library Association's Public Library Association is the main national coordinating agency for public library research, but many others exist, e. g. , Urban Library Council, U. S. National Commission for Libraries and Information Science.

One of the difficulties in many developing countries is that national public library system centers to collect and prepare research findings and standards do not yet exist. This has made these countries over-dependent on library reports and studies produced abroad and

prepared for other situations. Most of these reports need to be interpreted with great care in the light of differing local conditions.

The importance of a single national body with responsibility
for planning and developing a fully integrated library and information
system was clearly established by the Regional Meeting of Experts
on the National Planning of Documentation and Library Services
sponsored by UNESCO and held in Kampala, Uganda, in December
1970. One of the main objectives of that meeting was "to assess
the documentation and library needs of African States and correlate
a plan of development of these services for the region with a regional target for education, research and book development." Among the
tasks of the single national body to be established were the following:

    a.   the preparation, co-ordination and implementation of
          development plans for all types of library and informa-
          tion service
    b.   the costing of such plans and their inclusion in nation-
          al development plans
    c.   the harmonization of the allocation of all resources for
          library and information service whether from internal
          or external sources
    d.   the establishment of national standards for the efficient
          operation of library and information services
    e.   the development of a unified scheme of service and a
          common salary structure for the profession and the
          preparation in consultation with established schools of
          librarianship of the necessary manpower plans.

On an international basis, the function of reporting trends and
developments is shared by governmental and non-governmental agencies. The problems of rural and non-urban systems are of great
importance to international agencies, since the vast mass of the
world's population is still living in rural areas, and the greatest proportion of illiterates, now totalling over 850,000,000 persons, is
found there. In recent decades, the international governmental agencies of the United Nations, in particular UNESCO, the World Health
Organization and the World Bank, have assisted public library development.

Since UNESCO plays such an important role in coordinating
public library development, the programs of this body, as well as
their success, must be understood. In September 1974, UNESCO
held a major Inter-governmental Conference in Paris which adopted
a plan for national information development (NATIS). The purpose of
this plan is to establish a framework to deal with library, documentation and information needs in all member states. As adopted by
the Conference and subsequently approved by UNESCO, the basic
NATIS (National Information System) objectives are the following:

Objective 1. A national information policy.
A national information policy reflecting the needs of all community
sectors and of the entire nation should be established by each country in order to guide the national information plan.

Objective 2. Stimulation of user awareness.
In order to increase user awareness, appropriate bodies, including universities and other educational institutions, should include in their programs systematic instruction in information resource use.

Objective 3. Promotion of the reading habit.
In order to foster the reading habit, a network of school and public libraries within each country, in co-operation with other institutions, should develop programs designed to attract and sustain the interest of a wide body of readers.

Objective 4. Assessment of user needs.
Detailed analyses should be made of the requirements of governments and of the various groups of users in the areas of research, industry, and education, in order to ensure that the national information system is planned to meet their needs.

Objective 5. Analysis of existing information resources.
As a prerequisite to sound planning, comprehensive surveys should be undertaken of existing national documentation, library and archive resources.

In addition to these and other national objectives, a series of international objectives was adopted by the Conference:

Objective 13. Assistance to member states for the planning and development of NATIS.
UNESCO will promote the planning and development of a national information system and its elements in member states to achieve co-ordination at the national level and participation in world information systems.

Objective 14. Promotion of Universal Bibliographic Control (UBC).
UNESCO will promote universal bibliographic control in co-operation with the International Federation of Library Associations as a major policy objective to create a world-wide system for controlling information exchange.

The NATIS concepts were derived primarily from experience with special libraries and government information services rather than public library systems. This important consideration must be recognized in future public library system planning, since certain basic changes may be needed if public libraries attempt to work within the NATIS guidelines. The position taken by the UNESCO member governments and the objectives formulated at the Inter-governmental Conference will strongly affect all future library developments, including public library science.

UNESCO is publishing guidelines for planning national library, archive and documentation infrastructures. They deal with interaction among the user, the commercial publishing sector and new or existing library, archive and information institutions, nationally and internationally.

National Government Influences and Actions

In addition to the role which international inter-government
agencies play, various national governments are concerned with the
international dissemination of cultural and social services and their
relation to public library services abroad. Such concerns may be
based on the sales value of books, sound recordings, films and
other materials abroad. To some governments, public library systems play an important role in receiving and disseminating materials from abroad. Because public libraries are freely available to
citizens, many national governments pay close attention to the stock-
ing and supply of public libraries abroad. These matters are significant in dealing with comparative and international public library science, since the efforts of the larger governments are often directed
in this way. Such countries may have well developed interaction
policies with overseas public libraries. The effects of their policies
are important, particularly the effects on local library service of
pressure for distribution of foreign material.

In addition, many of the larger countries work to establish
public library methods abroad which are similar to those practiced
in their own countries. For this purpose they send visiting lecturers
to educate public librarians in other countries. Many public library
specialists from the USA, the UK, and the USSR assist libraries and
information services in developing countries.

In an effort to evaluate various proposals for change, certain
developing countries have established university degree courses for
the comparative analysis of public library policies and practices.
While few in number, the present trend indicates that more of them
will be developed in the future. Developing countries where comparative public library studies are being carried out include Jamaica,
Pakistan, Iran and Malaysia. Increasing effort is being made by developing countries to improve their national public library infrastructures and to adapt methods which meet their requirements.

During 1972, in the course of the International Book Year
(IBY), various symposia were convened by the USA, UK and USSR
governments. Many of them were directed to public library expansion. One of the most important meetings was convened December
10-13, 1973 at New Paltz, New York, by the U.S. National Book
Committee. This Conference reviewed the activities which should
be continued following the end of International Book Year. Arising
out of this meeting was a statement which indicated that the most
critical book needs must be met in the developing countries themselves, although books from abroad obviously have a certain role to
play. The path which lies ahead calls for creating domestic institutions in each country to improve the flow of books and other publications, educating authors and editors, fostering competent publishing, public or private, creating and strengthening book stores, libraries and other channels of distribution and encouraging the reading habit.

Most of the studies and meetings held during International Book Year wrestled with such questions as attempts to stop the flow of unwanted material into developing countries, achieving local support for domestic publishing and printing services, or improving the supply of material through translation with due regard to the controls normally exercised by foreign copyright owners. Such measures have been advocated in the past to relieve developing country problems. It is evident that the process of international information transfer does not imply uncritical acceptance of the methods, policies, ideas, and solutions of one country by another, but, instead, careful appraisal by library professionals seeking ideas which can be adapted locally, and introduced in appropriate circumstances.

Non-governmental Agencies Concerned with Advances

Among the international non-governmental agencies concerned with public libraries is the International Federation of Library Associations. For the past 25 years, IFLA has maintained a Public Library Section whose chairman has traditionally been a British, Dutch or Scandinavian librarian and whose program has been largely designed to deal with the needs and interests of European and North American public libraries. In 1971, at a Liverpool meeting of representatives from English-speaking developing countries during the 36th Annual Council, steps were taken to alter the IFLA program and to encourage work with library systems outside the developed countries. A working group on developing countries was established, with Joseph Soosai of Malaysia as chairman and two of the other members being public librarians.

At succeeding IFLA General Council gatherings in 1973 and 1974, there were meetings of working groups of librarians from developing countries whose languages were French and Spanish. In 1974, IFLA adopted a policy to establish a regional activity program for public, school, university and other library development in various regions of the world, with the first three regions being Asia, Africa, Latin America and the Caribbean.

It is still too early to determine IFLA's future program for public library science. The Association is still dominated by European and North American members who represent university, national, and special libraries and national government institutions. The role of the new IFLA Division of libraries for the general public approved in the new IFLA constitution in 1976, is awaited with great anticipation.

An IFLA sub-section, the International Association of Metropolitan City Libraries (INTAMEL), whose membership is concentrated in 100 large metropolitan cities, has been active both in meeting the needs of developed country members and in facing the problems of public libraries in developing countries. At the 1972 INTAMEL meeting in Rome a declaration offered support to city governments and public library agencies wishing to improve library service. INTAMEL inaugurated a research project in a developing country

as a pilot project. The Nigerian National Library, in cooperation
with the Lagos Public Library, secured a $27,000 grant from the
International Development Research Centre in Ottawa to study public
library user needs in the Lagos area.

National Library Associations

The role of national library associations in promoting public
library development has been of great importance. This is particularly true where new national associations have been formed in the
third world, often reflecting a need for public librarians to meet and
discuss their problems. Recent reports from Uganda, Jordan, Pakistan, and Kenya indicate the kinds of struggles which public libraries
are facing.

The lack of library association funds to support study of public library needs is a constant report theme. The fact that foreign
experience, largely from the UK, USA, USSR, West Germany, Canada and Scandinavia, is not always appropriate and helpful is a general theme. As the national associations in developed countries have
often patterned their services and objectives on each other, so do the
national associations in developing countries look to each other for
mutual guidance.

Contributions of Selected Public Library Systems

In addition to the role of international and national agencies,
the contribution of individual municipal, regional and rural public library systems is of some consequence. Many of them carry on extensive research in their own areas and use international and comparative studies. Staff members may be drawn from other nations,
also. Their presence has a decided effect on planning collection development and introducing new technical methods from abroad. Employing staff members educated abroad is an effective way of promoting international and comparative studies and exchanges.

Pre-Conditions for Useful Scholarship

Particular attention has been paid in this paper to the problems of public library systems in developing countries attempting to
meet user needs and to adapt practices used in the public libraries
of developed countries. This is a crucial area of public library concern. At the same time, the problems of public library systems in
developed countries are growing, and much study and research is being carried out to improve practices. This two-part situation is the
dominant characteristic of present-day public library research and
presents the main challenge in comparative and international public
library science. Library services in older countries must study developing country methodology, also, since very often a fresh look is
needed at some of the practices previously evolved.

One of the reasons why public library science has not evolved as effectively as information science or library management has been the poor international coordination of data gathering, research funding, and reporting of results. This is not as evident in socialist world countries as it is in Western Europe and North America. However, even within the socialist world, the presence of national bureaus for public library methodology and research has not altogether alleviated the problem. More attention needs to be paid to cooperative planning of public library research, and larger research and study allocations will be needed from national, regional and international agencies. Apart from one or two small research projects funded by INTAMEL on an international basis, no large scale public library studies have been funded and supported by public library systems internationally.

Organization of an International Association of Public Libraries under the auspices of the new IFLA Division could contribute to more effective coordination and planning of public library research. The same thing might be accomplished by existing national research institutions and library schools through international coordination of their work. Clearly, an important task lies ahead in this area. A much more effective cooperative sharing of research information and experience is needed to plan international public library activities.

BIBLIOGRAPHY

Abukutsa, J. L. The Role of Books in Development. Proceedings of the Fifth Biennial Conference, East Africa Library Association, Nairobi, September 25-29, 1972. Nairobi: Kenya Library Association, 1974.
Birch, F. M. "Problems Facing Jordanian Libraries," Rissalat Al-Maktaba IX (June 1974), pp. 8-20.
Campbell, H. C. Public Libraries in the Urban Metropolitan Setting. Hamden, Conn.: Linnet Books and Clive Bingley, 1973.
Chandler, G. (ed.) International Librarianship, Surveys of Recent Developments in Developing Countries and in Advanced Librarianship. London: Library Association, 1972.
Coombs, P. H. The World Education Crisis, A Systems Analysis. London: Oxford University Press, 1968.
Delhi Public Library. Annual Report 1972-73. Delhi, 1974.
Fang, J. and Songe, A. H. International Guide to Library, Archival and Information Science. New York: R. R. Bowker Co., 1976.
Gardner, F. M. Public Library Legislation: A Comparative Study. Paris: UNESCO, 1971.
Greenaway, E. "Progress in International Librarianship," American Libraries III (July-August 1972), pp. 803-806.
IFLA Annual, 1973, Proceedings of the 39th General Council Meeting, Munchen. Pullach: Verlag Dokumentation, 1974.
Kaltwasser, F. G. "The Library Plan 1973 in the Federal Republic of Germany," IFLA Journal I (March 1975), p. 135.
Kolodziejska, Jadwiga. "Powstanie Bibliotek Publicznych i Zasady

Gromadzeni Zbiorow" (The establishment of public libraries
        and the principles of collecting), in: Owspölczesnej Kulturze
        Literackiej, Vol. 2. Wrockaw: Ossolineum, 1973.
National Book Committee. International Book Year, 1972, Summary
        Report. New York: National Book Committee, 1973.
Nigeria: East Central State Library Board; Continuing Factor in our
        Nation Building, Annual Report 1973-1974. Enugu: State Cen-
        tral Library, 1974.
Robinson, J. L. National Planning for Libraries in the Developing
        Countries. Washington, 40th General Council, IFLA, 1974.
Sabzwari, G. A. "Library Authorities in Pakistan," Pakistan Li-
        brary Bulletin VII (September 1974), pp. 9-20.
Sallai, Istvan. A Közmüvelödesi Konyvtárügy Fejlödesi Iránya,
        Kulönös Tekintettel A Magyar Kösmüvelödesi Könyvtárügyre.
        2. atd. Változat. (Development Trends of Public Librarian-
        ship with Special Regard to Hungarian Public Librarianship.
        2. revised version). Budapest, 1968.
Ugandan Libraries. Special Issue on National Needs and Problems
        of Library Development in Uganda. Kampala: Uganda Li-
        brary Association, 1975.
UNESCO. International Conference on the Planning of National Docu-
        mentation, Library and Archive Infrastructures, Paris, Sep-
        tember 23-27, 1974. National Information Systems (NATIS);
        Objectives for National and International Action. Paris:
        UNESCO, 1974, COM 74/NATIS/3.
_____ . Intergovernmental Conference on the Planning of National
        Documentation, Library and Archive Services. Document
        COM. 74/NATIS/REF. 1, p. 7-8.
Whatley, H. C. British Librarianship and Information Science, 1966-
        1970. London: Library Association, 1972.
Whithers, F. N. Standards for Library Service; an International
        Survey. Paris: UNESCO, 1974.
World Bank. Education, Sector Working Paper. Washington, D.C.:
        World Bank, 1974.

CHILDREN'S LIBRARY SCIENCE

Anne Pellowski

Spread of Children's Library Services

A recent estimate of the world's child population under age 15 was 1,558,464,000. [1] Since about one billion of these children live in East and West Asian, African and South American countries, where children's library service is very limited or non-existent, clearly, world children's library service is not extensive. Even in many European countries and in Japan and China, children's library service is scattered and incompletely developed. Among the relatively few countries where such services do exist, however, there is a lively international exchange, although it tends to flow in one direction, rather than two.

Historical Influences

In the United States, Canada and England, children's librarians developed standards and established education programs (both inservice as well as academic) in the period 1876-1920. This service and education stressed the pleasureful aspects of introducing material to children. Since so few opportunities for free entertainment existed at that time, it was only natural for children to respond to their own libraries enthusiastically. These libraries were much less formal than school classes, encouraged the child to choose his own reading interests freely, and did not require book reports!

Such enthusiasm was unlikely to go unnoticed. Soon, many western European countries were sending young women to be educated in this type of library service. Among them was Sweden, and in particular, the librarian, Valfried Palmgren Munch-Petersen. During her 1907 visit to the United States she was so deeply impressed by the children's library work of Anne Carroll Moore at Pratt Institute and the New York Public Library that she returned to found the Born och Ungdomsbibliotek in Stockholm. She provided the main impetus for children's library service in Sweden. [2] Louise M. Boerlage, who trained with Effie L. Power, was credited with being an important initiator of children's service in The Netherlands. [3] In 1909, the Union of Ghent Women sent a young woman to be educated in library work with children at the Pittsburgh Public Library. Subsequently, she returned to establish library service for children in Ghent. [4]

Following the First World War, both France and Belgium were

the recipients of model children's libraries, called L'Heure Joyeuse,
from American benefactors, including the American Library Association. Other countries were influenced through the writings of early
children's librarians. Cynthia Paltridge of Australia stated: "The
American, Effie Power's Work with Children in Public Libraries
(2nd ed. , 1943), perhaps more than anything else, stimulated and
gave direction to pioneer workers."[6] Momoki Ishii of Japan credited
Lillian Smith and Jean Thompson of the Toronto Public Library with
having the deepest influence on her philosophy of children's library
service.[7] In Africa, it was both the writing and the exemplary work
of Evelyn J. A. Evans that helped to start the Ghana Library Board
as well as other national public library boards.[8] Modeled somewhat
on British subscription library systems (with very low fees), they
used British books since few local vernacular works were available.

Jella Lepman, founder of the International Youth Library in
Munich, West Germany, planned it to be both a model children's
service library and a research center on the international aspects of
children's literature.[9] In more than 25 years of service, it has
probably had more exchanges of children's librarians from other
countries than any other world library. However, most of these exchanges were made for the express purpose of literature study, and
rarely was there any opportunity for practical application of library
work with children. Therefore, although the International Youth Library's impact has been quite broad in terms of international children's book translation, publishing and study, its influence on the
theories and practices of children's library science has been negligi-
ble, in this writer's view.

The U.S. Information Service libraries spread throughout the
world might have had a far more dramatic local impact, if they had
been allowed to continue giving children's service. In 1950 Publishers Weekly stated:

> In the Philippines, 36,600 children have come to the Tondo
> Library in the past six months.... In Rangoon, Burma,
> children line up on the street every morning to wait for
> the library doors to open. A similar enthusiasm is shown
> in Ankara, Athens and Barcelona, where there are 1,000
> visitors to the library each day during the four hours it
> is open.[10]

Had such extensive library service continued for so many children
for a few decades, the impact, in international terms, would have
been even greater. This would have been especially true if the local
production of children's books had been encouraged and supported.

Present-Day Exchanges

For the most part, the pattern has continued to the present
day. Young persons from English-speaking African countries tend to
obtain their advanced children's library education in England; those

from Japan, Latin America and the Middle East go to the United
States or Canada. A small number of children's librarians from a
variety of nations now go to the Scandinavian countries, especially
Denmark and Sweden, and some Asians go to New Zealand and Australia. Perhaps because the socialist countries have similar education and library service patterns, long-term study or work exchanges
appear to be more unusual there. A few developing countries with
ideologies close to Marxist-Leninist principles send librarians to be
educated in leading socialist countries, but this writer has yet to
meet one educated in children's library service.

The preceding paragraph is not meant to imply that a large
number of children's library service exchanges has been carried out.
The opposite is more accurate. A November 1975 telephone survey
made by this writer in the 25 largest U.S. metropolitan library systems indicated that none of them had, at that time, an international
children's library exchange program. Neither one-way nor two-way
exchanges were operating. More than half of these libraries, however, had sponsored such exchanges in the past. A survey of university library schools would probably indicate only a small number
of overseas students studying children's services, also. This assumption is based on the author's personal observations while lecturing in several library schools.

Short-term exchanges, such as study tours of a few weeks
duration and international conferences sponsored by UNESCO, IFLA,
etc., account for some experience in exchanging ideas at the international level. However, this writer has observed very little except
surface exchanges on such occasions. What is achieved are personal contacts that may grow into substantive exchanges and an opportunity to see the physical conditions of children's library service in
urban areas. IFLA and UNESCO publications are more useful to
document the history and present status of children's library service
in a variety of countries than to serve as catalysts for further development or as comparative studies.

International Leadership

The reasons behind the spread of children's library service
internationally lie not so much, then, in institutions or organizations,
as they do in the dynamism of individuals who become enthused about
such service and spread their enthusiasm with the right amounts of
pragmatism and idealism. This appears to have been true in the
past, and in the present it can be seen strikingly in the work of such
leaders as Janet Hill of England, Virginia Betancourt of Venezuela,
Lily Amir-Arjomand of Iran, Mitsue Ishitake, Momoko Ishii and
Shigeo Watanabe of Japan, and Genevieve Patte of France.

Apparently Janet Hill used her New York Public Library experience to help clarify her ideas of what not to do in a large, inner
urban system of children's library service, even more than to define
the things she did wish to do. This is a singularly effective function

which can be performed by the large, well-established library systems in developed countries.   Many countries can be guided through the pitfalls of institution-building by studying the adaptability (or lack of it) that older institutions show.

Virginia Betancourt, while obviously using many aspects of U.S. library service as models for the Banco del Libro in Venezuela, still chose to disregard the American trends of the time and combined public and school library service to children under one agency.   This library may prove to be a long-lasting model of separate but equal school and public library service for children, organized under a common administration.

As she developed the children's libraries and cultural centers run by her Institute for the Intellectual Development of Children and Young Adults, Lily Amir-Arjomand was most strongly influenced by her Rutgers library science work under Mary Gaver.   Certain elements were structurally (but not ideologically) patterned after Soviet Union models, however, while architecturally following Scandinavian standards.   Recently the Institute was asked to assist in establishing, as part of an Iranian government-aid package, a similar type of service in Jordan.   Whether or not the Institute is well enough developed to carry out such a demanding task, in addition to its own system building, remains to be seen.

Groundwork for the Institute had been partly laid by various children's book groups working to spread reading among largely illiterate children.   The Children's Book Council, the Franklin Books Program and the Centre for Reading Materials for Literates (now called the Educational Publications Centre) can be cited.   The latter two groups combined skills and funds to launch the very successful Iranian children's magazine, Peik.   In this writer's opinion, Peik has achieved the most dramatic and consistent rise in children's reading habits in any developing country.   It cuts across rural, town and city populations.   A climate for better acceptance of the Institute's children's libraries was created by these earlier activities.

Mitsue Ishitake, director of the Ohanashi Caravan of the Hakuho Foundation, Tokyo, Japan, drew much of her inspiration from the United States and Canada, but her travels enabled the Caravan to learn from several countries.   Like the libraries mentioned above, the Ohanashi Caravan is a unique form of children's library service.   It provides group or extension activities for children on a contractual basis to municipal and prefectural libraries and other institutions.   It is unusual in drawing on public and private funds, also, and stressing heavy parental involvement in establishing children's library services.   Mrs. Ishitake was influenced by descriptions of certain Weston Woods Studio caravans and by the volunteer storytellers training film produced by Connecticut Films and Anne Izard of the Westchester County Library System.

Shigeo Watanabe, whose overseas experience and study included both public and school library service in the United States and

England, concentrated recently on introducing innovative Japanese
school library service through a still-developing model center at
Kato School, Numazu.

The home library movement, popularized by Momoko Ishii following World War II, continues to flourish in certain areas of Japan.
It is another form of public library service that combines public and
private sector funds.   Although a modest home library movement for
delivering children's service operated in the U.S., 1900-1920, the
movement did not continue and was not tried in other countries, so
no data are available for comparative study.

Genevieve Patte of France, who worked, studied and traveled
in a number of countries, used an amalgam of styles in directing
the model library at Clamart and in her frequent lecturing and advising in France.   Recent difficulties in that library have indicated the
problems of finding the right kind of institutional form and the most
effective types of service when dealing with customs as deeply em-
bedded as those in France.

Adaptation of Overseas Ideas

A dramatic change in the nationality of leading children's library service innovators has occurred in recent years.   Earlier,
Canadian and U.S. librarians were the leaders.   Now, developing
countries are more likely to produce such innovators.   The influence
of the United States and Canada remains strong, but the ideas are
likely to be of mixed nationality.

It is increasingly clear that cultural institutions cannot be
transplanted whole from one nation to the next and still function well,
especially when they have daily contact with both literate and illiterate persons.   The greater the adaptation to fit local political, ideological and social situations, the more lasting are the results.   Out-
wardly, services to children may look remarkably similar in a variety of countries, but the organizational structure and funding contain
many varieties of adjustment to local government, social structure
and temperament.

International Children's Library Science Research

The organizational aspects of children's library service are
rarely described in international library literature.   A search through
the last decade of Library Literature and the last five years of Dissertation Abstracts and Research in Education revealed no comparative study of children's library service, where two or more countries
were contrasted and compared in detail.   The student should be able
to identify such basic information as the following:

1. Child population in service areas
2. Number actually served

3. How the libraries perceived and described their clientele
4. How the clientele perceived and described the library
5. Physical description of library facilities
6. Library budget for children's work
7. How funds were obtained
8. Per cent of budget spent on personnel
9. Per cent spent on material and building maintenance
10. Number of personnel in relation to number of children
11. Administrative structure and how related to other departments
12. Background and education of staff members working with children
13. Annual hours of in-service education and meeting time
14. Annual hours of general service to children
15. Annual hours of programs and extension activities
16. Circulation and attendance statistics
17. Size of collection(s)
18. Methods of circulation and types of material circulated
19. Evaluative data of any kind.

Data can be obtained from a number of libraries and systems, but rarely in a form consistent enough for comparative library research use. For this reason, those persons responsible for establishing children's library service in new areas have difficulty providing reliable projections of costs, personnel and other needs. The philosophy and theory of children's library service is generally available in print, however. This is true for western children's libraries, as well as for socialist country models. The three volumes called Library Service to Children, sponsored by IFLA's Sub-section on Library Work with Children, contain several short passages indicating briefly the philosophy on which service is based in specific countries. Unfortunately, few of them contain comparative or international statements.

During the past five years, more than thirty papers have appeared in various journals around the world. One can find a few comparative statements related to the theory and philosophy of children's library service. A number of bi-national papers describe children's library services in one country, as viewed by someone from a second country. A high percentage of the international periodical literature describes the situation in terms of results, without giving its background. There is a lamentable lack of readily accessible statistical data. Children's librarians with overseas experience have used that experience to enrich their work but not as the subject of carefully documented and developed professional papers. While this improves immediate service, it frustrates research which could have long-term values.

A deep and persistent skepticism has existed in the minds of many North American children's librarians about the usefulness and accuracy of much research about children. A children's librarian can observe a wide variety of children's reactions to books, language and ideas in a less constrained situation than is common in schools.

However, most children's research has been carried out in association with schools and was thought to be much influenced by the system of grading in force. The results of such research often contradicted the daily observations of children's librarians. Research in a number of countries has shown that the theories of child development propounded by Jean Piaget, for instance, did not apply universally. [12] However, Piaget's methodology had such far-reaching implications that other limitations were thought to be of less importance.

Certain children's services library educators recommend such courses as child psychology, child sociology, and literacy processes. Nevertheless, children's librarians' questioning attitude toward research in these fields, especially that involving children's responses to reading, is still a serious limitation. This is a major reason for the lack of significant research in comparative children's library science in the western countries. In socialist countries, such research exists because educational methodology stresses child psychology and sociology. However, no long-term exchanges have occurred between western librarians with highly developed but different children's services. Consequently, comparative conclusions can only be general and speculative, since they must be based on secondary information sources.

Children's Literature

The related area of children's literature has produced much more research than children's library service. World-wide surveys or histories exist in five languages, and several national studies use bi-national viewpoints. Several children's books have been translated and used widely in children's libraries around the world. Even here one must admit a regrettable lack of objective studies, however.

The availability of a local children's literature of quality and variety impacts on the development of children's library service. This literature can be almost entirely imported from other countries using the same language, as was the case with Australia, Canada, New Zealand, and English-speaking African countries, and is the case in Venezuela and other Latin American countries. Or, it can come partially in translated form, as in the Scandinavian countries, The Netherlands, Iran, the socialist countries, South Africa, and postwar Japan and Germany. There is no example evident of a country which successfully started extensive children's library service without first having steady access to at least 300 children's book titles annually. In certain countries, notably the United States, the Scandinavian countries, Japan and Iran, the establishment of children's libraries stimulated an increase in the quality and quantity of local children's book production. [13] This was not the case in New Zealand, Canada and Australia. Instead, these countries are among those now struggling to develop a local literature. Progress is being achieved because of a new consciousness that the child's local and national identity should be evident in the children's literature given to him/her. [14] Children's librarians press for such literature, but cannot bring about its development alone.   If they had more influence, Canada, Australia, and New Zealand would have developed more extensive local children's literatures decades ago.

In the socialist countries, children's literature has been the determining factor.   Children's library service developed as one means of making sure that certain carefully selected types of children's literature would be read by all children.   Once the government established the policy of equal access to books for all children, it was logical that a system of children's libraries would be developed.   General public and school libraries were established, but their use by children appears to have been less than that of the children's public libraries established separately or as parts of the "palaces" or "houses of children's culture. "   They existed without control of a larger library unit giving service to the adult public. This was an extremely important factor arising from the great stress that socialist ideology gave to peer group education and social interaction.

The study of socialist children's library service can only be undertaken after understanding the ideology and methodology behind publication.   This statement should be true of China, also, which apparently has swerved radically from its earlier copying of Soviet models, but still places great emphasis on the careful selection, control and dissemination of all publishing for children.

Research Requirements

Useful comparative and international research in children's library science depends on the following conditions:

1. More cross-cultural and comparative international research in the general area of child development is needed.   This research must be studied by a wider number of children's librarians than are presently knowledgeable about it.

2. More international exchanges of longer duration are needed by children's librarians skilled in research methods as well as in direct children's service.

3. Dropping the library school language requirement must be re-examined.   Its effect seems to have been almost to eliminate the librarian who can function in more than one language.

4. General courses in international and area studies library science must include aspects of children's libraries.   A recent publication by Martin H. Sable cites 24 case studies but not one of them teaches reference sources and the skills related to international or area studies children's work. [15]   Library schools must make greater efforts to

locate and purchase the hard-to-find studies of children's
library service, also.

5. National and/or international library associations and organizations must develop guidelines for compiling the background and statistical data that are meaningful in international children's library service studies. They should encourage the publication of sets of statistics for individual
   libraries and systems in a variety of countries, as well as
   national and regional analyses.

When several of these conditions are met, perhaps children's
library science will obtain the attention it deserves from scholars
working inside or outside the field of library science.

NOTES

1. U. N. Population Unit, 1975.
2. Palmgren Munch-Petersen, Valfried. "Stockholms Barn och
   Ungdomsbibliotek," Biblioteksbladet XLVI (December 1961),
   pp. 750-9.
3. International Federation of Library Associations. Public Libraries Section. Subsection on Library Work with Children.
   Library Service to Children. Vol. 1, Lund: Bibliotekstjanst,
   1963, 125 pp. Vol. 2, Lund: Bibliotekstjanst, 1966, 92 pp.
   Vol. 3, Copenhagen: Bibliotekcentralen, 1970, 100 pp.
4. Limbosch-Dangotte, R. C. "Les Bibliothèques Pour Enfants à
   Gand," Revue des Bibliothèques et Archives de Belgique VII
   (July-October 1909), pp. 263-275.
5. Moore, Anne Carroll. "Report of a Sub-committee on Children's
   Work in Other Countries," American Library Association Bulletin XV (July 1921), pp. 148-52.
6. International Federation of Library Associations. Public Libraries Section. Subsection on Library Work with Children. Library Service to Children. op. cit. , Vol. 2, p. 8.
7. Conversation with the author, Tokyo, October, 1975.
8. Evans, Evelyn J. A. "Work with Children," in her A Tropical
   Library Service: The Story of Ghana's Libraries. London:
   Andre Deutsch, 1964, pp. 106-313.
9. Lepman, Jella. A Bridge of Children's Books. Trans. from
   the German by Edith McCormick. Chicago: American Library Association, 1969. Chapters V & VI.
10. "American Children's Books Around the World," Publishers'
    Weekly CLVIII (October 28, 1950), p. 1923.
11. International Federation of Library Associations. Public Li-
    braries Section. Subsection on Library Work with Children.
    Library Service to Children. op. cit. , Vols. 1, 2, 3.
12. Piaget, Jean. The Language and Thought of the Child. Cleve-
    land: World Publishing Co. , 1955, p. 29.
13. Scherf, Walter, "Observations on International Aspects of Chil-
    dren's Books," Top of the News XXXII (Jan. 1976), pp. 135-
    148. Mr. Scherf wrote among other things: "In many

countries, this influence on the literary market has seen considerable change during the last decades. In France, the public librarian does not yet play a serious role as purchaser of children's books. In the U.S., it is the very high sales figures for nonfiction titles that allowed and induced the tremendous production of nonfiction series and single titles for children. The main trading partner is the highly developed school library system. Leading American publishing houses have special sections for their collaboration with school libraries--an institution which is unknown in other countries."

14. Hurtig, Mel. "Never Heard of Them ... They Must be Canadian," A Report on the Results of a Canadian Student Awareness Survey. Toronto: Canadabooks, 1975, 16 pp.

15. Sable, Martin H. International and Area Studies Librarianship: Case Studies. Metuchen, N.J.: Scarecrow, 1973, 166 pp.

BIBLIOGRAPHY

Abric, Carol. Study of Children's Library Services in Australia. Research paper, State University of New York, Albany, 1969. 58 pp.

"American Children's Books Around the World," Publishers' Weekly CLVIII (October 28, 1950), pp. 1919-1923.

Arnoldowa, Maria, "Z Problemow Bibliotek i Czytelnictwa Dzieciecego w USA," Bibliotekarz (No. 3, 1966), pp. 72-7.

Bagshaw, Marguerite, "Children's Literature and Libraries Around the World," International Library Review I (January 1969), pp. 119-29.

"Children's Libraries and School Libraries," in: Ferguson, John Britton, Libraries in France. Hamden, Conn.: Archon Books, 1971, pp. 61-8.

Cohen, Lorraine Sterline, "Children's Library Services in Israel," Top of the News XXXI (January 1975), pp. 160-6.

Downs, Lavinia Davis, "Services for Children Provided by Public Libraries in Japan," Top of the News XXVI (January 1970), pp. 169-74.

Ellis, Alec. Library Services for Young People in England and Wales, 1830-1970. Oxford: Pergamon Press, 1971, 198 pp.

Evans, Evelyn J. A. "Work with Children," in her: A Tropical Library Service: The Story of Ghana's Libraries. London: Andre Deutsch, 1964, pp. 106-131.

Evertsen, Muriel H. "Library Services to Young People: Latin America," New Jersey Libraries III (Winter 1970), pp. 4-8.

Gallivan, Marion F. "Research on Children's Services in Public Libraries; an Annotated Bibliography," Top of the News XXX (April 1974), pp. 275-293.

Gaver, Mary V. "Good News from Iran: a Personal Report," Top of the News XXVII (April 1971), pp. 256-71.

Gosner, Pamela W. "Library Services to Young People: Denmark," New Jersey Libraries III (Winter 1970), pp. 24-6.

Harrod, Leonard Montague. Library Work With Children; With

Special Reference to Developing Countries. London: Andre Deutsch, 1969.

Hill, Janet. Children Are People: the Librarian in the Community. London: Hamish Hamilton, 1973, 123 pp.

Hiort-Lorenzen, Marianne, "Nogle Borne-og Ungdomsbibliotekeri USA," Bogens Verden LIV (1972), pp. 375-81.

Hopkins, Lee Bennett, "Once Upon a Slaughter House: the Biblioteca Publica de San Miguel de Allende," Horn Book XLV (February 1969), pp. 37-9.

Howard, Ruth B., "Library Services to Young People: Australia," New Jersey Libraries III (Winter 1970), pp. 13-15.

Hurtig, Mel. "Never Heard of Them ... They Must Be Canadian," A Report on the Results of a Canadian Student Awareness Survey. Toronto: Canadabooks, 1975, 16 pp.

International Federation of Library Associations. Public Libraries Section. Sub-section on Library Work with Children. Library Service to Children. Vol. 3. Copenhagen: Bibliotekcentralen, 1970, 100 pp.

Jones, Heather and Medlock, Lynne, "Children's Libraries in Scandinavia: a First Impression," Library Review XXII (Spring 1970), pp. 251-4.

Kirstein, Kirsten, "14 Dage i Ungarn," Bogens Verden LV (November 1973), pp. 540-1.

Kogochi, Yoshiko, "Children's Libraries in Tokyo from 1887-1945," Library and Information Science (Mita Society) No. 9 (1971), pp. 209-29.

Krumbach, Lis, "Children's Library; Children in Focus; Children's Centre," Scandinavian Public Library Quarterly V (Fall 1972), pp. 92-100.

Lepman, Jella. A Bridge of Children's Books. Trans. from the German by Edith McCormick. Chicago: American Library Association, 1969, 155 pp.

Limbosch-Dangotte, R. C., "Les Bibliothèques Pour Enfants à Gand," Revue des Bibliothèques et Archives de Belgique VII (July-October 1909), pp. 263-275.

Maclean, J. D., "Survey of Library Services to Children: Arrangements for the Survey and for a Follow-up Visit by an Overseas Librarian," New Zealand Libraries XXXV (February 1972), pp. 30-3.

Medvedeva, Nina, "Scientific Research on Children's Reading and Library Work with Children," UNESCO Bulletin for Libraries XXVI (July-August 1972), pp. 203-209.

Mikin, Ingrid, "Kinderbuch, Kinderbucherei in der CSSR: als Austauschbibliothekarin in Prag," Bücherei und Bildung XXI (August 1969), pp. 281-5.

Moore, Anne Carroll, "Report of a Sub-committee on Children's Work in Other Countries," American Library Association Bulletin (July 1921), pp. 148-52.

"Organizations of Professional Children's Librarians," International Library Review IV (July 1972), entire issue.

Palmgren Munch-Petersen, Valfried, "Stockholms Barn och Ungdomsbibliotek," Biblioteksbladet XLVI (December 1961), pp. 750-9.

Pellowski, Anne, "Notes from a Latin American Journey," Top of

the News XXIV (October 1967), pp. 209-15.
_____, The World of Children's Literature. New York: R. R.
      Bowker Co. , 1968, 538 pp.
Piaget, Jean.   The Language and Thought of the Child.   Cleveland:
      World Publishing Co. , 1955, 251 pp.
Ray, Colin H.   "Trends in Children's Librarianship," UNESCO Bul-
      letin for Libraries XXVIII (July 1974), pp. 188-92.
Saurman, Linda M.   "Library Services to Young People: the USSR,"
      New Jersey Libraries III (Winter 1970), pp. 27-9.
Scherf, Walter.   "Observations on International Aspects of Children's
      Books," Top of the News XXXII (Jan. 1976), pp. 135-148.
Slavik, Susan.   "Ivan Reads: an Examination of Children's Libraries
      in Russia," Top of the News XXVI (Jan. 1970), pp. 152-7.
Van Dyke, Flora Zoe.   "International Activities in the Field of Chil-
      dren's Libraries," International Library Review III (Oct. 1971),
      pp. 469-84.
Van Niel, Floise S.   "Children and the Penang Library," Hawaii
      Library Association Journal XXVIII (Dec. 1971), pp. 17-20.

SCHOOL LIBRARIANSHIP

Frances Laverne Carroll, with assistance from
the IFLA Section for School Libraries*

In the American development of school libraries in the early
1960s, the slogan, a school library for every child, was a popular
promotional phrase. This phrase should be the goal of every nation
in the 1970s. The statement is quantitative. Its existence indicates
that, in the United States, considered a leader in the area of school
librarianship, the provision for school libraries is unevenly distributed, particularly for children five to twelve years of age. School
libraries are rudimentary in many other countries--a few books in
locked cases. In many countries secondary school libraries continue
to receive the most attention. Population projections indicate that
primary school enrollment will increase after 1980, a situation that
can only widen the disparity between the two educational levels in the
provision of school libraries. School library growth is occurring in
a time when many new nations are being formed, but these nations
are not the only ones with limited school library development. Therefore, in a world assessment, the number of good school libraries is
severely limited.

Definitions and Objectives of School Librarianship

The development of school libraries is confined almost entirely to the twentieth century. In the 1920s and 1930s a few publications, mostly pertaining to school library management at both the
secondary and elementary levels, appeared in French, English, Spanish, and Swedish.[1] This was a period devoted to organizing, weed-
ing and inventorying the small collections, and only a few tools were
available to assist personnel who were just beginning to be educated
for a special type of librarianship. It was a period when those few
outstanding school librarians who expressed the contemporary viewpoint toward school libraries were considered visionaries. After
World War II, publishers gave greater support to school library development. A new genre of books written especially for young adults,
more nonfiction for children, and the highly artistic picture book appeared. The 1960 Standards for School Library Programs of the
American Association of School Librarians enlarged the official

---

*The IFLA Section for School Libraries membership was the follow-
ing: Readers--Linda Beeler, U.S.A.; T. Blazekovic, Yugoslavia;
Sigrun Hannesdottir, Iceland; and Contributors--Noelene Hall, Australia; Barbara Eddy, Canada; and Jennifer Shephard, England.

statement on materials and changed the terminology: "Instructional
materials include books--the literature of children, young people and
adults--other printed materials, films, recordings, and new media
developed to aid learning."[2] This widened the scope of materials to
be included in a school library to nonprint or audio-visuals and began the change of the library from a book-oriented room to a media
center. "A school media center is an area or system of areas in
the school where a full range of information sources, associated
equipment, and services from media staff are accessible to students,
school personnel and the school community."[3]

     The term, media center, will be used here only when refer-
ences are quoted which include it. The term, school library, will
be used throughout the text as having more widespread world understanding and application, although the school library may have other
than printed materials. Either term applies to the individual school
building. Students from five to eighteen years of age are usually
served. The media center provides facilities to enable teachers and
students to produce materials locally, most usually of the simpler
kinds such as graphics, slides, transparencies, and recordings. In
addition to those audio-visual devices previously mentioned, the following are often available: kits, games, programmed instruction,
film loops, filmstrips, video and oral tapes, microforms, sculpture,
models, and globes.

     The 1969 Standards had a tremendous impact on all U.S.
school libraries, and the implementation of both the philosophy and
the quantitative levels in a large number of schools has made viable
the emphasis of the 1970s: the integration of school library service
with instructional technique, to implement curriculum goals and to
support classroom instruction. Any nation can assess its own status
in school library development by: 1) the number of school libraries
and the educational levels served; 2) the extent and the types of materials and staffing provided; and 3) the type of utilization being
made of the material.

Problems Associated with the International
Spread of School Libraries

     World-wide educational change began in the decade after the
launching of Sputnik. In addition to the curriculum as the instigator
of interest in school libraries, countries use numerous other voices
to express the need for school libraries. In some countries the
source of school library development's thrust is the library school,
which feels a responsibility to the entire profession. In others it
may be the public library that sees the varied needs of patrons.
Some countries develop under the leadership or influence of another,
perhaps a neighboring, country. Some national and international organizations, notably the Organization of American States, Franklin
Books, and the Carnegie Corporation, have assisted indirectly in
school library development. Other countries are stimulated by creative authors and illustrators; others by small producers of print and

nonprint materials who realize the importance of a school market.
Some countries send persons to see school libraries in other countries and ask consultants to come to them.   Seriously affecting the
growth of school libraries is the recurring problem of a weak legal
base, with resultant low funding and unqualified personnel.   No single reason will be found to be the cause of underdevelopment or the
impetus for development.   However, ignorance of school libraries is
the most discouraging aspect because it should be the most unlikely
cause now of school library underdevelopment.

     A lack of understanding exists within and without the profes-
sion about the potential of the school library to contribute to both
education and librarianship and to society as a whole.   The school
library's greatest potential lies in the educational process.   The
learner is moving away from the passive role characteristic of formal education as the inquiry method is used increasingly.   The function of the school library "has broadened, from being purely suppor-
tive, humanistic and recreational to a new position of centrality in
the curriculum pattern."[4]   As curriculum revision has occurred
world-wide, as there has been a tendency for new knowledge to push
other knowledge out as obsolete or to change the old but not necessarily assimilate it, and as subjects have become more interdisciplinary, the school library has increased in importance to students
and teachers who need quantities of materials.   The school library
has become the site of learning, and the techniques of its usage, a
learning tool desirable beyond the school years.   For the student,
the school library is physically the closest information resource beyond the teacher at the moment he is motivated to learn.   The integration of both the concept and the skill of library usage into all
learning activities is most easily accomplished, with a greater depth
and a closer relationship to the curriculum, by librarians and teachers working together in a school library.   Cooperation of all libraries serving youth must be continued in order to provide special materials, fight censorship, and serve special groups within the youth
population.

     School librarianship's contribution to the library profession is
partly quantitative, but also, it contributes as a cooperating unit.
The actual and potential number of school librarians should be recognized by the profession.   By definition school libraries have the
greatest growth potential of any type of library, simply because of
the large number of school buildings.   The information system being
provided by school libraries for the age groups defined should be
recognized as collections are surveyed for the total resources available in national and international information networks.

     The school library is the logical initiator for its patrons of a
learning sequence concerned with the concept of a total information
system.   Society as a whole is just beginning to grasp the importance and responsibilities of living in a Communication Age.   Many
persons feel that it is humanly impossible to make decisions without
relevant information and that the resources commonly available for
securing information are inadequate.   Others feel that resources go

unused because of lack of knowledge of their existence or lack of the skill to use them. The inaccurate movement of information has been called public relations, advertising, and news management.[5] It is the school's responsibility, and particularly that of the school library, to be the source of information and of instruction in the skills of information gathering, and also to provide a broader background for understanding communications in the world today.

The weak legal base of the school library is evidence of the lack of commitment by educational authorities to school library development, which cannot be attributed to a conflict of goals, at either the international or national level; and the national level, for the foreseeable future, is where the responsibility for formal education lies. Illich has stated that the purpose of an educational system is to learn and share, a way to present a viewpoint to a public.[6] Recently, persons attending a UNESCO conference agreed on the importance in education of the following: the individual personality, the improvement of society, the development of values, and the utilization of knowledge.[7] National education goals are usually stated as: to transmit knowledge and the country's culture and to foster citizen responsibility and loyalty. A few nations must give technological success as a goal if that is what is most needed by the nation for survival. The methods used by countries to implement their educational goals, such as the number of years of schooling required or the selection process--either elitist or democratic for advanced education--are pertinent to the development of school libraries. The interest of the school librarian in the literacy rate and the concept of life-long learning adds to the proof that education and the school library have mutual goals.

The commitment of education authorities is not strong in pressing for legislation to establish school libraries or adequate budgets to continue them. One of the reasons for this is the slowness of change. The school library may assist teachers to do a better job, but it requires the teacher to change. "A course based on the use of certain sources cannot be the same, once these sources become available to the pupils."[8]

> In the system envisaged, the teacher has to alter his role, reappraise his work, give up being a vessel of knowledge to help pupils find a method. Such a transition calls for radical alteration of the teaching process and, therefore, for a change in the 'mentality' of the teacher, who must be willing (and ready) for this new venture.[9]

The rate and durability of change in educational methodology depends on the professional relationships and the mutual knowledge shared by teachers and librarians. The role of the librarian as a source of change in a school, as a catalyst who brings materials to teachers and students for effective learning, is familiar to the school librarian who has had specialized training in that role and who is employed full-time on the basis of that educational preparation to perform that role. The role is often misunderstood or not appreciated by the teacher.

The role of the teacher and the librarian and the terms
teacher-librarian and librarian-teacher are relevant to the perception
of school libraries. As far as utilization of materials is concerned,
the fine teacher whose command of subject matter is balanced with
alertness to new teaching methods and materials can be just as effective as the librarian in the intellectual guidance of a student.
However, the teacher does not always fulfill this role. The term
"teacher-librarian" has meant a teacher who was a part-time, un-
trained "librarian." To avoid confusion, the term "librarian-teacher" has been coined recently to indicate a full-time school librarian,
specially trained, equal to a teacher, who is involved in teaching a
subject in the library. These are the extremes of a continuum.
Generally, the school librarian works at a point on the continuum
where the librarian is one of a team of teachers, is teaching library-
related skills, and is a resource person in a group of teachers planning learning experiences for students.

Different aspects of "size" have been influential in the emergence of school libraries. First, the larger a school, the more likely it is to have a library. Schools tend to become larger today.
The democratization of schools, as well as the comprehensive school
as one of the forms which democratization has taken, seem pervasive
in educational reforms. Democratization goes along with the trend
to urbanization, both of which have fostered higher expectation in living standards and availability of education, resulting in an increase
in the school population. School libraries usually develop first in
urban centers, as part of a large system's tendency to give leadership and support for new ideas. Urban centers also have mobile population groups, whose needs tend to be expressed more rapidly. The
management function increases in initiation and expansion periods and
will continue if the size of a school--for example, a secondary
school with one or two thousand students--requires a school librarian
to manage facilities, routines, and supporting staff efficiently and
regularly. However, while administration may seem to be a more
obvious justification for the full-time, fully educated librarian, three
other factors--the information, consultation, and design functions--
must receive consideration as well. [10] If the school library staff is
not adequate in number, the effectiveness of the school librarian's
role in curriculum planning and the selection of materials is lessened.
Selection has been found to be one of the most critical areas in
school library development, demanding high competency and diploma-
cy by the school librarian who works with several subject areas and
wishes to provide materials worthy of collecting. Teachers agree on
the goal but are not always willing to accept the responsibilities of
evaluation.

Elementary school library development has been impeded by
the "littleness" which is associated with children in general. Many
collections have had little time to grow, few production sources
from which to secure material, small budgets, and philosophies that
have stifled growth. Especially at the elementary level, it has been
said that materials are not needed since teaching the 3R's does not
require a library. The child needs the largest collection possible,
to take him as far as he wants in any interest. The librarian,

supposedly not needed all day for a small collection, is needed as much one hour as another in the school day if the work is important to learning and learning is occurring in the school.   Generally, the arguments against elementary school libraries are advanced as an excuse for insufficient financial support for materials and staff, since the outlay is enormous in terms of the ratio of elementary schools to secondary schools--usually ten to one.

Some countries face technical problems--no electricity for lights by which to read or to run a motor on a projector.   Print and nonprint materials are not produced in sufficient languages or with content relevant to the needs of each country.   The latter is a particularly severe problem in countries with underdeveloped publishing houses and no audio-visual producers.   If the local language is not one of the major languages of the world, the acquisition or translation of materials is not easily accomplished; the needs are often split into two areas by the age of the students, the younger ones studying in their own language and the older ones starting a foreign or officially-adopted language.   The cost of transportation is added to other costs.   The current inflation of prices places a strong sense of accountability on libraries and strongly influences the priority given to the initiation of new library programs which involve special materials.

The controversy over the dual preparation of school librarians has delayed the growth of school libraries.   The general pattern of adding specialized education concerning school libraries to the previous education of a person who has qualified for a teaching position continues.   The small amount of specialized education has been criticized.   It is the procedure for securing dual preparation that is a serious drawback.   The higher education structure in some countries cannot readily accommodate the person who wishes to secure both qualifications, which are more and more being agreed upon as needed for the school librarian.

From a global view the problems associated with the international spread of school libraries may be summarized as the assumption of tremendous sociological responsibility during a relatively short period of expansion.   Despite the many problems associated with the growth of school libraries in the world, the groundswell of interest is being used to attract support; for the school library movement is flourishing and the increasing awareness is assisting nations to develop their systems of school libraries.

Geographic Centers of School Library Growth

Describing each nation's reaction to school library development is not the purpose of the chapter.   In attempting to highlight the development geographically a machine search of the ERIC and LIBCON data bases and a hand search of Education Index and Library Literature were made, using seven relevant subject headings.   In the search, which covered one hundred and fifteen nations, excluding the

United States, only forty-six nations were found to have been cited
in the literature during the five-year period, 1970-1975.   Of the
forty-six, thirteen countries were cited with one article each, seven
with two articles each, and seven with three.   Thirteen other countries ranged in the four to fourteen level.   The number of citations
for six countries ran from fifteen to over fifty.   The countries
whose developments in school librarianship have been most highly
publicized are: Australia, Canada, Denmark, Union of Soviet Socialist Republics (USSR), United Kingdom (UK), and West Germany.

Australia. --The late 1960s can be seen as a turning point for
libraries in Australian schools; the first federal funding came in
1969.   School libraries were developed through the State Departments
of Education.   This led to variations from state to state.   As the
financing of school libraries was dependent on local initiative, with
some government grants and subsidies, the result was inequities
among schools within states as well as between states.

The publication in 1966 of School and Children's Libraries in
Australia and Standards and Objectives for School Libraries gave impetus to moves by professional groups to correct the inequities that
had emerged.   The Library Association of Australia used these two
publications as a basis for an extensive campaign for federal aid.
Other associations of teacher-librarians, parents, teachers and interested citizens were involved in this campaign.   The successful
outcome was the States Grants (Secondary Schools Libraries) Act
1968, which provided for federal grants for secondary school library
buildings in a three-year program, 1969-1971.   Following a federally
funded research project to evaluate the impact of the federal aid program, it was extended for a further three years, 1972-1974.

A Schools Commission was established as a statutory body by
the Schools Commission Act, 1973, and a wider program of funding
for all Australian schools for 1974 and 1975 was authorized by the
States Grants (Schools) Act, 1973.   The Libraries Program was expanded to include primary school libraries and to provide bookstock
and audio-visual resources.   Some funding was made available for
State Education Departments to conduct special teacher-librarian
courses of varying length; at least 80% of this funding was for the
training of teachers from government schools.   By the end of 1975
the number of teacher-librarians enrolled in such courses was 932.
By the end of 1975 approximately 1,030 secondary schools had new
facilities; thus more than half of all Australian secondary schools,
serving nearly 60% of the national school enrollment, had reached an
acceptable standard.   Primary school libraries were progressing and
a further research project into library services and library resource
usage had been initiated.   Current developments in Australian Schools
Commission thinking indicate that the special Libraries Program will
be integrated into a general Services and Development Program plus
some provision for recurrent expenditure and an Australian Cataloguing Service.

These Services of the State Departments of Education are

appointing advisory and consulting officers to work with teacher-librarians in schools which are now given general grants for their total programs and services. The need for dual qualification in teaching and librarianship for teacher-librarians has been recognized and courses are now being developed to provide it.

Librarians and teacher-librarians are working through their professional associations at the state and federal levels to improve the provision of school libraries. There is a school library association in each state, federated into the Australian School Library Association of Australia. A Joint Committee of the ASLA and the LAA was formed in 1973 to focus on common interests. A new thrust currently under discussion is the concept of total community library service, in which the school library is seen as part of a national network of library and information services.

Canada. --Although there were libraries in every Vancouver school as early as 1939, the upsurge in Canadian school library development did not occur until the 1960s. As education, and hence school libraries, is constitutionally the responsibility of the provinces, the treatment and advancement of school library service in the provinces can differ drastically. All provincial governments give capital grants toward the cost of building and equipping libraries in new schools when they are approved by the provincial Department of Education. In addition, a direct grant for materials is usually given--anywhere from $1.00 to $13.00 per pupil. Every province, except British Columbia, has a provincial school library supervisor who is mainly a consultant and advisor to those who require such services. District and regional school library services are developing in most of the provinces to consolidate services in smaller areas. In 1971 Margaret Scott wrote, "Few school libraries in Canada--not more than five per cent--meet Canadian School Library Association standards for personnel, materials and facilities necessary to develop good (not superior) services. Many come close to reaching minimum standards for collection, but not for facilities or personnel."[11] Unfortunately, the statement is just as true today. Canada has come a long way in the last decade but it still has a long way to go in school library development.

Denmark. --The 1920 Danish Public Libraries Act made no provision for library services to children. Only when the Act was amended in 1931 was it stipulated that every public library should serve children and adults alike. An additional state grant was given if cooperation between the public and school libraries was established within the district. The school libraries were those in the primary schools (for ages seven to fourteen). After 1931 the main school library activity was lending children's literature.

A 1963 study showed that Danish children as a whole were much less well supplied with books than were adults. Soon after the study, separate book stock standards were compiled for the two types of libraries. By 1969, the purpose of the school library was to aid the teaching given in the school and to give all of the school's pupils

access to useful and stimulating reading matter in such a way that
the requisite guidance in book use could be given. Cooperation on
budgeting and book selection was organized in local committees, the
members of which were from the two library types. Purchasing,
binding, cataloging, etc. were handled by the public library, with
the assistance of the two central national institutions, Bibliotekscentralen (Library Bureau) and Indbindingscentralen (Binding Center).
With the development of pedagogic theory and new instruction methods, school libraries reached a stage at which they could be charac-
terized as pedagogic tools; they built up large stationary collections
which included audio-visual materials. The 1974 Act no longer required school libraries to cooperate with public libraries. School
libraries will come under the Primary Schools Act. "This should
be seen as a natural consequence of development, rather than a
break with tradition. Future co-operation is to be on a voluntary
basis, and should be shaped according to local conditions rather than
to a national pattern."[12]

        Union of Soviet Socialistic Republics. --The development of
school libraries in the USSR is linked to the philosophy of Lenin,
who tried to give priority to libraries. The libraries in existence
at that time, often attached to parish schools, were unsuited to the
needs of the new society--the abolition of illiteracy and the acquisition of knowledge useful for improving the country. A network of
mass (public) libraries has been developed which provides a library
within no more than a thirty-minute walk from the reader's place of
residence. In 1975, the Standard Position on the School Library was
affirmed by the Ministry of Education, USSR. In this important
document, which was accepted for the first time, the significance of
the library as a structural subdivision of the school, participating on
a level with the whole pedagogical collective in the Communist up-
bringing of pupils and promoting the raising of teacher qualifications,
is emphasized.[13] School librarians work with teachers and students
in literature classes, for example, in setting up the time for auto-
graphing the best children's book by all readers before sending it to
the author, the days with visiting laureate poets, and the performance
days for amateur theatricals based on children's favorite stories.[14]
A planned library network is consistent with the Communist ideology
of "engineering society," and the educational system utilizes all youth
agencies and libraries to assist in education. A child may work with
the librarian as an "agitator-propagandist" to interest other children,
usually two or three, in books and reading.[15] The USSR educational
model is admired since the seventy-three per cent illiteracy rate in
1917 has now been virtually wiped out. In the future the effect of a
newly and better educated people may change the goals and the type
of methodology in the educational system, which has operated on an
emergency basis up to the present time.

        United Kingdom. --The greatest change in the UK has probably
occurred since 1970, for 1970 could be called the year of the Resource Centre. Innovation in teaching methods, and the need for the
right support and materials, together with information on what was
happening in the resource centres in the United States, have made

people realize the desirability of bringing together in one place all
the support materials in the school. Many conferences were held
on this issue, books on the subject started to appear, and some
authorities started school library resource centres built specifically
as such. The Library Association produced its standards for school
library resource centres--recommendatory, but certainly causing
some Local Education Authorities to sit up and take notice. One
firm recommendation was for every secondary school of over eight
hundred pupils to employ a Chartered librarian. Out of the three
thousand secondary schools, four hundred currently comply with this
recommendation, and a few of these librarians are dual-trained, as
both teacher and professional librarian. It was the change in teaching methods which started to change the loan of supplementary reading materials from public libraries into a vital resource support
service. "It is the depth of resource provision needed and the quantity of items which I think makes it increasingly vital that the support services for education should remain closely integrated with
what is the largest resource centre in any authority in Britain, i.e.,
the public library."16 The Bullock Report on the Use of Literacy
was published and is perhaps one of the most useful supporting
statements for the creative role of librarians to have been produced
in England.

      West Germany.--The importance of a fully-fledged school li-
brary service in West Germany is just beginning to be urged, albeit
on a modest scale. 17 This comment was made ten years ago, and
significant progress in actually establishing school libraries has been
exceedingly slow. Several conferences on school library development
and demonstration school libraries have been publicized. In 1972, a
description of the media center, which included sufficient information
to be considered as the standard for the development of German
school libraries, was published. 18 A few of the schools are combining their separate collections of teachers' materials, textbooks,
and supplementary books for students in one place and seeking a librarian rather than a teacher to manage the library. There is some
evidence that less formal teaching methods are being used. At the
secondary level the German student needs and wants books to assist
in study. Many Germans, however, feel that the German school
pupil (elementary) does not utilize those years for very much study
so much as for socialization. Public library service has not been
extended into the rural areas to the degree desired, but in the large
cities it has been remarkably improved since World War II and includes services to children and young adults. In a few large cities,
notably Bremen, school-public library combinations exist.

      From this overview, which includes brief references to the
relationship of political, economic, and social characteristics of nations to school library growth in these specific countries, two aspects
seem to emerge. The number of public library-school library combinations is decreasing. The number of school libraries is slowly increasing and the remaining combinations are being altered, primarily
as a result of educational reform. Secondly, the learning activities

now taking place in school libraries are similar enough to suggest
that cross-national transfer of knowledge of technique is occurring.
These aspects of development give strong support for school librarianship since they are happening in countries with experience in library development.

The extent and type of American influence exerted on world
school library development can be summarized by singling out: 1)
the large amount of widely distributed material about school libraries,
primarily to assist the school librarian in improving day-to-day operation, and more recently, research-oriented; 2) a great number of
school library installations accompanying groups of mobile Americans
around the world, which have evidently aided knowledge transfer about
school library service programs; and 3) the existence of a large
American pool of human resources and demonstration libraries which
has fostered a flow of observers and consultants and served as a continual means of promoting school library development.   One of the
first projects of the American Association of School Librarians' International Relations Committee was the translation of a description,
"The School Library," into French, Spanish, and German.   The
committee also compiled a list of exemplary American and Canadian school library-media programs, which is updated frequently as
a service to international visitors.   These countries are the influential centers of school library development and the growth centers
which are apt to continue to be observed.

Significant Recent Literature

Few attempts have been made to approach the field of school
librarianship from an international viewpoint and the influence of this
material is, therefore, limited by its scarcity.   Anne Pellowski, in
The World of Children's Literature, attempted to include in her bibliography all the monographs, series, and multivolume works relating to public and school library work with children and books, in a
nation-by-nation approach for eighty-six nations and one region.   A
continental arrangement was used by Jean Lowrie in School Libraries:
International Developments, which covered nineteen countries.   A regional study, Library Development in Eight Asian Countries, by
David Kaser, reported on all types of libraries.   School libraries
were singled out in the sections devoted to each country which facilitated comparison.   However, the portions on school libraries are
short, usually only a page or two.   All of these are pre-1970 works.

Carolyn Whitenack's chapter, "School Libraries and Librarianship," in Comparative and International Librarianship, edited by
Miles M. Jackson, Jr., was devoted to the United States, while the
work as a whole presented different types of libraries in different
countries of the world.   This chapter was written soon after publication of the 1969 Standards and is a good discussion of the impact expected from them.   In the first volume of Advances in Librarianship,
Chase Dane, under the title, "The Changing School Library: an Instructional Media Center," attempted to put school library development in perspective on the basis of advances made in the USA.

Comparative studies are less available. The first French
doctoral thesis on public and school libraries, La Bibliothèque Institution Educative: Recherche et Developpement by Jean Hassenforder,
in Part I compares the histories of British and American school and
public libraries with the French experience. Another comparative
study is The Education Librarianship in Some European Countries
and in the Transvaal, by P. G. J. Overduin. The European countries are: Denmark, Sweden, Norway, Great Britain, and The Netherlands. The work is significant for its close adherence to the purpose and method of comparative studies. A portion of the book,
Standards for Library Services, by F. N. Withers, is devoted to a
brief comparison of the standards of school libraries in Australia,
Canada, West Germany, Hungary, Singapore, United Kingdom, and
United States. He attempted to find to what extent the standards
were reflecting the newer philosophy of the multi-media approach,
as well as how much variation existed in quantitative recommendations.

One type of literature is strikingly missing. One-volume historical, descriptive, and statistical accounts for each country, such
as A Brief History of School Library Service, 1952-1971 (Jamaica),
seem to be unavailable. A few of the journal articles, such as "The
School Library as an Instrument of Education in Nigeria," are almost of sufficient length to fulfill this need and are so well done as
to stand as substantial contributions to library literature. Comparative study would be more likely to flourish if such a body of literature were available to assist in the selection of nations for comparison. The literature in the English language about school libraries
in a number of countries is increasing, which allows some comparison. The journal article, for the most part descriptive in treatment,
remains the most plentiful type of literature available about school
libraries. The uneven coverage of nations by journals is attributed
to limited circulation of the material about school libraries outside
the country of origin and to inadequate indexing. The influence of
the literature would be greater if there were wider coverage of nations and more attempts at international studies of a single aspect of
school library science, such as the method of organization of resources for different age groups.

Contributions of International Organizations

The interest of international organizations in school library
development has increased in the last ten years and is assisting in
the natural growth of school libraries through leadership training and
planning conferences, rather than through direct aid for materials
and personnel, which are national responsibilities. Among the agencies affiliated to UNESCO are: International Bureau of Education
(BIE), the World Confederation of Organizations of the Teaching Profession, the International Institute for Educational Planning, the International Association of School Librarians (IASL), the International
Federation of Library Associations (IFLA), the International Federation for Documentation (FID), the International Council on Archives

(ICA), and the International Board on Books for Young People (IBBY).
Through contracts, memberships, committees, and liaison, these
groups are affiliated with each other.

The visibility of school librarians is one of the purposes of
the IASL. Its Newsletter, almost four years old, and its Directory
contribute to the world flow of information about school libraries.
The Section for School Libraries was organized in 1973 to provide
visibility for school libraries through IFLA, which represents
the whole of librarianship, and to survey what needs to be done to
assist in school library development. Both the FID and ICA have
committees concerned with the education of users. IBBY has national commissions in UN member-countries, and these boards can initiate and cooperate in projects concerning school libraries.

It is felt that "Unesco should take steps to get the general
rationale and purpose of media centers brought forward more sharp-
ly...."[19] In a recent UNESCO report devoted to creating and developing NATIS (National Information System) five of the sixteen objectives clearly support school libraries:

> Objective 2--Stimulation of user awareness calls attention
> to the use of libraries being a part of instruction offered
> from the primary school level onwards, so seeking infor-
> mation becomes a normal part of daily life.

> Objective 3--Promotion of the reading habit refers to the
> school library as having a great impact on a child's intel-
> lectual and cultural development. It is at that stage that
> the individual most easily learns to use books and libraries
> and acquires 'functional literacy,' thus ensuring that when
> he leaves school he does not relapse into illiteracy.

> Objective 5--Analysis of existing information resources
> states the need for higher priority for budgetary provisions
> for school and public libraries since their services are now
> recognized as needed in national information plans.

> Objective 10--Establishing a legislative framework for
> NATIS draws attention to the fact that individual elements
> of the information infrastructure which are not based on
> secure legal foundations may become vulnerable targets for
> budget reductions and that the national plan should provide
> for drafting and adopting any additional legislation required
> to reinforce the philosophical basis of the system.

> Objective 11--Financing NATIS has as a target the inclusion
> of the cost of all the elements of NATIS in the provisions
> for national development plans. In many countries eradi-
> cating illiteracy and improving education are main govern-
> ment targets, but the importance of school and public li-
> braries as instruments in these fields are not yet fully
> recognized, since the cost-benefits derived from these

128   Comparative/International

services are not as obvious as in such fields as industrial
information. When making budgetary provisions for the
national information plan, higher priority should be accorded to the development of these services. [20]

Effective International Patterns of Cooperation

        School library development is approaching a level, quantita-
tively and philosophically, at which similar problems are being noted
and planning as a step in development has a reasonable expectation
of success. International cooperation has not been tried, to any extent, to move school library development to another plateau or to
solve problems. An international survey of the education of users
is being undertaken, for example. The survey is the initial step in
an effort to develop international materials concerned with information awareness and information usage in a modern world. However,
the world education reforms are a beneficial backdrop for more international planning in the field of school librarianship.

        As national cooperation expands in the areas of copyright,
translation, and exchange of information, more representation from
the school library sector is needed on committees where laws,
agreements, and guidelines are being written. This demands an international representation, for the needs of school libraries in these
three areas are different in various nations. The international outlook, which reveals a multi-faceted potential for support for school
libraries, is important as encouragement to nations where the human
resources for promotion of school libraries are overtaxed. Scholarships, internships, and consultancies can also be sponsored at an
international rather than a binational level.

        Educational systems tend to resemble each other from one
country to another; each succeeding generation is a little more homo-
genous. Educational systems at the same time respond to local
needs. Where school libraries exist, the goal is not only to integrate the school library program into the school's educational program but to develop it into a tool worthy of integration, which meets
qualitative and quantitative standards. The latter idea seems to be
understood internationally; the former idea still awaits acceptance.
Where school libraries do not exist, the initiation of essential legislation is a responsibility of national planning, and this is now being
encouraged by international agencies. Development in all countries
can come about as attitudes are changed about school libraries; at
the same time, a school library service itself can contribute to
changing yet more attitudes. Judged critically, school librarianship
has made significant national progress and is entering a period where
there are already indications of significant international progress.

NOTES

1. Margaret Burton and Marion E. Vosburgh. A Bibliography of
        Librarianship. New York: Burt Franklin, 1970, pp. 66-68.

2. American Association of School Librarians. Standards for School Library Programs. Chicago: American Library Association, 1960, p. 11.
3. American Association of School Librarians and Association for Educational Communications and Technology. Media Programs, District and School. Chicago: American Library Association, 1975, p. 111.
4. Norman W. Beswick. "The Transformation of Secondary School Libraries into Multimedia Centres in the United Kingdom." Geneva: International Bureau of Education, UNESCO, 1974, p. 1.
5. Robert Theobald. "Theobald: Educating People for the Communications Era," in: Foundations of Futurology in Education, ed. Richard W. Hostrop. Homewood, Ill.: ETC Publications, 1973, p. 17.
6. Ivan Illich. "The De-schooling of Society," in: Alternatives in Education, ed. Bruce Rusk. Toronto: General Publishing Company Limited, 1971, p. 106.
7. William Van Til. "One Way of Looking at It," Phi Delta Kappan LVII (September 1975), p. 52.
8. Lucia Scherrer. "The Conversion of Secondary School Libraries into Multimedia Centres: an Experience in the Canton of Geneva." Geneva: International Bureau of Education, UNESCO, 1974, p. 3.
9. Jean-Pierre Delannoy. "A Multimedia Centre: the Individualized Documentation Centre of Audio-visual Secondary School at Marly-le-Roi." Geneva: International Bureau of Education, UNESCO, 1974, p. 18.
10. American Association of School Librarians and Association for Educational Communications and Technology, op. cit., p. 6.
11. Margaret Scott. "School Libraries in Canada," in: School Libraries: International Developments, ed. Jean E. Lowrie. Metuchen, N.J.: Scarecrow Press, 1972, p. 185.
12. Aase Bredsdorff. "Library Services for Children," Scandinavian Public Library Quarterly VII (1974), p. 52. See also Arne Holst, Keld Irgens, and Jorgen Tølløse, eds. School Libraries in Denmark. Copenhagen: Danish Association of School Libraries, Kirk Hyllinge.
13. M. I. Kondakov. "On a Level with Pedagogues...," Bibliotekar, No. 9 (1975), p. 2. (In Russian)
14. E. Murashova. "In the School Library," Bibliotekar, No. 3. (1971), p. 35-36. (In Russian)
15. L. Pozhivilko. "Not Guests but Hosts," Bibliotekar, No. 9 (1971), p. 19. (In Russian)
16. Jennifer Shephard. "The British Situation." Oslo, IFLA Pre-conference Seminar Lecture, 1975, p. 6.
17. P. G. J. Overduin. The Education Librarianship in Some European Countries and the Transvaal. Pretoria, S.A.: Mousaion, 1966, p. 4.
18. F. N. Withers. Standards for Library Service: an International Survey. Paris: UNESCO Press, 1974, p. 365.
19. Mary Virginia Gaver. "Multimedia Centers in Developing Countries," School Media Quarterly III (Fall 1974), p. 28.
20. Final Report, Intergovernmental Conference on the Planning of

National Documentation, Library and Archives Infrastructures, 23-27 September, 1974. Paris: UNESCO, 1975, pp. 25-30.

SELECTED BIBLIOGRAPHY

Aguolu, C. C. "The School Library as an Instrument of Education in Nigeria," International Library Review VII (January 1975), pp. 39-58.

American Association of School Librarians. Certification Model for Professional School Media Personnel. Chicago: American Library Association, 1976.

_____. Standards for School Library Programs. Chicago: American Library Association, 1960.

American Association of School Librarians and Association for Educational Communications and Technology. Media Programs, District and School. Chicago: American Library Association, 1975.

American Library Association and National Education Association. Standards for School Media Programs. Chicago: American Library Association, 1969.

Australia. Schools Commission, Primary Schools' Libraries Committee. Guidelines for Library Services in Primary Schools. Canberra, 1974.

Beswick, Norman W. "The Transformation of Secondary School Libraries Into Multimedia Centres in the United Kingdom." Geneva: International Bureau of Education, Unesco, 16 April 1974. (Mimeographed.)

Bredsdorff, Aase. "Library Services for Children," Scandinavian Public Library Quarterly VII (1974), pp. 48-52.

A Brief History of School Library Service, 1952-1971. Kingston: Jamaica Library Service, 1972.

Burton, Margaret and Vosburgh, Marion E. A Bibliography of Librarianship. New York: Burt Franklin, 1970.

Dane, Chase. "The Changing School Library: An Instructional Media Center," in: Advances in Librarianship, ed. Melvin J. Voigt. New York: Academic Press, 1970, pp. 133-157.

Delannoy, Jean-Pierre. "A Multimedia Center: the Individualized Documentation Centre of Audio-visual Secondary School at Marly-le-Roi." Geneva: International Bureau of Education, Unesco, 16 April 1974. (Mimeographed.)

Fenwick, Sara I. School and Children's Libraries in Australia. Melbourne: Cheshire, for the Library Association of Australia, 1966.

Final Report, Intergovernmental Conference on the Planning of National Documentation, Library and Archives Infrastructures, 23-27 September 1974. Paris: Unesco, 1975.

Gaver, Mary Virginia. "Multimedia Centers in Developing Countries," School Media Quarterly III (Fall 1974), pp. 27-29.

Great Britain. Secretary of State for Education and Science, Committee of Inquiry. Alan Bullock, Chairman. A Language for Life. London: Her Majesty's Stationery Office, 1975.

Hassenforder, Jean. La Bibliothèque Institution Educative: Re-
    cherche et Developpement (The library as an educative insti-
    tution: research and development). Paris: Lecture et Bib-
    liothèques, 1972.
Illich, Ivan. "The De-schooling of Society," in: Alternatives in
    Education, ed. Bruce Rusk. Toronto: General Publishing
    Company Limited, 1971, pp. 103-126.
Jackson, Miles M. Jr. , ed. Comparative and International Librari-
    anship. Westport, Ct. : Greenwood Press, 1970.
Kaser, David. Library Development in Eight Asian Countries.
    Metuchen, N. J. : Scarecrow Press, 1968.
Kondakov, M. I. "On a Level with Pedagogues," Bibliotekar, No.
    9 (1975), pp. 2-3. (In Russian)
The Library Association. School Library Resource Centres, Recom-
    mended Standards for Policy and Provision, Incorporating a
    Supplement on Non-book Materials. London, 1973.
Library Association of Australia. Children's Libraries Section,
    Standards and Objectives for School Libraries. Melbourne:
    Cheshire, for the Library Association of Australia, 1966.
Lowrie, Jean E. , ed. School Libraries: International Developments.
    Metuchen, N. J. : Scarecrow Press, 1972.
Murashova, E. "In the School Library," Bibliotekar, No. 3 (1971),
    pp. 35-37.
Overduin, P. G. J. The Education Librarianship in Some European
    Countries and in the Transvaal. Pretoria, S. A. : Mousaion,
    1966.
Pellowski, Anne. The World of Children's Literature. New York:
    R. R. Bowker Company, 1968.
Pozhivilko, L. "Not Guests but Hosts," Bibliotekar, No. 9 (1971),
    pp. 18-20. (In Russian)
Primary Schools' Libraries Committee of the Schools Commission.
    Guidelines for Library Services in Primary Schools. Woden,
    1974.
Riddell, Weihs. Non-Book Materials: the Organization of Integrated
    Collections. Ottawa: Canadian Library Association, 1973.
Scherrer, Lucia. "The Conversion of Secondary School Libraries
    into Multimedia Centres: an Experience in the Canton of
    Geneva. " Geneva: International Bureau of Education, Unesco,
    16 April 1974. (Mimeographed.)
Scott, Margaret B. "School Libraries in Canada," in: School Li-
    braries: International Developments, ed. Jean E. Lowrie.
    Metuchen, N. J. : Scarecrow Press, 1972, pp. 171-205.
Shephard, Jennifer. "The British Situation. " Oslo, IFLA/Unesco
    Pre-conference Seminar Lecture, 4-9 August 1975. (Mimeo-
    graphed.)
Statens Bibliotekskole, Oslo. School Library Services as a Compo-
    nent in National Library Systems. Papers of the IFLA/
    UNESCO Pre-Session Seminar, August 4-9, 1975. (In prepa-
    ration.)
Theobald, Robert. "Theobald: Educating People for the Communica-
    tions Era," in: Foundations of Futurology in Education, ed.
    Richard W. Hostrop. Homewood, Ill. : ETC Publications,
    1973, pp. 11-21.

Van Til, William. "One Way of Looking at It," Phi Delta Kappan
    LVII (September 1975), p. 52.
Whitenack, Carolyn. "School Libraries and Librarianship," in:
    Comparative and International Librarianship, ed. Miles M.
    Jackson, Jr. Westport, Ct.: Greenwood Press, 1970, pp.
    63-82.
Withers, F. N. Standards for Library Service: an International
    Survey. Paris: Unesco Press, 1974.

HEALTH LIBRARY SCIENCE

Joan Campbell

Health library science and health science libraries are emerging terms that are probably more generally used on the North American continent than elsewhere. Medical libraries are one component of this larger library science area, and many of them still use the narrower term, though their collections, services and users are diverse. With the concerted effort during the last two decades to connect and increase the effectiveness of resources and services through networks, the term health science libraries appears to be used increasingly. This use reflects the tendency towards team care and the greater utilization of para-professionals in health maintenance and patient care. In this paper, I refer to activities and programs under the broad term of health library science, which includes the wide range of library and information efforts facilitating health education, research and clinical practice.

Comparative Health Library Science

I have analyzed comparative and international health library science developments based on the guidelines offered by Danton and Harvey.[1,2] Comparative library science implies comparison of aspects of librarianship between two or more cultures or national entities, to identify similarities and differences and to arrive at principles or laws. This method of investigation requires the availability of data which can indeed be compared, information concerning the socio-political development and support of such activities and a firm grasp of the many variables affecting the situations. Such studies are hampered by the inconsistency or lack of standards of reporting which exist within geographical entities and the enormous disparities which exist between nations, regions and cultural groups. In health library science, as in the broader library science area, such studies cannot be undertaken satisfactorily without the existence of study programs which provide investigators with the diverse skills and methodology necessary to explore, select, evaluate and compare policies, procedures or operational systems.

Education for health science librarians as a sub-specialty of library science is a recent and not universally available opportunity. The content and nature of health science library educational programs has emphasized medical bibliography and more recently the application of electronic technology to the control and dissemination of scientific information. The rapid advances in the life sciences in the post-World War II period, with the accompanying increase in publication and sources of information, has required a growing knowledge and skillful use of the new devices of control and dissemination. Very immediate problems have captured the energy and ingenuity of many of the field's investigators. Comparative studies have not been viewed with the same degree of urgency, nor have many individuals had the extensive preparation and resources required for productive and long-term effort.

Many descriptive and some analytical reports of health library systems or activities have been produced by librarians traveling or acting as consultants abroad. They have not attempted substantial comparison but have nevertheless provided much needed awareness of the activity level existing elsewhere. Western travelers to certain other areas have described the library's access difficulties by students, the problems of obtaining overseas publications and the primary custodial activity of librarians. Exceptions have been noted, but in many centers books and libraries are scarce commodities to be savored by established scholars and not to be exposed or placed in a position of risk. Brodman and Izant allude to the complexity of the problems generally existing in developing countries.[3,4] Comparison is implied between health science libraries in developed and developing countries, but it was not the primary purpose of either author to analyze similarities and differences in depth.

International Health Library Science

International health library science has engaged individuals, organizations and government agencies, and support has been available from a number of sources. By international health library science, I am referring to the wide range of relationships, across national borders and within other countries, involving various methods of cooperation, assistance and exchange. As in all international programs, the concrete results of these efforts are difficult to measure and slow to materialize. The objective of international health library science is the more effective sharing of the information and dissemination techniques necessary for the productive response of all health professionals to existing problems. This implies a knowledge of conditions beyond one's own nation, and many individuals and organizations have contributed insights which have been the building blocks for planning. Good will and good intentions have been enhanced by constructive and persistent efforts to extend resources and services, to provide educational opportunities and to develop new technology for their utilization.

International health library science activity has been stimulated by major libraries, library associations, international organizations, and by the individuals in these agencies who have worked to reduce the barriers to the free flow of information. I will discuss significant contributions in the post-World War II period. Though selective, they represent national, regional, and international projects which have attained a measure of success. Major events and programs with long-range goals require a major investment of professional and economic collaboration. For international health library science, the immediate post-World War II period was one of rehabilitation and restoration. Individuals, libraries and organizations expanded exchange and assistance efforts to institutions where resources and services had been destroyed or greatly curtailed.

International Congresses

One of the more far-reaching events of the fifties was the first International Congress on Medical Librarianship, London, July 1953. [5] We will always be indebted to that rare combination of scholar activist in the British library world who found the resources to produce the event. I am referring to such individuals as W. J. Bishop, William R. Lefanu, C. C. Barnard, Hilda Clark, F. L. N. Poynter and the institutions which they represented. Three hundred librarians from 37 countries attended. Discussion subjects covered many issues: education and certification for medical librarians; theories of classification and indexing; history of medicine; and international medical library cooperation. Exhibitions and tours of London's medical libraries allowed delegates another opportunity to share experiences and ideas with colleagues. The Congress was catalytic and produced a structure for future planning.

A bridging committee appointed after the first Congress set about planning the second Congress held in Washington, D. C. , June 1963. The Congress was held simultaneously with the Medical Library Association annual meeting and Dr. Frank B. Rogers, Director of the National Library of Medicine and MLA President, was General Chairman. Approximately 900 individuals from 58 countries attended the Congress. Papers analyzed health science library education in various countries, new aspects of documentation and information dissemination and specific areas of progress or innovation. [6] MEDLARS (Medical Literature Analysis and Retrieval System), the automated indexing of biomedical serials by the National Library of Medicine, was a new term and concept there.

A third International Congress was held in Amsterdam, May 1969, with Scott Adams, United States, and Folke Ström, Sweden, as Honorary Presidents. [7] Collaborating organizations included the Royal Netherlands Academy of Sciences, the Netherlands' Union of Librarians and the Excerpta Medica Foundation. Earlier topics of education, classification and bibliographic control were on the program, but health science library computer applications became a more persistent theme. Networks and national and regional planning had assumed an urgency and a promise which appears to be dominating the seventies. At this writing, a fourth International Congress is a possibility for Yugoslavia in 1979.

The Medical Library Association

Among library associations that have provided strong support for international activities, possibly the foremost is the Medical

Library Association. Founded in Philadelphia in 1898, its membership has always been international, and in 1948, during the Presi-
dency of Mrs. Eileen Roach Cunningham, a Committee of International and National Cooperation (CINC) was established. A chronology
of the Association's international activities was compiled by M.
Doreen E. Fraser. [8] From 1948 to 1963, the Association's CINC
administered an International Fellowship program with funds totalling
$94,000 provided by the Rockefeller Foundation. Forty-three Fel-
lows from twenty-nine countries spent from six months to one year
in the United States on work-study-travel projects. Fellowship recipients were screened in terms of their ability to return to their
country of origin and participate actively in health library science.
Fellows had to obtain funds for travel to the USA, and many of them
were able to extend their opportunities for study and observation by
procuring additional funds from other agencies. A position to return
to in one's own country was another Fellowship stipulation. While
many Fellows have assumed leadership positions on their return, no
comprehensive project follow-up has been carried out. The present
MLA International Cooperation Committee is planning one, however.

     Mrs. Eileen Cunningham represented MLA on many interna-
tional agencies. [9] Her constructive support has continued through the
bequest in her will of a gift of $33,000 to the Association to provide
fellowships for overseas librarians. From 1970 to 1975, six awards
were made and two individuals are in the United States now on combined work-study programs.

     In 1974 the MLA International Cooperation Committee re-
ceived Board approval for the affiliation of other national or regional health science library groups with MLA. [10] The Committee sup-
ports a Library to Library project and has matched more than forty
pairs of libraries representing twenty-eight countries. [11] The libraries are encouraged to cooperate in reference referral, distribution of basic lists and directories, and translation services.

     The Medical Library Association Exchange program has been
a long-term cooperative activity. Following World War II, the Exchange collaborated with UNESCO to distribute duplicate material to
libraries in war-devastated areas. The Exchange continues as a
benefit of Association institutional membership. In 1975 there were
ninety overseas and fifty-five Canadian institutional members. The
delay in Exchange list receipt overseas has been somewhat mitigated
by an arrangement to send the lists airmail to one member institution in a country which can copy and distribute it rapidly to other
member libraries. The volume of material distributed in 1973 by
Exchange in the USA and overseas included 309,280 unbound journals,
20,002 bound journals and 13,641 books. [12]

     The Bulletin of the MLA actively solicits overseas papers
through its International Editor. From 1953 to 1970 a "Notes from
London" column was included in the Bulletin. In 1971, M. Doreen
E. Fraser expanded overseas news coverage by identifying international contributors. A monthly round-up of overseas health science
library activities appears in the MLA News.

The Medical Library Association has been an IFLA member since 1934. Few MLA members have been able to attend IFLA meetings, and without more active membership involvement it is difficult to stimulate interest in continued support. Let us hope that MLA and IFLA can work towards a more satisfactory liaison.

Great Britain

In Great Britain the Medical Section of the Library Association was organized in 1947 on the initiative of W. J. Bishop and C. C. Barnard. A Bulletin is published quarterly, an annual conference is held, and a duplicate exchange program is coordinated by the Wellcome Institute Library. [13] British health science librarians have given much assistance to libraries in other countries. The Section has produced a Directory of Medical Libraries in the British Isles which was issued in a fourth edition in 1976. It lists 452 libraries and provides a model for other countries to follow, both in format and in the amount of information provided. The British Council Medical Library provides book lists, publications, lecture-recordings and bibliographies to libraries in other countries. [14] The concentration of distinguished medical libraries in London has always attracted visiting colleagues.

The 1974 reorganization of the National Health Service, which established 14 Regional Health Authorities, should strengthen and extend hospital library resources outside the major metropolitan areas.[15] A network of regional hospital libraries will encourage more sharing more equably and distribute borrowing regionally. British hospital libraries have emphasized patient service and bibliotherapy. The hospital librarian is a member of a therapeutic team and has been referred to by one British physician as a "colleague in the art of healing."[16]

The Hospital Libraries and Handicapped Readers Group of the Library Association was organized in 1962, and in 1965 the Library Association issued Hospital Libraries: Recommended Standards for Libraries in Hospitals. A Newsletter has emerged into a quarterly, the Book Trolley, and contains a wide variety of articles on service to hospital patients, the handicapped, the elderly and the housebound.

Members of the Library Association Hospital Libraries and Handicapped Readers Group participate in the IFLA Libraries in Hospitals Sub-section. The sub-section publishes a News Bulletin which is an international clearinghouse for hospital library activities. In 1975, correspondents were identified in twenty-three countries. The sub-section is currently preparing an "International Bibliography of Hospital Librarianship," to be edited by Eileen E. Cumming of the Scottish Health Service Centre Library. [17]

Scottish health science librarians started meeting informally in 1970, and in January 1975 the Association of Scottish Health Sciences Librarians was organized, with Antonia J. Bunch as Chairperson. Members are from medical, nursing, patient and health

administration libraries.   Meetings are held twice a year and provide a forum for issues and problems of concern to all librarians in
the Scottish health service.   A large multi-disciplinary conference
sponsored by the Scottish Library Association is planned for May
1976, to be entitled "Libraries for Health. "   A recent publication by
Antonia J. Bunch traces the history and development of health science libraries in Scotland. [18]

Japan

        The Japan Medical Library Association is an organization of
institutional members tracing its origin to 1927. [19]   It has a central
secretariat in the medical library of Tokyo University.   In 1968, it
included fifty-one regular, thirteen associate and a small number of
supporting members.   To qualify as a regular member, a library
must have 15,000 volumes, and 80 per cent of the total must be
medical literature.   The organization has stressed cooperation, training for medical librarians and publishing.   By limiting membership
to larger libraries, the Association has attempted to improve standards of service.   A Union list of serials in Western languages held
in member libraries was published in 1961, and a list of Japanese
serials was published in 1963.   A MEDLARS center providing automated access to the data base of 2,244 biomedical serials was established at the Japan Information Center of Science and Technology
in 1972. [20]   This was negotiated as a bilateral quid pro quo arrangement with the National Library of Medicine, U.S.A.

Canada

        The impetus for strengthening Canadian health science library
information resources and services began with the Simon report,
1964. [21]   This report pointed out existing deficiencies in resources
and made recommendations for national planning.   In 1974 a Canadian overview of information services and sources edited by Phyllis J.
Russell was published. [22]   The guide provides information about library and other health science professional organizations participating in a Canadian network.   It describes the establishment in 1970
and the services of the Health Resources Centre at the National Science Library, Ottawa.   The Centre subscribes to all Index Medicus
titles not held by Canadian medical libraries.   The NSL is a MED-
LARS center and MEDLINE terminals are now available in nine Canadian university health science libraries.   The National Science Library offers current awareness service through tapes of nine data
bases.   CAN-OLE (Canadian-on-line enquiry) is available at several
locations throughout the country and provides on-line access to Biological Abstracts Previews, Chemical Abstracts Coordinates, COM-
PENDEX and INSPEC.

        A health sciences division of the Canadian Association of Spe-
cial Libraries and Information Services (CASLIS) was organized in
1970.   An annual meeting and workshop is held during the Canadian

Library Association Conference and a publication, Agora, is distributed quarterly.   There is an Associate Committee on Medical School
Libraries of the Association of Canadian Medical Colleges (ACMC).
The Committee meets annually with ACMC and includes the administrative librarian of each medical school and representatives of the
Health Resources Centre of the National Science Library.   The Committee has made recommendations for the number of serials and
serials' services to be included in medical school libraries.

U. S. S. R.

In 1956 a Department of Scientific Medical Information was
set up under the Academy of Medical Sciences of the U. S. S. R.   This
agency, in an effort to control and disseminate medical information,
established a medical abstracting service--Meditsinskii Referativnyi
Zhurnal. [23]   In 1962, the Department of Scientific Medical Information evolved into the All-Union Scientific Research Institute of Medical and Medico-Technical Information under the Ministry of Health
of the U. S. S. R. (VNIIMI).   Under the aegis of VNIIMI, Soviet medical bibliographical coverage has become more comprehensive, the
output of MRZ has expanded and there has been greater coordination
of information activities among all biomedical institutions.   To
strengthen and assist health science libraries in all of the Republics,
the State Central Scientific Medical Library of the Ministry of Health
has developed and encouraged other health science libraries to publish and distribute useful manuals and guides valuable to librarians.
Continuing education of medical librarians has been extended to the
Republics by training instructors in Moscow who are available to
conduct educational programs in other regions.   Technical assistance
is provided to enable libraries to introduce innovative information
services. [24]   Improved biomedical library management and coordination is a continuing concern.

The National Library of Medicine

The National Library of Medicine, U. S. A. , is unique among
national health science libraries in the scope of its activities domestically and internationally.   It has long been a major biomedical information resource but has always coupled this responsibility with
indexing capability and the publication and widespread distribution of
its efforts.   International exchange has had a long history, having
been initiated in 1881 during the administration of John Shaw Billings
when the library functioned as the Surgeon-General's Library.   By
1974, the library had 895 exchange partners in 85 countries throughout the world.   Its capability for more extensive activities was man-
dated by the Medical Library Assistance Act of October 1965.   Programs resulting from this legislation have been well documented. [25]
They have resulted in the establishment of 11 regional medical libraries in the United States and the emergence of a decentralized
biomedical information network.   Prior to this legislation, the NLM
had developed MEDLARS, the computerization of its indexing function,

which became operational in 1964. [26] This, too, has been decentralized and its capability expanded; in 1975, MEDLARS II became operational. [27] Approximately 300 user institutions in the United States
are on-line to the bibliographical data base which analyzes the contents of 2,244 biomedical serials.

NLM has always responded to international requests for service and information. In 1969, budgetary limitations required that a
fee be imposed for interlibrary and audiovisual loans overseas. By
arrangement with the U.S. Agency for International Development,
this did not apply to service to developing countries; the library has
been filling 20,000 annual service requests to 48 developing countries.
Service to developing countries has included MEDLINE, distribution
of Index Medicus, Abridged Index Medicus and the Current Catalog.
Much of this service is probably regarded as stop-gap until regional
programs become a reality overseas. Direct assistance from the
NLM was more general within the U.S.A. prior to the implementation of decentralization with the passage of the Medical Library Assistance Act in 1965.

Under the Special Foreign Currency Program (PL 480) which
originated with the Agricultural Trade and Assistance Act of 1954,
monies accruing to the U.S. government for the sale of agricultural
commodities have been available in certain countries. The NLM has
been able to use these funds within countries for the translation of
biomedical literature and more recently the development of bibliographic tools and the preparation of critical reviews. The latter
have been commissioned, and eminent scientists have analyzed and
synthesized progress within research fields. It is hoped that this
will stimulate and provide direction to other investigators working in
the field. Directories, monographs and handbooks have been produced through the availability of PL 480 funds, also.

International MEDLARS agreements on a bi-lateral quid pro
quo basis have been negotiated, and nine non-U.S. MEDLARS centers
have been established. These are arrangements to share the bibliographical data base developed by the NLM. Monies are not exchanged
between countries or institutions. NLM provides MEDLARS tapes,
technical documentation and training. The country desiring to participate must meet fiscal and personnel capability criteria and be able
to provide indexing input into the system. Mary Corning, NLM Assistant Director for International Programs, has described the arrangements for establishing overseas centers. [28] In 1975 centers existed in Australia, Brazil, Canada, France, Germany, Japan, Sweden,
Great Britain and at the World Health Organization Library in Geneva.
TYMSHARE nodes have been established in Paris and London for direct access to the NLM computer. MEDLINE terminals were first
operational overseas in Sweden and Great Britain, and training programs have been offered to the user community. Negotiations between NLM and the Director of the All-Union Research Institute for
Medical and Medical-Technical Information (VNIIMI) of the Ministry
of Health, U.S.S.R. have explored areas of cooperation. At present,
the U.S.S.R. does not have the computer hardware necessary to establish a MEDLARS center.

The National Library of Medicine internationally has found bi-
lateral agreements more possible of achievement than multi-lateral
agreements. It has in a relatively short period of time stimulated
many cooperative biomedical communication activities. They have
been of mutual benefit to the country involved and to NLM in seeking to test and evaluate its services in other locales. Participating
institutions have shared NLM goals, have demonstrated an ability to
utilize and extend such services and have become valuable collabora-
tors. International organizations attempting to develop such cooperative programs move slowly, probably due to the complex of socio-
political issues involved in negotiations.

The World Health Organization

Established in 1946 as a specialized agency of the United
Nations, the World Health Organization (WHO) has an office and library in Geneva and six regional offices throughout the world. It is
the agency concerned with the improvement of medical and public
health services and has had particular commitment to developing
countries. A series of medical school studies in the WHO Eastern
Mediterranean Region in the early sixties revealed the woeful inade-
quacy of their libraries. [29] Deficiencies of resources, organization,
staff and equipment were overwhelming. During 1964 and 1965,
WHO organized short-term summer refresher courses for medical
librarians at the American University, Beirut. In 1966, a six-week
work-study program in the WHO Geneva library was offered to middle eastern medical librarians. In all, thirty medical librarians
from eight countries attended the three courses. WHO has offered
longer-term fellowships to a few medical librarians from middle
eastern and Asiatic countries; new materials' support has been offered within the Eastern Mediterranean Region. Since 1966, twenty-
four libraries have been supplied with subscriptions to twelve medical periodicals.

Books and periodicals are supplied to libraries in member
states against payments in local currencies. The WHO Library in
Geneva operates an international exchange of duplicate medical literature with eighty-nine libraries in forty-one countries. In 1965, the
WHO Library expanded its acquisitions list into a publication which
included news items of biomedical library interest. Health Literature Topics is distributed widely to libraries in member states. In
the second issue, a report of the Library's 1974 MEDLINE activities
is given. During the experimental Center operation, searches were
processed primarily for the WHO technical staff, but from April to
December 1974, 769 searches were handled from requesters from
sixty-two member states. The WHO library had publicized the service to its member states, particularly to institutional teaching staffs,
and this group requested 43 per cent of the searches. [30] The provision of documents to support searches was not discussed, but undoubtedly the WHO Library was a major provider. From reports of
WHO library assistance programs, one is given the impression that
support to individual libraries having meager resources cannot improve the situation in the long run and that library regionalization

similar to the project evolving under BIREME leadership in Brazil
will provide more far-reaching and long-term benefits to health professionals.

The Pan American Health Organization

The Pan American Health Organization (PAHO) is the division
of the World Health Organization concerned with health care in the
Americas. It has worked with member states on programs of education for health professionals, improved clinical practice and the
control of communicable diseases. It has recognized that information services to health professionals have been inadequate and that
the existing fragmented approach should be replaced by substantial
regional planning. Other organizations became interested in the concept, and collaboration resulted in the Biblioteca Regional de Medicina (BIREME). How this productive liaison of agencies established
goals and mechanisms for their achievement should be analyzed in
greater depth, but, for the purposes of this summary, I will report
on certain results.

BIREME started in 1969 in Sao Paulo, Brazil as an international communications center for biomedical and scientific information in Latin America. An agreement signed on March 3, 1967 between the government of Brazil, the Director of the Escola Paulista
de Medicina and the Pan American Health Organization was the beginning. Subsequently, the Kellogg Foundation, the Commonwealth
Fund, the State of Sao Paulo and the National Library of Medicine
provided technical or financial support. The Escola Paulista de Medicina in Sao Paulo has provided physical facilities, a basic collection
and most of the staffing. The National Library of Medicine, through
credits with the U.S. Book Exchange, has assisted in collection development and has provided training for RLM personnel. BIREME
has not only developed a strong biomedical collection but from its inception recognized the importance of stimulating regional health library science development. Through agreements with the Federal
Universities of Brazil, eleven biomedical libraries have joined in a
communication network as subcenters for sharing resources and providing interlibrary loans. BIREME is the back-up library after local
resources and subcenter collections have been searched. Since 1969,
BIREME has supplied 235,937 photocopies of biomedical journal articles not available in Brazilian regional subcenters or in other Latin
American countries. [31]

Dr. Amador Neghme has been director of BIREME since 1969
and works with a Scientific Advisory Committee appointed by PAHO
to assist with policy and program development. Cooperative relationships have been activated internationally and include photocopy, loan,
and exchange agreements with the British Lending Library, the Institut National de la Santé et de la Recherche Medicale (INSERM) in
Paris, the Deutsches Institut für Medizinische Dokumentation und Information (DIMDI) in Cologne, the Istituto Italo-Latino Americano
in Rome, the Spanish Medical Documentation Center in Valencia, the

National Science Library of Canada and Keio University in Japan. BIREME participates in the MLA International Cooperation Committee's Library to Library project with the Lewis Calder Memorial Library at the University of Miami School of Medicine for the exchange of duplicates and some document delivery. A MEDLINE center has been established at BIREME, and the National Library of Medicine has provided technical assistance and training.

Regional centers linked to BIREME are being developed by PAHO in other Latin American countries. Union catalogs of biomedical serials will assist programs of sharing. Seminars for university faculty, librarians and health professionals have been held in Venezuela, Argentina, Colombia, Peru, Chile and Mexico. They have been planned to increase understanding of the importance of a biomedical information network in the support of research, education and health affairs. Latin American progress has been encouraging, and it has been due to a number of factors. The total health science community is being stimulated to seek more adequate information support for professional development. Institutions, foundations and libraries are being mobilized to direct their energy towards cooperative effort. Libraries, particularly, feel less isolated and their increased effectiveness is gradually becoming part of a more comprehensive plan to expand access to information.

UNESCO

UNESCO has worked with many other national and international agencies to improve access to educational opportunities. To gain some understanding of UNESCO operations one should peruse the Bibliography of Publications published in 1973. Libraries and documentation programs have received considerable support, and UNESCO has cooperated with other groups, particularly FID, FAO and WHO to produce bibliographical directories and guides.

UNESCO has recognized the need for more adequate preparation of library personnel in many areas of the world. In Africa, it collaborated in establishing the East African School of Librarianship at Makere University College in Kampala, Uganda for English-speaking countries, and the Centre Regional de Formation de Bibliothecaire de Dakar in Senegal for French-speaking countries. [32] It has cooperated with governments to set up national scientific and technical documentation centers. The first such center was established in Mexico City in 1950 and the second in New Delhi in 1952. The centers collect, classify and disseminate scientific and technical literature to research workers and organizations. In these efforts, UNESCO has provided experts, fellowships and equipment. The team of experts organizes and manages the operation for three to five years and trains local staff to assume responsibility.

Probably UNESCO's most ambitious project has been carried out in collaboration with the International Council of Scientific Unions, to study the feasibility of a world science information system (UNISIST).

Observers from many other agencies have attended planning sessions.
From 1964 to 1974, working parties explored and analyzed all aspects and components of existing systems and offered recommendations for planning. Providing developing countries with access to
such a system has been a primary concern if the gap between developed and developing countries is not to increase. By 1975, sixty
projects were defined and UNESCO budgeted $2.4 million for them.

UNESCO's impact on health library science has been indirect
but nevertheless beneficial. Its support for new library education
programs in countries where they did not exist will surely benefit
all libraries. Its establishment of scientific and technical documentation centers provides bibliographical control of many health-related
publications. UNESCO depository libraries in member states will
make available many of the directories, handbooks, guides and training manuals issued with its support. It is hoped that UNESCO can
continue productive relationships with other cultural and scientific organizations and that political differences will not hinder the considerable contribution it has made to all libraries.

For the purpose of this summary, I cannot refer to health
library science developments in every country or region, so I refer
to reports in the Proceedings of the Third International Congress of
Medical Librarianship. Biomedical information networks have
emerged in Czechoslovakia, Hungary and Germany. Developing countries in Asia and Africa are struggling to improve basic library services and some form of regionalization or coordination of effort seems
needed. Following the Third International Congress in 1969, health
science librarians in Germany organized the Arbeitsgemeinschaft für
Medizinische Bibliothekswesen and held annual conferences. The program for the 1975 annual conference was reported in MLA News,
August/September 1975. In July 1975, health science librarians in
South Africa held a symposium in conjunction with the Jubilee Congress of the Medical Association of South Africa. Librarians attending that meeting decided to organize a Medical Library Association
of South Africa. Such organizations will provide a more tangible
basis for national coordination of health science library resources
and services.

Health library science is at many different levels of development internationally. Many of the problems are common to library
science generally. Manpower, or the adequate supply of well educated professionals, appears to be a problem in many countries.
Direct access to resources is still uncommon for students and health
professionals. Regional planning, as at BIREME, appears to have
potential for success in developing countries. It requires the mobilization of government, association, institutional and foundation support
and strong assurance of ongoing commitment from all participants.
Automated data bases, such as MEDLARS, are a new phenomenon
and their availability internationally has stimulated national and regional support. The provision of documents to support the system in
developing countries is still dependent on outside resources. Health

library science is indeed more visible in countries or regions where
library science generally has become recognized as an important
facet of cultural life. It has various relationships to the larger discipline and is dependent on it for the establishment of universal
standards of bibliographical control and the accreditation of basic library education programs. Health library science has the advantage
of being a more closely knit sub-group of library science. The
Medical Library Association has provided a strong link internationally and international congresses have offered opportunity for the exchange of information and direct contact between individuals. The
prospect of a fourth International Congress on Medical Librarianship
will afford another opportunity for the exchange of ideas and experience.

NOTES

1. Danton, J. Periam. The Dimensions of Comparative Librarian-
      ship. Chicago: American Library Association, 1973, p. 52.
2. Harvey, John F. "Toward a Definition of International and Com-
      parative Library Science," International Library Review V
      (July 1973), pp. 289-319.
3. Brodman, Estelle. "Medical Libraries Around the World,"
      Bulletin Medical Library Association LIX (April 1971), pp.
      223-228.
4. Izant, H. A. "Problems of Medical Information Systems and
      Centres in Developing Countries: Survey of Work Being Done
      by WHO and UNESCO," in: Proceedings Third International
      Congress of Medical Librarianship, 1969. Amsterdam: Ex-
      cerpta Medica Foundation, 1970, pp. 413-419.
5. First International Congress on Medical Librarianship, 1953.
      "Proceedings," Libri III (1954), pp. 1-451.
6. Second International Congress on Medical Librarianship, 1963.
      "Proceedings," Bulletin Medical Library Association LII (Jan-
      uary 1964), pp. 1-352.
7. Third International Congress of Medical Librarianship, 1969.
      Proceedings. Amsterdam: Excerpta Medica Foundation,
      1970.
8. Fraser, M. Doreen E. "The Medical Library Association: the
      Span of Its International Activities, a Chronology," Bulletin
      Medical Library Association LIX (July 1971), pp. 495-510.
9. Langer, Mildred Crowe. "Eileen Roach Cunningham, 1894-
      1965," Bulletin Medical Library Association LIV (January
      1966), pp. 93-95.
10. "International Notes," MLA News, No. 67 (June 1975), p. 4.
11. "International Notes," MLA News, No. 72 (November 1975), pp.
      3-4.
12. Orfanos, Minnie. "Report of the Exchange Committee (MLA),"
      Bulletin Medical Library Association LXIII (January 1975),
      pp. 117-120.
13. Gaskell, Eric. "British Medical Libraries," in: Handbook of
      the Medical Library Association, edited by G. Annan and J.
      Felter. 3rd ed. Chicago: Medical Library Association,

1970, pp. 381-398.

14. Clark, Hilda M. "British Contributions to Medical Libraries Overseas," Bulletin Medical Library Association LIII (January 1965), pp. 35-42.

15. Stuart-Clark, A. C. , Clayton-Jones, E. and updated and revised by Hardie, M. C. "The British National Hospital Service," in: Hospital Libraries and Work with the Disabled, edited by M. E. Going. London: The Library Association, 1973, pp. 1-20.

16. Leys, Duncan. "The Place of Literature in the Art of Healing," in: Hospital Libraries and Work with the Disabled, edited by M. E. Going. London: The Library Association, 1973, p. 184.

17. News Bulletin (IFLA/FIAB Libraries in Hospitals Sub-section), No. 10 (July 1975), p. 1.

18. Bunch, Antonia A. Hospital and Medical Libraries in Scotland: an Historical and Sociological Study. Glasgow: Scottish Library Association, 1975.

19. Tsuda, Y. "Activities of the Medical Library Association of Japan," in: Proceedings of the First Japan-United States Conference on Libraries and Information Science, Tokyo, 1969. Chicago: American Library Association, pp. 280-284.

20. Corning, Mary E. "National Library of Medicine: International Cooperation for Biomedical Communications," Bulletin Medical Library Association LXIII (January 1975), pp. 14-22.

21. Simon, Beatrice V. Library Support of Medical Education and Research in Canada. Ottawa: Association of Canadian Medical Colleges, 1964.

22. Russell, Phyllis J. , ed. Guide to Canadian Health Science Information Services and Sources. Ottawa: Canadian Library Association, 1974.

23. Bagdasaryan, S. M. "The System of Medical Information in the USSR," in: Proceedings Third International Congress of Medical Librarianship, 1969. Amsterdam: Excerpta Medica Foundation, 1970, p. 345.

24. Glinkina, V. N. "Organization of Technical Assistance to the Medical Library Network in the Soviet Union," in: Proceedings Third International Congress of Medical Librarianship, 1969. Amsterdam: Excerpta Medica Foundation, 1970, p. 353.

25. Cummings, Martin M. and Corning, Mary E. "The Medical Library Assistance Act: an Analysis of NLM Extramural Programs, 1965-1970," Bulletin Medical Library Association LIX (July 1971), pp. 375-391.

26. Austen, C. J. MEDLARS, 1963-1967. Washington: U.S. Government Printing Office, 1968.

27. "MEDLARS II Acceptance Testing Completed," National Library of Medicine News XXX (February 1975), p. 1.

28. Corning, Mary C. , op. cit. , pp. 14-22.

29. Izant, H. A. , op. cit. , pp. 413-19.

30. "The WHO Medline Centre, 1974; A Report of Activities," Health Literature Topics I, No. 2 (1975), pp. 29-30.

31. Neghme, Amador. "Operations of the Biblioteca Regional de
    Medicina (BIREME)," Bulletin Medical Library Association
    LXIII (April 1975), pp. 173-179.
32. Izant, H. A., op. cit., pp. 413-19.

LIBRARY EDUCATION

Frances Laverne Carroll

A close link exists between libraries and library education.
In some countries library education is conducted exclusively in the
library, the staff imparting to recruits the policies and techniques
utilized in that library. Correspondence study, as well as external
and internal examining, has been used extensively in the world, also.
Approximately half of the nations utilize institutions which are usually associated with the country's system of higher education and which
employ a variety of methods to transmit the theoretical principles
and general practices of librarianship to neophytes. [1] "Education for
librarianship" is the term used to describe the instruction given by
these institutions. The United Nations Education, Scientific, and
Cultural Organization (Unesco) uses the word "training" when referring to the specialized education of librarians, documentalists, and
archivists, however. "Library education," when used in this chapter, includes all of the various processes being utilized to qualify
both entrants to the profession and those to be further qualified.

The diversity of library education around the world is understandable for a number of reasons. Library education reflects a
country's system of libraries, and the library system reflects the
culture of the nation, the "terminal community" of man as a social
animal. Libraries are not perceived in the same way in all countries; the library is not viewed as an educational institution in every
country. Cultures range from those of a "no book" type to those
perceiving the book only as an archive, to those with the multimedia
approach to information. Library education differs from country to
country as the educational systems vary. Largely because of such
origins, library education has a somewhat different orientation in
each country. Despite diversity in national library education considerable progress has been made in the past decade in the provision of regional and international library education.

International Library Education

The diversity resulting from nationalism should not be seen
as discouraging. In fact, the numerical smallness of the international library education field encourages a personal and professional ca-
maraderie. Some of the common goals and the spirit of international
library education are reflected in the following resolution:

As in many countries the methods of professional training

148

show minor differences, it should be possible to draw up
a programme on a common basis in order to exchange
professors and students, to acknowledge the equivalent
value of their diplomas, to publish common manuals, and
to grant scholarships for journeys [sic] and studying. 2

However, the current proposal for an International Library
School should be examined as a forecast of a new international library education to prepare international librarians.   International libraries exist.   The United Nations has two libraries, New York and
Geneva.   The International Youth Library in Munich and the International Atomic Energy Library in Vienna are examples, and an international copyright library has been mentioned. 3   The librarians working in international libraries were not trained in those libraries or
in an International Library School.   They are products of various
national library schools.   In the future the possibilities for working
with world networks of information may necessitate a type of education we have not yet instituted.

The first proposal for an International Library School was
made by an Italian.   "I hope to start this year [1904] in Florence an
international library school for the study of ancient culture and of
American improvements in a friendly exchange of mutual aids," said
Dr. Guido Biagi. 4   The time was still not ripe for the establishment of an international library school in the 1930s. 5   Among the
potential activities discussed in 1967 by Rose L. Vormelker of the
Library Education Division (LED), American Library Association
(ALA), was an international library school concentrating on aspects
of library education pertinent to developing nations and comparative
librarianship.

The idea of an International Library School was presented at
the 1969 conference of the International Federation of Library Associations (IFLA) in Copenhagen by Guy Marco, Kent State University,
USA. 7   His suggestion of a third approach to improve library education for emerging countries was based on the idea of centralizing efforts, in contrast to the two other approaches available for students:
national library schools or study abroad in another nation's schools.
His paper related too often to the organization and administration of
the school rather than exhibiting a serious concern for the philosophy
of library education to be embraced.   In the paper given immediately
afterwards, Knud Larsen did not feel that a similarity of core knowledge existed because the libraries of countries are in different stages
of growth.   He pointed out the need for course work for library instructors in developing countries.   In addition, he called attention to
the regional schools that already exist in East Africa and Latin
America, and their need for money rather than advice. 8

The International Library School issue remained before the
IFLA library education group until February 1973, when Marco,
Chairman of the International Education Committee, LED/ALA sug-
gested that a feasibility study be proposed to UNESCO by the IFLA
Executive Board.   This study would examine the idea of combining

the 1974 International Summer School to be sponsored by the Education and Training Committee of the International Federation for Documentation (FID) with the proposed International Library School. The summer school was not held until 1975.   "There is a sense in which the International Summer School is a part of the idea for an International School in that FID/ET has long envisaged a high-level International Academy and has seen progress towards this as being achieved via a succession of high-level Summer Schools. "[9]

At the IFLA meeting in Washington, 1974, the Section of Library Schools proposed the following resolution:

> Whereas the concept of an International University has been accepted and is being implemented by the United Nations, and having regard to the importance of library and information science in the transfer of world knowledge and information,
> It is recommended that the Executive Board request that its IFLA Section of Library Schools be consulted on the establishment of a faculty of library, archives and information science within the framework of the existing United Nations International University. [10]

The United Nations University, established by General Assembly vote in December 1972, will not be a university in the usual sense of the word, with a campus, students and degrees.   Instead, it will consist of a worldwide network of research and training centers dealing with key world problems.   The world headquarters is Tokyo.   A fair amount of skepticism has been expressed about the need for the university, however. [11]

> The unique characteristic of a world university lies in the freedom it can afford to the world's scholars to act on behalf of all the world's citizens, and to speculate, express themselves, report, study, and create in an atmosphere of global commitment.   In the history of the world there has never been an institution like that. [12]

One of the purposes of a world university is to train international leaders whose loyalties will be broader than the individual nation. "Here we have the full force of the paradox of our age.   The people of the world are possessed of little, if any, feeling of international responsibility.   Yet the characteristics of the times--the technology which brings us all together ... have led nations into international agreements. "[13]

Although the concept is one of the most important developments in library education, the International Library School has not yet developed widespread support from the library education community, partly because of the slowness of the communication process for ideas and partly because of indecision as to its purpose.   In early discussions of the purpose of the school, special courses in selection were considered of importance.   However, the international

nature of book stocks is decreasingly a distinguishing feature between libraries. Attention has been turned to cataloging and classification, where international cooperation is very apparent, but the
results are being incorporated into the curricula of national library
schools. Other functions suggested for an interational library
school are:

> to prepare teachers and study methods of teaching
> to serve as a resource to new and floundering library
> schools
> to provide a headquarters for an information system about
> library education
> to disseminate the new ideas and techniques being incorpo-
> rated into librarianship
> to conduct comparative studies on library education and
> library systems
> to interpret manifestations of the international world on
> library science
> to foster the study of documents dealing with libraries and
> library education which are international in scope, such
> as the Charter of the Book.

The offerings of the school must be on a level to prevent
duplication "at home" and be recognized internationally for their
uniqueness. International political systems and processes, international education, international law, and multinational corporations
should be studied before attempting to project a genuinely international library education which is significantly different from national library education.

International Aspects of National Library Education

Without an international library school, one must look at national and regional schools, since "the growing interrelationship between the nations of the world leads one to conclude that the need
for librarians with specialized knowledge and capacity for international activities will increase in the years to come."[14] Interested
schools should provide appropriate courses when a manpower survey
shows the extent to which librarians are involved in work abroad.
An attempt to discern occupational roles for librarians and to determine the feasibility of a special educational program with an international emphasis was made in 1969 at the University of Oklahoma.[15]
The roles were perceived to be those of the area-studies librarian,
the library consultant, and the librarian working in an alien information center. In determining the need for a course of study for these
roles, it was noted in 1965 that a shortage of area-studies librarians
existed and that the number of recruits with competency in languages
was diminishing.[16] The number of American consultants listed in
the Foreign Service Directory of American Librarians was only three
per cent of the ALA membership.[17]

At the time of the 1969 feasibility study, the proposed courses

were recommended for the advanced student and were to be handled
jointly by two schools from two countries.   The implementation near-
est to that idea does not yet involve an extended period of time
abroad, as was suggested.   Beginning in summer 1976, the School
of Library Science, Kent State University, Kent, Ohio, will accept
up to twelve quarter hours or eight semester hours of transfer credit on its Sixth Year Program from the International Graduate Summer School in Librarianship and Information Science, sponsored by
the College of Librarianship, Wales (CLW) and the University of
Pittsburgh Graduate School of Library and Information Science.   Previously, study abroad meant remaining abroad a sufficient time to
finish a credential in an overseas library school.

The occupational roles presuppose an international attitude
and necessitate professional mobility.   Also, the need for increasing
the rate of progress in implementing change requires flexibility and
adaptability. [18]   The occupational roles seem to be sufficiently demanding but not sufficiently important quantitatively to warrant a
large number of schools becoming involved with specializations for
international positions, but there is no current world manpower study
covering the availability and deployment of librarians on which to
base decisions.   A survey, done in accordance with UNESCO standards for data collection, should include the languages and the further
mobility plans of the individual.   Mobilization of surplus manpower
from nation to nation and further geographically-oriented career planning by individuals could then be done.

The primary or output goal of library education is the needed
manpower for the nation's libraries, the persons who complete the
course of study set for them and enter the world of work in a library or information center.   For the national schools, Sharify recommends revising the existing course content to make sure that
courses utilize the points of view expressed in international library
literature and that the concepts presented to students are not purely
national.   He feels that one or more courses, such as international
library resources and services, international bibliography, and the
foreign book trade, should be available in the study plan. [19]   The
American schools are responding slowly to the concept.   Other nations' library schools are more apt to include material about major
foreign library systems than the North American library schools do.

The national library school must also fulfill manpower obligations in terms of foreign students who may return home.   Many foreign students from Asia come to the United States; many African
students go to English or Russian library schools.   The mobility of
students has been a durable means for accomplishing an international
flavor, but it is felt that the number of foreign students is declining
in England[20] and, possibly, in the USA as new schools develop and
the quality of indigenous library education improves.   A strong plea
is made for an indigenous library education development matching
each nation's technological advancement. [21,22]   Indigenous professional education has the highest ranking by librarians of the twelve factors that help accelerate library development, and study abroad ranks
below it as only half as effective. [23]

There is agreement that the student's study abroad is more advantageous for advanced than for basic education. Unesco feels education abroad should be made available to senior librarians to encourage improvement through first-hand knowledge of activity in other countries, and that facilities for basic education should be available locally. As early as 1935, Munthe referred to the influence of the University of Chicago in attracting European librarians to learn the scientific method.[24] As a part of advanced education, a foreigner can expect to do basic research on the library needs of his country, assist in developing professional literature and bibliographic tools in an indigenous language, or plan to establish a library school at home. The extent of foreign student academic accomplishment in producing theses, dissertations, comparative studies and publications before or after graduation has not been sufficiently assessed, particularly for its contribution to library literature. Planned recruitment and financial support for librarians for continuing education would seem to be desirable for the advancement of librarianship and might be better justified after such an assessment.

The need for models of national schools which have achieved a significant degree of internationalism leads to inclusion of two descriptions of programs from directors of schools with international reputations. The present dean of the Pittsburgh school describes its well-rounded international library education program as follows:

> The Graduate School of Library and Information Science of the University of Pittsburgh has had a strong emphasis on international and comparative librarianship. The founding dean, Harold Lancour, has been pre-eminent among internationalists in the library and information fields. His interest in the international scene flourished at the University, which has long been noted for the international dimension.
>
> Both the faculty and the student body reflect a strong international aspect. The seven-member founding faculty included distinguished librarians from Australia, England, Austria, and Iran. Over the years, instruction has been enriched by a succession of visiting lecturers from abroad, currently Reverend Romano Almagno, Head Librarian, Collegio S. Bonaventura, Rome. The present twenty-two member full-time faculty includes six people born and/or educated outside the United States and ten individuals with significant teaching or consultant experience in Europe, Latin America, Asia, or Africa. Five members of GSLIS have major contractual assignments in Israel, Egypt, Saudi Arabia, or Nigeria in 1975-76. The student body is equally international in composition. Approximately fifteen per cent of our graduate students come from overseas, representing twenty-two nations. The School's curriculum reflects this, including a wide range of courses and seminars in international and comparative aspects of librarianship, as well as in regional materials and literatures such as Latin American and Asian bibliography.

A unique resource in support of the School's international curricular and research interests is the International Library Information Center. The Center comprises the collection of approximately 14,000 items in thirty-three languages, consisting chiefly of primary source material emphasizing library development in other countries.

Since 1970 the School has hosted three Multi-regional Seminars sponsored by the U.S. Department of State. This program, scheduled to be offered again in the Summer, 1976, brings mid-career practicing librarians to the United States for advanced seminars and individual programs of planned travel and internship in American libraries. Ten librarians from nine nations participated in the 1974 Pittsburgh Multi-regional Seminar.

In 1973, the School joined the College of Librarianship Wales to sponsor the first International Graduate Summer School in Librarianship and Information Science held at Aberystwyth, Wales. Dean Emeritus Lancour serves as Director of the Summer School, now in its third successful summer with continued University of Pittsburgh sponsorship. [25]

A program such as this is typical only of a very few schools, including, possibly, the school at Wales.

The director of another national library school of international stature describes another way to include international aspects:

We have always been aware that London's facilities and resources for study of other countries, and for study by visiting students and researchers, give us special responsibilities and opportunities. They enrich study for our students, for visitors and for ourselves. But 'international' study implies an international standpoint, and that is not something we have felt the need to satisfy. It may well be justified in an international body or within a large coherent area, but we have always preferred to individualise programmes of study so far as possible, whatever the level. We have had to grow out of bad habits that required students from other countries to pay undue attention to purely British subjects and contexts, but international comparisons are bound to be a part of any realistic, fruitful, professional and academic study. As for standpoints, we insist that these are established under tutorial arrangements. A student or researcher who aims for (or comes from) a post in the U.N. organization must have as special a programme as a visiting student from Asia or Africa who will return to work there; and in the nature of things most students and researchers will come from and return to British posts. I have no doubt that we could serve all students better with ampler resources, but I do not think we would ever wish to change our preference for offering opportunities for flexible individual study, instead of prescribed forms of attention to a specified range of employment contexts. [26]

Although it is not the purpose of this chapter to describe world patterns of library education or to identify the influence of one nation's type of library education on that of another, an example of such a transfer is the more formalized education for librarians, increasingly identified with higher education systems, a practice with which the USA has long been associated.

Regional Library Education

The national library school does have, however, a priority established by the very nature of its being a national school. The regional school may have some difficulty rising above the fact that it serves as the economically feasible center for a group of countries which lack national library schools. Both Sabor[27] and Larsen[28] seem to favor regional action.

A report from one of the most recently organized schools is a fair summation of a regional program:

> Having been with the Department, as one of the Unesco-provided staff, since soon after its establishment, I've no doubt that the programmes have been of service to librarianship in the English-speaking Caribbean. One notices the failures and the gaps, of course--we haven't been able to provide adequate programmes for some types of library specialisation; we haven't had students from some of the smaller territories like the British Virgin Islands--but some of our graduates are now contributing very usefully to library development in their own countries, and we have also been able to assist in other ways--with the drafting of new public library legislation for the Bahamas, for instance. A problem we have at the moment is in recruiting West Indian staff with appropriate teaching as well as professional library experience: a further period of Unesco assistance would help considerably with this staff development. [29]

Language has influenced regional school establishment. The regional library schools are: Inter-American Library School, Medellin, Colombia, established in 1956 for Spanish-speaking countries; University of Dakar, Dakar, Senegal, established in 1967 for French-speaking countries; University of West Indies, Kingston, Jamaica, established in 1971 for English-speaking countries; East African School of Librarianship, Kampala, Uganda, established in 1962 for English-speaking countries. The Indonesian area remains in need of education facilities supplementing those provided by the graduate library school and the documentation center in Djakarta. The Graduate School of Library Studies, University of Hawaii, is both a national and regional school since it has a unique program of Asian library studies.

A study of those goals which are unique to regional schools and can cause their development along new lines would clarify library education roles at other levels, the national and the international. The small number of students and the allusions in the literature to its precarious existence present another reason for studying the regional school's role.

International Short Courses

Programs of short duration, usually no more than three months, are plentiful. They have attracted international groups with a variety of backgrounds, by language, type of library, and previous library education. Notable among them is the International Graduate Summer School at Aberystwyth, Wales. Twenty-one students from eight countries (two-thirds from North America) took part in 1973. Four courses were offered and a ten-day guided tour to major points of library and cultural interest in Britain was included. In 1974, forty-seven attended from twenty-one countries; nearly half came from North America. Nine courses were added to the previous four. In 1975, the School took on a different complexion. The increased attendance (fifty-six from thirty-one countries) was no longer dominated by North Americans. An advanced level course on Library Development Planning was added. It was attended by twenty senior librarians from developing countries, their presence made possible by British Council scholarships.

The Department of Library and Information Studies, Liverpool Polytechnic, England, has had a one-week European Library Summer Seminar annually since 1973. Its purpose is to bring together future leaders and to give them an opportunity to discuss topics of current interest, such as Library Education in Europe and Libraries and Continuing Education. On each occasion, the seminar has attracted participants from about twenty countries.

Courses revolving around special topics for an international group may be given by agencies other than library schools or offered jointly by agencies and library schools. Since 1968, every two years, with UNESCO cooperation, the Royal School of Librarianship, Copenhagen, has organized a four-month course for library school instructors from developing countries. The course is not designed to give subject instruction but instruction in the methods of teaching subjects common to library schools.

Courses provided by agencies other than library schools offer no traditional award, such as a degree or diploma, but are very popular. Most of them deal with the newer areas of knowledge which are being incorporated into library school curricula, especially information science, scientific information, and the special needs of developing countries. One strong influence has been UNISIST, authorized by Unesco and the International Council of Scientific Unions, whose purpose is establishing a world science and technology information system.

UNISIST sponsored an international training course at Kato-
wice, Poland, in August 1974, for thirteen countries.   A course on
International Documentation was held by UNITAR (UN Institute for
Training and Research) in Geneva earlier that year, and another was
held in Athens.   The UN Industrial Development Organization's Inter-
regional courses on industrial information for developing countries
have been held in Moscow three times from 1970 through 1972.   The
ten-week course has been attended by seventy-one information scientists from thirty-five countries.   A five-day seminar on Cooperative
Library Automation was co-sponsored by the Asian Institute of Technology and Library Automation Research Communications (LARC) in
Bangkok, June 9-13, 1975.

International organizations have held pre- and post-conference
meetings dealing with library education: FID at Vesprem, Hungary
in 1972, and IFLA, notably at Liverpool in 1971 and Oslo in 1975.
Sponsored by the FID Education and Training Committee, the international seminar on Education in Information Science, at Vesprem,
was attended by forty-five people from eighteen countries.   The
IFLA conferences have dealt with other needed areas such as developing countries (in 1971) and school libraries (in 1975).   An FID Seminar was scheduled for the National University, Mexico City, in connection with the FID Conference, 1976.   The Program was to include
methods of teaching information science for different audiences and
new teaching aids.

The sponsors of the International Summer School which was
held in 1975 at Sheffield University (England) were IFLA, FID, and
UNISIST.   There was a consensus that the Summer School program
should reflect the natural relationship between the two disciplines by
locating it at a university in which education for library and information science is provided.   The program was prepared for teachers
of information and library science drawn from developing countries
and lesser developed industrial nations.   The courses were: computers and library information work, information retrieval, and systems approach to management.

This partial overview acts as a barometer for library education.   The decision on the value of incorporating into the national library schools the content or the teaching method of these short
courses is being facilitated by the continuation of evaluations, with
the assistance of Guidelines for the Evaluation of Training Courses,
Workshops and Seminars in Scientific and Technical Information and
Documentation by F. W. Lancaster.

International Cooperation in Library Education

Greater and more efficient international cooperation in library
education might result from the leadership of the proposed International Association of Schools of Librarianship, suggested by Harold Lancour in 1963. [30]   The establishment of an association has been proposed for library schools in the emergent countries, also. [31]   The

question of membership, by library school or by national library
school association, would influence the organization's size and voting
procedures.   Associations of library schools are few, probably existing only in Canada, Brazil, Britain, Africa, Latin America, and
the U.S.A.

The IFLA Section of Library Schools was created in 1972
to provide a platform for library educators to promote library education.   The section has already discussed a curriculum suggested
for international acceptance. [32]   In 1975 at Oslo, a document, International Standards for Library Education, was discussed. [33]
These standards related to Unesco's Level Three of Library Education, Stage One, leading to a first university degree, and Stage
Two leading to a post-graduate credential.   The projection of minimum standards has brought up the subject of international accreditation of library school programs.

Another area that library schools must consider is the trend
to include all fields of study related to information.   A "harmonized"
core curriculum has been suggested to educate library, information,
and archive staffs. [34]   Most library schools have offered introductory
courses in automation, but "the relationship between these two areas,
each claiming the title 'information science' or something similar,
will probably tend to remain rather vague until there is a wide-ranging, international body of expertise, based on real life experience of
successful computer operations in library and information services. "[35]   Due to the nature of archival work, the courses exhibit
variability and inequality in geographical distribution.   Developing
countries, usually with only one national archive, must often group
trainees in a regional school, such as the one at Dakar.   The chief
instrument of international cooperation in archives work is the international technical training course for archivists instituted in France
in 1951 for prospective French archivists and their foreign colleagues.
This course constitutes, for some, an initiation to the profession,
and for others, a complement to training already received at home.
Spain gives Latin Americans access to instruction in archives work.
Many others, including the Vatican, USSR, USA, and UK, have authorized foreign nationals to engage in study periods of varying duration in their archives and to enroll in their archives schools. [36]
The International Standards for Library Education does not cover
the new alliance with archivists, but it does include documentalists.

Tours and conferences in foreign countries provide opportunities for students and faculty members to learn and to develop international understanding that will facilitate cooperation in international
activities.   Since 1966, approximately twenty short summer tours,
mostly to European libraries, have been sponsored for credit by
North American library schools.   Study abroad and study tours are
used regularly by British and European library schools.   The first
reciprocal international exchange of librarians and student-librarians
occurred between the UK and the USA in 1968, organized by the College of Librarianship, Wales as one of its foreign study tours.   The

local host was the University of Pittsburgh. Seventy-four persons
were on the tour led by Frank Hogg, Principal of CLW. A group
of Americans, led by J. Clement Harrison, Associate Dean of the
Pittsburgh library school, went to England for three weeks.

The tour of librarians from the People's Republic of China,
in the fall of 1973, enabled Chinese library educators to meet library
educators in the USA.   The five-week visit was designed to give the
delegation an opportunity to observe library administration and services using modern techniques.   The cooperation of library schools
with libraries increases the possibilities of students and faculty members being able to go abroad.   The concept of sending British library school students, whose specialties involve a foreign language,
to work for a year in the library of an appropriate country is a
good one, but many of the attempts to arrange these attachments are
overly time-consuming.   The meager pay and uneven student guidance are unsatisfactory aspects.   At Brighton, England, a new B. A.
course combines library education and modern languages, taught
wholly within a European context.   The College of Librarianship,
Wales and the University's Russian Department are proposing a year's
exchange for a Russian librarian to work in the CLW Library and a
CLW library school student to work in a Russian library.   Since
1970, CLW has sent thirty students to Europe for a year's practice
work.

Study abroad for American library school students for extended time periods does not compare favorably to that available for
other library school students or for students in other American professional schools.   One hundred and sixty-one American library
school students went abroad from 1946 to 1955, and fifty-one in the
1956-65 period. [37]   A six-week summer work-study program at the
University of the Americas in Mexico is available for two Spanish-
speaking librarians.   Guy Marco is director of a new Program of International Partnership (PIP) which was formalized in 1975.   One
purpose of PIP is to avoid overlapping among American and Canadian
library schools in formulating cooperative programs with other library schools in the world.   This plan should increase faculty mobility and perhaps assist in study-abroad programs.   The greatest
amount of mobility has been demonstrated by the faculties of British
library schools, encouraged by the British Council.   In the area of
international cooperation the activities of library education remain
more on the level of binational cooperation, while the planning for
the future of library education is evidencing an international approach.

Significant Recent Literature

Basic to efficient international cooperation in library education
have been the published directories of library schools, personnel, and
associations, such as the World Guide to Library Schools and Training Courses in Documentation and the International Guide to Library,
Archival, and Information Science Associations.   They have established a practical means of communication.   An interface of the
World Guide with a list of schools for archivists is now needed.

Short descriptive articles about library education programs in various countries are plentiful and valuable. An effort needs to be made, however, to cover systematically the library education programs about which little has been written. Nineteen countries with library education programs have had no articles indexed since 1970. The highest concentration of these, six countries, is in South America. Articles on library education appear sporadically as journals initiate and discontinue special international issues, series, and columns. Analyses, comparison, or conclusions transcending national boundaries are difficult, since this type of material is not written for these purposes. The absence of statistics is lamented, also. International library education does not have its own journal and must rely principally upon the Unesco Bulletin for Libraries, International Library Review and Libri for articles of any length.

Larry Earl Bone produced a significant contribution to international library education when he edited the twenty papers presented at the 1967 International Conference on Librarianship, Library Education, an International Survey. The papers are organized around issues transcending national boundaries, such as practice work, recruitment, and advanced study. The paper by Haynes McMullen represents the international approach hoped for in the majority of the papers. McMullen presents the number, type, and subjects of student-guided research in the USA, England, Continental Europe, the Soviet Union, and Latin America. The format of Bone's book complements an issue of Library Trends, entitled Education for Librarianship Abroad in Selected Countries, which had lengthy articles but a scope limited to thirteen countries and three regions. One of the most recent publications is World Trends in Library Education, by George Bramley. The author deliberately concentrates on Anglo-American library education, ranges around the world to cover major patterns, and attempts to trace the influence of British and American library education in the developing countries. The text is descriptive of accreditation in the USA and Canada and the certification of individuals in the UK, both by library associations and via the state examination method used elsewhere in the world.

A small proportion of library literature is in languages other than English. With the objective of breaking down this literature's language barriers, the College of Librarianship, Wales, in 1973, appointed a specialist, Anthony Thompson, who has developed SPEL (Selected Publications in European Languages), published in English five times a year.

Textbooks are needed which treat library school subjects from an international viewpoint. Instructors in foreign library schools should attempt to write these texts. Unesco authorized two manuals: Education for Librarianship and Methods of Teaching Librarianship, and should continue to up-date and add relevant library education volumes to this excellent series.

In summary, the many international library education activities should continue, and they will be nurtured by the forces of an

international society. Unesco support has created a more international library education world, but its resources alone have not been
able to implement the plans sufficiently. The cooperation of groups
and individuals concerned with international library education is expected. One planning group at the international level which represents documentalists, librarians, and archivists should inventory library education activity and study the needs geographically. South
and Central America apparently have fewer library education programs in the 1970s than hitherto, and only five nations have new
schools, one in Africa, three in the Middle East, and the regional
school in Jamaica. The inequalities extend to computer education
facilities, which are mainly located in the USA, Canada, and Japan.[38]
The planning group could carry out or identify an agency to perform
many of the centralizing and disseminating functions suggested for the
International Library School. The function of the International Library School, in review, tends to be the education and reeducation
of teachers of library schools, particularly those adept at preparing
students for new types of internationally-oriented work, as with information networks. If this function is carried on by a number of
library schools, perhaps on a regional approach, as suggested by
UNISIST, further clarification as to what is really meant by an International Library School may be forthcoming.

International understanding and advancement of knowledge are
traditional international goals. They are secondary or support goals,
and their achievement does not rest on library education alone.
Many of library education's activities can be subsumed under these
two goals. In the advancement of knowledge through the production
of new knowledge, the few existing comparative studies are weak support. One comparative study of interest could be on the approaching
agreement of American and English library education; progress here
has been remarkable. Another comparative study could begin with
the eight countries about which a great deal has been written--from
ten to sixty-five articles on each in the past five years. Persons
who write in this area must be encouraged and must learn to appreci-
ate the international aspects of library education. International understanding provides a strong basis for continuing professional relations
under stress, whether natural or man-made, which adds stature to
librarianship and belies the weakness and vagueness often attributed
to this goal. Since benefits accrue to the profession as a whole,
this goal needs group support.

The preconditions for developing a greater interest in international library education must include a better international employment market. The international mobility of librarians is low, and
current labor restrictions outside the European Economic Community
are detrimental to its increase. The professional as a world citizen
expects in the future to "deal with cultural differences in the same
way that he now deals with individual differences. " He expects "a
heightened sense of supranational colleagueship. " Further, the profession may expect the "expanded knowledge to be helpful in improving practice and developing the underlying theory on which effective
practice must be based. "[39] Developmental growth among nations can

be advanced by the employment of overseas professionals if occupational environments permit them to make a contribution. The responding libraries in the Campbell survey placed those foreign-edu-
cated librarians whom they hired largely in regular positions, not
in non-professional, specialist, temporary, or trainee positions. [40]

The profession has attempted to establish the equivalencies
of academic credentials for fifty years. Only ten countries were
recognized in 1969 by employers in the USA and Canada as having
library education programs considered the equivalent of the American degree, Master of Library Science. [41] The status of librarians
is a concern of international library education. More students are
seeking full-time university level courses, and their career expectations are higher than before. Equivalencies and reciprocities in educational credentials and employment in libraries worldwide will
raise professional status as well as increase mobility, one characteristic of an international profession. Another characteristic, voluntary cooperation among library educators, has made and will continue to make international library education a reality.

NOTES

1. World Guide to Library Schools and Training Courses in Docu-
    mentation. Paris: Unesco, 1972; London: Bingley, 1972.
2. Joachim Wieder. "Twenty-sixth Session of the IFLA Council,
    Lund and Malmo, 7-11 August, 1960," Libri X, No. 3 (1960),
    p. 258.
3. George Chandler. Libraries in the Modern World. Oxford:
    Pergamon Press, 1965, p. 142.
4. Guido Biagi. "A Note on Italian Library Affairs," Library Jour-
    nal XXIX (December 1904), p. 59.
5. John D. Cowley. "The Development of Professional Training for
    Librarianship in Europe," [quoting conclusion reached by Dr.
    G. Henriot in his survey "La formation professionelle des
    bibliothécaires," Revue des Bibliothèques XXIX (1929), pp.
    121-154], Library Quarterly VII (April 1937), p. 173.
6. "From the LED President," American Library Association, Li-
    brary Education Division Newsletter No. 63 (October 1967),
    p. 2.
7. Guy A. Marco. "The Idea of an International Library School,"
    Library World LXXII (December 1970), pp. 191, 193.
8. Knud Larsen. "Comments on the Idea of an International Library
    School," Copenhagen, 35th General Council Meeting, Interna-
    tional Federation of Library Associations, August 25-30, 1969,
    p. 1-2.
9. Wilfred Saunders, January 6, 1976, Sheffield, England, letter.
10. "40th General Council Meeting, Washington, 18-23 November,
    1974," IFLA Journal I (February 1975), p. 127.
11. Harold Taylor. A University for the World: the United Nations
    Plan. Bloomington, Ind.: Phi Delta Kappa Education Founda-
    tion, 1975, p. 29.
12. Ibid., p. 30.

13. Michael Zweig. The Idea of a World University. Carbondale: Southern Illinois University Press, 1967, p. 7.
14. Marietta Daniels Shepard. "International Dimensions of United States Librarianship," American Library Association Bulletin LXII (June 1968), p. 706.
15. Frances Laverne Carroll. Feasibility Study for Incorporating a Year Abroad in the Library School Curriculum. Norman: University of Oklahoma, 1969.
16. Howard W. Winger. "Education for Area-studies Librarianship," Library Quarterly XXXV (October 1965), pp. 361-362.
17. Lewis F. Stieg. "American Librarians Abroad 1946-65," Library Quarterly XXXVIII (October 1968), p. 317.
18. Herbert Schur. Education and Training of Information Specialists for the 1970's. Paris: Organization for Economic Cooperation and Development, 1973, p. 16.
19. Nasser Sharify. "The Need for Change in Present Library Science Curricula," in: Library Education, An International Survey, ed. Larry Earl Bone. Urbana: University of Illinois Graduate School of Library Science, 1968, pp. 184-185.
20. John Roe. "Internationalism in British Library Schools," in: Proceedings, Gorebridge, Scotland, Library Association International and Comparative Librarianship Group Conference, June 28-July 1, 1974, p. 72.
21. John Dean. Planning Library Education Programmes, A Study of the Problems Involved in the Management and Operation of Library Schools in the Developing Countries. London: Andre Deutsch, 1972, p. 30.
22. Ibid., p. 14.
23. Carl M. White. "Acceleration of Library Development in Developing Countries," in: Advances in Librarianship, ed. Melvin J. Voigt. New York: Academic Press, 1970, p. 270.
24. Wilhelm Munthe. American Librarianship from a European Angle. Hamden, Conn.: Shoe String Press, 1939, p. 152.
25. Thomas J. Galvin, August 6, 1975, Pittsburgh, Pa., letter.
26. Ronald Staveley, July 3, 1975, London, England, letter.
27. Josefa Emilia Sabor. "International Co-operation in the Training of Librarians," Unesco Bulletin for Libraries XIX (November-December 1965), p. 296.
28. Larsen, op. cit., p. 2.
29. Roderick Cave, July 7, 1975, Kingston, Jamaica, letter.
30. Harold Lancour. "Introduction," Library Trends XII (October 1963), p. 122.
31. Dean, op. cit., p. 114.
32. H.-P. Geh. "Current Problems in Library Training with a Proposal for a Curriculum," Grenoble, 39th General Council Meeting, International Federation of Library Associations, August 26-September 1, 1973, p. 8.
33. Guy A. Marco. "International Standards for Library Schools," Oslo, 41st General Council Meeting, International Federation of Library Associations, August 9-16, 1975.
34. Havard-Williams, P. "Education for Library, Information and Archives Studies." Oslo: 41st General Council Meeting, International Federation of Library Associations, Aug. 9-16, 1975, p. 5.

164   Comparative/International

35. Douglas Foskett. "Survey of Training Programmes in Informa-
    tion and Library Science," Unesco Bulletin for Libraries
    XXIX (January-February 1975), p. 30.
36. Robert-Henri Bautier. "Twenty Years of Co-operation in Ar-
    chives Work," Unesco Bulletin for Libraries XIX (November-
    December 1965), p. 322.
37. Stieg, op. cit., p. 316.
38. Foskett, op. cit., p. 30.
39. Irvin T. Sanders. Professional Education for World Responsi-
    bility. New York: Education and World Affairs, 1968, pp.
    27-28.
40. Henry C. Campbell. "Employment of Foreign Trained Librari-
    ans in the U.S. and Canada, an Enquiry on Behalf of the
    LED Committee on Equivalencies and Reciprocity, Final Re-
    port." Detroit: Institute on International Library Manpower,
    Wayne State University, June 26-27, 1970, p. 6.
41. Ibid., p. 8.

SELECTED BIBLIOGRAPHY

Asheim, Lester. Librarianship in the Developing Countries. Ur-
    bana: University of Illinois Press, 1966.
Bautier, Robert-Henri. "Twenty Years of Co-operation in Archives
    Work," Unesco Bulletin for Libraries XIX (November-Decem-
    ber 1965), pp. 317-323.
Biagi, Guido. "A Note on Italian Library Affairs," Library Journal
    XXIX (December 1904), pp. 57-60.
Bone, Larry Earl, ed. Library Education, an International Survey.
    Urbana: University of Illinois Graduate School of Library
    Science, 1968.
Bonn, George S., ed. Library Education and Training in Developing
    Countries. Honolulu: East-West Center Press, 1966.
Bramley, George. World Trends in Library Education. London:
    Bingley, 1975; Hamden, Ct.: Shoe String Press, 1975.
Campbell, Henry C. "Employment of Foreign Trained Librarians in
    the U.S. and Canada, an Enquiry on Behalf of the LED Com-
    mittee on Equivalencies and Reciprocity, Final Report." De-
    troit: Institute on International Library Manpower, Wayne
    State University, June 26-27, 1970. (Mimeographed.)
Carnovsky, Leon. The Foreign Student in the American Library
    School. Washington, D.C.: U.S. Department of Health, Edu-
    cation, and Welfare, Office of Education, Bureau of Research,
    1971.
Carroll, Frances Laverne. Feasibility Study for Incorporating a
    Year Abroad in the Library Science Curriculum. Norman:
    University of Oklahoma, 1969.
Chandler, George. Libraries in the Modern World. Oxford: Perga-
    mon Press, 1965.
Cowley, John D. "The Development of Professional Training for Li-
    brarianship in Europe," Library Quarterly VII (April 1937),
    pp. 169-195.

Danton, J. Periam. Education for Librarianship. Paris: Unesco,
    1949.
Dean, John. Planning Library Education Programs, a Study of the
    Problems Involved in the Management and Operation of Li-
    brary Schools in the Developing Countries. London: Andre
    Deutsch, 1972.
Fang, Josephine R. and Songe, Alice H. International Guide to Li-
    brary, Archival, and Information Science Associations. New
    York: R. R. Bowker, 1976.
"40th General Council Meeting, Washington, 18-23 November, 1974,"
    IFLA Journal I (February 1975), pp. 119-137.
Foskett, Douglas. "Survey of Training Programmes in Information
    and Library Science," Unesco Bulletin for Libraries XXIX
    (January-February 1975), pp. 23-32.
"From the LED President." American Library Association, Library
    Education Division Newsletter No. 63 (October 1967), pp. 1-3.
Geh, H. -P. "Current Problems in Library Training with a Proposal
    for a Curriculum." Grenoble, 39th General Council Meeting,
    International Federation of Library Associations, August 25-
    30, 1973. (Mimeographed.)
Havard-Williams, Peter. "Education for Library, Information and
    Archives Studies." Oslo, 41st General Council Meeting, In-
    ternational Federation of Library Associations, August 9-16,
    1975. (Mimeographed.)
Lancaster, F. W. Guidelines for the Evaluation of Training Courses,
    Workshops, and Seminars in Scientific and Technical Informa-
    tion and Documentation. Paris: Unesco, 1975.
Larsen, Knud. "Comments on the Idea of an International Library
    School." Copenhagen, 35th General Council Meeting, Interna-
    tional Federation of Library Associations, August 25-30, 1969.
    (Mimeographed.)
McMullen, Haynes. "The Place of Research in Library Schools,"
    in: Library Education, an International Survey, ed. Larry
    Earl Bone. Urbana: University of Illinois Graduate School of
    Library Science, 1968, pp. 345-372.
Marco, Guy A. "The Idea of an International Library School," Li-
    brary World LXXII (December 1970), pp. 191, 193.
    . "International Standards for Library Schools." Oslo,
    41st General Council Meeting, International Federation of Li-
    brary Associations, August 9-16, 1975. (Mimeographed) Also
    in: IFLA Journal II (1976), pp. 209-223.
Munthe, Wilhelm. American Librarianship from a European Angle.
    Hamden, Ct.: Shoe String Press, Inc., 1939.
Phillips, Janet C., ed. Foreign Service Directory of American Librari-
    ans. Pittsburgh: University of Pittsburgh Book Center, 1967.
Roe, John. "Internationalism in British Library Schools," Proceed-
    ings, Gorebridge, Scotland, Library Association International
    and Comparative Librarianship Group Conference, June 28-
    July 1, 1974, pp. 68-74.
Sabor, Josefa Emilia. "International Co-operation in the Training of
    Librarians," Unesco Bulletin for Libraries XIX (November-
    December 1965), pp. 285-296.
    . Methods of Teaching Librarianship. Paris: Unesco, 1969.

Sanders, Irvin T.   Professional Education for World Responsibility.
     New York: Education and World Affairs, 1968.
Schur, Herbert.   Education and Training of Information Specialists
     for the 1970's.   Paris: Organization for Economic Co-opera-
     tion and Development, 1973.
Sharify, Nasser.   "The Need for Change in Present Library Science
     Curricula," in: Library Education, An International Survey,
     ed. Larry Earl Bone.   Urbana: University of Illinois Gradu-
     ate School of Library Science, 1968, pp. 171-196.
Shepard, Marietta Daniels.   "International Dimensions of United
     States Librarianship," American Library Association Bulletin
     LXII (June 1968), pp. 699-710.
Stieg, Lewis F.   "American Librarians Abroad 1946-65," Library
     Quarterly XXXVIII (October 1968), pp. 315-322.
Taylor, Harold.   A University for the World: the United Nations
     Plan.   Bloomington, Ind.: Phi Delta Kappa Education Founda-
     tion, 1975.
White, Carl M.   "Acceleration of Library Development in Developing
     Countries," in: Advances in Librarianship, ed. Melvin J.
     Voigt.   New York: Academic Press, 1970, pp. 241-285.
Wieder, Joachim.   "Twenty-sixth Session of the IFLA Council, Lund
     and Malmo, 7-11 August, 1960," Libri X, No. 3 (1960), pp.
     255-265.
Winger, Howard W.   "Education for Area-studies Librarianship,"
     Library Quarterly XXXV (October 1965), pp. 361-372.
World Guide to Library Schools and Training Courses in Documenta-
     tion.   Paris: Unesco, 1972; London: Bingley, 1972.
Zweig, Michael.   The Idea of a World University.   Carbondale:
     Southern Illinois University Press, 1967.

THE COMPARATIVE AND INTERNATIONAL LIBRARY SCIENCE
COURSE IN AMERICAN LIBRARY SCHOOLS

Martha Boaz

In the Spring of 1975 the author wrote to ask each one of the
62 graduate library schools accredited by the American Library Association for the outlines of their Comparative and International Library Science courses and for recent comprehensive school catalogs.
Fifty-six schools responded, those which had such courses and outlines. Certain schools noted their plans for adding content from
this field to future curricula. Much of the material that follows has
been summarized from this information.

Interest has been shown in this subject area by several library school-sponsored institutes: 1) The University of Chicago Institute on the International Aspects of Librarianship, 1953; 2) The
University of Pittsburgh Institute of International Comparative Librarianship, 1965; 3) The University of Illinois Institute on International Librarianship, 1966; and 4) The University of Oklahoma Institute on Internationalism in Education for Librarianship, 1969.[1,2,3,4]
In addition, the International Federation of Library Associations' Library Education Committee has sponsored public program meetings
at several conferences, the Library Association (UK) contains an active section discussing comparative and international library science
in all of its aspects, and the International Federation for Documentation has shown a strong interest in library education.

Individual scholars and library leaders have conducted studies
and promoted educational and research programs in Comparative and
International Library Science, also: J. Periam Danton, Professor,
School of Librarianship, University of California, Berkeley; Nasser
Sharify, Dean, Pratt Institute Graduate School of Library and Infor-
mation Science, Brooklyn; and John F. Harvey, Dean of Library
Services, Hofstra University, Hempstead, New York, to name but a
few in the United States; and Sir Frank Francis, retired Librarian,
British Museum, London, and Douglas J. Foskett, University of Lon-
don Institute of Education, in Great Britain.

As a formal course offering, Comparative and International
Library Science is of recent origin. Danton wrote about "the increased interest in the general subject of comparative librarianship
in recent years."[5] In the following statement he commented on library school programs:

In the first year, 1963, in which the programs of American

167

(and Canadian) library schools were broken down by fields
and specializations in the Journal of Education for Librarianship, five schools--California, Berkeley; California, Los
Angeles; Chicago; Columbia and Wisconsin--were listed as
offering work in comparative librarianship. The corresponding figure today is forty-five. [6]

Furthermore, the latter figure above was not completely indicative
of North American course coverage, for several schools had units
or materials which dealt with the area, although they did not list
full courses. [7]

Apparently, formal courses were taught in few other countries,
however. Bone listed no such course for Latin America but did note
plans to include a course in Comparative Library Science. [8] Nor did
Bone list such a course in continental Europe.

Schools in other countries giving some attention to the subject
included the Institut für Bibliothekswissenschaft und Wissenschaftliche
Information, Humboldt University, Berlin; the Royal School of Librarianship, Copenhagen; and the Institute of Librarianship, Ibadan
University, Nigeria. Danton pointed to the "Absence from this list
of the several strong library schools of West Germany, the Soviet
Union and the two strong schools of Czechoslovakia. "[9]

Laverne Carroll of the University of Oklahoma has provided
information concerning comparative and international library science
course work in the library schools of the Federal German Republic.
Kluth indicated that several of these schools--Hanover, Frankfort
and Berlin--provided material on libraries abroad inside other
courses. [10] Berlin covered library science in Denmark and Sweden
in certain of its courses. In other cases, an entire semester course
was offered on the libraries of other countries. Hamburg had such a
course, Göttingen had a course in public libraries in foreign countries, Cologne taught regular courses in this field, and offered seminars, study tours, and theses. Stuttgart provided a course of lectures on world library science and Bonn planned a greater emphasis
in this subject field in the future.

As far as could be determined, few, if any, of the library
schools of third world countries offered international or comparative
courses. Almost their entire library school curricula were borrowed
and adapted from other countries, and so were international in a
sense. Shores commented on their dependence on American and
British models. [11]

According to Simsova and MacKee, "The two countries where
comparative librarianship has been receiving attention for some time
are the United States of America and the U. S. S. R. "[12] These authors
noted that, "In the U. S. S. R. , comparative librarianship is not in the
syllabi of library schools. Instead, considerable research is being
carried out by the Lenin Library, which publishes a periodical called
Bibliotekovedenia ze rubeahom (Librarianship Abroad). "[13]

In a discussion of Comparative and International Library Science in Britain, Simsova and MacKee pointed out that this subject had been introduced into the post-graduate "and later into the two-year course syllabus of the Library Association and the higher degrees in librarianship at the University College, London."[14] This change occurred after D. J. Foskett's 1964 visit to the United States.[15] The Polytechnic of North London was the first British library school to teach the course, in January 1966. Since then, the subject has been introduced into the College of Librarianship, Wales[16] Other schools offering courses included Leeds Polytechnic and the University of Sheffield. Simsova pointed out that the instructors of these courses were meeting annually in the Comparative Librarianship Study Group to exchange information.[17] Comparative and International Library Science was included in many library school curricula but on an optional basis. The Library Association syllabi listed it as an optional subject. Students choosing it were required to produce two pieces of written work during the course. The course appealed to students with some overseas experience or students who wished to take a challenging course.

Roe collected information on internationalism in 1974 in British library schools.[18] He found a good deal of this kind of activity. Five schools had non-British teaching faculty members, and many schools had non-British students. In Wales, Ealing, Sheffield, Liverpool, London and North Polytechnic, students from abroad accounted for up to ten per cent of the student body. A separate course in international library science was present in ten schools. In a few other cases, curricula were said to have been to some extent internationalized. International library science courses allowed overseas students to study their own countries. Eight schools mentioned encouraging students to carry out international research work. Conferences on international themes had been organized by two schools. Certain faculty members were active in IFLA and other international association work. A number of papers were produced which related to international themes. While all schools collected some international library science material, no school had attempted to build a comprehensive collection. Of course, the international summer school at Aberystwyth was well known.

Course Objectives and Contents

Study and research in Comparative and International Library Science may be based on a set of theoretical principles but are more likely to be focused on practical objectives.[19] Among these, as Dorothy Collings pointed out, are the following:

> (1) To provide guidelines for a proposed new library program in one's own country or in a foreign country; (2) to contribute to the critical analysis and solution of widely found library problems, viewed in their respective contexts; (3) to stimulate and assist judicious consideration and possible adaptation of promising practices and solutions to

library problems from one area to another while guarding
against indiscriminate emulation; (4) to provide background
information for use in foreign library work assignments,
study visits, consultation and aid programs; (5) to facilitate the exchanges of library material or information particularly among different countries; (6) to strengthen scholarly content and practical relevance of library education
and training both for national and foreign students, through
the consideration of library development and problems in
differing cultural contexts; and (7) to contribute to the advancement of international understanding and more extensive and effective cooperation in library planning and development. [20]

Three major types of studies fall within the parameters of
Comparative and International Library Science: area studies, cross-
national or cross-cultural studies, and case studies.   Area studies
concentrate on a given country or area.   Cross-national or cross-
cultural studies deal with such factors as technical or functional library problems in two or more countries, or, with a particular type
of library situation or development in a particular country.

An overall statement of the purpose of study in Comparative
and International Library Science might be generalized as: To study
the international aspects of library science and to provide students
with knowledge and understanding of the objectives, values and poten-
tials of these library services.   Generally, the objectives and coverage of these courses are similar among the library schools.   Several
typical examples follow. [21]

Columbia University brought in research as a first objective,
when, in its course outline, it listed:

(1) To introduce the students to the concepts and methodology of comparative research; (2) to broaden the professional viewpoint and gain a better perspective of one's national
library system through comparative study of library organization and practice in other countries; and (3) to acquire
an understanding of international aspects of librarianship
and areas of international cooperation.

Columbia's course covers a brief history of comparative library science concepts, definitions, terminology, methodology and techniques
of comparative research, types of comparative studies and sources
of data.   In addition, Columbia takes up selected comparative topical
studies: national libraries, the library profession, legislation, planning, librarianship in developing countries, comparative studies by
type of library and in technical services, information networks and
other topics.   Among area studies, Columbia includes a unit on "general," then goes to individual continents.   The last unit of the outline
discusses the international aspects of library science.

The course outline of the State University of New York, Geneseo, lists as course objectives:

(1) To study available data concerning the library systems
and problems of selected countries; (2) to develop perspective on and better understanding of one's own national library system and problems; (3) to assist in the advancement of better international understanding and cooperation
in library development.

The course covers:

The development and present status of libraries and librarianship abroad in comparison with the United States;
international relations, emphasis upon the contemporary
status of library resources and services, activities of professional organizations and international agencies, world
literacy, publishing and distributing materials abroad, problems of national and international bibliography, national libraries, trends of librarianship in developing countries.

Indiana has similar objectives, according to its course outline.
It deals with books and libraries in Africa, Asia, Latin America,
Europe and the British Commonwealth, covering in these countries
historical as well as current topics for various types of libraries and
bibliographic control, documentation, library education, professional
associations and national planning, also. Indiana concludes with a
study of international library activities and worldwide programs such
as the International Federation of Library Associations, International
Federation of Documentation, UNESCO, and the international exchange
of publications.

The University of North Carolina's course, as described in
the 1975-76 Bulletin, covers "Library and information system characteristics in selected European and developing countries; world
trends and international cooperation in library organization and service." According to Professor Lester Asheim, "The emphasis is not
on a country by country description of library practice, but rather on
more general problems of international cooperation, exchange, and
the role of the American librarian and American library concepts on
the international scene. "22 Asheim goes on to say that the general
theme of the course is the phenomenon of culture shock and the need
for greater understanding and empathy for the ideas, ways of life and
practices of other peoples.

Some of the objectives of the international services course at
Pittsburgh, as listed in its outline, are: 1) to analyze the nature of
library, information and communication sciences; 2) to compare their
processes within the same country; 3) to formulate suggestions for
their improvement throughout the world; 4) to formulate principles of
comparative librarianship study based on generalizations in various
countries; 5) to enable United States and foreign students to understand activities of library, information and communication outside of
their own countries and to apply this understanding to their own country; 6) to give students from various countries opportunities to discuss experiences in these fields; 7) to provide background information about the library, information or communication professions in

a particular country or region of the world for librarians, information scientists, or communication specialists working there.

Pittsburgh identifies the factors relevant to library science
within a country. They include, in the course outline: historical
background, population, education, government, culture, economy,
geography, transportation and communication. A more specific "analysis of librarianship within a country" includes the historical background, the profession, librarians, professional associations, education, library literature, financial support, types of libraries, services, and future planning.

The objectives of the Rosary College course are "to provide
a survey and evaluation of international organizations serving libraries and librarianship; and to study library systems, library and
bibliographic services, library operations and library education in
selected areas or countries." The course consists of three parts:
international, European and Asian library science. An interesting
extension of the course in January 1975 was an optional tour to Japan, Hong Kong, Taiwan and Honolulu.

Kent State University has a course, "European Librarianship,"
which covers patterns of library services in a selected group of
European countries and presents, according to the course syllabus,
"International perspectives on such problems as library objectives,
urban services, finance, cooperation and library education." In the
1975 Winter quarter, Kent offered a seminar in "Latin American Librarianship," also.

The University of Chicago offers a course, "Development of
International Bibliographic Organization," which deals with the international evolution of systematic bibliography. Toronto describes its
course as "An introduction to the methodology of comparative research as it may apply to librarianship."

Oregon offers a seminar, "Libraries Abroad," with objectives
"to explore the state of the art of librarianship in various parts of
the world and to encourage critical examination of American library
theory and practice in the light of different conceptual and procedural
approaches abroad."[23]

Courses are offered in some schools under the title, "Comparative Librarianship," and in some under the title, "International
Librarianship." Others are offered under such titles as "Comparative and International Librarianship" or "International and Comparative Librarianship." Certain schools add an "Information Science" to
the end of the title. "International Library Services and Resources"
is the title at another school. In still other schools, these courses
are offered under a general seminar format without a distinctive title,
or units on the topic are offered within other courses.

Obviously, these courses are introductory and explanatory,
primarily instructional, rather than research-oriented. They attempt

to introduce the student to a survey of policies and practices abroad and to contrast the American with the overseas. Learning how to study the library status of an entire nation is stressed. Certain courses describe comparative research methodology for the student. Identifying patterns of library systems, development levels, state of bibliographic development, studying the work of international organizations, comparison of national philosophy, objectives and the influence thereon of socio-political and economic factors are commonly included.

An outline that might serve as a model for a comprehensive year-long course is found in Danton's The Dimensions of Comparative Librarianship. [24] The outline is comprehensive, thorough, carefully and logically arranged and well planned. Readers should consult the book for the complete outline. In addition, Sable and Deya provided a model introductory course. [25]

Advanced Courses

Advanced courses are needed in certain schools. Such courses could be offered in the selection and acquisition of foreign material; international bibliographical and reference sources; the cataloging, classification and organization of international documents; indexing and abstracting foreign library and information material; and administration of library services on an international cooperative basis. This list could be expanded. Almost every one of these course titles could be narrowed and made more specialized to fit a particular geographic area, such as the acquisition of Asian materials or the study of Latin American bibliographic and reference tools. A knowledge of the foreign languages involved in a particular country could be studied, also. Such courses are especially valuable to Americans and other persons who want to work in libraries abroad.[26]

In constructing a curriculum or major in this field, a separate course may be provided in comparative library science proper, in order to explore that difficult field thoroughly. Specialized courses by region of the world can be recommended, as well as a specialized course on the work of international organizations. The specialized bibliography of each continent can be useful. And finally, opportunity can be provided for a special problems course and for thesis research in comparative and international library science.

Several schools list more than one course. Pratt offers seven international library science courses. Among them are "Foreign Languages for Librarians and Information Specialists," "Documentary Services of International Organizations," "Comparative International Book Production," and "Planning Libraries and Information Centers in Developing Countries."

Hawaii offers several courses: "Technical Services for Far Eastern Collections," "International Publishing and Bibliography," "Administration of Libraries in Asia," "Asian Reference Sources," and a "Seminar in Library Development." According to the 1974-75 School bulletin, the latter course requires each student to "report on the state of development of library services in a particular country and to outline a program for library development to provide an optimum scheme for library services on all levels in that country." Hawaii has offered study tours to Asia and a specialized institute on the information industry in Asia, also. Historically, Drexel was the first accredited school to offer for credit a study tour of overseas libraries, in the Summer of 1964.

Pittsburgh offers four related courses: "Seminar in Comparative Librarianship," "Latin American Bibliography," "Asian Bibliography," and "Languages for the Library and Information Sciences." In another form, Carroll of Oklahoma proposes a way of providing additional work in the field. She suggests a year abroad as part of the curriculum. [27]

M. M. Jackson, Geneseo, lists his course values:

(1) Broadens professional viewpoint by assisting the understanding of library systems and problems of other countries; (2) Stimulates consideration of one's own national library system and problems in the light of ideas and practices in other countries; (3) Affords useful knowledge for possible foreign library service, study or visitation.

Educational objectives at Catholic University are:

Upon successful completion of the course, students are expected to (1) describe the library's effect on social change as well as the effects of social change on the library; (2) identify library theories as related to various foreign countries; (3) compare professional issues, problems, and solutions abroad with those in the United States, (4) describe the work of international associations, and (5) discuss the totality of librarianship as viewed through an international awareness.

An observation made by Norman Horrocks, Dalhousie, is appropriate here:

This is a course which should not only emphasize the comparative approach as an area worthy of serious study but should also be taught by those who have had experience in situations which call for some familiarity with comparative studies. An interesting course can be made at a descriptive level of international library activities but the comparative element makes it a more challenging and satisfying course. [28]

Richard Krzys hoped that international and comparative library science study would result in the involvement of

library phenomena in their intranational, cross national or
cross cultural contexts for the purpose of deepening library
science through explanation, prediction and control of library phenomena and for the ultimate purpose of improving
libraries through comparison of library practice variants
throughout the world. The total effect of library science
on society may be greatly assisted by planning and careful
study. Such courses should enable students to study, compare and analyze various approaches to library, communication and information sciences and to formulate plans and
programs to improve local, national and international bases.
And, such study should enable students to determine basic
principles, structures and philosophies of library systems
and to identify some of their problems through cross national, cross-cultural and cross-societal studies. [29]

Some Problems in Courses

Should the graduate library curriculum include a course or
two in comparative and international library science, or should the
entire curriculum be impregnated with internationalism, or both?
Probably most internationalists would recommend both and would suggest further that the latter exceeds the former in importance.   To
encourage the provinciality of teaching merely American or British
library science is unthinkable.   Yet, the presentation should not de-
part to an extreme degree from the library policies in effect locally
or else the students will not be satisfactorily prepared for work in
local libraries.   Theory needs an international presentation much
more than practice.   A considerable upgrading of qualifications is
required before the majority of library educators will be well prepared to impregnate their courses with the international approach.

Is a course in this field appropriate in a beginning-level curriculum?   Until they have a basic foundation of knowledge about libraries in their own country, students may have difficulty understanding overseas libraries.   Library school catalogs suggest that most of
these courses are offered as electives at the advanced master's or
doctor's level without specific prerequisites.   On the other hand, this
subject can be taught in the form of units within the introductory curriculum, in such courses as Introduction to Library Science and in
basic reference and cataloging courses.   Students can be given opportunities to use any overseas experience or knowledge they possess.
Still other critics have recommended both introductory and advanced
courses, particularly in the advanced certificate or doctoral curriculum.   While Foskett recommends a course at the advanced level,
Sable recommends both an introductory and an advanced course, and
Campbell recommends infusing the curriculum with internationalism. [30,31,32]

Another problem is the availability of qualified faculty members to teach these courses.   Those best qualified to teach should
have worked and taught in other countries.   Danton points out the
requirements for a qualified professor:

At the best, satisfactory teaching and especially research
call for some command of foreign languages and cultures;
a sound knowledge of library history and some particular
aspects of libraries and librarianship; the knowledge of research methodology in the social fields; and insight into
the intellectual, ideological and sociological forces which
have produced the world, and probably substantial foreign
travel. Very few librarians possess all of these desid-
erata. [33]

Is the comparative and international library science instructor
teaching internationalism or teaching a research method? Is the
course intended to emphasize the international approach to library
problems or the comparative research methodology? The answer for
most courses is that both subjects need to receive some attention.
Many courses give greater emphasis to one or the other, usually the
former, since the latter is only a small and specialized research
subject within the large field of international library science. Both
are important to an understanding of the entire field, however.

What is the value of interdisciplinary course work to the international library scientist? It is considerable, because certain
other subject fields have made more progress in internationalizing
their research than library science has, and their work can provide
useful models. In addition, the bibliographic and library development
of an overseas area cannot be understood without reference to its
political, economic, social and cultural development.

Yet another problem in the field relates to the papers which
students prepare for these courses. Many of them are merely descriptive, rather than analytic and comparative. Instructors mention the problem of getting more than mere description from student
papers. Suffice it to say, the comparative research method is difficult to apply and too much should not be expected of students who
are being introduced to this research methodology.

A continual problem is the lack of information on overseas
library systems. [34] Pittsburgh's large enrollment of international
students makes international and comparative study an area of special curricular and research emphasis and contributes to a solution
to this problem. "In connection with this," says Dean Thomas Galvin,

The School has developed an International Library Information Center which is directed by Richard Krzys and which
presently includes approximately 14,000 items in 33 languages. Its object is to act as a clearing house of data on
library development, documentation, book production, and
distribution with regard to both the United States and overseas resources and to serve as a training and research
center in the field of international librarianship. [35]

To some extent, this material is available for use by scholars

everywhere.   According to Aman, Pratt Institute maintains a Center
for International Librarianship Studies, also. [36]

Trends, Predictions and Recommendations

Interest in Comparative and International Library Science
course work is increasing, as is shown by the increase in the number of such courses offered.   Trends seem to suggest that education
is likely to become more internationalized in spite of us; why should
it not become so because of us?

In a pioneering paper delivered at the 1966 Illinois Institute
on International Library Education, Sharify urged more internationalism in professional schools generally, and suggested specific course
areas for library schools. [37]   His program to internationalize the library school led to an eventual required course in Comparative and
International Library Science and to a sixth-year curriculum in this
field.

In a paper presented at the 1972 IFLA meeting in Budapest,
Sharify predicted that, "As technology expands even further in the
future, interest in international information will continue to grow
rapidly."[38]   And he pointed out later, "Certain universities have already realized that they cannot remain great unless all relevant aspects of their curricula are internationally oriented."   He continued:
"It is quite possible that by the year 2000 most important universities will have completely internationalized their curricula, and it is
very unlikely that by the end of the twenty-first century any university could still call itself a university without teaching and producing
a body of international knowledge."

In this vein, Carroll presented a method of evaluating the extent to which the curriculum had been internationalized. [39]

This author recommends that:

1. Courses be included in library school curricula on Comparative and International Library Science in order to
   broaden the curriculum and reflect the remainder of world
   library science.
2. Programs of research dealing with such courses and with
   general plans for international library science be instituted
   in educational curricula, since research should accompany
   all curricular programs.
3. Such courses and programs be supported and endorsed by
   professional organizations and associations to give them
   greater attention and respect.
4. Financing for promotion and support be sought from local,
   national and international sources.

NOTES

1. Leon Carnovsky, ed. International Aspects of Librarianship. Chicago: University of Chicago Press, 1954.
2. Nasser Sharify and Roland R. Piggford. "First Institute on International Comparative Librarianship," Pennsylvania Library Association Bulletin XXI (November 1965), pp. 73-80.
3. Larry Earl Bone, ed. Library Education: An International Survey. Champaign: University of Illinois, Graduate School of Library Science, 1968.
4. H. C. Campbell. "Internationalism in U.S. Library School Curricula," International Library Review II (April 1970), pp. 183-6.
5. J. Periam Danton. The Dimensions of Comparative Librarianship. Chicago: American Library Association, 1973, p. 4.
6. Ibid., p. 4.
7. Beverly Brewster. "International Library School Programs," Journal of Education for Librarianship IX (Fall 1968), pp. 138-43.
8. Bone, op. cit., p. 27.
9. Danton, op. cit., p. 95.
10. Kluth, R. "Vergleichende Bibliothekswissenschaft in der Bundesrepublik Deutschland." Grenoble, 39th General Council Meeting, International Federation of Library Associations, August 25-30, 1973. (Mimeographed.)
11. Louis Shores, ed. "Comparative Library Education: Homework for a National Plan," Journal of Education for Librarianship VI (Spring 1966), pp. 231-317.
12. Silva Simsova and Monique MacKee. A Handbook of Comparative Librarianship. 2nd ed. Hamden, Conn.: Shoe String Press, 1975, p. 61.
13. Ibid., p. 62.
14. Ibid., p. 62.
15. D. J. Foskett. "Comparative Librarianship," in: Progress in Library Science 1965. Washington: Butterworths, 1965, pp. 142-5.
16. Simsova and MacKee, op. cit., p. 62.
17. Ibid., pp. 62, 71.
18. Roe, John. "Internationalism in British Library Schools," Proceedings, Library Association, International and Comparative Librarianship Group, Gorebridge, Scotland, Conference, June 28-July 1, 1974, pp. 68-74.
19. Silva Simsova. "Comparative Librarianship as an Academic Subject," Journal of Librarianship VI (April 1974), pp. 115-25.
20. Dorothy G. Collings. "Comparative Librarianship," in: Encyclopedia of Library and Information Science. New York: Marcel Dekker, 1971, Volume V, pp. 493-4.
21. Footnotes are not used hereafter for excerpts from course outlines and bulletins from the various library schools. Credit is given by using the name of the school. When excerpts are directly quoted, they are enclosed in quotation marks. This is done to avoid repetitious notes. The author has obtained permission from these schools to quote from their bulletins

and course outlines.
22. Excerpt from a letter from Lester Asheim to the author, April
    7, 1975.
23. Excerpt from a note from P. D. Morrison to the author, April
    19, 1975.
24. Danton, op. cit., pp. 157-66.
25. Martin A. Sable and Lourdes Deya. "Outline of an Introductory
    Course in International and Comparative Librarianship," Inter-
    national Library Review II (April 1970), pp. 187-92.
26. Howard Winger. "Education for Area Studies," Library Quarter-
    ly XXXI (October 1965), pp. 361-72.
27. Frances Laverne Carroll. "International Education for Librari-
    anship," International Library Review II (January 1970), pp.
    19-39.
28. Excerpt from a letter from Norman Horrocks to the author,
    April 14, 1975.
29. Richard Krzys. "International and Comparative Study in Librari-
    anship, Research Methodology," in: Encyclopedia of Library
    and Information Science. New York: Marcel Dekker, 1971,
    Volume XII, pp. 327-330.
30. D. J. Foskett, op. cit., p. 144.
31. Sable and Deya, op. cit., pp. 187-92.
32. H. C. Campbell, op. cit., p. 184.
33. Danton, op. cit., p. 102.
34. The following title attempts to remedy this situation, in part:
    Jefferson, George. Public Library Administration: An Ex-
    amination Guidebook. Hamden, Conn.: Archon Books, 1969,
    pp. 28-44.
35. Excerpt from a letter written by Thomas J. Galvin to the author,
    April 15, 1975.
36. M. M. Aman. "Pratt Institute Center for International Librari-
    anship Studies," International Library Review I (October 1969),
    pp. 469-86.
37. Nasser Sharify. "The Need for Change in Present Library Sci-
    ence Curricula," in: Larry Bone, ed. Library Education:
    An International Survey. Champaign: University of Illinois,
    Graduate School of Library Science, 1968, pp. 171-96.
38. Nasser Sharify. "Beyond the National Frontiers; The Interna-
    tional Dimension of Changing Library Education for a Chang-
    ing World." Paper presented to the Committee on Library
    Education at the General Council Meeting of the International
    Federation of Library Associations, August 30, 1972, at Buda-
    pest. (Mimeographed.)
39. Frances Laverne Carroll. "Internationalism in Education for
    Librarianship," International Library Review IV (January
    1972), pp. 103-26.

BIBLIOGRAPHY

Asheim, Lester. Librarianship in Developing Countries. Urbana:
    University of Illinois Press, 1966.

Bone, Larry Earl, ed. Library Education: An International Survey.
    Champaign: University of Illinois, Graduate School of Library
    Science, 1968.
Bowles, Frank. "American Responsibilities in International Educa-
    tion," The Educational Record XLV (Winter 1964), pp. 19-26.
Collings, Dorothy G. "Comparative Librarianship," in: Encyclo-
    pedia of Library and Information Science. New York: Marcel
    Dekker, 1971, Volume V, pp. 492-502.
Danton, J. Periam. The Dimensions of Comparative Librarianship.
    Chicago: American Library Association, 1973.
Foskett, J. Douglas. Science, Humanism and Libraries. London:
    Crosby, Lockwood, 1964.
Krzys, Richard. "International and Comparative Study in Librarian-
    ship, Research Methodology," in: Encyclopedia of Library
    and Information Science. New York: Marcel Dekker, 1971,
    Volume XII, p. 330.
Parker, J. Stephen. "International Librarianship--A Reconnais-
    sance," Journal of Librarianship VI (October 1974), pp. 221-
    31.
Sharify, Nasser. "Beyond the National Frontiers: The International
    Dimension of Changing Library Education for a Changing
    World." Paper presented to the Committee on Library Edu-
    cation at the General Council Meeting of The International
    Federation of Library Associations, August 30, 1972, at Buda-
    pest. (Mimeographed.)
Shores, Louis. "Why Comparative Librarianship?" Wilson Library
    Bulletin XLI (October 1966), pp. 200-206.
Simsova, Silva and MacKee, Monique. A Handbook of Comparative
    Librarianship. 2d ed. Hamden, Conn.: Shoe String Press,
    1975.

INFORMATION SCIENCE

B. C. Vickery and A. G. Brown

Library service is essentially a practice, aiming to make adequate provision of documents and their contents to the members of a particular community. The pattern of each service is shaped by the needs of its community and the social environment in which it is operating. Variation between services--whether within an individual country or internationally--is therefore the norm. Comparative and international studies of this variety are therefore a valuable field of work, distinguishable from the study of common problems or of the practice of a particular library system.

Can the same be said of "information science"? The answer will depend upon the meaning we give to "information science," since there is no agreement as to the scope of this phrase. We find it helpful in the first place to distinguish between "information science" and "information studies." We think of the latter as studies of information service, which is one aspect of the functions performed by the library/information profession. As such, it is as dependent on community needs and social environment as any other aspect of library service. Comparative and international studies of information service are therefore fully justified, even though not readily distinguished from studies of special library service: any special library worthy of the name is also concerned with information service to its clients. There are, of course, information services not directly linked to a library, and they will be considered below.

If we exclude studies of information service from our remit, what is the scope of "information science"? We believe that four areas of meaning can be identified:

1) The particular problems of the communication of information in the sciences and their applications (this is better called "science information"). Study of this is concerned with the nature and methods of the sciences, pure and applied; communication activities within scientific and technical communities; forms of publication; the nature of information service in this field (here is the link with "information studies"); national and international systems of scientific and technical information transfer.

2) The use of technology--particularly computers and telecommunications--in information handling (sometimes called "information technology"). Study of this covers data

181

processing and its applications to library and information systems; computer communications and networks.

3) The application of scientific method to practical library
and information activities (this might be called "information
systems science"). Study of this includes the nature of systems; levels of library and information system; analysis, design and evaluation; systems as organizations; planning and
forecasting.

4) The scientific study of the communication of information
in society (this is the true "science" of information). Study
of this explores research method; the nature of a science of
information; the methodologies applicable; types of investigation in information science; statistical techniques.

All four areas of meaning must be included within the scope
of information science. Now it is true that activities in these areas
can sometimes have "local" features that may lend themselves to
comparative study, but, by and large, science--in all the meanings
used above--is itself international. It is precisely concerned with
principles that transcend local and national boundaries. Science uses
the comparative method as a matter of routine in order to isolate
generalities. It is difficult to identify "comparative studies" as a
special area of information science. We would certainly not advo-
cate setting up a course on "comparative and international information science" as though it were a separately definable area of study.

Nevertheless, for the purpose of this book it is possible to
pick out certain studies within information science that are relevant
to these themes. We identify them as follows:

1) Comparison of the communication patterns of scientists and
   technologists in different countries and cultures.
2) Studies of the transfer of science/technology information between countries or cultures.
3) Comparison of the national STI systems.
4) International STI systems and networks.
5) The activities of international STI organizations.
6) Studies of international cooperation in any aspect of information science.
7) International conferences on information science.
8) Comparison of national schools of thought in information science.

Examples of activities within these themes will be given below. We
have made no attempt to be comprehensive, but have sampled the
literature to illustrate the kinds of studies undertaken in recent years.

An apt illustration of the international character of information
science is provided by the report prepared by Schur on education and
training of information specialists for the 1970s. This was based on
an international review of papers, reports and curricula, and dis-

cussions with a hundred educators and practitioners in France, the Federal Republic of Germany, the Netherlands, Sweden, the United Kingdom and the USA. Again, a review of "informatics" by Foskett cites Soviet, American, British, Israeli, French, Dutch and Czech contributions.

Communication Patterns

The study of information use and users in science and technology has been extensive. For some years, studies have been regularly reported in the Annual Review of Information Science and Technology. A valuable general account of communication in science has recently been published by Meadows, and Kochen's book on information retrieval also contains relevant material.

However, most studies concentrate on a particular community, and rarely cover more than one country. Almost the only investigation deliberately undertaken in a comparative mode was the study of physicists' requirements in current awareness, carried out by Slater and Keenan on behalf of the American Institute of Physics and the U.K. Institution of Electrical Engineers. This study directed closely comparable inquiries to physicists in the two countries.

A more recent example of a survey that drew respondents from a number of countries is the investigation by Gralewska-Vickery and Roscoe of the information needs of earth science engineers. Scientists and technologists from a dozen countries were interviewed, and postal questionnaires analyzed, to build up a picture of communication patterns in a variety of environments.

Apart from studies of this kind, international comparison can only be made by looking at roughly comparable investigations in different countries. The significant word here is "roughly," since differences in research approach, methodology, terminology, and analytical categories make valid comparisons extremely difficult. Moreover, few adequate studies of scientific or technical communication have been carried out in countries that most need comparative insights--namely, countries of the developing world. Consultancy visits to such countries are rarely able to include a proper survey of user information needs.

The study of the communication patterns of social scientists is, in all respects, less developed than that of natural scientists and technologists. A very useful survey of relevant studies is provided in the monograph by Brittain, and more recently, the contribution by Martyn to volume 9 of the Annual Review of Information Science and Technology (1974) is indicative of general trends in this area.

In that area of study centering upon the user/producer of information, little significant attention was devoted specifically to the social sciences before the late 1960s. An important exception is that series of studies carried out by the American Psychological

Association which commenced in 1961 and which is usefully surveyed
by Garvey and Griffith.   This large and detailed project, however,
concentrated upon the existing information system in one discipline
and upon the flow of information between persons in that system.
Moreover, concentration was inevitably upon psychologists working
in the USA.

It was the very absence of data relating to the social sciences
that helped to instigate the Investigation of Information Requirements
in the Social Sciences (INFROSS), a research project conducted in the
UK between 1968 and 1970, and this was designed to cover the whole
of the social sciences and to provide a broad survey of information
requirements in these disciplines.   Much useful data was obtained,
particularly that relating to the use of formal and informal channels
of communication by different groups of users in different disciplines
and contexts of work, but it was essentially a national survey relating to the situation in the UK (see reports from Bath University Library).

Comparative studies as between different countries and cultures are undeveloped.   As in science and technology, certain studies
may yield data of a comparative nature even though the study itself
is not essentially comparative in conception.   This is true, for example, in the results of the UK DISISS project (Design of Information
Systems in the Social Sciences, reported by Line and Roberts), a
large-scale bibliometrical study of the literature of the social sciences.   Data on the structure, growth and size of this literature are
in certain cases comparable on a national basis, e.g., the publication of social science serials and monographs by country.

Skelton, in her paper on the comparison of scientists and social scientists as information users, points out the need for attention
to the conscious use of methodologies which facilitate the comparison
of the results of relevant studies.   In this particular case, comparison was between the results of the INFROSS project and those of
thirteen science "user studies" previously conducted.   In the still
relatively untapped field of the social sciences per se, and to a far
greater extent, of course, in the humanities, the opportunity to devote attention to the methodology and conceptual nature of studies in
order to produce valid comparisons of communication patterns should
not be foregone.

Information Transfer Between Countries

The study of the transfer of information in the context of the
utilization of information is an integral part of the study of communication patterns.   Any attempt to investigate patterns of communication must inevitably involve data on the transfer of information
through the existing formal and informal channels which make communication possible.

Although variations occur between disciplines, and between

specializations within disciplines, the essential character of science is international rather than national or local. Despite the existence of political barriers, one anticipates that the information transfer within such disciplines is equally international, potentially ignoring both national and cultural boundaries. Consequently a study involving information transfer in the sciences, even though it centered on the system in a single country within a single discipline, would be likely to involve information transfer on an international scale. In this area we are not so dependent on the existence of "international" studies to comprehend an international phenomenon as we are on comparative studies to comprehend a comparative phenomenon. Thus, most of the studies which do have something of relevance to say about the international transfer of information have not taken this as the central theme of their investigation. It is much more likely to occur as one among several themes.

For example, traditional elements in citation studies are breakdowns of citations by language and/or by country. Such analyses help to give some indication of the degree to which information emanating from countries other than that of the citing author is utilized. We may give a few examples. Nalimov and Mulchenko, in their book on "scientometry," report a study showing levels of inter-citation between Soviet, German, U.S., French and other authors in a number of physicochemical subjects. It is clear that writers in English are far more confined to that language in their citations than are those who write in other languages. Broadus, in his survey of citation studies relating to the social sciences, also reveals a uniformly low level of use by English-speaking social scientists of foreign language sources. This was true of studies conducted both in the USA and in the UK. This sort of finding tends to raise more questions relating to the international and intercultural transfer of information than it does to provide answers.

Moreover, data derived from citation studies, such as the ones reviewed by Broadus or the later DISISS project, are of relevance only to the use of formal channels of communication. When considering the international transfer of information, the use made of informal channels is potentially of considerable significance. Study of informal networks is of relatively recent origin and it is doubtless more difficult to arrive at viable data on the way in which research workers use informal channels than on the way they use formal channels. Much significant work on the informal system, e.g., Price or Menzel, stems from the sciences rather than the social sciences. Attention to this aspect of the social sciences has not, however, been lacking, e.g., the American Psychological Association studies of the 1960s and the INFROSS survey of the early 1970s. Sufficient is now known to accept the importance of such channels and their implications for the total system of information transfer.

A significant element in the informal system is the "invisible college," a group of scientists, linked only by common interests, who exchange information largely through the medium of personal contact. Such groups may, of course, be composed of individuals drawn from

a single country but it is likely, particularly if one considers the
more elite colleges, that they will be international in membership.
Zaltman has recently investigated just such an elite group of high
energy physicists and its functioning as an informal channel for the
international transfer of information. The existence of such groups
has obvious implications not only for the functioning of informal channels but also for the use made of formal channels; as Zaltman points
out, this is an area which merits further research.

An important area of investigation is the study of the transfer
of technological information, well surveyed by Douds. Studies of
technical innovations within UK industry were reported by Langrish.
Of 158 key ideas leading to innovations, 53 had been obtained from
industrial, government or academic sources outside the UK. The
same author looked at a series of review articles written by UK industrial chemists, and found that half the papers cited came from
outside the UK. These are notable examples of international technology transfer.

National Information Systems

There have been many studies of the scientific and technical
information system of a single country--the best-known recent example being the SATCOM report of the U.S. National Academy of Sci-
ences/National Academy of Engineering (1969). There are relatively
few instances of studies comparing the systems of different countries.
Going beyond information to science policy itself, there have been a
series of national reviews prepared under the auspices of the Organisation for Economic Co-operation and Development--e.g., on national
science policy in the US (1968), USSR (1969), or Spain (1971). These
have laid the basis for some comparative studies, e.g., a comparison of the research systems in France, Germany, UK, by Salomon
and others. Against the same background, Rozsa has written a general analysis of scientific information and society.

Studies of the world output of scientific information, analyzed
by language or country of publication, permit international comparisons to be made. Examples of this are the article by de Solla Price
on "measuring the size of science," or Barr's estimate of the number of currently available scientific and technical periodicals. Nalimov and Mulchenko have summarized a number of studies of this
kind. An example in a single subject field is the analysis of world
agricultural documentation services by Boyle and Buntrock.

The experience of national science documentation centres was
drawn upon by an FID group under the direction of Schütz, who drew
up a manual for Unesco on the function and organization of a national
documentation center in a developing country.

International comparisons of specific information services
within different countries are not often encountered, but review papers sometimes provide material of this kind--for example, Leggate's

study of computer-based current awareness services. In an endeavor to establish costs for computer information services, Vickers visited and reported on 18 centers in the U.S. and in European countries. Earlier examples of reviews crossing national boundaries are de Grolier's study of general categories applicable to classification and coding; Coyaud's linguistic analysis of retrieval languages; and Robertson's review of retrieval test measures. On a more practical level, Haringsma has reported on a survey of information handling practices in industrial research and development. This covered 65 firms in the main European countries and is therefore a useful comparative study.

International Information Organizations and International Cooperation in Information Science

The actual and potential importance of international scientific and technical information organizations in the present context is obvious. The existence, growth and functions of such organizations are international phenomena of relevance to information science in themselves. Moreover, if one were to pursue any of the themes referred to in this article in any depth--comparative studies, national information systems, the international transfer of information, etc. -- one would almost inevitably encounter the impact of international organizations in some capacity. Their work pervades all international and comparative aspects of information science. Here we have chosen to exemplify such organizations and their work by reference to the theme of international cooperation in information science. International scientific and technical information organizations are prolific and proliferating and they are diverse in nature. Often the very existence of such an organization depends on international cooperation to some degree; moreover, international cooperation itself can take many different forms. Consequently, we stress once again that this paper is highly selective, serving only to indicate the extent of a pertinent field.

No matter how selective, no survey could justify a failing to grant due prominence to the work of Unesco. For over twenty-five years Unesco has played a leading role in developing international cooperation in scientific and technical information matters. As far back as 1949, Unesco convened an international conference on science abstracting, where the subjects discussed went far beyond the scope of the title. As a direct result, in 1952 the International Council of Scientific Unions (ICSU) set up an Abstracting Board, which in time established uniform policies and procedures, in several disciplines and countries, for the preparation of abstracts, the exchange of article proofs, and so on. A further international survey of abstracting was prepared for the United Nations Economic and Social Council in 1962.

Through the technical assistance program of the United Nations, Unesco has contributed experts, fellowships, publications and equipment for the establishment of science documentation centers in developing countries. During 1974, for example, the following were organized:

> Seminar for industrial information officers from Latin America (Moscow)
> Seminar on computerization techniques (Paris)
> Seminars on information for planning and decision-making (3 African cities)
> Seminar on the interactive library (Stockholm)
> European colloquium on information systems in education (Prague)
> Group on systems of techno-economic information (Paris).

In 1967, ICSU and Unesco came together on a joint project to study the feasibility of a world scientific information system, and the study report was published by Unesco in 1971 under the title of UNISIST. All Unesco conceptual and operational activities related to scientific and technological information are now concentrated in the UNISIST program.

A selection of the work carried out in 1975 and proposed for 1976 serves to illustrate the activities of the UNISIST program. As in previous years, these activities can be grouped into three broad areas:

> 1) Conceptual (studies and information policy proposals). During 1975 there was active UNISIST participation in feasibility studies for an International Development Information System (DEVSIS), an International Information System for Architecture (ARKISYST), and a World Information System on Informatics (WISI).

> 2) Normative (development of guidelines and recommendations). In this area, UNISIST activity is characteristically in close cooperation with other important international organizations, e.g., the International Federation of Library Associations (IFLA) and the International Federation for Documentation (FID). The concept and methodology for the UNISIST Manual for Information Handling Procedures was defined in 1975. Guidelines under preparation in 1976 include those on the development of multi-lingual thesauri and the training of managers of information systems and services.

> 3) Operational (training courses, workshops, technical assistance to Member States). Among the international training courses held in 1975 were:
> a course for managers of information systems and services in Latin America (Mexico);
> a nine-month postgraduate course on the training of specialists in scientific information and documentation (Grenoble and Paris).
> During 1976 this training program continued with, for example:

an international summer school on modern information systems (Paris), and
an international seminar on indexing (Poland).

As an indication of the increasingly important role of the UNISIST program in the sphere of international cooperation in scientific and technological information, we may note that several relevant United Nations Development Programme (UNDP) projects have been transferred to UNISIST, for example:

Water and power information system (India)
National scientific and technical documentation center (Senegal)
Automated center for scientific and technical information (Bulgaria).

The future should see a continuing expansion of the UNISIST program. In their initial conception the UNISIST proposals were aimed at the natural sciences and their associated technologies. Already UNISIST is being extended to the social sciences and ultimately it will include other areas of knowledge. The first important stage towards the incorporation of the social sciences was the Unesco-sponsored meeting of experts held at Valescure, France in 1974. In broad terms this meeting considered the characteristic needs of the social sciences and the extent to which they could be incorporated into the UNISIST proposals. A final report of this meeting was published by Unesco in 1974.

Apart from this top-level sponsoring of international cooperation, there are many cases of individual international organizations evidencing cooperation within particular subject fields, within particular activities, and to differing degrees of internationalism. For example, Mongar has described the activities of the International Road Research Documentation network, a cooperative system of some twenty centers throughout Europe and North America, set up in 1965 by OECD. The centers each select, abstract and index current work on road research, and exchange records in standardized magnetic tape format. Delbos and Gravestein similarly describe a European network for geological documentation: in this case each center contributes worksheets for keyboarding in Paris.

Another international organization founded under the auspices of OECD (1961) is the European Translations Centre (ETC), which has its Central Bureau at Delft and national centers or cooperating organizations in a number of countries throughout the world. The aim of the ETC is to coordinate the individual policies of member countries on the following points:

1) The integration of the scientific and technical knowledge of Eastern European and Asiatic countries into the total knowledge of western countries.
2) The exchange of knowledge by means of translation.
3) The prevention of duplication of work in this field.

The national centers and cooperating organizations take responsibility for the collection and notification of translations in their
own countries and send them to Delft. The Central Bureau verifies
the bibliographic descriptions and publishes a monthly classified list
with journal titles, author and keyword indexes.

A more parochial example of international cooperation within
a single discipline is provided by the Latin American Center for
Physics (CLAF). The CLAF headquarters in Rio de Janeiro maintains a library and provides an information service for member countries. The organization is instrumental in promoting cooperation in
physics documentation through publication and in the arranging of
meetings and conferences throughout Latin America.

Before leaving the consideration of international cooperation
we should remember that this is not coterminous with the work of
international organizations. Still in Brazil, but this time in the field
of education in information science, we have the example of the
M. Sc. Information Science program conducted at the Brazilian Institute of Bibliography and Documentation (IBBD), Rio de Janeiro. This
course was started in 1971 and is open to students from all parts of
Latin America in the absence of any directly comparable course elsewhere in the continent. Between 1971 and 1975 the course was conducted largely by visiting lecturers from the USA and the UK and was
partially funded by, among other agencies, the UK government,
Unesco and the Leverhulme Trust.

Yet another form of international cooperation was the planning
of a science and technology center for Iran, as part of the consultancy undertaken for the proposed Pahlavi National Library in 1975/
76. One international team led by Martha Williams prepared a detailed specification of the functions, procedures, organization and
computer back-up for a modern information center to serve Iranian
scientists and technologists (report not yet available).

International cooperation is thus an intrinsic element in information science in all spheres and at all levels, and the activities of
international organizations are obviously of vital importance in stimulating and facilitating this cooperation. As information science continues to develop, so also will international cooperation, for, as we
have stressed elsewhere, information science, both in its theoretical
base and its practical applications, is essentially international in
character.

International Systems and Networks

International cooperation in preparing abstracts--referred to
earlier--was a first step towards the development of an international
system or network in science information. A more formally organized cooperative system was initiated in 1968 by the International
Atomic Energy Agency, which commissioned a study on an international nuclear information system, subsequently realized in 1971 as

INIS. In this system (described, for example, by Pelzer) a number
of national centers collect relevant documents in their countries, index them and record their details (either on worksheets, paper tape
or magnetic tape). The records are dispatched to Vienna for input
to the computerized system, and from this a monthly publication,
Atomindex, is produced. Also sent to Vienna are abstracts in English, French, Russian or Spanish, and microfiche copies of them
can also be delivered as output to users. The data base on magnetic
tape can be supplied to those who wish to process it for SDI or retrospective search.

A few years later, a similar development was initiated by the
Food and Agriculture Organisation in Rome, leading to the establish-
ing in 1975 of its AGRIS system (described by East and Martinelli).
This also receives input from national centers, publishes a bulletin,
Agrindex, and makes its magnetic tape data base available. The
facilities and computer programs of the INIS system are employed.
A third international system is planned--DEVSIS, an information sys-
tem for development science.

The international aspect of these systems lies particularly in
their cooperative input, though their products are of course available
to the world. Internationally organized output--in the form of a network for on-line access to a central data base--was established in
1969 by the European Space Agency. Its Space Documentation Service (at first based in Darmstadt, now in Frascati) holds a series of
data bases, mainly of US origin, which can be accessed via terminals using dedicated lines. Limited dial-up facilities are now becoming available (studies of the system are provided by Martin and by
Isotta).

A substantial development of networking in Europe is outlined
by Rolling. The planned EURONET, using Post Office telecommunications, will, by 1979, link major centers in the nine countries of
the European community, to give on-line access to a wide range of
data bases. At present, dial-up access in Europe is basically limited to the use of Tymshare to gain entry to the DIALOG and ORBIT
systems in California, and to MEDLINE, but increasing use is being
made of these facilities (see a comparative study by Wilmot).

International Conferences

Because information science--in its various connotations--is
a new and developing area, it has given rise to a number of conferences of international scope, and their proceedings are a most important source of material for the study of the subject. Two classi-
cal early conferences are still a rich mine for investigators: the
Royal Society Scientific Information Conference of 1948, and the International Conference on Scientific Information, Washington, 1958.

Next to be mentioned is the conference on mechanized information processing, organized in 1967 jointly by the International

Federation for Documentation (FID) and the International Federation
for Information Processing (IFIP), the proceedings being edited by
Samuelson. After introductory reviews by Pietsch, Vickery and
Berul, the conference considered a variety of papers on file organization and search strategy, the economics of mechanized systems,
computer-aided publications, and on-line systems.

The year 1967 also saw the first International Conference on
Mechanized Information Storage and Retrieval Systems, held at the
Cranfield Institute of Technology in England. Five such conferences
have now been held, attended by active information scientists from
many countries. The latest (in 1975) included papers from the UK,
US, USSR, Norway, Belgium, Canada, Egypt, Czechoslovakia, Japan,
Netherlands and Switzerland. Proceedings are not separately pub-
lished, though individual papers find their ways into journals.

The FID has published a series of collections of more theoretical papers, the third of which was based on a Moscow conference.
The first collection, on Theoretical Problems of Informatics, appeared in 1968; the second, on Problems of Information Science, in
1972, and the third in 1975.

Meanwhile, NATO has sponsored two advanced study institutes
in information science, held in Pennsylvania, 1972, and in Wales,
1973. The proceedings have been edited by Debons. The first included papers on the nature of information, information technology,
social and professional impacts of information, and concluded with
an overview by Licklider. The second added sessions on the nature
of a science of information, information systems, and the use of information.

The Commission of the European Community has been associated with two congresses on documentation systems and networks,
held in Luxembourg in 1973 and 1975. The proceedings of the first
are available from the Commission, the second awaits publication.
The emphasis has been on the design and evaluation of computerized
information systems. The same is true of a symposium on the interconnection and compatibility of information systems, organized by the
International Atomic Energy Agency in Bulgaria in 1974; and of a
seminar on the interactive library held in Stockholm, 1974, whose
proceedings have been edited by Schwartz.

More wide-ranging overviews of information science are to be
found in the European conferences on research into information management (EURIM), organized by Aslib at Paris in 1974 and Amsterdam in 1976. The proceedings of the first have been edited by Batten. The second awaits publication, but its range can be indicated
by the session titles: influence and expectations of research in the
information field; research carried out by permanent research units;
bibliometrics; economic problems of information; cooperative systems
and networks; indexing languages; machine systems; interlingual problems; user studies; and dissemination of research results.

One last item to be mentioned is an international forum on the theoretical basis of information science, initiated by Brookes and held at University College, London in 1975. This concentrated on the phenomena of interest to information science, the kind of science needed to tackle its problems, the formalisms to be used, and implications for research and teaching.

International Character of Information Science

In the science of information there are many individual theoretical approaches. It begins to be possible to distinguish "schools of thought," or at any rate to recognize common ways of thinking. Wersig and Neveling have recently reviewed information science from this aspect. It may be that researchers within a particular country or culture share a common viewpoint, and Belkin has discussed Soviet concepts of information science. In general, however, rather than national schools of thought we have a variety of individual outlooks. What is true is that research interest in information science is by no means confined to one country, but is to be found in many parts of the world.

In such a rapidly growing and fluid field of study, it is risky and perhaps invidious to pick out a few names for mention, but there are a number of workers, now well-established, who would perhaps recognize each other as members of an "invisible college." The Russians (such as Mikhailov, Chernyi, Shreider, Polushkin and Ursul) are discussed by Belkin and will not be mentioned further here.

Moving westwards, we meet Dembowska of Poland, whose main work is an outline of problems and trends in scientific information; Merta of Czechoslovakia, with articles in several of the conference proceedings noted earlier; and Rozsa of Hungary, who has explored the role of scientific information in society. In the German Federal Republic we may note Wersig, with a work on the sociology of information; Dahlberg, who is chief editor of the journal International Classification and author of a book on the foundations of knowledge classification; and Soergel (now in the US), a student of indexing languages. The same subject is the concern of Gardin in France. Turning north, we must mention Samuelson of Sweden, who has published many papers on international network problems. For practical contributions to system development and evaluation in Europe we have already noted such names as Rolling, East and Isotta, and should add those of Tell and Gluchowicz, who developed the search system at the Royal Institute of Technology in Stockholm.

The United Kingdom is perhaps too close to the authors for an impartial choice, but we would note Fairthorne, a pioneer thinker in information retrieval; Brookes, who applies quantitative methods to information problems; Lynch, active on chemical information systems; and Sparck Jones, concerned with linguistic aspects of retrieval. It is even more difficult to select a few US names who have made international contributions, while omitting many others, but we must certainly mention, alphabetically, Allen, Garfield, Garvey, Goffman, Griffith, Hamburg, Hayes, Kochen, Lancaster, Leimkuhler, Salton, Saracevic, Slamecka, Martha Williams and Yovits, as well as the editors of the Annual Review of Information Science and Technology.

The names given in this section illustrate the view of information science put forward in this paper. We have not been able to cite workers eminent in "comparative and international studies" of the field--they are simply internationally eminent in information science.

Need for Comparative and International Studies

Despite this view, we believe that a case can be made for an increase in such studies within the field.

Many generalizations within information science are based upon studies made wholly within the more highly industrialized countries. In such cultures there is a surfeit of information, and those who need it must seek what is relevant within the mass, while at the same time shielding themselves from the irrelevancies with which they are bombarded. In less developed countries there is a paucity of information, and user problems differ. We need more international and comparative studies of information needs and behavior in a variety of social and cultural environments, so that more firmly based generalizations can be derived. This is in line with a similar demand encountered in sociology as a whole (see, for example, Berger).

This is of practical as well as theoretical importance. As seen above, experts from industrialized countries are frequently called upon to advise developing countries on information science problems and systems. If assumptions and conceptions are transferred wholesale to a different environment, the advice given may be faulty, the systems designed may be inappropriate, and user needs may not be satisfied. A more broadly based information science will improve information practice.

For the same reason, international or comparative studies are needed of the working of science information systems in different countries, in order to evaluate the effectiveness of different system patterns in different environments.

Information science, like other studies in our profession, is still too provincial, with too little cross-fertilization between the workers of different countries. This is partly because of the obvious language difficulties, but it also arises from ingrained attitudes. A deliberate attempt to undertake more international studies, and to compare data and theories from different countries, would help to alter these attitudes.

A further factor prompting such studies is the growing importance of international information systems and networks.   To develop
such systems requires an adequate study of conditions in each of the
cooperating centers, located in different countries and social environments.   Once developed, such international systems need to be
studied in their own right, so that future designers can learn from
the successes and failures of the past.

Comparative studies have an important role to play in information science education.   In the industralized countries, many institutions offering information science courses now enroll candidates
from developing countries.   One fruitful type of individual study project is for the candidate to define a problem encountered in his home
country, study its solutions in the industrialized environment, and
relate those solutions to conditions back home, often concluding with
a recommended course of action to be explored on his return there.
Such a project both advances comparative studies and results in an
international transfer of knowledge and understanding.

The development of internationalism within the information
field is having profound effects upon information science.   The widening of horizons, the need to explore information problems in varied
environments, has already been mentioned.   A second factor is that
international systems are often an order of magnitude more complex
than systems appropriate to an individual information center, and
thus present much greater problems of analysis, design and evaluation.   Moreover, the nature of the problems encountered is altered:
as well as the relatively familiar problems of technical design and
performance evaluation, international cooperation raises organizational, economic, political and even ethical issues that have not figured
largely in simpler systems.   To investigate and solve these problems, information science is led into modes of analysis and areas of
study analogous to all the social and behavioral sciences.   The nature of information science itself thus begins to alter.

This in turn creates considerable difficulties for both research
and teaching.   Sociological, behavioral, economic and other methodologies are now of much greater importance in information science
studies.   Systems analysis and design must take more into account
the institutional and political environments of the actual information
system.   The mainly technical orientation of US information science
courses, surveyed by Belzer and colleagues, already begins to look
outdated.   How can a wide-ranging understanding be imparted to students?   Undoubtedly, this can be helped by an examination of case
studies that themselves range widely, and it is likely that comparative and international studies in this field will provide useful teaching
material.

To conclude: we do not believe that a clearly defined area of
"comparative and international studies" can be usefully demarcated in
information science.   But greater attention to such studies within the
subject will aid the development of information science, make it surer
in practical application, and contribute to educational courses.

BIBLIOGRAPHY

1. Barr, K. P. "Estimates of the Number of Currently Available
    Scientific and Technical Periodicals," Journal of Documenta-
    tion XXIII (1967), pp. 110-116.
2. Bath University Library. Design of Information Systems in the
    Social Sciences (1970-75): Working papers Nos. 1-11, and
    Research reports, Series A Nos. 1-5, Series B Nos. 1-4.
3. _____. Investigation into Information Requirements of the
    Social Sciences (1968-1971): Research reports Nos. 1-5.
4. Batten, W. E., ed. Proceedings of European Conference on Re-
    search into Information Management. London: Aslib, 1974.
5. Battrick, B., ed. The Future of Co-operative Information Pro-
    cessing in Europe. EUSIDIC, Frascati, 1974.
6. Belkin, N. J. "Some Soviet Concepts of Information for Infor-
    mation Science," Journal of the American Society for Informa-
    tion Science XXVI (1975), pp. 56-64.
7. Belzer, J. and others. "Curricula in Information Science,"
    Journal of the American Society for Information Science XXVI
    (1975), pp. 17-32.
8. Berger, B. Societies in Change--an Introduction to Comparative
    Sociology. New York: Basic Books, 1971.
9. Boyle, P. J. and Buntrock, H. Survey of the World Agricultur-
    al Documentation Services. Rome: Food and Agricultural
    Organization of UN, report FAO/DC/AGRIS 6, 1973.
10. Brittain, J. M. Information and Its Users: a Review with Spe-
    cial Reference to the Social Sciences. Bath: Bath University
    Press, 1970.
11. Broadus, R. N. "The Literature of the Social Sciences: a Sur-
    vey of Citation Studies," International Social Science Journal
    XXIII (1971), pp. 236-243.
12. Brookes, B. C. "Numerical Methods of Bibliographic Analysis,"
    Library Trends XXII (January 1973), pp. 18-43.
13. Bureau Marcel van Bijk, ed. Seminar on Wholesalers of Docu-
    mentary Information. Brussels, 1974.
14. Cleverdon, C. W. "Evaluation Tests of Information Retrieval
    Systems," Journal of Documentation XXVI (1970), pp. 55-67.
15. Clifford, L. National Scientific and Technical Information Co-
    ordinating Organisations--a Comparative Survey. Dublin: In-
    stitute for Industrial Research and Standards, 1975.
16. Commission of the European Communities. First European Con-
    gress on Documentation Systems and Networks. Luxembourg,
    1973.
17. Coyaud, M. Introduction a L'Étude des Langages Documentaires.
    Paris: Klincksieck, 1966.
18. Dahlberg, I. Grundlagen Universaler Wissensordnung. Munich:
    Verlag Dokumentation, 1974.
19. Debons, A., ed. Information Science--Search for Identity. Pro-
    ceedings of 1972 NATO Advanced Study Institute. New York:
    Dekker, 1974.
20. _____ and Cameron, W. J., eds. Perspectives in Information
    Science. Proceedings of 1973 NATO Advanced Study Institute.
    Leyden: Noordhoff, 1975.

21. Delbos, L. and Gravestein, J. Reseau Européen en Documentation Géologique. Free communication presented at First European Congress on Documentation Systems and Networks, Luxembourg, 1973.
22. Dembowska, M. Documentation and Scientific Information. Warsaw: Central Institute for Scientific, Technical and Economic Information, 1968.
23. Douds, C. F. "The State of the Art in the Study of Technology Transfer," R. & D. Management I (1971), pp. 125-31.
24. East, H. and Martinelli, M. T. The Development of AGRIS as an Example of Systems Interconnection. Paper in International Atomic Energy Agency symposium, 1975 (see below).
25. FID (International Federation for Documentation). Problems of Information Science. Publication FID 478, 1972.
26. _____. Research on the Theoretical Basis of Information. Publication FID 530 1975.
27. _____. Theoretical Problems of Information. Publication FID 435, 1968.
28. Fairthorne, R. A. Towards Information Retrieval. London: Butterworths, 1961.
29. Foskett, D. J. "Informatics," Journal of Documentation XXVI (1970), pp. 340-69.
30. Gardin, J. C. "Document Analysis and Linguistic Theory," Journal of Documentation XXIX (1973), pp. 137-68.
31. Garvey, W. D. and Griffith, B. C. "Scientific Communication as a Social System," Science LLVII (1967), pp. 1011-1016.
32. Gluchowicz, Z. Selective Dissemination of Information and Retrospective Searches. Stockholm: Royal Institute of Technology Library, 1973.
33. Gralewska-Vickery, A. and Roscoe, H. Earth Science Engineers--Communication and Information Needs. London: Imperial College Rock Mechanics Report 32, 1975.
34. Grolier, E. de. A Study of General Categories Applicable to Classification and Coding in Documentation. Paris: UNESCO, 1962.
35. Hamburg, M. and others. Library Planning and Decision Making Systems. Cambridge, Mass.: MIT Press, 1974.
36. Hayes, R. M. and Becker, J. Handbook of Data Processing for Libraries. 2nd ed. Los Angeles: Melville, 1974.
37. International Atomic Energy Authority. Information Systems--Their Interconnections and Compatibility. Vienna, 1975.
38. Isotta, N. E. C. ESRO's Interactive System. Paper in conference edited by Schwarz, 1974 (see below).
39. Kochen, M. Principles of Information Retrieval. Los Angeles: Melville, 1974.
40. _____. "WISE--a World Information Synthesis and Encyclopaedia," Journal of Documentation XXVIII (1972), pp. 322-43.
41. Laisiepen, K. and others. Grundlagen der Praktischen Information und Dokumentation. Munich: Verlag Dokumentation, 1972.
42. Lancaster, F. W. Vocabulary Control for Information Retrieval. Washington, D.C.: Information Resources Press, 1972.
43. Langrish, J. "Technology Transfer--Some British Data," R. &

D. Management I (1971), pp. 133-5.

44. Leggate, P. "Computer Based Current Awareness Services,"
    Journal of Documentation XXXI (1975), pp. 93-115.
45. Line, M. and Roberts, S. "The Size, Growth and Composition
    of Social Science Literature," International Social Science
    Journal XXVIII (1976), pp. 122-159.
46. Lynch, M. F. Computer Based Information Services in Science
    and Technology. Stevenage, England: Peregrinus, 1974.
47. Martin, W. A. Comparative Study of Terminal User Techniques
    in Four European Countries. Paper in Commission of Euro-
    pean Communities Congress, 1973 (see above).
48. Meadows, A. J. Communication in Science. London: Butter-
    worths, 1974.
49. Menzel, H. "Informal Communication in Science: Its Advan-
    tages and Its Formal Analogues," in: E. B. Montgomery, ed.
    The Foundations of Access to Knowledge. Syracuse: Syra-
    cuse University Press, 1968, pp. 153-163.
50. Mikhailov, A. I., Chernyi, A. E. and Gilyarevskii, R. S.
    Osnovy Informatiki. Moscow: Izdat, 1968.
51. Mongar, P. E. IRRD and Its Role in an Evolving Transport
    Research Information Network. Free communication present-
    ed at First European Congress on Documentation Systems and
    Networks, Luxembourg, 1973.
52. Nalimov, V. V. and Mulchenko, Z. M. Naukometriya. Mos-
    cow: Izdat Nauka, 1969.
53. National Academy of Sciences/National Academy of Engineering.
    Scientific and Technical Communication. Washington, D.C.,
    1969.
54. Organisation for Economic Co-operation and Development. Re-
    views of National Science Policy--a Series. Paris, 1967 on.
55. Pearson, A. W. "Fundamental Problems of Information Trans-
    fer," Aslib Proceedings XXV (1973), pp. 415-423.
56. Pelzer, C. W. "The International Nuclear Information System,"
    Aslib Proceedings XXIV (1972), pp. 38-54.
57. Price, D. J. de Solla. "Measuring the Size of Science," Pro-
    ceedings of Israel Academy of Sciences and Humanities IV,
    no. 6 (1969), pp. 98-111.
58. _____. "Networks of Scientific Papers," Science LXLIX
    (1965), pp. 510-515.
59. Robertson, S. E. "The Parametric Description of Retrieval
    Tests, parts I-II," Journal of Documentation XXV (1969), pp.
    1-37, 94-107.
60. Rolling, L. "International Networks--the European Situation,"
    Bulletin of the American Society for Information Science V,
    no. 4 (1975), pp. 18-19.
61. Rozsa, G. Scientific Information and Society. The Hague and
    Paris: Mouton, 1973.
62. Salomon, J. J. and others. The Research System, vol. 1,
    France, Germany and UK. Paris: OECD, 1972.
63. Salton, G. Dynamic Information and Library Processing. Engle-
    wood Cliffs, N.J.: Prentice-Hall, 1975.
64. Samuelson, K., ed. Mechanised Information Storage, Retrieval
    and Dissemination. Proceedings of the FID/IFIP Joint

Conference, Rome 1967. Amsterdam: North-Holland Publishing, 1968.
65. Saracevic, T. , ed. Introduction to Information Science. New
York: Bowker, 1970.
66. Schur, H. Education and Training of Information Specialists for
the 1970s. Sheffield: Postgraduate School of Librarianship
and Information Science, 1972.
67. Schttz, H. , ed. Function and Organisation of a National Documentation Centre in a Developing Country. Paris: UNESCO
Press, 1975.
68. Schwarz, S. , ed. The Interactive Library. Stockholm: Swedish Society for Technical Documentation, 1975.
69. Skelton, B. "Scientists and Social Scientists as Information
Users: a Comparison of Science User Studies with the Investigation into Information Requirements of the Social Sciences,"
Journal of Librarianship V (1973), pp. 138-155.
70. Slater, M. and Keenan, S. "Methods of Conducting a Study of
Physicists' Requirements in Current Awareness in the US and
the UK," Proceedings of American Documentation Institute IV
(1967), pp. 63-67.
71. Soergel, D. Indexing Languages and Thesauri--Construction and
Maintenance. Los Angeles: Melville, 1974.
72. Sparck Jones, K. Automatic Indexing--a State of the Art Review.
Cambridge, England: University Computer Laboratory, 1974.
73. _____ and Kay, M. Linguistics and Information Science.
New York: Academic Press, 1973.
74. UNESCO. International Conference on Science Abstracting.
Paris, 1951.
75. _____. Meeting of Experts on the Problems and Strategies
of Incorporating the Social Sciences into the World Science
Information System (UNISIST): Final Report. Paris, 1974.
76. "UNESCO'S Documentation, Library and Archives Activities in
1973-74," UNESCO Bulletin for Libraries XXIX, no. 3 (1975),
pp. 136-47.
77. "UNESCO'S Information and Documentation Programme for 1975-
76," UNESCO Bulletin for Libraries XXIX, no. 3 (1975), pp.
124-35.
78. UNISIST Newsletter. Paris: UNESCO, 1973 onwards.
79. UNISIST Study Report. Paris: UNESCO, 1971.
80. University College, London. International Research Forum in
Information Science--the Theoretical Basis. London: British
Library Research and Development Report 5233, 1975.
81. Vickers, P. H. "Cost Survey of Mechanised Information Systems," Journal of Documentation XXIX (1973), pp. 258-80.
82. Vickery, B. C. Classification and Indexing in Science. 3rd ed.
London: Butterworths, 1975.
83. _____. Information Systems. London: Butterworths, 1973.
84. _____. "Little SI, Big SI--a Review of UNISIST," Journal of
Librarianship III (1971), pp. 267-74.
85. Wersig, G. Informationssoziologie. Frankfurt: Teilbereich, 1973.
86. _____ and Neveling, U. "The Phenomena of Interest to Information Science," Information Scientist IX (1975), pp. 127-
40.

87. Wilmot, C. E.   "On-line Opportunity--a Comparison of Activities in America and the UK," Aslib Proceedings XXVIII (1976), pp. 134-43.
88. Zaltman, G.   "Note on an International Invisible College for Information Exchange," Journal of American Society for Information Science XXV (1974), pp. 113-17.

THE CHANGING ROLE OF AUDIOVISUAL MEDIA

Donald P. Ely

To provide a context for this chapter, it is necessary to consider the relationship between library science and educational technology. The precursor of educational technology was audiovisual education (or audiovisual communications), which reached its development peak during the 1955-1965 decade. The major thrust of the audiovisual movement was to provide a variety of resources and to assist individuals in using them appropriately. The impact of the programmed instruction movement in the 1960s, which was embraced by the audiovisual field, accelerated change in the field to include a comprehensive concern for the design of instruction. Currently, educational technology is defined as "... a systematic way of designing, carrying out, and evaluating the total process of learning and teaching in terms of specific objectives, based on research in human learning and communications, and employing a combination of human resources to bring about more effective instruction."[1] While educational technology incorporates the use of audiovisual media, the media no longer dominate.

As the audiovisual field was going through its metamorphosis, the field of library science was becoming increasingly concerned about audiovisual (or nonprint) media. During the 1960s more librarians began to feel that their professional responsibility included the acquisition and dissemination of information regardless of the medium in which it was stored. Consequently, more libraries began to include a variety of print and nonprint media in their collections. For many years libraries had provided recordings and art prints, and some more progressive libraries had established motion picture collections. Some special libraries already had collections of maps, slides, and music recordings. Other libraries which were almost entirely print-oriented began to acquire microforms in a variety of formats. Since microforms required display equipment some librarians felt that they were dealing with a new medium. This fact helped alert professionals to the idea that information can be stored and displayed in several ways.

Most of the significant developments in integrating audiovisual media into traditional libraries were first championed by school libraries. Except for the specialized libraries in music, art and architecture for which audiovisual media were already an integral part of the discipline, most academic and public libraries have only recently begun to consider audiovisual media as viable information sources for users.

The current status of audiovisual media in libraries could be summarized as follows: 1) school libraries are rapidly becoming learning resource centers with a variety of media in their collections; 2) academic libraries are moving at a somewhat slower pace to incorporate nonprint media in their collections; and 3) public libraries are at the early stages of expansion to include nonprint media. Special libraries are more flexible in providing information for a defined clientele and more difficult to categorize.

The trends described above are written from the perspective of the United States. While there is some evidence to indicate that the same developments are occurring in other nations, the extent of change is somewhat less and the rate of change is slower. There are no comparative or international studies which describe country-by-country trends in integrating audiovisual media within library collections.

Definition of Terms

The term "media" is often used to connote audiovisual media, although its generic definition refers to media as a means for communicating information, which would include people and all printed material. "Nonprint (or nonbook) media" has emerged as a sufficiently non-ambiguous term with the appropriate disclaimer--non (all that which is not). "Audiovisual media" is preferred by some persons but excludes certain categories of media such as objects, dioramas and machine-readable data formats. In educational circles, the modifier, "instructional" or "educational" is often used. The term "nonprint media" will be used here because it has gained acceptance among librarians, even though "audiovisual media" seems to be a more descriptive term.

When referring to nonprint media, most librarians are talking about the products (sometimes referred to as "software" or materials). Individuals working in libraries are primarily concerned with the identification, acquisition, classification, cataloging, storage and retrieval of these nonprint materials. However, in the context of the learning resource center (formerly the school library), personnel are often concerned with producing nonprint media and consulting about their use. The school librarian has become a media specialist with an expanded job description.

Again, these developments are described from the perspective of the United States, but there is some evidence of similar growth in the more developed nations of the world--Japan, most of the European countries, Canada and Australia. Certain developing nations have moved in the same direction through the efforts of UNESCO teams and specialists from other nations, but there is no concentration of these efforts in specific countries.

In exploring nonprint media status in any nation today, one would need to seek out persons in mass communication programs

(primarily radio and television), in audiovisual programs (most likely support services) in schools, colleges, industrial training and
military education, and in libraries (where there is probably very
little activity). If any research is going on, it would be marketing
research by the broadcasters and studies by educators comparing the
effectiveness of one medium with another.

One of the difficulties in attempting to assess international
and comparative developments in nonprint media is to locate the individuals who are working in this field. The field is not as clearly
defined as library science. Professional education programs in audiovisual communications (educational technology) exist in only a few
of the most developed countries, with an occasional small developing
country program. Several professional library programs have developed nonprint courses, but they tend to be added onto an existing
library science program. Individuals who work with nonprint media
often do not learn about these media during their professional education but more often learn on the job.

The personnel problem is further compounded by the functions
performed by people who work with nonprint media. Some are pre-
occupied with developing good collections and making them available
to users; others are more concerned with producing media, and still
others focus on consulting to help users design programs of instruction which incorporate nonprint media. Some personnel are general-
ists concerned with managing a program including the full range of
media and such functions as evaluation, instruction, production, information storage and retrieval, design and logistics. Others are
specialists who emphasize one function (such as production of media)
or one medium (such as television). Technicians are necessary to
assist in producing material (graphic artists, for example) and maintaining and operating equipment. Usually the nonprint media personnel team includes clerks or aides who handle much of the day-to-day
distribution. When one attempts to determine the status of nonprint
media activity, the functions performed by all of the above personnel
must be taken into account.

Evidence of Increasing Cooperation

Even with the difficulties of attempting to discover the locus
of audiovisual activity in any country and identifying the personnel
associated with it, there appears to be increasing cooperation between library and audiovisual personnel. Through international organizations, individuals concerned about nonprint media are beginning
to cooperate on such matters as standards, statistics, copyright,
terminology, exchange of materials and other matters. The two most
active nongovernmental organizations are the International Council on
Educational Media (ICEM) and the International Federation of Library
Associations (IFLA).

The International Council on Educational Media (ICEM)

ICEM was founded in 1950, and its objectives are:

(a) To provide a channel for the international exchange of
information and experience in the field of educational
technology, with particular reference to pre-school, primary, secondary education, to technical and vocational
training, and to teacher and continuing education.
(b) To encourage international liaison amongst individuals
and organizations with a professional responsibility for
the design, production, promotion, distribution and use
of educational media in member countries.
(c) To promote an understanding of the concept of educational technology both on the part of educators and on
the part of those involved in the training of educators.
(d) To contribute to the pool of educational media available
to member countries by the sponsorship of practical
projects involving international cooperation and co-production, exchange and other means.
(e) To advise manufacturers of hardware and producers of
software on the needs of education in member countries.
(f) To act as an information service on developments in
educational technology and to provide consultancy for the
benefit of member countries.
(g) To co-operate with other international organizations in
promoting the concept of educational technology.

ICEM consists of 33 members, from as many countries.
Each country is entitled to have only one representative. The member of each country is to be a person who speaks on behalf of a national body within that country with responsibility for the provision
of educational technology in the areas specified in the objectives and
for the production and/or distribution of educational media.

ICEM has been granted consultative status A by UNESCO
through the International Film and Television Council. [2]

ICEM holds a general assembly each year in one of the member nations. Topical conferences are held on a variety of themes,
e. g. , "The use of modern media in developing countries" and "Audiovisual media and technical education. " Since 1965, ICEM has sponsored the annual International Film Week in Brussels.

Working committees exist in six areas of interest: administration of audiovisual services, equipment, research, production, developing countries, and video production. The Council and its committees have completed several significant accomplishments:

Educational Media International is a quarterly journal (in
English) published since 1964. French and Spanish editions
are published, also.
An Agreement on the Free Flow of Audiovisual Media was

developed and implemented by ICEM. A film catalog of 650 titles permits member nations to purchase films at laboratory prices.

A Film Reference Library has been established at the Council Secretariat with the help of UNESCO. Member countries can send representative titles of their productions to this center.

Co-production of films has occurred. When films can be made only by putting together the resources of several countries for geographic, scientific or financial reasons, ICEM serves as a vehicle for co-production.

Studies and Reports. ICEM has published reports, some with UNESCO assistance. Examples of current reports are: 1) a glossary of technical terms in the field of educational films and audiovisual media in seven languages; 2) a report published by UNESCO on the contribution of teaching films in primary education; and 3) a series of reports on the organization of audiovisual services in Western Europe, in socialist countries, in North America and Africa.

The International Federation of Library Associations (IFLA)

IFLA is a large international organization with many areas of interest concerned with library science. Interest in nonprint media is focused in three committees: Audiovisual Media in Public Libraries, Statistics and Standardization, and Cataloging. IFLA's purpose is "to promote cooperation in the field of librarianship and bibliography, and particularly to carry out investigations and make propositions concerning the international relations between libraries, library associations, bibliographers, and other organized groups." UNESCO contracted with IFLA in 1974 to complete a survey of existing systems and current proposals for the cataloging and description of nonbook material collected by libraries, with a view to arriving at preliminary suggestions for international coordination. The study was conducted by C. P. Ravilious of the University of Sussex (England) and was published in 1975. It was an attempt to arrive at procedures for an International Standard Book Description for Nonbook Media (ISBD/NBM).

The International Film and Television Council (IFTC)

IFTC is an organization of organizations. Its 1976 roster of full members included 38 international organizations related in some way to the audiovisual movement, with primary emphasis on film and television.[3] IFTC has been concerned about the cataloging of nonbook media since its inception in 1959. A 1968 Paris conference discussed the relevance of computer science to the documentation of audiovisual material. A second conference held in London in 1973 continued exploration of the topic. In 1975, IFTC, under the name, International Council for Film and Television and all Other Audiovisual Media of Communication, received a UNESCO contract to study

nonbook cataloging practices on a worldwide basis. Dr. Christopher
Roads directed the project as IFTC's Chairman of a Special Commission on Cataloging.

United Nations Educational, Scientific and Cultural Organization (UNESCO)

The fountainhead for much of the international audiovisual
media activity is UNESCO. This is a quasi-governmental organization rather than an association organized in an informal manner with
membership depending upon individual initiative.

Nonprint media activities are centered in the Education Sector
(Department of Programmes, Structures and Methods of Education;
Division of Methods, Materials and Techniques) and, to a lesser extent, in the Department of Documentation, Libraries and Archives.
The principle task of the Division of Methods, Materials and Techniques (MMT) is to promote, develop and maintain the use of educational technology for in-school and out-of-school educational systems
in the member states. MMT cooperates with the Information Sector
within UNESCO, especially in matters pertaining to the application
of communication systems to education.

The activities of MMT are related more closely to the process definition of educational technology than to the product definition
of nonprint media. While nonprint media are the primary vehicles
within the programs managed by MMT, they are not a dominant emphasis. Activities include:

1. Studies related to: the development of strategies of innovation in education; and the promotion and transfer of new
   techniques in education which would be applied within the
   member states and in operational projects.
2. Perfecting international instruments and mechanisms which
   facilitate the widespread use of modern materials and techniques in the member states;
3. The development of various information and training activities; and
4. The development of assistance to member states.

The Paris Headquarters staff is augmented by staff located in
cooperating institutions: the Latin American Institute for Educational
Communications (ILCE) in Mexico City; the Asian Centre of Educational Innovation for Development (ACEID) in Bangkok; and the International Centre for Advanced Technical and Vocational Training in
Turin. Educational technology specialists are assigned to UN Regional Offices for Education in Bangkok, Santiago (Chile), Dakar and
Beirut.

The Division is responsible for publishing Prospects, a forum
for the exchange of ideas and experiences in educational innovation.
It is not media-oriented.

MMT is an organization which provides international leadership and services regarding audiovisual media to the educational programs of member states. It sponsors conferences, gathers and disseminates information about methods, materials and techniques in
education, serves as a clearinghouse, provides assistance and consultants to developing nations and is alert to new technological developments with implications for education.

The Department of Documentation, Libraries and Archives
within the Communication Sector of UNESCO is involved with matters
of national library planning and education. Through the use of its
staff and short-term experts, assistance is given to member states
as requested. There is an extensive publication program emphasizing state-of-the-art studies in various aspects of library organization
and management. The Department publishes UNESCO Bulletin for
Libraries bimonthly and Bibliography, Documentation, Terminology,
which contains short notes on the most important activities relating
to documentation and bibliography in education, culture and communication. It appears that very little activity within this Department
is devoted to the nonprint media.

Council of Europe

The 21 European nations which comprise the Council of Europe
have joined together in a Council for Cultural Cooperation. Since
1963, the Council has published a series of works about education in
Europe. One such study, conducted by Robert LeFranc of France,
surveyed the procedures being employed to train teachers to use audiovisual media. The 1973 publication is a catalog of such programs.

Another project sponsored by the Council of Europe seeks to
develop standardized cataloging of audiovisual materials as part of the
European Documentation and Information System for Education
(EUDISED). The project is directed by Leslie A. Gilbert of the
Council for Educational Technology for the United Kingdom. In 1976
the first field-testing of the system was underway in five countries.

The Nature of International Cooperation

Most of the international cooperative efforts regarding nonprint
media have been accomplished through international organizations.
These activities occurred in four areas: 1) definitions and terminology; 2) classification and cataloging; 3) equipment and material standards; and 4) exchange of materials. Other activities have been promoted by individuals or institutions who have interests in international affairs, but these isolated efforts have had very little impact on a
worldwide basis.

Definition and Terminology. --In an attempt to create a universe of discourse among practitioners concerned with nonprint media,
several attempts are underway to develop an approved list of terms

which can be used for classification and cataloging, data gathering, and production of materials.   ICEM has a glossary which has been used by members of that organization but which has no widespread acceptance.   The IFLA Committee on Statistics and Standardization has an active working group which has developed a list of terms and definitions and is attempting to bring about consensus.   The Nonprint Media Committee of the Anglo-American Cataloging Rules Revision, sponsored by IFLA, is working with the Statistics and Standardization Committee.   The International Standards Organization has joined forces with these organizations to help with the problem.   There should be an internationally accepted list of terms and definitions by 1980, if not before.

Classification and Cataloging. --The cooperative effort of the Canadian Library Association, the American Library Association and the Library Association of the United Kingdom produced Nonbook Materials: The Organization of Integrated Collections.   This volume was a precursor to the publication of Chapter 12 of the Anglo American Cataloguing Rules (North American Edition), a revised guide to classifying and cataloging of nonprint media.   Additional work is being done by the IFLA Committee on International Standard Bibliographic Description for Nonbook Media.   The Council on Educational Technology in the United Kingdom has published Non-Book Materials Cataloguing Rules.

Equipment and Material Standards. --The leadership of the International Standards Organization has brought about technical agreements on such topics as cinematography (e. g. , projection, sound recording and reproduction) and documentation (e. g. , microfiche, bibliographic content designators for machine processing).

International Exchange of Materials. --As noted earlier, the 33 member countries in ICEM have developed and implemented an agreement for international exchange of audiovisual media.

Recent Literature

Most of the literature on the international aspects of nonprint media takes the form of descriptive reports emphasizing the organization and activities of nonprint media (or educational technology) programs within each country.   The ICEM reports on audiovisual services in Western Europe, in European socialist countries and in North America have already been mentioned.   The Commonwealth Secretariat in the Centre for Educational Development Overseas published a comprehensive comparative survey of all Commonwealth countries: New Media in Education in the Commonwealth (1974), with 1972 data.

In a similar vein, the U. S. Office of Education funded two area studies regarding nonprint media in other lands, but they are dated.   Survey of Educational Media Research in the Far East (1963) and Survey of Educational Media Research and Programs in Latin

America (1965) offer locations, names of persons and activities from the early 1960s.

The Academy for Educational Development, a non-governmental consulting organization in Washington, D. C. , published Big Media, Little Media by Wilbur Schramm in 1974. Schramm described on a comparative basis the educational television systems in American Samoa, El Salvador, Niger and the Ivory Coast. UNESCO published World Communications, a survey of press, radio, television and film in 200 countries, but it does not relate directly to noncommercial media uses.

Most of the international literature, other than that indicated above, are descriptive reports of specific projects, reports on research (which are usually found in professional journals), status reports of activities within a single country, or conference reports.

Significant Centers and Personnel

A directory of significant international programs and well-known leaders compiled by one person is limited by the contacts and perceptions of that person. There are more programs and people than those mentioned here but they have not come within the author's purview. The problem is further compounded by the transition of the audiovisual field to educational technology and the evolving acceptance of nonprint media into the library milieu. Therefore, the first criterion to qualify for inclusion in the list of institutions and people is an orientation to production, use or distribution of nonprint media. This would exclude many references to educational technology programs and personnel oriented more to the process of instructional design. If the first criterion is met, then one or more of the following must be met: 1) visible contributions to the research and literature about nonprint media; 2) offices held in national or international organizations; or 3) administrative head of a significant visible program.

Europe. --In England, Geoffrey Hubbard is the Director of the Council for Educational Technology of the United Kingdom, a nongovernmental organization which serves as a national clearinghouse for information about nonprint media in the context of innovative programs in education. CET has an extensive publication program including a quarterly publication, the British Journal of Educational Technology (BJET). The Editor of BJET is C. J. Duncan, Head of the Department of Photography at Newcastle-Upon-Tyne, which has an excellent academic program emphasizing the technical aspects of audiovisual production. The National Committee for Audio-Visual Aids in Education and the Educational Foundation for Visual Aids have been the principal leaders in the production and distribution of nonprint media. They provide a National Audio-Visual Aids Centre which serves as an information clearinghouse and a training and demonstration unit. They operate the National Audio-Visual Aids Library and sponsor the annual trade show, INTER NAVEX, in London. The organization's

official journal is Visual Education (monthly), and there is an extensive publication program.

The British Open University has had significant national impact and is now reaching out to other countries. A large part of the
credit must go to the staff of the Institute of Educational Technology
directed by David G. Hawkridge. The audiovisual research activities
are headed by A. W. Bates.

In Scotland the prime mover of audiovisual activity has been
the Scottish Film Council, directed by R. B. Macluskie. This organization promotes the use of films and other media as instructional and cultural resources. They work closely with the Scottish Central Film Library and the Scottish Educational Film Association.
Academic programs for the study of educational technology and nonprint media have been established at Dundee College of Education
(A. M. Stewart) and Jordanhill College of Education (D. C. Butts).

In Wales, the School of Librarianship at the University College of Wales in Aberystwyth has recently added nonprint media
courses to its curriculum and is championing the integrated approach
of nonprint media in libraries.

In France, Robert LeFranc is probably the best known person
in the field. He directs the Centre Audio-Visual at Ecole Normale
Supérieure in St. Cloud and serves as the Executive Director of
ICEM. Henri Dieuzeide is the Director of the UNESCO Division of
Methods, Materials and Techniques in Education.

In the Netherlands, H. J. L. Jongbloed directs the Dutch Institute for Audiovisual Teaching Aids. He served as President of
ICEM during 1975-76. Other organizations involved in media activities include the Department of Educational Affairs, University of
Nijmegen, the Media Institute, University of Utrecht and the Educational Research Section, University of Amsterdam.

In Belgium, J. H. Mertens heads the Audio-visual Aids program in the National Ministry of Education. Other persons involved
in the field include M. R. Rarar, Institut National Supérieur des
Arts (Brussels), L. D. Mainaut at the Université de l'Etat à Muns,
and G. de Landsheere, Université de Liege.

North America. --In Canada, the pioneer work with film has
been accomplished by the National Film Board of Canada. This gov-
ernment-sponsored organization is responsible for producing and distributing audiovisual media for education and for the general public.
A comprehensive study of audiovisual programs in Canadian colleges
and universities was completed by G. A. B. Moore of the University
of Guelph, which has an extensive media program. Aside from the
National Film Board, most of the research activity dealing with nonprint media has been accomplished through the Ontario Institute for
the Study of Education where Fred Rainsberry leads nonprint media

activities. The Association for Media and Technology in Education in Canada (AMTEC) is a new organization formed by the amalgamation of the Educational Media Association of Canada, the Educational Television and Radio Association of Canada and the Canadian Science Film Association. Good academic and service programs exist at the University of Alberta (Kenneth Bowers) and the University of British Columbia (Daniel Peck).

The United States has the most extensively developed nonprint media programs in the world. The Association for Educational Communications and Technology (formerly the Department of Audiovisual Instruction of the National Education Association) is the largest organization of its type in the world (membership about 10,000); Howard B. Hitchens is Executive Director. There is an extensive committee and division structure within the organization and an active publications program. The International Division is concerned with activities involving nonprint media in all parts of the world. The Information Systems Division considers the various practices in handling nonprint media. A committee on cataloging has published four editions of Standards for Cataloging Nonprint Materials: An Interpretation and Practical Application. The Association's monthly journal is Audiovisual Instruction, and the research-oriented quarterly is AV Communication Review. AECT holds the U.S. membership in ICEM and cooperates with many international organizations. It screens U.S. nontheatrical films for showing in international festivals through a committee known as CINE--Council for International Nontheatrical Events.

Within the American Library Association, several organizations and groups are concerned with nonprint media. The largest and most active is the American Association of School Librarians (AALS), which publishes School Media Quarterly. The Executive Secretary is Alice E. Fite. Committees on Video Communications, Instructional Media and Media Center Facilities relate most closely to the nonprint media in school library settings.

Within the Public Library Association is an Audiovisual Committee which has published Guidelines for Audiovisual Materials and Services for Large Public Libraries and Recommendations for Audiovisual Materials and Services for Small and Medium-Sized Public Libraries. Primary leadership has come from Wesley Doak of the Los Angeles Public Library. A recent report, New Media in Public Libraries has been written by James W. Brown.

Information about developments in nonprint media is coordinated by the two large organizations (AECT and ALA) and by the Educational Resources Information Clearinghouse (ERIC) on Information Resources at Syracuse University. This Clearinghouse gathers, abstracts and makes available information about educational technology, library science and information science. It has a large publication list on all phases of nonprint media. The other information sources regarding specific nonprint media are: the Multi-Media Review Index, a comprehensive listing of nonprint media reviews by C. Edward Wall and the National Information Center for Educational Media (NICEM) which publishes a series of indexes listing nearly all titles in each format: 16mm films, 35mm filmstrips, 8mm film cartridges, disc recordings, tape recordings, slide sets, transparencies and videotapes.

Other journals carrying current information about nonprint media are Previews (R. R. Bowker Co.), Educational Technology and the International Journal of Instructional Media.

Several universities offer graduate programs in educational technology. Each of the programs grew out of the audiovisual tradition but now emphasizes instructional development with nonprint media as a related area. The universities are Indiana University (John Molstad, Chairman), Michigan State University (Castelle Gentry, Chairman), Syracuse University (Richard Clark, Chairman) and the University of Southern California (William H. Allen, Chairman). Certain universities have developed good working relationships between educational technology and library science: Arizona State University (Howard Sullivan, Chairman), Auburn University (Thomas Miller, Chairman), California State University, San Jose (Leslie H. Janke, Chairman), and the University of Maryland (James Liesener). Well-known school library-media programs exist at Florida State University (Harold Goldstein), St. Cloud State University (Luther Brown), Purdue University (Carolyn Whitenack), Millersville State College (Joseph Blake), Western Michigan University (Jean Lowrie), and the University of Washington (Eleanor Ahlers).

Other organizations concerned with nonprint media are the University Film Association, the Educational Film Library Association and the Producers Council of the National Audio-Visual Association, an organization of producers of materials and manufacturers of equipment.

The Educational Media Yearbook, published annually by R. R. Bowker and edited by James W. Brown, provides a wealth of information on current national and international developments.[4]

Latin America. --A useful article, "Educational Media in Latin America" by Richard Kent Jones, appears in the 1974 edition of the Educational Media Yearbook.

In Chile, the Oficina de Planifacación Docente de la Vicerrectoria de Sede Sur at the University of Chile is headed by Lydia Miquel and serves as a focal point for audiovisual activity.

In Peru, the Centro de Teleducación of the Pontificia Universidad Catholica, directed by Estela Barandiaran de Garland, is in the early stages of developing nonprint media for national use. The Universidad Nacional de Trujillo has established a Center for Educational Technology concerned with nonprint media. There is an Association for Educational Technology, of which Alejandro Solis is President.

In Mexico, the Instituto Latinamericano para Communación en Educación (ILCE) provides leadership and guidance in educational communications in Latin American countries by offering training courses, providing technical assistance to all countries served, producing media in all formats, doing research and conducting seminars. It has organized the Center for Audiovisual Documentation for Latin America (CEDAL). Within the Ministry of Education is the Dirección General Audiovisual (DGAV) which serves schools throughout the country.

In Venezuela, the Centro Audiovisual Nacional offers courses for students from all parts of Latin America and coordinates activities within the country.

Middle East. --In Iran, audiovisual activities are growing rapidly through the Ministry of Education and National Iran Radio and Television (NIRT). During 1975-76, a team of media specialists from Indiana University, Syracuse University, Michigan State University and the University of Southern California helped to develop a media training program for Iranian teachers.

Asia. --In India, the Centre for the Development of Instructional Technology in New Delhi serves the entire country. Some universities, especially those with agricultural curricula, have developed audiovisual support services.

In Japan, there is the Japan Audiovisual Association which sponsors the Japan Audiovisual Information Centre for International Service.

Africa. --The application of instructional technology for enrichment, improvement, and compensation has been very slow in taking a place in the African educational scene. In Nigeria, the wealthiest, most populous and most advanced African country, many elementary school teachers still buy such a common item as chalk with their own money. Children still have to bring stools from their homes to sit on in classrooms. In some schools, teachers and pupils squat on the floor. In the secondary schools, emphasis on audiovisuals has not caught on except in a very few private schools. At the university level, the University of Lagos is foremost in the application of educational technology. The other universities suffer from lack of personnel and money to meet the cost of supplementing and improving instruction with the use of instructional media.

Australia. --In Australia, as in other countries, there is a dichotomy between those persons involved with nonprint media and those in educational technology. La Trobe University in Melbourne has a major educational media department. Smaller programs are offered at the University of New South Wales, the teachers college at Monash and the Tasmanian College of Advanced Education. Most of the major universities and colleges of advanced education (colleges offering bachelor's degrees and sometimes master's degrees) have audiovisual sections in the library which generally acquire, store, catalog and distribute nonprint materials but do not produce them.

The primary producers of material for use in educational settings are the Television Unit at the University of Sydney, the Closed Circuit Television Department at the University of New South Wales (J. H. Shaw, Head), the Center for the Advancement of Teaching at MacQuarie University (G. R. Meyer, Director), and the Educational Media Centre at the Royal Melbourne Institute of Technology.

The list above is incomplete, limited by the knowledge and contacts of the author. If an individual wishes to inquire about developments in a specific country, initial contact should be made with the Ministry of Education or the National Library. The MMT Division of UNESCO serves as a clearinghouse of information regarding nonprint media developments in all member states. The ICEM publications on North America, Western Europe and socialist countries in Europe are useful sources. The survey of the Commonwealth Secretariat is a current and comprehensive report of Commonwealth countries.

Audiovisual Activities--A Status Summary

When the entire world is reviewed, much activity in the audiovisual field can be seen, but there appears to be a dearth of academic programs outside the United States and the quantity and quality of research is limited.

Part of the problem relates to the newness of the field. The major thrust of the movement began in the late 1940s, with acceleration in the late 1950s and new technologies added in the 1960s. The audiovisual field has changed both in name and concept as educational technology emerged in the late 1960s and early '70s, but its heritage is clear. At the same time, the expanded concept to include information in nonprint formats has invaded the established library field. This is clearly a time of transition, and such times do not stimulate establishment and expansion of academic programs, nor research. Most efforts of professionals are concentrated on organization and spelling out a philosophy and rationale. This activity will, no doubt, help to create hypotheses about nonprint media--its production, use and distribution. This problem is compounded by the introduction of new audiovisual formats and distribution systems--cable TV, satellite distribution and videodiscs, for example.

Any new field is likely to attract persons from a variety of fields who discover new interests and applications related to their original discipline. So it is with the audiovisual movement. Educators were first to grasp the new field and, later, psychologists, film makers, communication specialists and, finally, librarians. Each field adds its own perceptions to those which already exist and usually alters the field in some fashion. When the period of early development becomes more solidified, it is likely that more academic programs will be established with research components. The content and structure of the field has not been established.

Part of the evolution is the demand for personnel. Most of the personnel working with nonprint media have gained their skills and competencies on the job. As long as people within organizations exhibit interest in assuming new responsibilities in the nonprint area, there is little demand for new personnel. As the field becomes accepted and grows, employers begin to look for individuals with professional education. However, programs for professional education are not begun until there is some evidence of demand from the field. It would appear that a sufficient number of programs exists now in the United States. Recent AECT publications indicate 67 programs for professional education[5] and 15 for paraprofessional training.[6]

Only a handful of such programs exist in other parts of the world--in Canada, England, Scotland, Australia, India and perhaps a few others. The Commonwealth survey revealed that most of the programs were short courses of less than one year and many of them were largely technical, e.g., production of radio, television, film and photography.[7] In one of the conclusions to this study, it was stated that "... the range of training centres is much less extensive than the range of media projects.... Training is time-consuming and expensive. In realization of this, there is now a growing tendency for much more care to be given to the problems of recruitment. Effective recruitment is the sine qua non for effective training."[8]

The nature of audiovisual education makes it an expensive venture. Besides the usual faculty and library resources, there must be laboratories for production of graphics and photography and studios for television and film. Many types of equipment are required for producing and using nonprint media. There must be nonprint resources available as well. To a country which is having difficulty in supplying sufficient chalk, paper and textbooks, audiovisual resources seem to be less important and too costly.

Institutional standards for audiovisual programs are beginning to be accepted and used in North America. Media Programs: District and School and the audiovisual guidelines and recommendations for public libraries help to establish the concept that programs should be developed. Apparently there are no such standards in other parts of the world. If standards do not exist, it is unlikely that programs will be considered an integral part of the institutional scheme.

Research is another matter. A minimal amount of research precedes the establishment of a program. The bulk of the research during the first 20 years of the field's growth (1945-1965) concentrated on the validity of audiovisual media. Most of the research sought to compare traditional teaching with the use of one medium or another. Most of this research showed no significant difference, which was interpreted by some to mean that audiovisual media had no effect and therefore should not be used. Others argued that if there were no difference, why should a teacher be used when media could accomplish the same result at far less cost? Both arguments

are moot, however, since most of the research was poorly designed
and has been repudiated by researchers.

Another research strain explored production variables (color
vs. black and white; narration vs. no narration; angle of view; in-
serted questions, etc.) with the purpose of discovering optimum production standards. This type of research continues at a minimum
level, mostly in doctoral dissertations. It may be of some help
when a sufficient number of variables has been studied. Another dimension of current research is to relate learner aptitudes to media
treatments in an attempt to discover the "best" medium (or attributes
of a medium) to help an individual learn a specific type of information or skill.

Research occurs when demonstrated needs and problems must
be resolved. This requires money. Even when pressing medical
problems are identified, it is often difficult to secure sufficient funds
to perform the research which might lead to solutions. Educational
research has a much lower priority than other types of research in
most countries. Abundant funds for media research were made available from 1958 to 1968, in the United States, but very little media
research has been funded since then because of fiscal pressures on
government and foundation supporters. Some of the best media research today is going on within the Audiovisual Research unit of the
British Open University under the direction of A. W. Bates.

Important research questions do not appear to be dominant at
the present time. This appears to be a time of consolidating previous research to develop generalizations on what is known before
formulating new dimensions for further research.

Preconditions for Useful Contributions from
Comparative and International Audiovisual Studies

The preconditions for further development of comparative and
international audiovisual studies are: competent personnel, an agreed-
upon structure and definition of the field, and an understanding of media's role in education and society. If these preconditions existed in
every country, comparative and international activities would be facilitated.

Competent Personnel. --There is no substitute in any field for
competent professionals. In the case of the fields which incorporate
the audiovisual media (educational technology and library science, primarily), most of the personnel who deal with nonprint media have
very little professional education in the audiovisual area. Most of
the individuals who have day-to-day responsibility for the selection,
use and distribution of nonprint media are administrators--persons
who manage a service to users through libraries, audiovisual centers,
learning resource centers and the like. It is rare to find researchers, philosophers and theoreticians among management personnel.
The combination of minimal professional preparation and holding

management positions retards research and development progress in
the field.

Times are changing, however.   There are more training programs in more countries and the developers of these programs are
asking about the structure and content of the field.   In the U.S., the
recent concern for competency-based professional education programs
has caused professional associations to study the functions performed
by media professionals. [9]   New standards for professional certification in many states within the United States are helping to establish
parameters for the field.   Most of the activity is occurring within
the United States.   If it is to happen in other countries, the need for
personnel must be made known through a new concept of education.
Media professionals are not needed where traditional education patterns continue, but as new structures are developed and as problems
of instruction are identified, it is likely that media professionals will
be needed.   As for libraries, in the more highly developed nations
increased demands for nonprint media personnel can be expected.   It
will be a long time before most of the African and Latin American
countries, for example, will need nonprint media specialists because
of strong traditions and lack of resources.

A Structure for the Field. --The syllabi for new, applied fields
usually grow out of activities which are performed on the job and are
augmented by chapter headings from the first books to appear in the
field.   This content is further modified by individuals from related
fields who embrace the new field and add their own special interests.
Thus, the content and structure of the field is delayed until there is
a critical mass of personnel who, through meetings, writings and experience, gradually develop a scope and sequence of content and objectives which is labeled as a curriculum.   This point has not yet
been reached in the nonprint media field.   There are still too many
new inputs to decide what constitutes the field.   Most of the ferment
is in the more developed countries.   Comparative and international
studies will not be possible until there is international agreement on
the basic concepts, structure and philosophy of the field.

One step in the direction of international agreement is the ongoing effort to develop an acceptable list of terms and definitions.
If this agreement occurs, as is likely, the opportunity for a universe
of discourse is enhanced.   The ability to develop comparable statistics, for example, would be possible for the first time.

More fundamental than agreement on definitions and on the
content and structure of the field, is a basic understanding of what
the field is about.   Currently, audiovisual media means different
things to different people, even those who are working within the field.
To some, this would mean that a statement of philosophy is required;
to others it would mean that a rationale for doing what they are doing
is needed.   While there is substantial agreement about the technical
aspects of production, many who work in the field do not know why.
There are many schools of thought about how nonprint media can or
should be used.   There probably will never be agreement on use--

and perhaps that is as it should be.   At least there ought to be
some concurrence about what medium will best accomplish a specific purpose for a defined audience, however.

Understanding Media's Role. --The contemporary paradox regarding the role of nonprint media in society is that the general public uses these media extensively as they are distributed on a mass
basis in the form of television, radio and film.   Yet, when the use
of the same media are considered for education, libraries and other
public institutions, there is reluctance to accept them.   Perhaps individuals suffer from the media = entertainment syndrome.   Perhaps
it is a preoccupation with the traditional; i. e. , libraries are for
books; teachers are in schools to help students learn and they don't
need "aids. " Perhaps the initial costs of providing audiovisual media are resisted by taxpayers and government officials who develop
budgets.

Another paradox is that audiovisual media are being used in
many countries for industrial and military training, while schools
and libraries are neglected.   There appears to be an acceptance of
nonprint media use when it is employed for specific purposes with
defined outcomes.   Yet, schools do not appear to qualify under this
condition.   Again, we are faced with attitudes toward the use of audiovisual media in public institutions.

The future for nonprint media will be determined by the needs
of the people and the ability of the professionals to meet them.   In a
pluralistic world, it would appear that pluralistic means must be provided to meet individual information needs.

NOTES

1.   Sidney G. Tickton, ed.   To Improve Learning.   New York:
      R. R. Bowker, 1970.
2.   The Activities of the International Council for Educational Media.
      Paris: ICEM, October, 1974, p. 1.
3.   Full members of IFTC include:
      Asian Broadcasting Union (ABU)
      Comité International des Films de L'homme (CIFH)
      European Broadcasting Union (EBU)
      International Animated Film Association (ASIFA)
      International Association for Art and the Audiovisual Media
         (AIAMA)
      International Association of Documentary Film Makers (IAD)
      International Broadcast Institute (IBI)
      International Catholic Association for Radio & Television
         (UNDA)
      International Catholic Film Organisation (OCIC)
      International Centre of Films for Children and Young People
         (Cinema and Television) (ICFCYP)
      International Committee for the Diffusion of Art and Letters
         by the Cinema (CIDALC)

International Confederation of Technical Film Sectors of the
Film Industry
International Council for Educational Media (ICEM)
International Council of Graphic Design Associations
(ICOGRADA)
International Experimental and Art Film Theatres Confedera-
tion (CICAE)
International Federation of Actors (FIA)
International Federation of Audio-Visual Workers (FISTAV)
International Federation of Film Archives (FIAF)
International Federation of Film Critics (FIPRESCI)
International Federation of Film Distributors (FIAD)
International Federation of Film Producers Associations
(IFFPA)
International Federation of Film Societies (IFFS)
International Federation of Musicians (FIM)
International Federation of Producers of Phonograms and
Videograms (IFPI)
International Inter-Church Film Centre (INTERFILM)
International Liaison Centre for Film and Television Schools
(CILECT)
International Music Centre (IMZ)
International Newsreel Association (INA)
International Radio and Television Organisation (IORT)
International Scientific Film Association (SFA)
International Union of Amateur Films (UNICA)
International Union of Cinematograph Technical Associations
(UNIATEC)
International Union for Film and Television Research
International Union of Film Exhibitors (UIEC)
International University of Radiophonics (URTI)
International Writers Guild (IWG)
Pan African Federation of Film Producers (FEPACI)
World Association for Christian Communications (WACC)

4. James W. Brown, ed. Education Media Yearbook 1975-76. New
York: R. R. Bowker Co., 1975, p. 197.
5. Instructional Technology Graduate Degree Programs in U.S. Colleges and Universities, 1969-71. Washington, D.C.: AECT,
1971.
6. Training Programs for Media Support Personnel: An Annotated
Directory. Washington, D.C.: AECT, 1970.
7. New Media in Education in the Commonwealth. London: Commonwealth Secretariat, 1974, pp. 172-174.
8. Ibid., p. 288.
9. American Library Association. Behavioral Requirements Analysis Checklist. Chicago: ALA, 1973.
Jobs in Instructional Media. Washington, D.C.: AECT, 1971.

BIBLIOGRAPHY

Anglo American Cataloguing Rules. Chapter 12, Revised. Chicago:

American Library Association, 1975.

Brown, James W. New Media in Public Libraries. Syracuse, N. Y. : Gaylord Bros. , Inc. , 1976.

Chisholm, Margaret E. and Ely, Donald P.   Media Personnel in Education: A Competency Approach. Englewood Cliffs, N. J. : Prentice-Hall, Inc. , 1976.

Ely, Donald P. Survey of Educational Media Research and Programs in Latin America. Syracuse, N. Y. : The author. ERIC # ED 003166.

Guidelines for Audiovisual Materials and Services for Large Public Libraries. Chicago: American Library Association, 1975.

Media Programs: District and School. Chicago, Illinois and Washington, D. C. : American Library Association and Association for Educational Communications and Technology, 1975.

Media Review Digest. Ann Arbor, Mich. : Pierian Press, 1975.

Moore, G. A. B. "The Growth of Educational Technology in Canadian Higher Education," British Journal of Educational Technology III (January 1972), pp. 32-47.

New Media in the Commonwealth. London: Commonwealth Secretariat, 1974.

Non-Book Materials Cataloguing Rules. (Second Edition). London: Council on Educational Technology, 1974.

Recommendations for Audiovisual Materials and Services for Small and Medium Sized Public Libraries. Chicago: American Library Association, 1975.

Schmid, Fridolin. Comparative Study on the Administration of Audio-Visual Services in Advanced and Developing Countries, Part I: The Audio-Visual Services in Western European Countries. Paris: International Council on Educational Media, 1974.

Schramm, Wilbur. Big Media, Little Media. Washington, D. C. : Academy for Educational Development, 1974.

Standards for Cataloguing Non-print Materials: An Interpretation and Practical Application. Washington, D. C. : Association for Educational Communications and Technology, 1975.

Survey of Educational Media Research in the Far East. Washington, D. C. : U. S. Government Printing Office, 1963.

Tickton, Sidney G. , ed. To Improve Learning. New York: R. R. Bowker, 1970.

Weihs, Jean R. , Lewis, Shirley and Macdonald, Janet. Nonbook Materials: The Organization of Integrated Collections. Ottawa: Canadian Library Association, 1973.

World Communications. London: Gower Press, 1975.

COMPARATIVE AND INTERNATIONAL BIBLIOGRAPHY

Mohammed M. Aman

As biography follows from the existence of human beings, bibliography follows from the existence of printed books. In this sense, bibliography has been described as the biography of books. Much of the early interest in bibliography was dilettante, to express appreciation and delight in the exquisite execution of artistic embellishment of an example of fine craftsmanship. Here incunabula have had a leading place. The fascination and mystery connected with the invention of printing by movable type, the story of its growth and spread, and the perfection of many early products led to book study and ultimately to the introduction of descriptive, analytical and enumerative bibliography. [1]

From the beginning it was recognized that books must be known to exist and survive before they could be studied as material objects. One of bibliography's first tasks, therefore, became enumeration, which later became an art and science by itself. Enumeration involved technical description, and description involved studying the books described. Thus, enumeration and description became the main foundations of today's bibliography. The "listing of titles" in their printed form appeared as early as 1494, only a few years after the invention of printing. Their origin, in manuscript form, is much more ancient, as ancient as the libraries of Babylon and Alexandria.

The earliest "pure" enumerative bibliography was the Liber de Scriptoribus Ecclesiasticis of Johann Tritheim (1462-1516), printed by Amerbach in Basle in 1494. [2] It is "pure" in the sense that it was produced specifically as a biographical list and not with secondary purposes. Other lists followed by such bibliographers as Greg, Maittaire, Panzer, Hain, Stillwell, Copinger, and Reichling, who described, studied and enumerated the early output of Gutenberg's invention. [3]

Throughout the sixteenth, seventeenth and eighteenth centuries bibliographic lists proliferated and national or subject bibliographies emerged. From the seventeenth century onwards, trade lists emerged but they were slow in establishing themselves on any sizable scale. Perhaps this was due to the small amount of any country's book production.

The advent of the mechanized book industry in the nineteenth century brought about the most revolutionary changes since Gutenberg. It is estimated that world book production doubled between 1858 and

1898.[4] In addition, the number of periodicals nearly quadrupled
from 1866 to 1898.   This growth caused some learned men to become absorbed in collecting lists of works published.

During the nineteenth century, scholars, chiefly in Germany
and France, published vast numbers of retrospective bibliographies.
In France, Charles Jacques Brunet, a Parisian bookseller, was responsible for one of the most famous of all universal bibliographies
on a selective basis.   Brunet's first edition of Manuel du Libraire
was published in 1810.[5] For the next fifty years it remained Brunet's chief preoccupation and was enlarged significantly with each issue, until the fifth edition of 1860-1865, for which he is now best
remembered.

While Brunet was absorbed in collecting a universal bibliography for Europe, American bibliographers were keen to register and
identify every publication brought to the American shores.   Sabin's
Dictionary of Books Relating to America from Its Discovery to the
Present Time[6] and Charles Evans' American Bibliography[7] were excellent examples of early American retrospective bibliography.

According to Heaney, "The listing of books about America,
including those in what is now the United States, antedates the founding of the republic by almost a century and a half."[8] The listing of
American imprints may be traced from the work of Isaiah Thomas,
a collector and writer on printing history in America.   Charles
Evans listed American imprints from 1639 through 1820.   Ralph
Shaw and Richard Shoemaker's American Bibliography: A Preliminary Checklist for 1801-1819 updates Evans' work.   Checklists of
state imprints began to emerge in the 19th century.   Now, a checklist of early imprints exists for almost every state in the Union.
Most of these bibliographies owe their existence to the hard work of
individual scholars.

In certain Latin American countries, specific examples show
what can be done by individuals who have the knowledge, energy and
resources to deal with very difficult bibliographic situations.   In Bo-
livia, two bibliographers have contributed significantly to national
bibliographic development: Marcela Meneses, a librarian, and Werner Guttentag, Managing Director of Editorial Los Amigos del Libro,
Cochobamba.   The annual volumes of Bibliografía Boliviana continue
to appear under the name of Werner Guttentag.   Another individual
who compiled a Bolivian retrospective bibliography was Arturo Costa
de la Torre.   His influential work was published in La Paz, Catalogo
de la Bibliografía Boliviana: Libros y Folletos 1900-1963.   The
period covered extends from the last major work of the noted Bolivian bibliographer, Gabriel René Morene (1836-1908), to 1963.[9]

Chile is another South American country where a strong bibliographic tradition was founded by outstanding bibliographers, in this
case, José Toribio Medina and Sr. Zamorano y Caperan, whose
Servicio Bibliografico Chileno (1940-) has supplied the only consistent Chilean publication record for three decades.

In Colombia, the first Anuario Bibliográfico Colombiano was compiled by Pedro R. Carmona and published in Cali in 1951. Its contents were incorporated into the next volume, 1951-1956, compiled by Rubén Pérez Ortiz, as were subsequent volumes through 1962.[10]

Venezuela owed the appearance of its first Anuario Bibliográfico Venezolano to a Spanish émigré, Pedro Grases. Under his direction, an Anuario covering material published in or about Venezuela in 1942 was completed in 1944. A later effort was made by Felipe Massiani and Carmen Luisa Escalante to update the Anuario.

Haiti is another country which owes most of its national bibliographic record to the effort of one man, Max Bissainthe, former Director of The National Library. His Dictionnaire de Bibliographie Haitienne, from 1804 through 1949, was published by the Scarecrow Press in 1951.[11] A supplement, covering 1950-1970, was published in 1973.

In Cuba, Fermín Peraza y Sarausa (1907-1969) was the person responsible for compiling the Anuario Bibliográfico Cubano in 1938. It established an unmatched record for continuous assembling, editing, and publishing a country's current national bibliography by one person. After he left Cuba and moved to Gainsville, Florida in 1965, Dr. Peraza's bibliographic work continued.

Notable bibliographers like Jacinto Jijón y Caamaño, Carlos Rolando and Miguel Angel Jaramillo have been primarily responsible for collecting Ecuadoriana and developing Ecuadorian bibliography.

Asian and Middle East scholars developed an early interest in enumerative bibliography, and many current projects began in their contributions. Most of the earliest Middle Eastern bibliographies were the works of individuals, with little or no outside financial or moral support. These projects were due entirely to the determination and dedication of Middle Eastern scholars like Father Qanawati, Sirkis 'Awwad and others.[12] Other Middle Eastern bibliographies were published outside the region.

Bibliographic Societies

The bibliographic traditions and monuments published through the dedication of generations of scholarly bibliographers have led to the establishment of bibliographic societies. While varying from one country to another, the societies established in Europe and the United States made substantial contributions to national bibliographical control.

European societies promoted bibliographic studies and compiled bibliographies. They accomplished their objectives through periodic meetings, presentation of papers, and publication programs. The first record of a bibliographical society is that of the Société

Bibliographique, established in 1868 in France.   Its monthly publication, Polybiblion, ceased in 1920.   Under the auspices of the Société
the International Bibliographical Congress held three meetings: 1878,
1888, and 1898. [13]   Another French Society, the Société Française
de Bibliographie, founded in 1906, published several important works.
In 1948 the Société Internationale de Bibliographie Classique was
formed in Paris and published L'Année Philologique. [14]

In the United Kingdom, and perhaps throughout the English-
speaking world, the first bibliographical society was the Edinburgh
Bibliographical Society, formed in 1890.   George Waterson, a director of the family firm of printers and stationers, George Waterson
and Sons, originated the idea and became the Society's second president in 1891.   The Society's Transactions published important contributions on Scottish bibliography, printers and presses, bibliographies of authors like that of Sir George Mackenzie or the poetical
works of Sir Walter Scott, and articles on libraries, such as one on
the first twenty years of the National Library of Scotland. [15]

In 1892, the Bibliographical Society of London was formed.
The need for this Society was expressed as early as 1868 in an article in Notes and Queries by W. E. A. Axon.   He wrote, "If such a
society was formed, a general literary index would be something of
a possibility, the vexed question of cataloging would probably find a
solution, much light would be thrown upon literary history, special
bibliographies of particular subjects might be brought out. "[16]   In his
paper on "The Necessity for Its Operations," Copinger envisaged
compiling "a general English literature bibliography, a list of fifteenth
century books on Hain, producing facsimile specimens of every known
fifteenth century press, a complete bibliography of bibliographies ...
with catalogues of public and private libraries, also of the more extensive and remarkable book auction sales...."[17]

The Society's main objectives were finally conceived as "...
the acquisition of information upon subjects connected with bibliography.   The promotion and encouragement of bibliographical studies
and researches.   The printing and publishing of works connected with
bibliography. "[18]   The Society continued to publish biennially the Bibliographical Society Transactions (1893-1920), supplemented by News-
Sheet (1894-1920) until it was incorporated into The Library in 1920.

Before World War I the Society undertook what has undoubtedly, to the world at large, been its most important publication: Pol-
lard and Redgrave's Short-title Catalogue of Books Printed in England, Scotland and Ireland and of English Books Printed Abroad,
1475-1640.   It was completed in January 1927. [19]

In 1901 the Lancashire Bibliographical Society was formed for
one year to publish Gordon Duff's work on English printing on vel-
lum.   The Welsh Bibliographical Society was established to publish
Welsh bibliographies.   It published the Bibliography of Quaker Literature Relating to Wales, also.   In 1918 the Bibliographical Society of
Ireland held its first meeting and began publishing its Transactions.

The Oxford Bibliographical Society began publishing Proceedings and Papers in 1922, in addition to the annual Bibliography in Britain. The Cambridge Bibliographical Society, founded in 1949, published its annual Transactions and occasional Monographs.

In Italy, the Società Bibliografica Italiana was founded in 1895. Its official publication, the Bolletino, was published for one year. In 1907 it began to publish Il Libro e la Stampa, which continued until World War I. During the same year, the Chilean Sociedad Bibliográfica de Santiago was founded. It published a history of the Ecclesiastical Province of Chile.

In 1901 the Gutenberg-Gesellschaft (Society) was founded in Germany to publish research on the book printing art from Gutenberg to the present. Among its publications were Gutenberg-Jahrbuch Kleine Drucke and Veroffentlichungen. In Canada, the Bibliographical Society was founded in 1946, and in 1955 its semi-annual Newsletter began distribution.

In the United States, S. S. Josephson, chairman of the Bibliographical Society of Chicago organizing committee, arranged several preliminary meetings in the Spring of 1899. At the organization meeting in October of that year he expressed the hope that "the organization of this society may lead to the founding of a national bibliographical society. "20

From its beginnings until today, the Bibliographic Society of America adopted the "broadest possible idea of bibliography. " Among the papers published in the first volume of Proceedings and Papers, 1904-1907, were "The Need of Bibliographies in Literary History," contributions to the "Theory and History of Botanical Bibliography," and "Material in the Library of Congress for a Study of United States Naval History. " Recent volumes cover contemporary issues in bibliography. After the 1904 organization of the American Bibliographical Society, many important articles were published in its Papers, as well as in the publications of the New York Public Library and the Harvard College Library.

While most of these societies are well established and recognized, their main preoccupation is catching up with the past rather than keeping up with the present or planning for the future. Recognizing this dilemma, new generations of bibliographers have called for the establishment of national bibliographic centers or institutes to deal with pressing issues in national bibliographical planning. The role of these centers has been recognized by Unesco and national and regional bodies. Whether they are divisions of national, university or major research libraries, they act as national centers for bibliographic information and in some cases as the national exchange centers. A good example is the Australian Advisory Committee on Bibliographical Services (AACOBS) which has, since 1956, served as a coordination center for Australian bibliographical service. The Committee includes representatives of many libraries, of the authorities responsible for their administration and of the Library Association

of Australia. It undertakes projects already planned or ensures their
implementation by other bodies in accordance with the Committee's
directives. The functions of AACOBS are to prepare and recommend
to appropriate authorities projects for the further development of
Australian library and bibliographical services.

In Denmark, the Bibliotekscentralen acts as a bibliographical
center and publishing house for public and research libraries. In
other countries, like West Germany, the National Commission for
Bibliography, usually affiliated with Unesco, functions as the nation's
bibliographic center. The Iranian National Commission for Bibliography was established in 1955 at the instance of the National Iranian
Commission for Unesco. Its aim was to fill the gaps in Iranian
bibliography.

Other less fortunate countries, like Iraq, Liberia, Libya and
Lebanon, have no national commissions for bibliography or similar
agencies.

Aside from the general bibliographic information centers on
which Unesco has reported regularly since 1962 when it first published a Guide to National Bibliographical Information Centers, other
specialized centers have been created. Unesco has published two
guides to these centers: World Guide to Science Information and
Documentation Services, and World Guide to Technical Information
and Documentation Services.

Bibliographic Publishing

Individual efforts exerted in compiling and collecting bibliographies in various countries, especially the United States, led to a
commercial publishing business dominated by two publishing firms,
R. R. Bowker and H. W. Wilson.

United States bibliographic publishing began with Orville A.
Roorbach, born in New York in 1803. In 1849, he published the first
volume of his Bibliotheca Americana. It listed 25,000 titles published
between 1820 and 1849. A supplement of 2,000 more titles was published the following year.

In 1851, Charles B. Norton, a purchasing agent for libraries
and bookstores, decided to continue Roorbach's labors by establishing Norton's Literary Advertiser, a monthly journal with book listings. The Advertiser was adopted by the New York Book Publisher's
Association and continued under various names until it merged with
another magazine to become the present Publishers Weekly.

In 1866 a young German immigrant, Frederick Leypoldt,
joined Henry Holt, a recent Yale graduate, to establish a publishing
firm. One of the company's publications was the annual Literary
Bulletin, which in 1869 appeared as a "Monthly Record of Current
Literature," a subject catalog of the principal books issued the

previous year. It was followed two years later by the American Catalogue of Books for 1869, the first annual catalog since Norton's. By 1872 Leypoldt severed his connection with Holt to publish his own trade journal. That journal, combined with a descendant of Norton's original Advertiser, became Publishers' Weekly. [21]

The American Catalogue represented the second part of Leypoldt's plan for United States book trade bibliography. His monumental quartos set the standard to be followed in American national bibliography, not only in the publications emanating from Leypoldt and Bowker, but in their successors, the United States Catalogs of H. W. Wilson, also. The second American Catalogue was completed under Bowker's direction after Leypoldt's death. The great quarto series continued until 1911, by which time the United States Catalogs of H. W. Wilson Co. covered the field.

In 1873, Leypoldt started the Publishers' Trade List Annual. In its first issue, the Annual bound in alphabetical order the catalogs of 101 publishers, with advertisements from 114 others. [22] Like PW, it has been in continuous publication since its founding. PTLA's first edition was the progenitor of all that followed, both in the United States and in many European countries. It was only a year later that the British firm of Whitaker began publishing the British book trade bibliography, the Reference Catalogue of Current Literature, fashioned after Leypoldt's efforts. Later, Bowker distributed that work in the United States.

In its more recent history, the Bowker Co. commissioned and compiled a host of bibliographical tools and listings. Merle Johnson's authoritative American First Editions was first published in 1929. Edward Lazare edited American Book Prices Current, and Carolyn Ulrich edited the first Periodicals Directory published in 1932, which is currently known as Ulrich's International Periodicals Directory.

The advent of Bowker's Books In Print was a major breakthrough in the company's bibliographic service, as well as in the development of production processes to accommodate publication of immense amounts of directory information. Recent editions of BIP, now in two volumes, carry full information on the current offerings of more than 2,000 publishers. A Subject Guide to Books in Print began in 1956. From this vast body of data, librarians now have access by title, subject and publisher to full bibliographic information on thousands of United States titles in print. In combination with Forthcoming Books, LJ's "Books to Come," Paperbound Books in Print, Textbooks in Print, the PW "Weekly Record," the American Book Publishing Record, and the other Bowker bibliographies, the U.S. book output is relatively well covered.

Computerization of Bowker bibliographies began modestly in the early 1960s. The new technology promises to allow development at Bowker of a national bibliographic data bank from which can be extracted information on books yet to be published, those already in print, and those no longer available.

An equally important company in U. S. bibliographic publishing is The H. W. Wilson Co. The company's most important contribution to the field was the 1897 publication of the Cumulative Book Index, which is still being published today. In 1899 Wilson first published the United States Catalog. Other editions followed in 1902, 1912, and 1928.

Wilson's activities in serials bibliographical control were unprecedented. The company started with the Reader's Guide to Periodical Literature, which created a demand for more specialized indexes. The International Index to Periodicals, originally released as a supplement to the Guide and later as an independent publication, began in 1907. In 1913 the company issued the first number of the Industrial Arts Index, a guide to the increasing numbers of technical magazines. Later, the Index to Legal Periodicals and the Public Affairs Information Service were published. Many other Wilson indexes were published in the following years: in 1916 it published the Agricultural Index, followed in 1929 by the Education Index and Art Index and in the 1930s by the Vertical File Service Catalog, the Abridged Reader's Guide, the Motion Picture Review Digest, Library Literature, and Bibliographic Index. During the 1940s the company began to publish Current Biography and Biography Index. In the 1950s the company began to publish Business Periodical Index.

Few countries outside the U. S. A. can claim the kind of bibliographic coverage given to American publications by Bowker and Wilson. In most European countries, national libraries are responsible for most of the control over the country's book output.

Recent developments show an increased number of specialized agencies concentrating on specific subjects or regions. In Africa, the East African Literature Bureau was founded, in 1947, as the publishing outlet of the East African community. During the past three years EALB has published a rapidly increasing amount of scholarly bibliographic work. It has published a monumental 700-page Bibliography of Health and Disease in East Africa, with 30,000 entries covering all aspects of medicine and associated subjects.

The African Bibliographic Center, located in Washington, D. C. , publishes subject bibliographies. Africana Publishing Co. , located in New York, occasionally issues bibliographies on African countries or topics as part of its African bibliography series. The latest in the series is Mark and Delancey's Bibliography of Cameroon.[23] The East African Literature Bureau in Tanzania is active in bibliographic publishing. The Library of the United Nations Economic Commission for Africa publishes a series of excellent bibliographies, also.

Trade Bibliographies

The increased awareness of the value of information on books published has resulted in more trade bibliographies. Bowker's

American Book Publishing Record, Publishers Weekly, Publishers
Trade List Annual, and especially Books in Print have been imitated
abroad.

Daniel Melcher's dream of a Latin American Books in Print
came true when Libros en Venta en Hispanoamérica y España was
first published in 1964. Libros en Venta provided complete bibliographic information on the book production of Spanish and Latin
America, in classified subject order with author and title approaches.
Comentarios Bibliográficos Americanos (CBA) began as a quarterly
in 1969 to provide annotations on the books listed, news notes about
literary contests and prizes, Uruguay and Argentina best-seller lists,
and other items.

The British equivalent of BIP is British Books in Print, which
is subtitled: "The national inclusive book-reference index of books
in print and on sale in the United Kingdom with details as to author,
title, and other bibliographic elements." The trade bibliography for
Canada is Canadian Books in Print. First published in 1972, it attempts to cover English and French books as well as books published
in other languages, e. g. , German, Ukranian, Polish, etc. The current issues of Cumulative Book Index (CBI) and Whitaker's Cumulative Book List provide a wide coverage of books printed in the English language and available on the current market.

Catalogue del' Edition Française was first published in 1971.
The second edition published in 1973 covered 176,000 French-language
books from 2,300 publishers in 41 countries. The difference between
BIP and Catalogue is that the first is limited to material published
in the U. S. A. and includes foreign books only if they have U. S. distributors willing to report them through Bowker channels. The Catalogue attempts to list all French-language books, as the subtitle indicates: "Une liste exhaustive des ouvrages disponsibles publiés, en
Français, de par le monde." In this respect, the Catalogue is very
much like CBI.

Another French equivalent of CBI is Francophone Edition: Revue Bibliographique del' Edition de Langue Française dans le Monde
(Paris, France-Expansion, Nov. 1972- , no. 1-). This bibliography
lists "all the expressions of intellectual endeavor produced in all the
French-speaking countries and available from publishers." It includes books, new periodicals, transparencies, films, instructive
games, microformats, gramophone records, tapes, etc.

In West Germany the Verzeichnis Lieferbarer Bücher, which
appeared first in 1971, provides bibliographic information on current
German book production. The author and title volumes list 152,000
books of all kinds currently available from 1,104 publishers in West
Germany, Austria and Switzerland. The author volume provides full
bibliographic information for each listing. The title volume lists all
books by title and includes several useful indexes.

The first edition of Australian Books in Print, now in its

eleventh edition, was published in 1911. The list includes an alphabetical listing of books and government publications in print by author, title and subject. It is the most comprehensive Australian
trade bibliography.

Indian Books in Print was first published in 1969 in the English language. Another publication covering the same material is
the Reference Catalogue of Indian Books in Print, first published in
1960 as Impex Reference Catalogue of Indian Books in Print in English. The Reference Catalogue claims to be more comprehensive--
56,000 titles in Reference Catalogue, and 47,000 in Indian Books in
Print. These trade bibliographies are restricted to publications in
the English language, published in India. A third trade bibliography
is Indian Books, an annual bibliography first published in 1969. Unlike the first edition, the recent edition (1973-74) covers government
publications. In addition to author, title, and subject listings, this
volume contains a publishers' directory.

In Africa, a number of trade bibliographies have emerged recently, especially on a regional level. In 1969, the Nigerian Publishers Association, with the support of Franklin Book Programs,
Inc., issued Nigerian Books in Print, now in its third edition. In
Ghana, an equally useful publication was issued by R. J. Moxon in
1971 under the title, Ghanaian Books in Print. No subsequent editions have been reported. In the Republic of South Africa several
lists were published. C. Struik's Catalogue of Books (English) Published in Southern Africa, Still in Print (1970) listed over 1,000
titles including reprints.

The International African Bibliography was transferred from
the International African Institute Library to the School of Oriental
and African Studies Library, London, in 1973, and has since been
published by Mansell, beginning with volume 3. [24] The quarterly bibliography lists writing in the field of African Studies, excluding the
natural and technical sciences, fiction and school textbooks.

A most recent and valuable publication is the new African
Books in Print, 1975, edited by Hans M. Zell and published by Mansell Informational Publishing, Limited, London, in association with
the University of Ife Press, Nigeria. This publication is issued in
two parts, with the English/African and French volumes to be issued in alternating years. Its objective is "to provide a systematic,
reliable and functional reference tool and buying guide to African published materials currently in print." ABIP is based on data supplied
by African publishers. The first part lists 6,000 titles published in
nineteen African nations by 188 African publishers, research institutions and learned societies, as well as publications available from
university libraries or bookshops acting as distributors on behalf of
university departments, institutes, etc. [25]

The bibliographic listings in the African Book Publishing Record[26] are compiled in collaboration with over 200 African publishers,
research institutions, learned societies, professional associations,

and other organizations with publishing programs. The ABPR covers books in English and French as well as significant new titles in the African indigenous languages, which are listed selectively. It covers books, pamphlets, reports, series (including regular series), but does not include periodical publications other than yearbooks or annuals. For the time being, at least, government publications are excluded. ABPR bibliographic listings provide a supplementary updating service to African Books in Print.

The Middle East, except for Israel, has no BIP equivalent, and librarians must search various resources, especially literary magazines, to learn what has been published. Perhaps the only resource for Middle Eastern, especially Arab, publications is the Accession List: Middle East compiled and published by the U.S. Book Procurement Office in Cairo. [27]

The Israeli one-volume version of Books in Print is the General Book Catalog. It appeared in 1973 in a new format, arranged by author, title and subject, and produced by computer. It lists almost all Israeli publications in Hebrew. An updated, improved edition, which will include all languages, is promised annually (General Book Catalog, 1961-irregular. Available from: Book Publishers' Association of Israel, 29 Carlebach Street, Tel Aviv, Israel).

National Bibliography

Comprehensive national bibliographies did not appear until late in the 19th century. However, there were earlier attempts to compile what came to be known as a national bibliography. The Catalogue of English Printed Books, published by the English bookseller Andrew Maunsell in 1595, can be considered a national bibliography since the compiler did not try to determine whether or not the books were for sale. It was an attempt to list everything known to have been published during the period.

Similar attempts were taking place at the end of the 16th century in Belgium, in the low countries in the 17th century, and in Spain in the second half of the 17th century. Scholars in these countries produced remarkable bio-bibliographies of regional writers which may be regarded as the first signs of national bibliography. [28]

During the 18th and 19th centuries, booksellers like Wilhelm Heinsius and Joseph Marie Quérard began to publish what could have been the nuclei of national bibliographies. In Germany, Wilhelm Heinsius (1768-1817) published his Allgemeines Bücher-Lexikon, which listed all works published in Germany, 1700-1797. In France, Joseph Marie Quérard began, in 1839, through the house of Dejuin and under the title of the Littérature Française Contemporaine, to publish the continuation of La France Littéraire for the years 1827-1840.

In the U.S. in 1868, Joseph Sabin inaugurated his Dictionary

of Books Relating to America which, along with Evans' American
Bibliography, became the most important national bibliographies of
their kinds. Other bibliographies covering the nineteenth century in-
clude: Roorbach's Bibliotheca Americana (1820-1861); Shoemaker's
Checklist of American Imprints (1820-1861); James Kelly's American
Catalogue of Books (1861-1871 and 1876-1910); and H. W. Wilson's
United States Catalog (1899-1927).

A national bibliography in the modern sense is a tool "to
make quickly available in published form suitable records of the current output by all countries of publications of research value."
Helen Conover's idea of a current national bibliography is "... a
complete listing of all books, documents, pamphlets, serials, and
other printed matter published within the bounds of a single country
and within the time limits of the previous year or less...."[29]

The modern concept of national bibliographic control was widely recognized when Unesco was established. In its Constitution,
Unesco stated that one way to achieve its purpose was "to maintain,
increase and diffuse knowledge ... by initiating methods of international cooperation calculated to give the people of all countries access to the printed and published material produced by one of them."[30]

In 1946, the Unesco General Conference held its first session
in Paris. At the second plenary meeting the interests of bibliographers were called to the attention of the Conference by the Prepara-
tory Commission report. According to this report, Unesco was responsible for formulating concrete projects, one of which ought to
be a world bibliographic center. At the end of that year, a Conference on International, Cultural, Educational and Scientific Exchanges,
held at Princeton University, recommended that Unesco and other
suitable agencies stimulate each country to issue comprehensive current national bibliographies.[31]

Since the 1950s, Unesco has prepared regional and national
conferences and seminars to provide platforms for exchanging information, sharing experiences and training bibliographers. As part of
its activities to promote and disseminate information about bibliographical services, Unesco has published its bibliographic handbook,
Bibliographical Services Throughout the World, which began in 1958.
The latest edition covers 1965-69. The information is being updated,
a few countries at a time, in the quarterly issues of Bibliography,
Documentation, Terminology. Unesco Bulletin for Libraries contains
articles and news about national and regional bibliographic activities,
also.

Today, under Unesco stimulation, valiant beginnings at national bibliography are being made in various parts of the world, especially in developing nations where bibliographic controls are lacking.
Bibliographic services are developing rapidly throughout the world,
and a bibliographic tradition is being firmly established. Governments and bibliographers have learned how to compile an inventory
of the material contained in libraries and archives.[32]

While Unesco is concerned with global bibliographical services, regional organizations attempt to develop effective bibliographic control in specific geographic areas. The Pan American Union
publishes the quarterly Inter-American Review of Bibliography. It
has a notes-and-news section arranged by countries, and "Recent
Books" includes a listing on bibliography. "The List of Books Ac-
cessioned and Periodical Articles Indexed, published monthly by the
Pan American Union's Columbus Memorial Library, devotes sections
in both categories to bibliography and may be depended upon to note
items concerning national bibliography."[33] The seminars on the Acquisition of Latin American Library Materials which began in 1956
were originally sponsored by the Pan American Union, but in 1968
they were formally incorporated under the acronym SALALM. An
annual SALALM working paper devoted to bibliographic activities for
the past year provides information on national bibliography developments.

Publishers and booksellers have taken interest in the bibliographic control of Latin American publications. The Stechert-Hafner
LACAP program, which ceased in 1973, provided, among other
things, bibliographic information regarding current publications made
available through the Latin American Cooperative Acquisition Program. In the 1960s Stechert-Hafner began to publish a special series of numbered lists under the general title, New Latin American
Books: An Advance Checklist of Newly Published Titles Just Acquired Under the Latin American Cooperative Acquisitions Project
(LACAP). Although these lists are booksellers' instruments rather
than bibliographic aids, they provide much information on Latin
American publications.

The R. R. Bowker Company began experimenting in Latin
America with the equivalents of Publishers Weekly and Books in
Print in 1961. In October, 1971, the company published the first
issue of its quarterly bulletin, Fichero Bibliográfico Hispanoamericano: Catálogo de Toda Clase de Libros Publicados en Las Améri-
cas en Español. Fichero was prepared at the New York Public Library until 1964, when it was transferred to Buenos Aires. The
present Fichero Bibliográfico Hispanoamericano is a monthly trade
bulletin, published by Bowker Editores Argentina, S. A. It provides
a listing, arranged by the D. D. C. , of books and pamphlets recently
published in Spanish-speaking countries.

In Africa a move is under way to establish an Africa Bibliographic Center (ABC). The sponsors of the project hope to enlist
the long-term interest of the OAU (Organization of African Unity),
African governments and citizens in an ambitious new pan-African
venture, a proposal that envisages setting up a central information
and bibliographic center and library base to serve the whole of Africa. Some of the Center components would include an "African Lending Library" which would collect all African published materials, and
an "African Audiovisual Depository" which would systematically collect non-print material, such as films, photographs, and tape recordings. Other functions and activities might include "African

Bibliographic Publishing," current awareness services, and an "African Microfiche and Publications Center" which would secure copies
of difficult to preserve source materials on contemporary African affairs including confidential government and official publications. [34]

     In the Middle East, the League of Arab States expressed in-
terest in developing and coordinating a regional bibliography for the
Arab World.   Unfortunately, nothing beyond rhetoric was achieved.
It is hoped that the Middle East Studies Association will play an active role in the field of Arab bibliography.

     In Asia, while it is extremely difficult to obtain region-wide
coverage, due to the diversity, the Association for Asian Studies has
played an excellent role in Asian bibliography.   The Association's
most important contribution is its Bibliography which began in 1930.

     The American Libraries Book Procurement Centers in Africa,
Asia and the Middle East provide up-to-date current bibliographies
for select countries.   Although these are primarily accession lists
of the material purchased by these centers and shipped to American
libraries, they provide up-to-date information on publications.   In
some cases, such as the Middle East, Africa, and Asia, the lists
are the only up-to-date comprehensive bibliographies published from
these countries.

The Role of Legal Deposit and Copyright Laws
in the Development of National Bibliographies

     Unlike previous methods used to compile bibliographies of
publications issued in a given country, most of today's national bibliographies rely on the introduction and enforcement of legal deposit
laws.   The value of legal deposit for developing a national bibliography was recognized by UNESCO in 1954, when a model copyright deposit law was suggested.   In spite of these UNESCO developments
and encouragements, there are still countries today with no legal deposit laws, and in others archaic laws have not been revised to meet
modern needs and recent publishing developments.

     Although legal deposit was originally introduced for different
purposes, in a number of countries it is primarily used today to provide the national bibliography of a country.   This recently recognized
purpose of legal deposit is strongly emphasized in the new Belgian
and West German Acts, although both countries had national bibliographies, issued on a private basis, before the introduction of legal
deposit.

     In spite of the well established legal deposit there, national
bibliographies in the Scandinavian countries are based primarily upon
copies delivered voluntarily by publishers; they are only later compared with the legal deposit copies for the purposes of control.   This
system is a consequence of the long delay (up to six months) allowed in the Acts for delivering deposit publications. [35]

Because of the reliance of the national bibliography on legal deposit or copyright laws, it is safe to assume that in most countries the national bibliography is accurate only if these laws are comprehensive, up-to-date and enforced. Limitations inherent in legal deposit laws and their enforcement make the national bibliographies of some countries far less comprehensive than their producers expected. In many countries, national bibliographies must be supplemented with other bibliographic tools such as accession lists, bibliographies of theses, government publications and other types of library material.

In some Latin American countries, depository laws are consistently ignored by publishers and current national bibliographies are non-existent. Although the Boletin Bibliográfico Nacional should be the official source for the Argentine national bibliography, its history and present status illustrate the full range of difficulties of such publications. One difficulty is the ineffectiveness of the ley de depósito legal, which deprives the Library of receiving current material to provide the information needed. 36

In Brazil, the legal deposit law is poorly observed, and government publications are not sent to the Biblioteca Nacional, Rio de Janeiro. Since the Boletin Bibliográfico (1886-) is prepared by the library acquisition department on the basis of material received, the record is incomplete. Another official Brazilian bibliography is Bibliografía Brasileira (1938/39-). It is prepared and published by the Instituto Nacional do Livro, an agency of the Ministerio de Educacao e Cultura, and is more up-to-date than the Boletin. In spite of difficulties with Brazil's legal deposit law, the country is fortunate that publishers, book-dealers, and bibliographers recognize their common interests. A cooperative arrangement between the Instituto do Livro and the Library of Congress has contributed to relatively prompt and complete coverage by the Bibliografía Brasileira Mensal. This arrangement was established in Rio de Janeiro, in about 1967, to provide LC with selective but improved Brazilian publication coverage.

In the family of South American countries, Chile has the strongest bibliographic tradition. This can be attributed to a number of notable bibliographers including José Toribio Medina. His efforts were carried on largely through Don Guillermo Feliu Cruz. His Anuario de la Frensa Chilena is being continued by the Biblioteca Nacional. In Peru, the Biblioteca Nacional provides excellent coverage in its Anuario Bibliográfico Peruano of all material acquired. The Anuario appears too late to provide a current record, however.

In Africa, the bibliographic situation is similar to that in Latin America. A few years ago, Africa constituted no problem to bibliographers, since the titles published were too few to warrant special bibliographic coverage. African publisher output for the years 1965 and 1966 was a mere 1,310 books and pamphlets, or only 1.5 per cent of the world's annual book production. Unesco's estimate of Africa's book production in 1972 was 10,000 titles, reflecting

a rapid change. It is estimated that each of eleven indigenous African publishers has over 100 titles in print, and this count excludes
South Africa. New university presses have been established on African campuses, thus enhancing scholarly publishing. Many research
institutions maintain active publishing programs presenting vital research material. [37]

As a result of these developments there has been considerable progress in providing bibliographic services. National bibliographies in one form or another exist for Algeria, Botswana, Ethiopia,
Ghana, Ivory Coast, Malagasy Republic, Malawi, Mauritius, Moroc-
co, Nigeria, Rhodesia, Senegal, Sierre Leone, South Africa, Tanzania, and Uganda. Most notable among them for standards of organization and comprehensiveness are the bibliographies of Nigeria
and South Africa, and perhaps Ghana and Tanzania more recently.
In many cases, however, African bibliographers and librarians fail
to enact or enforce legal deposit laws.

The francophone nations in black Africa are not as fortunate
as the anglophone nations, with the exception of the Malagasy Republic and the Ivory Coast, which publish fine annual bibliographies.
The University of Dakar Library School, under the leadership of Dr.
Bousso, has published bibliographies, some with Unesco support.

In spite of recent bibliographical gains, many of the recommendations of the International Conference on African Bibliography
held at University College, Nairobi, 4-8 December 1967, have not
been enacted. Most African governments have not promoted the compilation of national bibliographies. Legal deposit laws, when they
exist, are not being enforced, and "ephemeral" materials are not included in national bibliographies. The best established bibliographies
in the continent are African Books in Print, the Nigerian National
Bibliography, the South African National Bibliography, the Ghana National Bibliography, and the Library of Congress Accessions List:
Eastern Africa published by the LC Office in Nairobi, Kenya.

Asian bibliographic control was formerly accomplished by the
colonial powers, especially Britain and France, whose legal deposit
laws extended to their colonies. In the late nineteenth and early
twentieth centuries, the British Museum and the Bibliothèque Nationale issued a series of catalogs for various Asian countries. When
these two powers gave Asia its independence they did not leave behind a bibliographic tradition. Instead, many Asian countries have
had to develop this tradition after independence. In Asia, as in Africa, numerous aspects contributed to a bibliographic tradition. The
rise of literacy and nationalism have produced a greater amount of
publishing in local languages than had been thought possible a decade
ago.

India was among the first new independent nations in South
Asia to develop a legal book deposit; it is now part of the Public Library Act of 1956. Books deposited in compliance with the Act are
listed in the monthly Indian National Bibliography, which includes

publications in fourteen Indian languages and in English.   In spite of
the strict Act, recent study has shown that 40 per cent of the material published in India is neither deposited in the National Library
nor listed in the Bibliography. [38]   Like many other Asian national
bibliographies, the INB is several years behind in current coverage.
A more complete and current coverage can be obtained in the Library of Congress PL 480 accessions list which began in 1962.

Another ambitious bibliographic project is the National Bibliography of Indian Literature, 1901-1953.   This list is sponsored by
the Sahitya Akademi (National Academy of Letters).   Volumes have
appeared so far for the following languages: Assamese, Bengali,
English, Gujarati, Hindi, Kannada, Kashmiri, and Malayalam.

Bibliographic control of Pakistani material began officially in
1947, although numerous publications on the area were published as
parts of earlier series.   In 1952 the Stationery and Printing Department began publishing a Catalogue of the Government of Pakistan
Publications. [39]   A decade later the Pakistan National Bibliography
appeared. [40]   The national bibliography, like the Indian National Bibliography, follows UDC and is divided into government and non-government sections.   The LC PL 480 office accession list is the most
up-to-date bibliographic control for the country. [41]

Sri Lanka's bibliographic activities have been summarized by
H. A. I. Goonetileke: "What little bibliographic activity there is,
is regrettably haphazard and unplanned, with the single exception of
the Ceylon National Bibliography. "[42]   The Ceylon National Bibliography is published monthly with no annual cumulation. [43]   It includes
books published in the country, official publications, university theses, and dissertations and bibliographies of bibliographies.   The
work is divided into three sections, one each for the three official
languages of Ceylon, namely English, Sinhala, and Tamil.   Within
each section the works are arranged by UDC with appropriate author
indexes.   The LC PL 480 program for Ceylon issues an accession
list which provides up-to-date data on material acquired under this
program.

In developed countries, a national bibliographic tradition was
established early in the century.   Their legal deposit laws have been
enforced and the national bibliographies became the beneficiary.   In
Canada, for example, the deposit law was written into the constitution.   Provision was made for two copies to be deposited in the Canadian National Library of items originating in that country or relating to it.   These items appear in Canadiana, the country's monthly
national bibliography.

A strict deposit law can be found in France.   According to
the last decree, November 21, 1960, publication deposit in the Bibliothèque Nationale must occur at least 48 hours before it appears
for sale.   A recent amendment, August 1, 1963, extends the legal
deposit to phonographic works which must be deposited in the Phono-
thèque Nationale.   These publications are then listed in the Bibliographie de la France-Biblio, the country's current national bibliography.

In Italy, where a legal deposit law is being enforced, the National Central Library, Florence, in cooperation with the national
center for the Union Catalog of Italian Libraries, edits and publishes
the Italian National Bibliography, Bolletino delle Pubblicazione Ital-
iane Ricevuto per Piritto di Stampa dalla Biblioteca Nazionale Centrale di Firenze. It began publication in 1886 as a monthly; in 1957
the title was changed to Bibliografia Nazionale Italiana.

In some of the Western European countries, legal deposit
laws were enacted very recently. In Belgium, the Act of April 8,
1965, which promulgated legal deposit, enables the Royal Library
for the first time in its history to compile an official and comprehensive national bibliography, Bibliographie de Belgique. Although
the bibliography was founded in 1875, only recently has it relied on
legal deposit.

A system of legal deposit has existed in Denmark since the
seventeenth century. The present law dates from 1927 and stipulates
that one copy of every printed work (book, pamphlet, periodical,
newspaper, map, etc.) must be deposited in the Royal Library and
one copy in the State University Library, Aarhus. These titles are
then listed in the Danish current national bibliography, Dansk Bog-
fortegnelse.

According to the Finnish legal deposit law, printers are required to send copies (usually five) of all works they publish to the
Helsinki University Library, which is responsible for distributing
them among the legal deposit libraries. The Library is responsible
for compiling and publishing the Finnish national bibliography, Suo-
men Kirjallisuus Finlands Litteratur.

Bulgaria's legal deposit has existed since 1897 and is com-
pulsory for all types of publications. The Kiril i Metodi (National
Library), which is the center of bibliographical activity, produces
Bulgarski Knigopis. It gives a list of books, pamphlets, musical
scores, maps, atlases, and periodicals published for the first time.
Since 1962 it has issued a quarterly supplement listing official publications, standards, works in Braille, theses, etc.

In Norway, the Norsk Bokfortegnelse, the Norwegian national
bibliography, lists books, pamphlets and periodicals published in the
country, as well as publications printed abroad for Norwegian publishers and original works by Norwegian authors published abroad.
The bibliography is based on material deposited at the Royal University Library, Oslo, in compliance with the legal deposit law of June
9, 1939.

In Portugal, the National Library in Lisbon publishes a current national bibliography in the form of a bulletin entitled Boletin
de Bibliografia Portuguesa. It is based on material deposited in the
Library in compliance with the legal deposit law.

The comprehensiveness of an effective legal deposit system

can result in an equally comprehensive bibliography which is a true
record of the nation's cultural and intellectual production. The enforcement of the Australian legal deposit act results in a comprehensive Australian National Bibliography which lists books published in
Australia and books of Australian authors published overseas, maps,
prints, films, sheet music, government publications, both commonwealth and state, and the first issue of each new serial. Government publications are listed in a separate annual volume, Australian
Government Publications, which includes serials as well as monographs.

    In nations with a federal structure, such as the USSR, legal
deposit laws require that copies be deposited with the central and
the state libraries. Thus, the USSR Book Chamber and the book
chambers of each one of the republics receive free copies of all publications according to the 1917 decree. These book chambers are
responsible for registering publications and publishing national bibliographies, Knizhnaja Letopis (Book Chronicles). These bibliographies, however, exclude certain publications which the Soviet government chooses not to publicize.

    Although the U. S. does not have a compulsory deposit sys-
tem, a copyright law of 1909 (Title 17, U. S. Code) governs the legal registration of material. This law provides for the deposit of
two copies of all copyrighted published material and one copy of unpublished works in the Library of Congress Copyright Office. Only
one copy of a foreign work is required for deposit. These titles
and others are listed in the National Union Catalog.

    Like the U. S. , West Germany does not have a general law
relating to legal deposit. However, through an agreement with the
German Book Chamber, the Deutsche Bibliothek, Frankfurt, receives
a copy of all German publications. These publications are included
in the weekly Deutsche Bibliographie Wochentliches Verzeichnis,
which has been Germany's national bibliography since 1947.

    The National Diet Library is responsible for the Japanese na-
tional bibliography, Zen Nihon Shuppan-butsu Sô-Mokuroku, which
lists all works published in Japan, including books in Braille. The
bibliography is divided into two parts--official publications and unof-
ficial publications--and contains several indexes and a directory of
publishers. The Library is responsible for publishing Nohon Shuho
(current publications), a weekly list of works deposited in the library,
also.

    In spite of recent developments, the national library measures
in Asia are fraught with the difficulties inherent in local publishing
conditions, their deposit arrangements and the nature of the material
published. Valiant efforts are being made by the Library of Congress, through the various accessions lists produced by PL 480 programs, and by the Association of Asian Studies through its bibliographic series, especially the annual Bibliography of Asian Studies
(Ann Arbor: Assoc. for Asian Studies, 1941- annual).

In the Middle East the situation is equally complex, and legal
deposit laws are not being enforced properly. As a result, national
libraries, when they exist, cannot enforce the laws and, therefore,
are deprived of receiving publications that should be listed in the national bibliographies. In Lebanon, for example, the National Library
cannot enforce the legal deposit law of 1941, since the law is far
from being comprehensive for Lebanese publications, and thus it is
unable to produce a regular current national bibliography. As a result, only a few issues of the irregular Bulletin Bibliographique Li-
banais have appeared since 1964-65.

In Jordan, material acquired through legal deposit is listed
annually in The Library Journal published by the Jordan Library Association. The University of Jordan publishes the Monthly List of
Books Added to the Library (in Arabic and English). In Iraq, the
National Library publishes the Iraqi Publications Pamphlet.

Of all the Middle East countries, Israel and Egypt have the
most advanced national bibliographic control systems. In the former,
the National and University Library continues to publish its Kirjath
Sepher, a bibliographic quarterly which lists material deposited in
compliance with a 1953 law. In Egypt, the National Library is responsible for publishing the Egyptian National Bibliography which is
based on deposited material.

Union Catalogs

While national and trade bibliographies are important tools to
identify the intellectual and cultural published output of the country
covered, the national union catalog (or catalogs) is an inventory common to a group of libraries. It contains all or some of their publications, foreign and domestic, listed in one or more orders of arrangement. 45

Union catalogs may be general or special. The general ones
aim to be exhaustive and to list both national production and the foreign works held by the country's libraries. Special union catalogs,
on the other hand, are selective and confined to a single category of
publication on the basis of the origin of material (e.g. , foreign publications); its nature (periodicals, theses, manuscripts, etc.); date
of publication (incunabula, old books, recent acquisitions, etc.); or
the branch of knowledge concerned (e.g. , social sciences, medicine,
agriculture, etc.).

The need for a national union catalog was first recognized by
Goethe in 1798 when he proposed a scheme for a union catalog of
Weimar libraries. In 1884, the historian Heinrich von Treitschke
put forward the proposals which eventually led to the Prussian Union
Catalog (Preussische Gesamtkatalog). 46 The Gesamtkatalog was originally expected to replace individual library catalogs. "By 1929 when
the printed union catalog was closed, it listed all books published before January 1, 1929 which were in possession" of 18 libraries,

including ten Prussian university libraries and the Prussian State Library. [47] Between 1929 and World War II, a card union catalog containing entries from other German and Austrian libraries extended the endeavor into a more comprehensive Union Catalog. This project was carried on through the Berliner Titledrucke, maintained through the Auskunftsbureau in Berlin. From the letter B onward, the printed catalog was expanded into a German Union Catalog (Deutscher Gesamtkatalog). Today, most of the union catalogs in existence in East and West Germany are regional in approach. [48]

Developments in U.S. national union catalogs can be traced to Herbert Putnam, former Librarian of Congress. Under his leadership, the National Union Catalog was begun in card form in 1901. In addition to the Library of Congress there were four cooperating libraries: the New York Public Library, Boston Public Library, Harvard College Library and John Crerar Library, Chicago. The NUC had over two million cards and was physically located at the Library of Congress. The problem was later solved by sending duplicate cards to large key libraries throughout the United States. In the early 1940s, work began on a printed book catalog. In January 1956 the printed catalog was expanded to include not only Library of Congress holdings, but those of other libraries, also. In July of the same year the book catalog bore the new name: The National Union Catalog.

U.S. regional union catalogs can be traced to California, where the oldest one began in its State Library in 1909. It was first a union list of periodicals in California libraries. Later, cards were added for book holdings. In 1914, a Library of Congress depository catalog was acquired and used as a foundation for further expansion.[49] During the 1930s, regional union catalogs were founded on a large scale, thanks to the WPA (Works Project Administration) free labor program. Today, regional and local union catalogs can be found in almost every state and in some large cities.

The British National Central Library possesses a series of union catalogs which are kept up to date. Among others, they include the national union catalog, containing a list of books in the libraries belonging to the regional library system. In addition, each regional office has a union catalog, and a duplicate list of all additions is forwarded to the national union catalog.

The National Library of Australia launched a 1960 project to compile and maintain a union catalog of monographs held in major Commonwealth libraries. The union catalog of current monograph accessions contains entries for works acquired since 1959 by all the larger and an increasing number of small libraries. Publication of this union catalog is planned along the lines of the U.S. National Union Catalog. Publications bearing imprints earlier than 1960 are included in the retrospective bibliography which has been microfilmed. [50] Australian Bibliography and Bibliographical Services lists nearly forty union catalogs. More recent ones are identified in the current survey published in Bibliography, Documentation, Terminology.

Good inventories of published library catalogs, including union catalogs, have been compiled by such well-known bibliographers
as Robert Collison, Robert Downs and Lee Ash. [51] The most recent
one is Collison's Published Library Catalogues: An Introduction to
Their Contents and Use (1973), which lists 600 library catalogs, including union catalogs, from the English-speaking world. In a series of survey chapters it narrates eleven subject areas that they
cover: general catalogs, auction sale catalogs, book industries,
philosophy and religion, social sciences, science and technology,
arts and architecture, literature, history and biography, music and
geography.

While tremendous efforts have been exerted in developing
countries to develop current national bibliographies, few attempts,
if any, have been made to compile and publish national or regional
union catalogs. As one looks at Asia, Africa, the Middle East and
Latin America, one finds only a few countries, usually large and
economically advanced ones, in these regions that have compiled or
are compiling union catalogs. Others are not as fortunate. Considering the value of union catalogs in facilitating access to library
collections, one can conclude that readers in these countries remain
deprived of free access to book and non-book material, and that
those who live far from the metropolitan centers where major libraries exist suffer the most. This is not entirely a library problem. It is a communication problem, also, since developing countries suffer from backward postal service and delivery systems.

A country like Brazil has, through the cooperation of the Instituto Brasileira de Bibliografia e Documentacao (IBBD) and the Instituto Nacional do Livro, produced an automated Catalogo Colectivo
Nacional as the nucleus of a Brazilian national union catalog. However, the country's postal service is so poor that one wonders if the
purpose behind a national union catalog, namely interlibrary loan,
can be achieved under the present circumstances.

Other countries are not as fortunate as Brazil since no attempts have been made to identify library holdings in order to establish a union catalog. Even in countries with large and numerous
university libraries like Egypt, no attempt has been made to compile
a union catalog so that students and faculty can have easy access to
information without traveling from one campus to the other.

In Africa, the University of Dar es Salaam Library has published a useful catalog which brings together details of all the publications produced by the various university departments and research
institutes.

Bibliographic Control of Serials

Serials remain the most important means of rapidly disseminating the new knowledge in all fields. Their great profusion makes
it imperative that bibliographers identify the serial publications

published and available in their countries.   The large increase in
the number of bibliographies and abstracting services published in
developed and developing countries is a clear indication of the enormous number and increased importance of serials published throughout the world.   In many countries, dedicated efforts are being made
to identify the periodicals published by compiling serials directories,
identifying libraries with holdings of periodical titles (union lists of
serials), showing the contents of these periodicals (periodical indexes) and showing the contents of the articles included in these
periodicals (abstracting services).

       The U.S. has long been the undisputed leader in these areas.
As with other bibliographic ventures, individuals played an important
role in publishing periodical bibliographies.   William Frederick
Poole issued his first bibliography in 1848, a 154-page booklet titled
Index to Subjects Treated in the Reviews and Other Periodicals.   It
was followed by a new edition in 1853, and in 1876 ALA took over
the project with Poole as editor.   Another bibliographer, W. I.
Fletcher, entered the field in 1883 when he published Cooperative Index to Periodicals.   It was later absorbed by Wilson's Readers'
Guide to Periodical Literature which began in 1901.   Other indexes
followed which made the Wilson Company a giant in periodical bibliography.   Sophisticated indexes are now being published.   Some cover specialized journals, and many are compiled by automated indexing methods.

       Periodical indexes have increased in various parts of the
world, an indication of their extreme usefulness.   India leads the developing nations in the quality and quantity of its periodical indexes.
They range from the most general, like the Guide to Indian Periodical Literature (social sciences and humanities), to Index to Indian
Economic Journals and Indian Library Science Abstracts. 52,53,54
While these and other indexes appear regularly in India, other developing countries are not so fortunate.   The Ceylon Periodical Index
is a case in point.   Even in a leading African country like Nigeria,
the few indexes that are published, including Index to Selected Nigerian Periodicals, are not issued regularly, and therefore their value
is diminished.

       While indexing and abstracting services in developing coun-
tries are lagging, bibliographic identification of periodicals in these
countries is dramatically improving.   As the Western countries have
developed good bibliographic coverage for their periodicals, so have
the Eastern and developing nations.   The American Standard Periodical Directory has its equivalents in the Canadian Serials Directory,
Current Australian Serials and Guide to Current British Journals. 55

       Similar directories have had modest beginnings in Nigeria and
Ethiopia.   In the former, the National Library publishes Serials in
Print in Nigeria, and for the latter, S. Chojnacki and Ephraim Haile
Selassie publish a List of Current Periodical Publications in Ethiopia
every two years.

Comparative/International

In Asia, India leads the developing nations with its Indian Periodicals in Print, which contains an alphabetical listing of 16,483 periodicals and serials. The Ceylon Periodical Directory, published by the Department of National Museums, Colombo, lists the new periodicals and the title changes in 1973. The office of the Registrar of Books and Newspapers, in Sri Lanka, publishes its Catalogue of Newspapers, which attempts to cite all Ceylon non-monographic items.⁵⁶

The USSR, Japan and China have their own directories. The Letopis' Periodičeskih Izdanij SSSR lists USSR periodical publications every five years. The contents of Japanese periodical articles are given in the Zasshi Kiji Sakuin, published monthly by the National Diet Library. An Annotated Guide to Taiwan Periodicals has been published, also.

In some national bibliographies, new periodical titles are included under the heading "periodicals" and bibliographic information is given about them. Examples can be found in Bulgaria's national bibliography, Bulgarski Knigopis. Other European countries have their separate lists. Among them are: Repertório das Publicacões Periódicas Portuguesas, published by the Portugese National Library in Lisbon; Handbuch Österreichs Presse, which lists Austrian periodicals; and the current supplement to J. Van Hove's Répertoire de Periodiques Paraissanten en Belgique, published in 1961, which lists Belgian periodicals.

Since new directories appear frequently, the era of bibliographic fragmentation may be ending, and international control of new periodical titles and literature about to begin.

Union Lists of Serials

Related to the process of identifying serial publications is the identification of the libraries holding them. With today's profusion of serial publications, even the richest libraries in the most developed nations have difficulty obtaining and keeping more than a part of the titles needed. In developing countries, where budget and currency problems cannot be avoided, the idea of sharing resources should be gaining support. To share each other's resources, librarians have found the union list of serials to be the most convenient device by which to identify libraries with specific periodical holdings. Union lists have facilitated interlibrary loans and photocopy procurement and can support other forms of library cooperation, such as exchanges and transfers, cooperative acquisition and storage.

The earliest known union list of serials was compiled by Luciano dell'Acqua and published in Milan in 1859. Dell'Acqua's list appeared in two subsequent editions, 1861 and 1864. They were followed by the publication in 1866 at Oxford University of a Provisional Catalogue of Transactions of Societies, Periodicals, and Memoirs Available for the Use of Professors and Students, which was revised

in 1871, 1876, and 1887. Other early union lists were issued in
Belgium in 1881; Geneva, 1879; Amsterdam, 1884; and Italy, 1885.
In the U.S., the earliest union list, a Check List of Periodicals, was published by Johns Hopkins University in Baltimore in
1876. A second edition appeared in 1878, the same year in which
two lists for the Boston-Cambridge area were first published. The
first regional American list was issued in California in 1880, and
the first one offering national coverage was Bolton's Catalogue of
Scientific and Technical Periodicals, published by the Smithsonian Institution in 1885. The representation of Canadian library holdings,
which has become a standard feature of the major American union
lists, began with Bolton, also.

The monumental American Union List of Serials appeared
first in 1927 and contained entries for 75,000 serial titles located in
225 libraries. By comparison, the third edition contained 156,449
titles which began prior to January 1, 1950 and were held by 956 libraries. New Serial Titles brought about significant bibliographical
control for those periodicals which began publication after January 1,
1950.

The British counterpart of ULS and NST is the British Union
Catalogue of Periodicals, a four-volume basic work updated by quar-
terly supplements. The German equivalent is Gesamtuerzeichnis der
Zeitschriften und Serien in Bibliotheken der Bundesrepublik Deutsch-
land Einschliesslich Berlin (West). In Canada, the Union List of
Scientific Serials in Canadian Libraries is published by the National
Science Library. In Japan, several union lists have been compiled,
each covering a given subject area: the Chikuji Kankobutsu Sogo
Mokuroku is a union list of music periodicals and the Igaku Zasshi
Sogo Mokuroku is a similar list of medical periodicals.

Such lists are the kinds that librarians and bibliographers in
developing countries aspire to compile. Successful attempts, albeit
limited in scope and coverage, were made in such countries as Nigeria, where the Lagos Special Libraries Information Service published a Union List of Periodicals in Member Libraries; in Pakistan,
where a Union Catalogue of Scientific Periodicals in Pakistan libraries has been published by the National Scientific and Technical
Documentation Center; and in the Republic of China, where the National Library is in charge of compiling a Union Catalogue of Chinese
Periodicals in the Humanities and Social Sciences. In Sri Lanka, a
union list of scientific periodicals appeared in 1953.[57]

The value and importance of union lists is amply confirmed
by their proliferation during the past 105 years, and especially in
recent decades. Sixty per cent of the editions reported in Freitag's
bibliography of union lists of serials were published after the end of
the Second World War.[58] As these lists become well established in
many countries, the prospects for regional union lists in Asia, Latin
America and the Middle East look good. In Latin America, the
seeds for limited regional cooperation have been planted. The

Catalógo Colectivo de Publiçacoes Periodicas de América Latina (CAPPAL), first published in 1962, contains information received by the Instituto Brasielieiro de Bibliografia e Documentaçâo concerning collections of reviews of cultural value to be found in the libraries of seven Latin American countries, Argentina, Chile, Columbia, El Salvador, Guatemala, Mexico and Venezuela.

Impetus for more international cooperation may come from the International Serials Data System (ISDS) and the International Center for the Registration of Serials as part of the UNISIST program. As part of its system, ISDS has set about to create a network of serial centers. A number of those already in operation have been established in national libraries: for example, the National Library of Australia, National Library of Canada, British Library, Library of Congress, Bibliothèque Nationale, and Deutsche Bibliothek, Frankfurt am Main. [59]

Bibliographies of Theses and Dissertations

Few countries outside Europe and North America have established complete and regular bibliographic identification of theses submitted to their academic institutions. Although the number of theses and dissertations available from these countries is very small, no mechanism has been established to deposit copies with libraries responsible for identifying them. Copies may be deposited in the university library, but in many cases no record of their existence is made public except occasionally in university yearbooks or specialized works.

Among the countries with advanced bibliographic control of theses are: Canada, where the National Library compiles Canadian Theses/Thèses Canadiennes, published by the Queen's Printer; the U.K., where Aslib continues to publish the Index to Theses Accepted for Higher Degrees in the Universities of Great Britain and Northern Ireland; and France, where the Ministry of Education continues to publish an annual Catalogue des Thèses de Doctorat Soutenues Devant les Universités Françaises; another specialized list is the Table des Thèses Soutenues Devant la Faculté de Médecine de Paris.

An equally good source for dissertations is Japan. The titles of doctoral theses are listed by the Research Institute of Educational Administration in the annual Nihon Hakushi Roku. The most comprehensive of all lists are the American Dissertation Abstracts and American Doctoral Dissertations, both published by University Microfilms, Inc., Ann Arbor, Michigan.

While these lists are published separately, other countries include theses in their national bibliographies or in supplements. This practice is followed in the USSR where theses appear in a supplementary edition of Knižaja Letopis, and in Hungary in Magyar Nemzeti Bibliográfia.

In developing countries, university libraries are normally re-
sponsible for publishing bibliographies of theses and dissertations.
In Nigeria, the University of Ibadan publishes a List of Theses on
Nigerian Subjects and of Theses by Nigerians. The National Library
in Lagos has published a more comprehensive list under the title
Theses and Dissertations Accepted for Higher Degrees in Nigerian
Universities. In Argentina, the Instituto Bibliotecológico at the Uni-
versidad Nacional de Buenos Aires publishes Tesis Presentadas a la
Universidad de Buenas Aires.

Bibliographic control of theses in developing countries is further complicated by the fact that many doctoral candidates complete
their theses in European or American universities without depositing
copies in their native libraries. In some countries where the candidate may deposit copies in the Ministry of Education or the agency
for higher education, the work may never be bibliographically identified since the country lacks the appropriate bibliography for theses.

The great profusion of U. S. doctoral dissertations has prompted University Microfilms, Inc. to computerize bibliographic access.
The project is known as DATRIX (Direct Access to Reference Information; a Xerox Service). This service provides computer searching and listing of relevant references, complete microfilm and xero-
graphically reproduced copies of requested dissertations. Hundreds
of thousands of dissertations are available through this data base.

Bibliographic Coverage of Other Types of Material

The emphasis on non-book material, especially in Europe and
North America, has resulted in relatively improved bibliographic coverage of such material as government documents, maps and atlases,
musical scores, patents, standards, and audiovisual records. In developing nations, too few of such publications, except for government
documents, are produced to warrant special bibliographic coverage.

Government Documents. --Special bibliographies for official
publications are being compiled in many countries. International
agreements govern the exchange of publications or documents and require states to possess the bibliographical tools needed to honor
their international obligations. [60]

A country with a centralized government printing house is
well equipped to produce regular lists of official publications. The
Monthly Catalog of United States Government Publications is an excellent source for identifying a large number of U. S. documents. State
publications are identified in the Monthly Checklist of State Publications compiled and published by the Library of Congress. Similar
lists can be found for Canada, Great Britain, and some European
countries. In others, where separate bibliographies do not exist,
government publications are included in the national bibliography.

Audiovisual Material. --The most complete coverage of

audiovisual material has been achieved in the U.S. , and, to some
extent, in Europe.   Gramophone records, for example, have been
included in the bibliographies of Bulgaria, Czechoslovakia, Poland,
Rumania and the Democratic Republic of Germany.   The registration
of films is still beyond the scope of the national bibliography except
in a few countries, Great Britain, Australia, Canada, Nigeria.

Computerization and Bibliographic Control

With the expansion of computer use in libraries and bibliographic centers and with increased awareness of the value of national bibliographic access, networks are developing rapidly in both developed and developing nations.   With the development of the MARC
project, regional data banks are emerging in the U.S.   A good example of a bibliographic data bank is the Ohio College Library Center.   Its computerized, on-line cataloging system stores catalog
copy and location information for all items cataloged by its members.

National bibliographies are now being compiled via computers.
The Deutsche Bibliothek at Frankfurt on Main, the bibliographical
center for the Federal Republic of Germany, began, in 1966, to use
a computer to compile and print the Deutsche Bibliographie.   Computers have been used to produce the British National Bibliography,
the Canadian National Bibliography and the Australian National Bibliography, also.   In countries where national bibliographies have been
compiled by computer, librarians and bibliographers have acknowledged the speed and accuracy of compilation.

This survey shows that fragments of national bibliographies
in various countries come from a variety of uncoordinated sources,
such as the national library, the publishing industry, the government
printing office, university libraries and many other channels.   Lack
of coordination has resulted in duplication without providing complete
coverage of national production.

Even in the most advanced countries, no organization can undertake all of the tasks often performed efficiently by the many information and documentation facilities scattered throughout the country.   An up-to-date bibliographic network must be based on the existing infrastructure by coordinating activities, articulating various
services, developing the strong points, helping and guiding private
initiative in the right direction, and bridging the gaps which remain. [61]

In developing nations a dire need exists to issue bibliographies
regularly and currently.   This may convince publishers and authors
of the value of national bibliographies for promoting their work, and
consequently, win their cooperation in enforcing legal deposit laws.

Universal Bibliographic Control

Ever since printing was invented man has dreamed of a

universal bibliographic control which would record all books in existence throughout the world. Gesner dreamt of the idea and put himself to work on what became known as Bibliotheca Universalis, published in 1545. The Allgemeines Europäisches Buche Lexicon was compiled by the Leipzig bookseller Gottlieb Georgi and published from 1742 to 1758 in five folio volumes with three supplements in two volumes. The list was unique in attempting to cover the printed works of all countries up to 1757. It was arranged alphabetically by author and anonymous titles. Parts I to IV were mainly devoted to German books; Part V was limited to French books.

The Parisian bookseller, Charles Jacques Brunet (1780-1867) brought universal selective bibliography to its highest degree of perfection. His was a classic of this type and the most highly regarded work of the last quarter of the 18th century, both in France and abroad. Later compilers such as Johann Graesse attempted to compile universal bibliographies, also. Like Gesner, none went beyond Western Europe.

Other attempts were made to compile universal bibliographies on one subject. Among these specialized efforts were: the Concilium Bibliographicum, established in Zurich in 1890 to cover the world's literature of the biological sciences and kindred areas, and the International Catalogue of Scientific Literature (London: Royal Society, 1902-19), started at the beginning of the 20th century, with the object of covering all fields of science.

In 1895, the International Institute of Bibliography was established in Brussels. It was financed by the Belgian government, but in all other respects it was the achievement of two Belgian lawyers, Paul Otlet (1868-1944) and Henri La Fontaine (1853-1943). "It was the central organism of a vast federation of enterprises, scientific associations, and government organizations, intended to be the editorial center for a bibliography on cards of everything printed since the 15th century, in all countries and on all subjects. The arrangement was to be a double one, consisting of a classified catalog and an author list."[62] Otlet and La Fontaine saw their project as an enterprise which would flourish by international agreement among cooperating countries and begin to bring some measure of standardization to the extremely variable bibliographic practices of various countries. Much thought was given to these and other ideas until the beginning of the Second World War when so many dreams were shattered.

Since 1945, another new approach to the idea of universal bibliographic control has taken shape. The old idea, never completely abandoned since the days of Gesner, was revived in a more practical form. The emphasis, however, was placed on national bibliographies throughout the world. Bibliographers began to share in the belief that effective national bibliographic organization must precede international or universal coverage and that a universal bibliography must of necessity be grounded upon the work of individual countries.

To determine the state of the art of national bibliographic

control throughout the world, Unesco sponsored a survey carried out by the Library of Congress in the early post-war years. The report was published in 1950 under the title, Bibliographical Services, Their Present State and Possibilities. Since then, overall coverage has improved steadily, as shown in the third survey, 1969. This report shows most countries to possess bibliographical tools and current national bibliographies compiled by their national libraries or, in countries that have no national library, by national bibliographical institutes. [63]

Unesco's role in promoting national bibliographic development has been extremely influential. In its attempt to implement a workable universal bibliographic control, Unesco urges member countries to look beyond national boundaries and to develop and maintain links abroad, since no country today can be self-sufficient. [64]

A new concept for Universal Bibliographic Control (UBC), adopted by IFLA as its major policy objective, aims at the creation of a worldwide system to exchange bibliographic information. The purpose of the system is to make universally and promptly available, in an internationally accepted form, basic bibliographic data on all publications issued in all countries. The present UBC concept presupposes a network of component national parts which cover a wide range of publishing and library activities and are integrated at the international level to form a united system.

In the operation of the UBC system, the first stage begins at the national level, where bibliographic control is established. The second stage is located at the international level, where national bibliographic agencies will be integrated in a total system. To achieve the desired purpose behind this integration, the following conditions must be met: a) each national bibliographic agency is responsible for establishing the authoritative bibliographic record of its own country's publications; and b) international standards are applied in the record's contents (elements to be included in the description, on the order of those elements, the means of distinguishing those elements and their functions) and its physical form. Standardization is one way of achieving compatibility, a basic UBC requirement.

With agreement to these two conditions by all countries and wide-scale computer application, bibliographic records from one country can be speedily transferred to every other country in machine readable form. Such exchanges are already occurring among major European and American research libraries. There is the exchange of bibliographic machine-readable tapes between the Library of Congress and the British National Bibliography, for instance. Other "national and regional projects are using as their data basis the MARC machine format originally developed by L.C."[65]

Recently, there has been a widespread growth of interest in the possibility of improving bibliographic cooperation by connecting bibliographic centers with modern facilities for data and information transfer. Mechanized means to exchange and communicate bibliographic data to and from libraries are available and have been used in some developed nations. Other countries are adopting plans to connect with these networks. [66]

The possibilities of using satellite links to data bases and information services in Japan, Europe, and the United States are being canvassed by libraries and bibliographic centers in developing nations. Most of the available bibliographic networks, however, are beginning with library catalogs. The exchange of catalog data from many libraries can give users bibliographic access to a greater wealth of library resources--something which is needed in every country including the most advanced. Thanks to the MARC project, this exchange is presently materializing.

In the context of Universal Bibliographic Control, the Canadian National Library exchanges its Canadian MARC tapes with other countries. The National Library policy for this exchange is to supply tapes free of charge to another national library or bibliographic center which can disseminate and use them in any publication as long as the Canadian National Library receives reciprocal privileges.

In the fall of 1973, West German libraries adopted a common exchange format for bibliographic data, MAB1 (Maschinelles Austauschformat für Bibliotheken, Version 1). MAB1 is one of the youngest formats although it has not been designed along the well-established lines of older MARC formats. Nevertheless, the German MAB1 format conforms to the principles of design laid down by the international standard ISO 2709-1973: Format for Bibliographic Information Interchange in Magnetic Tape.

The form of the national bibliographies of both Singapore and Malaysia is styled on that of the BNB (British National Bibliography) and ANB (Australian National Bibliography). The logical extension of their participation in the MARC project would be a single system of data processing.

International information networks in subject fields have been developing. Operational systems are: MEDLARS (Medical Literature Analysis and Retrieval System), INIS (International Information System for Atomic Energy), and AGRIS, the international information system in agriculture.

New efforts aiming at a world-wide science information system have resulted in the establishment of UNISIST. Like UBC, UNISIST is not a new concept. It has been the response to a need felt in the scientific information world to the wider problem of bibliographic control. [67] Project UNISIST reinforces and in no way conflicts with UBC. The two projects depend on strengthening a flexible network of existing and future library systems.

The National Information System (NATIS) is a new system designed to provide an umbrella-like framework within which information activities of nongovernmental organizations and of UNESCO itself

can be brought together.   The NATIS concept implies that the govern-
ment--national, state or local--should maximize the availability of
all information through documentation, library and archive services.
As with UBC, NATIS aims can be achieved only through a national
information plan which must be developed and implemented in each
country in accordance with an established information policy, taking
into account the priorities of overall national and sectoral planning.[68]

Librarians and bibliographers, especially in developing countries, must urge their governments to establish national information
systems (NATIS) with a prospect for regional cooperation.   During
its recent meeting, the Tunisian Association of Librarians, Documentalists and Archivists adopted a resolution deeming it useful in establishing NATIS to pursue the objectives recommended for national
action by the intergovernmental conference, to subscribe to international standards, and to support Unesco efforts in documentation, libraries and archives.   It recommended that national bibliographic
control be introduced to allow for effective participation in universal
bibliographic control.[69]

The launching of NATIS by UNESCO was approved at its
18th session after taking into account the amendments
made by the Intergovernmental Conference in Paris.   A
resolution authorizes the director general of UNESCO to:

1.   Promote the general concept of overall planning of
national infrastructures of documentation, libraries and
archives, and to invite member states to take appropriate steps to create or improve their national information systems.

2.   To assist member states, especially the developing
countries, to plan and develop their national information
systems in such a way as to ensure coordination at the
national level and to prepare the bases for active participation in world information systems.

3.   To draw up a long-term program to this end and
submit it to the next general conference of UNESCO.

4.   To take into account: the recommendation approved
by the Intergovernmental Conference, the UNISIST program, and other relevant international programs in
order to avoid the development of overlapping activities.

Since the main objectives of NATIS are to enable each
country to develop its information systems so as to provide
information for all categories of users, UNESCO regards
UNISIST as a complementary program and as a culmination
of efforts towards achieving a systematic approach to the
problems involved in the transfer of information.[70]

Librarians and bibliographers are beginning to accept the fact that no national system can flourish on its own. It is increasingly necessary to achieve the maximum practical level of international cooperation so that information can be available to all countries. Among the prerequisites to this kind of international cooperation is international standardization, so that records and information can be shared without difficulty.

NOTES

1. John Ferguson. Some Aspects of Bibliography. Edinburgh: George P. Johnston, 1900, p. 13.
2. Roy B. Stokes. Bibliographical Control and Service. London: Andre Deutsch, 1965, p. 58.
3. For a detailed study of the bibliographic coverage of incunabula see John P. Immroth and Romano S. Almagna, "Incunabula," in: Encyclopedia of Library and Information Science. Allen Kent, Harold Lancour and Jay E. Daily, eds. New York: Marcel Dekker, 1974, vol. XI, pp. 265-84.
4. Stokes, op. cit., p. 59.
5. Jacques Charles Brunet. Manuel du Libraire et de L'amateur de Livres. 7 vols. 5th ed. Paris: Didot, 1860-1880.
6. Joseph Sabin. Bibliotheca Americana, A Dictionary of Books Relating to America, from its Discovery to the Present Time. 29 vols. New York: Bibliographical Society of America, 1868-1936.
7. Charles Evans. American Bibliography: A Chronological Dictionary of All Books, Pamphlets and Periodical Publications Printed in the United States of America from the Genesis of Printing in 1639 Down to and Including the Year 1820. 12 vols. Chicago: Printed privately for the author by the Columbia Press, 1903-34.
8. Howell J. Heaney. "Bibliographical Scholarship in the United States, 1949-1974: A Review," College and Research Libraries XXXVI (November 1975), p. 497.
9. Irene Zimmerman. Current National Bibliographies of Latin America: A State of the Art Study. Gainesville: University of Florida, 1971, p. 27.
10. Ibid., pp. 40-41.
11. Ibid., p. 110.
12. Sirkis Awwad, comp. Mùjam al-matbu'àt al-Árabiyah (Dictionary of Arabic Books). Cairo: Matba àt Sarkis, 1928-31.
13. Savina Roxas. "Bibliographical Societies," in: Encyclopedia of Library and Information Science. Allen Kent and Harold Lancour, eds. New York: Marcel Dekker, 1969, vol. II, p. 385.
14. Ibid., p. 385.
15. J. R. Seaton. "Edinburgh Bibliographical Society," in: Encyclopedia of Library and Information Science. Allen Kent and Harold Lancour, eds. New York: Marcel Dekker, 1972, vol. VII, p. 400.
16. Roxas, op. cit., p. 401.
17. Ibid., p. 402.

18. Ibid. , p. 402.
19. A detailed list of the Society's publications can be found in Roxas' article in the Encyclopedia of Library and Information Science and a comprehensive list from 1892 to 1942 can be found in the Bibliographical Society, 1892-1942: Studies in Retrospect. London: Bibliographical Society, 1945, pp. 199-211.
20. J. M. Edelstein. "Bibliographical Society of America," in: Encyclopedia of Library and Information Science. Allen Kent and Harold Lancour, eds. New York: Marcel Dekker, 1969, vol. II, p. 395.
21. John Berry. "Bowker, R.R. Co. ," in: Encyclopedia of Library and Information Science. Allen Kent and Harold Lancour, eds. New York: Marcel Dekker, 1970, vol. III, pp. 133-48.
22. John Tebbel. A History of Book Publishing in the United States, vol. 2: The Expansion of an Industry, 1865-1919. New York: Bowker, 1975, p. 590.
23. For up-to-date lists of these bibliographies see the various issues of the U.S. Library of Congress, National Program for Acquisitions and Cataloging. Accessions List: Eastern Africa. Nairobi, Kenya: Library of Congress Field Office, bi-monthly.
24. Gordon Harris and Michael B. Driskell, eds. International African Bibliography: Current Books, Articles, and Papers in African Studies. Vol. III, ed. under the general direction of J. D. Pearson. London: Mansell, 1975.
25. Hans M. Zell. African Books in Print. An Index by Author, Title and Subject. Part I-1975, English Language and African Languages. London: Mansell Information/Publishing Ltd. , 1975, pp. xi-xii.
26. African Book Publishing Record. Oxford: African Book Publishing Record Co. , 1975- .
27. U.S. Library of Congress. American Book Procurement Center, Cairo. Accessions List: Middle East. Cairo: Library of Congress Field Office, 1962- .
28. Louise Noële Malclès. Bibliography, trans. Theodore C. Hines. Metuchen, N.J. : Scarecrow Press, 1973, p. 47.
29. U.S. Library of Congress. General Reference and Bibliography Division. Current National Bibliographies, comp. by Helen Conover. New York: Greenwood Press, 1968, p. 1.
30. Unesco. Constitution, Article 1. Clause 2 (c).
31. U.S. Library of Congress, Current National Bibliographies, op. cit. , p. 1.
32. Paul Avicenne, ed. Bibliographical Services Throughout the World, 1965-1969. Paris: Unesco, 1972, p. 10.
33. Zimmerman, op. cit. , p. 6.
34. Full details about the planned Center, as well as an ABC Newsletter, are available from the Africa Bibliographic Center, Box 5089, Addis Abada, Ethiopia.
35. Estrid Bjerregard. "Legal Deposit: Purpose and Scope in Modern Society," Libri XXIII (1973), p. 344.
36. Zimmerman, op. cit. , p. 20.
37. African Book Publishing Record. Oxford: African Book Publish-

ing Record Co. , 1975- .
38. Dorothy Anderson. Universal Bibliographic Control. Pullach,
    München: Verlag Documentation, 1974, p. 27.
39. Catalogue of the Government of Pakistan Publications. Karachi:
    Manager of Publications, 1965.
40. Liaquat Memorial Library. Pakistan National Bibliography.
    Karachi: Government Printing Office, 1962.
41. U.S. Library of Congress. American Libraries Book Procure-
    ment Center, Karachi. Accessions List: Pakistan. Karachi:
    Library of Congress Field Office, 1962- , monthly.
42. H. A. I. Goonetileke. Bibliography of Ceylon, a Systematic
    Guide to the Literature on the Land, People, History and Cul-
    ture Published in Western Languages from the Sixteenth Cen-
    tury to the Present Day. 2 vols. Zug, Switzerland: Inter-
    Documentation Co. , 1970.
43. Ceylon National Library Services Board. Ceylon National Bib-
    liography. Colombo: Government Printing Office, 1963- .
44. U.S. Library of Congress. American Libraries Book Procure-
    ment Center, New Delhi. Accessions List: Ceylon. New
    Delhi: Library of Congress Field Office, 1967- .
45. Silvere Willemin. Technique of Union Catalogues; a Practical
    Guide. Paris: Unesco, 1966, p. 6.
46. John H. P. Pafford. Library Cooperation in Europe. London:
    Library Association, 1935, p. 132.
47. Robert D. Stueart. "German Union Catalogs," in: Encyclopedia
    of Library and Information Science. Allen Kent, Harold Lan-
    cour and Jay E. Daily, eds. New York: Marcel Dekker,
    1973, vol. IX, p. 387.
48. For a complete history of the Gesamtkatalog, see Pafford, Li-
    brary Cooperation in Europe, pp. 127-47.
49. Yadwiga Kuncaitis. Union Catalogs and Bibliographic Centers:
    a State-of-the-Art Review. Columbus: The State Library of
    Ohio, 1968, p. 8.
    Robert B. Downs. Union Catalogs in the United States. Chica-
    go: American Library Association, 1942.
50. John Balnaves and Peter Biskup. Australian Libraries. 2d ed.
    Hamden, Conn. : Linnet Books and Clive Bingley, 1975, p.
    84.
51. Lee Ash, comp. Subject Collections; A Guide to Special Book
    Collections and Subject Emphases as Reported by University,
    College, Public and Special Libraries and Museums in the
    United States and Canada. New York: R. R. Bowker Co. ,
    1974.
    Robert Collison. Published Library Catalogues: An Introduction
    to Their Contents and Use. London: Mansell Information
    Ltd. , 1973.
    Robert B. Downs, see footnote 49.
52. Guide to Indian Periodical Literature (Social Sciences and Human-
    ities). Gurgaon (Haryana): Prabhu Book Service, 1964- .
53. Index to Indian Economic Journals. Calcutta: Information Re-
    search Academy, 1966/67- .
54. Indian Library Science Abstracts. Calcutta: Indian Association
    of Special Libraries and Information Centres, 1967- .

55. David Woodworth, comp. Guide to Current British Journals.
    London: The Library Association, 1970.
56. Sri Lanka, Office of the Registrar of Books and Newspapers.
    Catalogue of Newspapers. Colombo: Government Printing
    Office, 1961.
57. M. U. S. Sultan Bawa. List of Scientific Periodicals in the
    Libraries of Ceylon. Colombo: Ceylon Association for the
    Advancement of Science, 1953.
58. Ruth S. Freitag, comp. Union List of Serials: A Bibliography.
    Washington, D. C.: Library of Congress, 1964; reprinted,
    Boston: Gregg Press, 1973, p. v.
59. Dorothy Anderson. Universal Bibliographic Control. Pullach,
    München: Verlag Dokumentation, 1974, p. 27.
60. Avicenne, op. cit. (1960-64), p. 84.
61. Guy Silvestre. "The Developing National Library Network of
    Canada," Library Resources and Technical Services XVI
    (Winter 1972), pp. 48-60.
62. Malclès, op. cit. , p. 123.
63. Avicenne, op. cit. , p. 25.
64. Anderson, op. cit. , p. 17.
65. Ibid. , p. 25.
66. David P. Waite. Library Networks, Book 1. Reading, Mass. :
    Information Dynamics Corp. , 1972, p. 4.
67. Anderson, op. cit. , p. 24.
68. C. R. Sahaer. "National Information Systems and Unesco," in:
    The Bowker Annual of Library and Book Trade Information.
    20th ed. Madeline Miele and Sarah Prakken, eds. New
    York: R. R. Bowker Co. , 1975, pp. 336-338.
69. Unesco. Natis News, No. 2 (1975), p. 3.
70. Sahaer, op. cit. , p. 337.

MULTI-CULTURALISM, LIBRARIES AND INTERNATIONAL TERMINOLOGY

Anthony Thompson

Each culture is based on a language, on that wonderful in-
heritance which we all enjoy--the "mother-tongue." Most of us
grow up with one mother-tongue, learned literally from our mothers;
and any other languages which we may acquire later are learned la-
boriously in the classroom, and seldom come to life sufficiently to
replace the original tongue. We may have learned French, German
or even Spanish or Russian in this way at school, ploughing through
grammars and vocabularies, and reading selected texts or "set
books" like studying a dead language.

Some of us, however, have been lucky enough to have grown
up with parents having different mother-tongues, or in a country
whose language was different from our own. In these circumstances
we have had the privilege and the luxury of learning two really living languages at an early age, so that we could enjoy equally the
fruits of two cultures. Some countries have two official languages,
such as Canada with English and French, Belgium with Flemish and
French, South Africa with Afrikaans and English, and Wales with
English and Welsh; while Switzerland boasts four languages--French
and German as the most used, but also Italian and Romansch in certain southern districts. In the USA, "colonies" of European immi-
grants have settled and remained in groups, and have preserved their
original languages and cultures.

I have stated above that for a child to grow up with more than
one language is a privilege, and indeed it has been shown that such
a situation stimulates the intelligence of the child, who will grow up
with a wider outlook on other cultures which he meets in his adult
life, also. This is the phenomenon of multi-culturalism, and so it
is the duty of libraries to provide literature in the mother-tongues
of all the larger linguistic groups in the community.

Two examples of good library provision for multiple cultures,
of international library science within a country, which come to my
mind are:

1) The foundation at the National Library of Canada of a multi-
cultural centre, and the pioneering provision in Toronto for readers
of languages other than English. This was one of the results of the
statement by the Prime Minister, M. Trudeau, in the Canadian Parliament in October 1971, in which he said:

Although many public libraries in Canada do have collections of books in non-official languages, the supply is well below the demand. The Canadian Library Association has studied the problem and has recommended the creation of a multi-cultural language and literature centre at the National Library. The Library will embark immediately on a preliminary study leading to the creation of this centre. The centre will administer a programme designed to deposit in local libraries books in languages other than English and French.

The call was answered by the Toronto Public Library, [1a] also, and in 1968 was taken over by the Metropolitan Toronto Library Board, including the boroughs of Etobicoke, Scarborough, York, East York and North York, with their independent library systems. In 1973 a "language co-ordinator" was appointed to administer the "Languages Centre" in the Central Library for the whole metropolitan area of over two million inhabitants, of whom over half a million had mother-tongues other than English or French, and had come from all the corners of the earth to settle in Canada. The acquisition of books in over a dozen European languages was at first problematical, but this was eased when the language co-ordinator produced a bibliographical aid, [1b] by the appointment of some multilingual library staff, and by gifts of books and other media from European countries. The Centre has met with an enthusiastic response from readers, and its success has stimulated multi-culturalism in other Canadian libraries. [1c]

The Multilingual Biblioservice at the National Library of Canada, Ottawa, completed its first year of operation in March 1976. Eleven thousand books in languages other than English and French were distributed during this first year to twenty-three provincial and regional library centres. These books are in the eight most demanded languages: Chinese, Dutch, German, Italian, Polish, Portuguese, Spanish and Ukrainian. However, this represents only about one-third of the total number of volumes requested; and collections are to be built up to include all the 72 languages spoken in Canada. The Multilingual Biblioservice is run by a staff of eleven, with the help of some specialists.

2) The Library of Literature of the Peoples of the USSR in Moscow. This specialized branch of the Moscow Public Libraries was started a few years ago to serve the many nationals from the non-Russian parts of the Soviet Union who were working in the Moscow region. The Soviet Union has 120 different languages, and the special task of this library is to provide collections of literature in the principal languages of the non-Russian republics. There are, for example, a collection of Ukrainian literature, a collection from the Baltic republics (in Estonian, Latvian and Lithuanian languages), and other growing collections in Uzbek, Tadzhik, Georgian, Azerbaidjanian and other languages of the peoples of the USSR.

Such libraries need multilingual staff, and multilingual

librarians need to know the technical terminology of library science
in several languages.   To take two simple examples: the French
term "éditeur" may in English mean "editor," but more often it
means "publisher"; and the German term "wissenschaftlich" is much
broader than the English "scientific," and should be translated, according to context, as "learned" or "scholarly," and not as "scientific."

Terminology is the basis, often the unconscious and rather
uncontrolled basis, of communication in all types of work.   Terms
(words) are the basis for formulating and recording information, but
they are also the vital elements used for indexing and retrieving information which has been recorded.   The recent rapid development
of science and technology has depended on international cooperation
based on detailed vocabularies and dictionaries of specialized fields
which give equivalents and definitions in different languages.   Because of this, during the last decades some outstanding efforts have
been made to coordinate terms, at least in the European languages,
and to work towards a measure of standardization; and this includes
our field of library terminology.

ISO/TC 37

As early as 1935, work on international principles of terminology was undertaken, when ISO (International Standardization Organization) set up its Technical Committee 37 on Terminology:
Principles and coordination, in which now 40 ISO member-organiza-
tions, as well as 40 international organizations, are participating.
The ISO/TC 37 Secretariat has been held since its foundation in
1935 by the Österreichisches Normungsinstitut (Austrian Standards Institute).   Studies had been undertaken by Professor Wüster which resulted, in 1931, in the publication of the first edition of his book on
the international standardization of engineering terms,[2a] and it was
largely this book, as well as other untiring work by Professor Wüster, which led to the foundation of ISO/TC 37 in 1935.   After the
long interruption of the second world war this technical committee
resumed its work only in 1951.

Up till now ISO/TC 37 has produced six ISO Recommendations
and one ISO Standard, as follows:

ISO/R 1087--1969 Vocabulary of Terminology.   Contains the
terms and definitions of 95 concepts frequently used for
the theory of terminology and linguistics.
ISO/R 919--1969 Guide for the Preparation of Classified Vocabularies.   Instructions on the technical work of compilers of vocabularies.
ISO/R 704--1968 Naming Principles.   On the principles to be
observed in constructing concepts, systems of concepts,
terms and definitions.
ISO/R 860--1968 International Unification of Concepts and
Terms.   Sets out the advantages, possibilities and limits

of the international unification of concepts and terms.
ISO/R 1149--1969 The Layout of Multilingual Classified Vocabularies. Recommendations on the technical details of
lexicography.
ISO/R 639--1967 Symbols for Languages, Countries and Authorities. Symbols recommended for use in terminological
work, arranged in tabular form.
ISO 1951--1973 Lexicographical Symbols. An international
standard on these symbols and their application.

At the INFOTERM Symposium of April 1975 it was formally
proposed that these ISO/TC 37 publications should be gathered together and published as a booklet, in order to facilitate and promote
their wider use by the compilers of dictionaries and vocabularies.
The last of these, now an international standard, provides symbols
to facilitate the relations of one term to another in a classified vocabulary. Terminological work has been done in the past, and much
of it is still done today, by comparing terms in two different languages and compiling dictionaries or vocabularies in which the terms
are arranged alphabetically. A more advanced and more efficient
method is to investigate the relations between all the concepts in a
given field, and to arrange these in a classified order. The result
is the clarification of the whole subject by bringing together all related concepts and terms. Often no precise equivalent for a given
term can be found in another language, and the symbols recommended in the standard ISO 1951 should be used to express the relations
between terms. For example, a generic concept is marked >, and
a specific concept <; and where there is no normal equivalent term,
five dots ..... should be used; an obsolete term should be marked
†; and two terms which are not exact synonyms should be separated
by the sign ≠. The result of such work is a classified vocabulary
which may be with or without definitions. The addition of definitions
is necessary for absolute accuracy, and the act of classifying the
concepts facilitates the process of making the definitions. A good
example of the use of these symbols and of the terminological principles of ISO/TC 37 is the vocabulary of "The Machine Tool" prepared by Professor Wüster for the Economic Commission for Europe
of the United Nations. [2b]

In some scientific fields, such as biology, chemistry, medicine and physics, terminology is advanced, whereas in library science and documentation it is still at the stage of gradual coordination.

INFOTERM

In the field of terminology in general the need had long been
felt for an international center to coordinate and provide information
on terminological work on all subjects. It was not until 1971, however, that the International Information Centre for Terminology
(INFOTERM) was established within the framework of UNISIST, and
with the aid of UNESCO. At INFOTERM's first international

symposium in 1975, UNESCO representatives explained that UNESCO was trying through the UNISIST program to interconnect national information systems, and for this purpose to make them more compatible; thus the need for standardization became obvious, and terminology was one of the first aspects. With UNESCO recommendation and support, INFOTERM was set up in 1971 at the Austrian Standards Institute in Vienna. Work on international terminology had already been stimulated there by the initiative of Professor Eugen Wüster. INFOTERM now works in Vienna in liaison with ISO/TC 37.

In accordance with a contract between the Austrian Standards Institute and UNESCO, INFOTERM tasks are: 1) coordination of terminology through contact with terminological agencies and clearinghouses for thesauri throughout the world, and advice for compilers of vocabularies, including the application of terminological principles; 2) Documentation and information on terminology, through the bibliography and collection of terminological publications, inventories of terminology agencies, research projects, courses and lectures, and investigations into the development of word-banks.

The ambitious INFOTERM program includes all subjects and all languages and aims at developing a world-wide network. It has already published The Road to Infoterm, by E. Wüster,[3a] and prepared in March 1975 a draft of a World Guide to Terminological Activities,[3b] arranged by subjects and using the Universal Decimal Classification. INFOTERM plans later to publish up-dated versions of the UNESCO bibliographies of monolingual and interlingual scientific and technical dictionaries.

In April 1975, INFOTERM held in Vienna its first "Symposium on Cooperation in International Terminology," at which papers were read on work being done in various subject fields. Some important information was given on:

--Bio-chemical terminology. In 1921, the Commission on Nomenclature in Biological Chemistry (now Commission on Biochemical Nomenclature), under the auspices of the International Union of Biochemistry, with members from Austria, Belgium, France, Germany, UK, USA and USSR, published a series of recommendations on nomenclature which are followed throughout the world.

--Electrotechnology. The Commission Electrotechnique Internationale, founded in 1904, produced its first vocabulary in 1911, with 340 terms. This work developed very slowly, and the Vocabulaire électrotechnique international, with 2,000 terms, appeared only in 1938. The second edition, with 8,000 terms, appeared in 1970, with English and French definitions, and the equivalent terms in German, Italian, Spanish, Dutch, Polish and Swedish. Now, Russian has been added, with Russian definitions, and altogether 10,000 terms appear in 34 separate volumes. In 1967, the

Siemens Company in Munich set up a terminological data-
bank. The firm has several hundred translators and in-
terpreters and thousands of employees engaged in technical writing and marketing, and so it has been necessary
for the firm to standardize terminology, even terms not
yet standardized by national or international bodies, and
to make the terms immediately available. The Siemens
data-bank with its programming system is called TEAM
(Terminologie-, Erfassungs- und Auswertungsmethode, or,
in English, Terminology Evaluation and Acquisition Method).
Terms are stored in English, French, Spanish, Russian,
Italian, Portuguese, Dutch and German. Two kinds of input media are used: a six-channel perforated paper tape,
and typewriting on ordinary paper typed with OCR-B machine-readable characters. The lexical entries are based
on concepts, i.e., on defined units of meaning, and the
information units are given two-digit numerical codes (with
100 units for each lexical entry). Thus, the program can
ask for the equivalents of the constituent parts of multi-
word terms, and the system is therefore flexible. There
are several output programs, off-line and on-line, for the
data, which is prepared by high-speed print-out. The
first dictionary in the world produced by computer from a
terminological data-bank was the Siemens English-German
& German-English Dataprocessing Dictionary, which appeared in 1970.

--Law and administration. In 1967, the International Institute
of Legal and Administrative Terminology was founded in
Berlin. It grew out of a working group of German and
French experts in this field, mainly from government departments, with the aim of facilitating understanding within
the European communities. This has developed into 30
groups, with a total of about 90 experts working on French,
German, English and Italian. The Institute is publishing
the Glossaire Européen de Terminologie Juridique et Administrative in fascicules.

These descriptions of terminological work, which were given
in full at the INFOTERM Symposium, indicate some important international achievements in several subject fields, and may serve as
examples for future terminology work in our own field of documentation and libraries. In this field, much work has been done, or is
in progress on the terminology of archives, documentation and library
science.

It is clear from the conclusions and recommendations of ISO/
TC 37 that specialized vocabularies should be classified, to facilitate
the correlation of terms both for the compiler and for the user, that
they should be compiled by experts in the subjects and the languages
of the vocabulary concerned, and that they should give definitions according to TC 37's recommendations. Now let us examine some of
the more important work done in our own field.

Terminology of Archives

    The principle work on the terminology of archives is the Lexicon on Archive Terminology of 1964, compiled by a special committee of the International Council on Archives and bearing its authority, as stated by Professor J. Herbert in his preface.[4] There are 175 terms with their equivalents in French, German, Italian, Spanish and Dutch; i. e., it is a Western European work with no Russian terms and no Arabic or Asian languages.

Terminology of Library Science and Documentation

    Monolingual vocabularies. Here there is a massive background of monolingual vocabularies, of which some of the most important, in the major European languages are:

In English:	The Librarian's Glossary (Gt. Britain), 1971[5a]
	The A. L. A. Glossary (USA), 1943[5b]
In German:	Kirchners Lexikon des Buchwesens (Western Germany), 1952-56[5c]
In Russian:	Slovar' Knigovedčeskih Terminov (USSR), 1958[5d]
In Spanish:	Diccionario de Bibliotecologia (Argentina), 1963[5e]

All of these works give definitions of various lengths and in various forms but none follows the principles recommended by ISO/TC 37; nor is there any attempt at international coordination, which begins only when a second language is added. None of them attempts to classify the terms, except The Librarian's Glossary which in an appendix divides the terms under the following broad groups, to which I have added the number of terms, to provide an analysis by subject:

	Number of terms
Bibliography	538
Book acquisition & processing	126
Book production	447
Bookbinding	567
Cataloging & indexing	689
Classification	295
Illustrations	170
Information retrieval	361
Libraries & library work in general	374
Library services, buildings & equipment	278
Palaeography & archives	110
Paper & paper-making	262
Printing	957
Reprography	282
Special librarianship	67
Total	5,523

Bilingual vocabularies. The work on international terminology began with bilingual vocabularies. Of those linking English with other European languages, here are some of the good recent publications, all with their terms arranged alphabetically:

With French: Vocabulaire technique de la bibliothéconomie (Canada), 1969[5f] (with French definitions).

With Spanish: Diccionario técnico de biblioteconomía (Mexico), 1965.[5g]

With Russian: English-Russian Dictionary of Library and Bibliographical Terms (USSR), 1958[5h] (no definitions, illus.).

English-Russian Bookman's Glossary (USSR), 1962[5i] (no definitions).

Dictionary of Terms on Informatics (USSR), 1971.[5j]

With Afrikaans: Biblioteekwoordeboek/Dictionary of Library Terms (South Africa), 1971 [5k] (no definitions).

Two of these works were produced in the favorable milieu of bilingual countries; no attempt was made to classify the terms, since it was simpler to arrange them alphabetically under one language with an alphabetical index of the second language.

Multilingual vocabularies (alphabetical). It was only when faced with the problem of equating terms in several languages that compilers had to seek a truly international approach. Most compilers of dictionaries and vocabularies arranged the terms alphabetically in their native language, and provided a series of alphabetical indexes from the other languages, beginning with Moth's pioneering work of 1915,[5l] and continued in works by Cowles,[5m] Orne,[5n] Lemaitre,[5o] Mamiya,[5p] Schlemminger,[5q] Więckowska,[5r] Olmütz University Library,[5s] the Comité européen des assurances,[5t] Pipics,[5u] Ždanova,[5v] Kunze,[5w] Clason,[5x] Neveling & Wersig,[5y] and others.

Multilingual vocabularies (classified). In the year 1805, P. M. Roget made a small classified catalog of English words, to help with literary composition. However, he became Secretary of the Royal Society, London, and it was not until he retired from this exacting post that he was able to expand the list into the now famous and indispensable Roget's Thesaurus of English Words and Phrases, first published in 1852. In the introduction to this work he wrote: "The present work is intended to supply ... a desideratum hitherto unsupplied in any language; namely, a collection of the words it contains and of the idiomatic combinations peculiar to it, arranged, not in alphabetical order as they are in a dictionary, but according to the ideas which they express.... We seek in vain the words we need.... The appropriate terms ... cannot be conjured up at will. Like 'spirits from the vasty deep,' they come not when we call...."

Roget elaborated and completed his Thesaurus, and explained further: "The assistance it gives is that of furnishing on every topic

a copious store of words and phrases adapted to express all the recognizable shades and modifications of the general idea under which
those words and phrases are arranged.... The review of a catalogue of words of analogous signification will often suggest by association other trains of thought, which, presenting the subject under
new and varied aspects, will vastly expand the sphere of our mental
vision. "

     This quotation from Roget, and the great and lasting reputa-
tion of his Thesaurus, are sufficient to establish the practical value
of a classified dictionary, however difficult it may be to compile.

     In 1949, the Vocabulaire Technique du Bibliothècaire of Le-
maître[5o] was sent by UNESCO to three critics, Mme. S. Briet, of
the Bibliothèque Nationale, Paris, W. B. Ellinger, of the Library
of Congress, Washington, and myself; and at the end of the same
year I myself undertook the revision and expansion of this work,
which later became the Vocabularium Bibliothecarii.[6] The three
critics had reported a lack of balance of subjects, and many terms
had to be added, especially from the fields of cataloging, classification and documentation. The best way to achieve a proper balance
was by classifying the terms. This was done, not only as an aid to
the compiler in achieving a balance of subjects, but with the aim of
providing a conceptual survey of our professional terminology, an international classified thesaurus of the terms used by a librarian.
The classification scheme had to be international since it was
UNESCO's intention that this vocabulary, initially in English, French
and German, should gradually be extended to include other languages,
of which many would not be in the Latin alphabet. The Universal
Decimal Classification, with its notation of internationally accepted
Arabic numerals, and because it was already widely known to librarians, the future users of the work, was the obvious choice. The
UDC was preferred to the Dewey Classification because of its syn-
thetic structure; the point, colon and parentheses, which analyze the
terms into their elements, were found to be very useful as an international cross-referencing device which is expressed, not in any one
language, but in Arabic numerals.

     The first edition of the Vocabularium Bibliothecarii (English,
French and German) appeared in 1953,[6a] and a second improved edition, with the addition of two Unesco languages, Russian and Spanish,
ten years later.[6e] It had always been the intention of UNESCO that
other languages could be added to this basic vocabulary, now in five
major European languages, and a blank column was provided for
this purpose. The successful result of this policy was the independent publication of a number of further editions, with the permission,
of course, of UNESCO. The first of these were in Italian,[6b] Rumanian,[6c] and Turkish,[6d] translated from the first edition. Later,
translated from the second edition, there followed Arabic,[6f] Serbo-
Croat,[6g] Netherlands,[6h] Scandinavian,[6i] and Hungarian[6j] editions.

     Thus, UNESCO's policy of initiating international projects and
then handing them over for continuation by individual nations has
been largely fulfilled in the field of library terminology.

It was, however, intended from the beginning that the Vocabularium Bibliothecarii should later be supplemented by the addition of
the essential terms from the field of documentation and information
science. A start was made in 1964, with my unpublished draft supplement, Vocabularium Documentationis, and this was developed into
a greatly improved draft of English, French and German terms with
definitions in 1971.[6k] The final version of this was published by
UNESCO in 1976, giving English definitions and the terms in English, French, German, Spanish and Russian. An interesting parallel
to this has already been published in 1975 in Germany[5y] with German
definitions.

A recent, extremely scholarly publication explaining the elements and grammar of all the European languages has just been published by Bowker,[61] and will serve as an excellent reference work
for ambitious multilingual librarians.

The terminological works described above, and those referred
to in the bibliography, indicate that librarians and documentalists are
steadily preparing for the development of multiculturalism. Libraries
with multicultural collections and multilingual staff members will surely contribute in the near future to UNESCO's aim of "constructing the
defences of peace in the minds of men" through mutual understanding
between different cultures based on their different languages.

BIBLIOGRAPHY

1. Multiculturalism

    a. Campbell, H. C. "New Canadians Tune in to the Public
       Library," UNESCO Bulletin for Libraries XVII (March-
       April 1963), pp. 63-4.
    b. Wertheimer, Leonard. Books in Other Languages: Aids
       to Selecting and Ordering. A Preliminary List. Metro-
       politan Toronto Library Board, 1973, 41 pp.
    c.   . "New Canadians and the Public Library: a
       Decade Later," UNESCO Bulletin for Libraries XXVIII (May-
       June 1974), pp. 139-48.

2. ISO/TC 37

    a. Wüster, Eugen. Die Internationale Sprachnormung in der
       Technik (The International Standardization of Language in
       Engineering). 3rd ed. Berlin: VDI-Berlag, 1970, 507 pp.
    b.   . The Machine Tool/machine-outil; and Grundbe-
       griffe bei Werkzeugmaschinen. London: Technical Press,
       1968, 2 vols.

3. INFOTERM

    a.   . The Road to Infoterm; Two Reports Prepared
       on Behalf of UNESCO. Pullach bei München: Verlag

Dokumentation, 1974, 142 pp.
b. Krommer, Magdalena Benz. World Guide to Terminological Activities. Vienna: Infoterm, 1975 (draft).

4. Terminology of archives

International Council on Archives. Lexicon of Archives Terminology. (English, French, German, Italian, Spanish, Dutch). Amsterdam: Elsevier, 1964, 183 pp. 175 terms.

5. Terminology of library science and documentation

a. Harrod, Leonard Montague. The Librarian's Glossary of Terms Used in Librarianship and the Book Crafts. 3rd ed. London: Deutsch, 1971, 784 pp.
b. Thompson, Elizabeth H. ALA Glossary of Library Terms, With a Selection of Terms in Related Fields ... under the direction of the Committee on Library Terminology. Chicago: American Library Association, 1943, 159 pp.
c. Kirchner, Joachim. Lexikon des Buchwesens. Stuttgart: Hiersemann, 1952-56, 2 vols.
d. Šamurin, E. I. Slovar' Knigovedčeskih Terminov. Moscow: Sovietskaya Rossiya, 1958, 340 pp. circa 4,500 terms.
e. Buonocore, Domingo. Diccionario de Bibliotecologia; Terminos Relatives a la Bibliología, Bibliografía, Bibliofilia, Biblioteconomia, Archivologia, Documentologia, Tipografia y Materias Afines. Santa Fé (Argentina): Castellví, 1963, 336 pp. 2,249 terms.
f. Rolland-Thomas, P., Coulombe, V. and Chabot, Juliette. Vocabulaire Technique de la Bibliothéconomie et de la Bibliographie. Montreal: Association Canadienne des Bibliothécaires de Langue Française, 1969, 187 pp. circa 3,250 terms. (French, English)
g. Massa de Gil, Beatriz, Trautman, R. and Goy, P. Diccionario Tecnico de Biblioteconomía Español-Inglés, Inglés-Español. Mexico: F. Trillas, 1965, 387 pp.
h. Saringulian, M. H. English-Russian Dictionary of Library and Bibliographical Terms. Moscow: All-Union Book Chamber, 1958, 284 pp. 11,000+ terms.
i. Elizarenkova, T. P. English-Russian Bookman's Glossary. Moscow: Sovietskaya Rossiya, 1962, 510 pp. circa 20,000 terms. (Covers librarianship, bibliography, publishing, bookselling, printing, computers, reprography and sound-recording.)
j. Akademiya Nauk SSSR. V. I. N. I. T. I. Slovar' Terminov po Informatike. (Compiled by G. S. Ždanova & others. Russian and English.) Moscow: Nauka, 1971, 359 pp. 3035 terms.
k. Vaktaalburo, Pretoria. Biblioteekwoordeboek/Dictionary of Library Terms. (Afrikaans, English). Pretoria: South African Library Association, 1971.

l. Moth, A. F. C. M. Glossary of Library Terms (in 8
Western European languages). Boston, Mass.: Boston
Book Co., 1915.
m. Cowles, Barbara. Bibliographer's Glossary of Foreign
Words and Phrases. New York: Bowker, 1935. (20 languages, based on English)
n. Orne, Jerrold. The Language of the Foreign Book Trade:
Abbreviations, Terms and Phrases. Chicago: A.L.A.,
1949 & 1962. (10 languages, based on English)
o. Lemaître, Henri. Vocabulaire Technique du Bibliothécaire.
Paris: UNESCO, 1949. (English, French, German)
p. Mamiya, Fujio. A Complete Dictionary of Library Terms.
Revised and enlarged ed. Tokyo: Japan Library Bureau,
1952. (Chinese, Japanese, English, French, German)
q. Schlemminger, Johann. Fachwörterbuch des Buchwesens.
2nd ed. Darmstadt: Stoytscheff, 1954. (German, English, French)
r. Więckowska, Helena and Pliszczyńska, Hanna. Podręczny
Slownik Bibliokarza. Warsaw: Państwowe Wydawnictwo
Naukowe, 1955. (Polish, Russian, English, French, German)
s. Universitnî Knihovna Olomouci. Slovnîk Knihovnických
Terminů v Sesti Jazychích. Prague: Státnî Pedagogické
Nakladatelstvî, 1958. 632 pp. (Czech, Russian, Polish,
German, English, French)
t. Comité Europeen des Assurances. Terminologie de Traite-
ment Electronique de l'Information. Würzburg: Triltsch,
1962. (French, German, English, Spanish, Italian, Algol
60)
u. Pipicz, Zoltán. A Konyvtáros Gyakorlati Szótára/Diction-
arium Bibliotecarii Practicum. Budapest: Akadémiai
Nyomda, (1963) (20 European languages), 317 pp. 300
terms.
_____. Dictionarium Bibliothecarii Practicum. 6th ed.
Munich: Verlag Dokumentation, 1971. (22 languages)
v. Akademiya Nauk SSSR. V.I.N.I.T.I. Russko-Anglo-
Frantsuzskiî Terminologičeskiî Slovar' po Informatzionnoi
Teorii i Praktike, by Zdanova & others. Moscow: Nauka,
1968, 239 pp. 1281 terms. (Russian, English, French)
w. Kunze, Horst and Rückl, Gotthard. Lexikon des Biblio-
thekswesens... Leipzig: Bibliographisches Institut, 1969,
769 pp. 3,250 terms, with equivalents in English, French
& Russian.
x. Clason, W. E. Elsevier's Dictionary of Library Science,
Information and Documentation... Amsterdam: Elsevier,
1973, 597 pp. (English, French, Spanish, Italian, Dutch,
German)
y. Neveling, Ulrich and Wersig, Gernot. Terminologie der Information und Dokumentation, herausgegeben von ... der
Deutschen Gesellschaft für Dokumentation, Frankfurt-am-
Main. 307 pp. (German, English, French) Munich:
Verlag Dokumentation, 1975.

6. The Vocabularium Bibliothecarii

a. Thompson, Anthony. Vocabularium Bibliothesarii, English, French, German; begun by Henri Lemaître, revised and enlarged... Paris: UNESCO, 1953, 296 pp. 2,500 terms.
b. Gambigliani-Zoccoli, Battistina. Dizionario de Terminologia Bibliografica, in: La Ricerca Scientifica, 1956-59.
c. Georgescu-Tistu, N. Vocabularul Biblioecarului...(Rumanian, German, French, English, Russian, Hungarian), in: Călăuza Bibl. R. P. R. (Bucharest) 10(4) 1957, pp. 19-21 & continuations.
d. Şenalp, Leman. Dört Dilde Kütüphanecilik Terimleri Süzlügü... Türkeeterimleri... Ankara: Türk Tarih Kurumu Basimevi, 1959, 379 pp.
e. Thompson, Anthony. Vocabularium Bibliothecarii. 2nd ed., English, French, German, Spanish, Russian. Collaborator for Russian: E. I. Shamurin; for Spanish: D. Buonocore. Paris: UNESCO, 1962, 627 pp. 2,800 terms.
f. Hussien, N. A., Kabesh, A. and Sheniti, M. Vocabularium Bibliothecarii. 2nd ed., with Arabic translation... Cairo: UAR National Commission for UNESCO, 1965, 692 pp.
g. Čučkovič, Dana and Šime, Jurič. Rječnik Bibliotekarskih Stručnih Izraza. (Serbo-Croat) Zagreb: Izdavačko Poduzecê "Skolska Knjiga," 1965.
h. Algemene Conferentie der Nederlandse Letteren. Sectie Bibliotheekwezen. Bibliotheekterminologie...Bewerkte Uitgave van het Vocabularium Bibliothecarii, 2de uitg. 1962... The Hague: Centrale Vereniging voor Openbare Bibliotheken, 1967, 294 pp. (English, French, German, Dutch)
i. Nielsen, Torben. Vocabularium Bibliothecarii Nordicum... udgivet af Nordisk Videnskabeligt Bibliotekarforbund. Copenhagen: Bibliotekscentralen, 1968, 278 pp. (English, Danish, Norwegian, Swedish, Finnish)
j. Pipics, Zoltan. Vocabularium Bibliothecarii ac Supplementum Hungaricum... Budapest: Akadémiai Kiadó, 1972. (English, French, German, Spanish, Russian, Hungarian)
k. Wersig, Gernot and Neveling, Ulrich. Vocabularium Documentationis, first draft... Paris: UNESCO, 1971, 258 columns. (English, French, German)
l. Allen, Geoffrey C. A Manual of European Languages for Librarians. London: Bowker, 1975, 803 pp.

ART LIBRARY SCIENCE: A FRESH START

Judith A. Hoffberg

Although there have always been art books, art libraries and art library science are relatively young specializations. What distinguishes art libraries is that art itself can be one of the most voluminous non-specialties in libraries; what makes an art library special and art library science a profession apart from general library science is not the existence of art books, but the fact that these libraries and this library science have as their theoretical basis the methodology of art history and, more concretely, the observation of how visual arts scholars use libraries. This is especially important in libraries providing visual non-book or non-print resources which must interact with the printed word, also.

In addition, special collections have been the foundation of art libraries, those bothersome formats such as portfolios, collections of loose plates, photographs, slides, filmstrips, microfiche, etc. -- these ephemera which document the twentieth century and earlier visual worlds are the substance of art or visual libraries. Large encyclopedic libraries in which, however, art history is not recognized as a history of thinking or creating in forms--but simply as a branch of history, or worse, as "illustrated history"--do not need art librarians. Of course, they need acquisitions librarians who know art literature and may even be good bibliographers--but in such libraries the user must be his own art librarian!

Art library science, or at least the curatorship of great visual treasures, was not formally initiated until perhaps the fourteenth century in France, when Gilles Mallet was named Keeper of the Royal Library of John the Good of France, and made custodian of many art books. Similarly, in 1770, in England, Francis Hayman, book illustrator, was named first librarian of the Royal Academy. However, the earliest attempts at organizing the profession took place in America. The first fine arts library in the United States was established by the San Francisco Art Association and housed in the Mark Hopkins Institute. The Boston Museum of Fine Arts had a library room and an allocation of money by 1875, and the Metropolitan Museum of Art started a library in 1880, ten years after its founding. By the end of the nineteenth century, public libraries developed specialized art departments, and museum libraries grew rapidly, also. The Sacramento Public Library set up the first known art department in 1879.

The growth and development of art libraries culminated in the

need for organization. The Special Libraries Association formed a
Museums Group in 1929 which attracted art librarians, though SLA
did not see the need for a separate group for art librarians. In
1924, the American Library Association established the Art Reference Round Table. This group attracted 63 people, who represented
public library art departments, art school libraries, museum libraries, and other organizations. For the first time, a cross-sec-
tion of art librarians could meet, share ideas, and create a forum
for problems and solutions.

The ALA Art Reference Round Table had one great advantage
over the later form of ALA art librarians organization; clearly this
group was open to all types of librarians--public, museum, academic,
and special--as well as publishers and others. The Round Table
flourished through the 1930s and 1940s, but little contact was made
with art librarians in other countries, save for those in Canada who
felt the need to join American librarians in their national library organizations. As far as domestic cooperation and communication, the
only joint meeting between the Special Libraries' Museum Group and
the ALA Art Reference Round Table was held in 1933.

After World War II, art library science no longer held a special place and was submerged in the Specialized Libraries Division,
later to become a subsection of the Special Libraries Section of
ALA's Association of College and Research Libraries. In a still
later reorganization, the ACRL Subject Specialists Section was further divided into subsections, and one of them became the Art Section. Only in 1972, at the very moment ARLIS/NA was being formed,
did ACRL agree to the goal of many Art Subsection chairmen to
"raise" the art subsection to the status of a Section. In addition, in
1971, SLA's Museums Division changed its name to Museums, Arts
and Humanities Division to attract a larger art librarian audience.

Yet a new dawn was coming for art librarians, for the scope
of art library science no longer kept to hemispheric borders, but
turned to England where a new organization, ARLIS (Art Libraries
Society), evolved in 1969. A group of art librarians throughout the
United Kingdom felt the need for an independent, vigorous organization divorced from the Library Association. To facilitate communication amongst themselves, they published a quarterly Newsletter,
which acted as a binding force among their members.[1,2] U.S. art
librarians had met the same year in Buffalo at an Institute for Art
Librarians where they realized how important it was to gather, share
problems and find solutions to manifold questions. In both countries,
the need for a forum of ideas and continuous communication network
was clear.

Attempts were made to coordinate the American groups existing at that time. The Art Section of ACRL, the Museums Division
of SLA, and the newly formed Art Libraries Section of the College
Art Association needed to channel their energies and interests in the
same direction. Although these three groups inspired academic and
museum librarians in the fine arts, many unaffiliated art librarians

could not afford the time, energy or dues to join them, and many needs could not be met. There were problems to solve, and the communication need was urgent, but the groups met only once a year. After many years of attempted coordination, a new approach was needed.

In November 1972, ARLIS/NA (Art Libraries Society of North America) came into existence and promised two things: effective communication to ameliorate the professional problems plaguing art librarians, and affiliation with a strong regional chapter for art librarians in all kinds of institutions. These promises were realized with the ARLIS/NA Newsletter and regional chapters in New York City, Boston, Southern California, Northern California, Georgia, the Twin Cities, Texas, and Kansas-Missouri; other chapters soon started in New Jersey, the Lake Erie area, Western New York, and Indiana-Illinois. [3] The call to join went out to all art librarians-- those in public libraries, museums, galleries, art institutes, art academies, universities and colleges. In addition, persons interested in visual resources library science, although not art book librarians per se, were invited to join, with the result that art book publishers, book dealers, students, retired and unemployed librarians--those persons deeply concerned with art collections--were able to identify and share ideas with similarly-oriented people.

When ARLIS/NA's membership voted unanimously to affiliate with the Art Libraries Society in the United Kingdom, international art library science was born. Thus began in 1973 the basis of cooperation and communication among art librarians in Great Britain and North America. Both organizations have attracted art librarians from Germany, The Netherlands, Israel, France, Japan, Italy, Sweden, Australia, and New Zealand. The building of bridges has begun to create the feeling of an international fraternity.

One difficulty among art librarians is lack of self-identification. There is neither directory nor list to identify them throughout the world. Thus, both Newsletters have included articles about library science in various countries, such as the Germanies, Colombia, Israel, and France. Discussing common problems allows art librarians to solve some of them.

Cross-fertilization of ideas has been encouraged by American and British librarians' exchange visits. The sharing of systems, problems, solutions and ideas has been of the utmost importance in understanding and generating new answers to old problems. It is not surprising to discover that art library science is far better developed in the United Kingdom, the United States and Canada than elsewhere, at least in an organized and structured manner. It is surprising to discover, however, that the facts and figures of art libraries throughout the world are relatively unknown to other art librarians. With the tools of communication and cooperation, art library science is now entering a new phase of international understanding.

Under the guidance of the dynamic Jacqueline Viaux, head

librarian of the Bibliothèque Forney, Paris, the Subsection of Art Librarians in the French Library Association is an active group. In addition, certain countries have organized art library science differently from the Anglo-American model, i.e., as a conglomerate of institutions rather than of individuals. The German "Arbeitsgemeinschaft der Kunstbibliotheken" (Association of Art Libraries, for instance, is now a formal body which has initiated a coordinated acquisitions plan, covering special subject areas assigned to librarians in Berlin, Florence, Cologne, Munich, Nuremberg and Rome.[4] Uniform interlibrary loan and photocopy policies are followed by all cooperating Association librarians. Librarians responsible for this German-oriented program are Horst-Johannes Tummers, Peter Tigler, Thomas Lersch of the Library of the General Institute for the History of Art in Munich, Elisabeth Rucker of the Library of the Germanic National Museum in Nuremburg, and Ernst Gulden of the Hertziana Library in Rome.

The first international conference organized by art librarians was held in London and at the University of Sussex in April 1976. More important than the conference theme--Art Periodicals--or the location, was that this was the first of its kind. European, North American, Australian and African librarians convened with their ARLIS/UK hosts to talk about art periodicals in particular and art librarianship in general.

Judith A. Hoffberg, Executive Secretary of ARLIS/NA, and major proponent of the international concept of art librarianship (the practice of the art) stated eight points which characterize the goal of a proposed international organization:

1) to foster cooperation among art librarians
2) to stimulate and coordinate their activities
3) to help realize projects in bibliography and art librarianship
4) to encourage the international exchange of art library material in all media
5) to stimulate the establishment of international guidelines for cataloging art library material
6) to promote the conservation of art library material
7) to cooperate with other national and international bodies, and
8) to meet together periodically as a congress.

As a result of stimulating discussion, it was suggested that an international committee be formed to investigate areas where art librarians can work together and contact other countries and to draw up a structure for ARLIS/INTERNATIONAL. This information will be presented to the membership of each national group by late 1977. What can be envisioned is an international organization, with affiliated chapters in many countries, a quarterly scholarly journal, and biennial conferences in different countries, with an international gift and exchange program. In addition participation should be encouraged with other international organizations such as IFLA, in developing international standards for documentation and bibliographical control.

Jane Wright's "cri de coeur" in 1908 aptly stated that

> the art library so far has been little known or appreciated,
> and has existed mainly for the use of museum curators
> and a very few students.... But there is a future--to my
> mind, a great future--for the earnest art librarian....
> Can there be a more inspiring work for any librarian than
> to develop the usefulness of these rich legacies of the ages
> stored away in her books and engravings and photographs,
> etc. ? Can there be a more absorbing and necessary ambi-
> tion in these dollar and cents days of ours, than to make
> accessible to the few seekers the inspiration and knowledge
> of past artistic accomplishments so that the common life
> of our own cities and people may be beautified, their
> vision enlarged?[5]

To be sure, this could be the plea of all art librarians who
feel themselves part of an international fraternity of visual information specialists, of those who enhance others' lives and expand their
vision. International art library science is just beginning, but its
future looks very promising.

NOTES

1. ARLIS Newsletter, 1969. Art Libraries Society, 1969- , quarterly.
2. Hunnisett, Basil. "The Art Librarian," ARLIS Newsletter (England) (February 1972), No. 10, pp. 9-12.
3. ARLIS/NA Newsletter, 1972. Art Libraries Society of North
   America, 1972- , bimonthly.
4. Arbeitsgemeinschaft der Kunstbibliotheken. Deutsche Kunstbibliotheken. Berlin, Florenz, Köln, München, Nürnberg,
   Rom, München: Verlag Dokumentation, 1975, 101 pp.
5. Wright, Jane. "Plea of the Art Librarian" (letter to the editor),
   Public Libraries (1908), pp. 348-9.

NOTES ON CONTRIBUTORS

MOHAMMED M. AMAN was born in Alexandria, United Arab Republic. He graduated from the Department of Library Science, Cairo University, and has degrees from Columbia University and University of Pittsburgh Graduate School of Library and Information Sciences (Ph. D.). After a period of work in Cairo, Aman came to the United States where he was employed at the University of Pittsburgh, Duquesne University, Pratt Institute, St. John's University, and Palmer Graduate Library School, C. W. Post Center, Long Island University, where he is now Dean. He is chairman of the ALA International Relations Round Table and serves on the consulting editorial board of International Library Review. He has written extensively in the fields of cataloging and classification, library automation and bibliography as well as international library science. Aman is fluent in English, Arabic, French and German.

MARTHA BOAZ is a graduate of Madison College, Virginia, U. S. A. , Peabody College Library School, and the University of Michigan School of Library Science (Ph. D.). She has been Dean and Professor, School of Library Science, University of Southern California, Los Angeles, for the past 24 years. Dr. Boaz has been President, American Association of Library Schools; President, Library Education Division, American Library Association; and President, California Library Association. In 1961-62 she served as Hobart Professor, University of Karachi, and in 1966 she was a library consultant in Vietnam.

ALAN GEORGE BROWN is a graduate of University College London, B. A. (Honors) and a postgraduate diploma in librarianship. He was formerly employed by J. Walter Thompson Co. , Ltd. and was previously a Lecturer, School of Librarianship, North Western Polytechnic, London. Presently, he is a Lecturer, School of Library, Archive and Information Studies, University College London, London, England.

HENRY CUMMINGS CAMPBELL is a Canadian who secured his education at the University of British Columbia, Toronto University and Columbia University. During World War II he was a librarian and film producer for the Canadian National Film Board. After a career with the United Nations in New York and with UNESCO in Paris, he became Chief Librarian of the Toronto Public Library in 1956, and has been there ever since. Currently, Campbell is First Vice President of IFLA. He has made significant contributions to the literature through the UNESCO Bulletin for Libraries, through his Handbook on the International Exchange of Publications, Metropolitan Public Library Planning Throughout the World and other monographic publications.

MARY JOAN CAMPBELL was born in Canada and has degrees from the University of Manitoba, McGill University, and the University of Chicago. After beginning her professional career at the University of Manitoba, she moved to Chicago in 1948 and has been a medical librarian there ever since. She is presently Assistant Director for Technical Services, Library of the Health Sciences, University of Illinois, Chicago, and has taught several medical library science courses. She has been President, Chicago Library Club, a member of the Society of Typographic Arts, the Chicago Council on Foreign Relations, and edits the International Relations Section of the Medical Library Association Newsletter.

FRANCES LAVERNE CARROLL is a graduate of the Kansas State College, Pittsburg, University of Denver School of Librarianship and Western Reserve University School of Library Science (Ph. D.), U. S. A. After a career as a public school teacher and elementary, secondary and junior college librarian in Kansas, she joined the faculty of the School of Library Science, University of Oklahoma, in 1962. Climbing through the ranks, Dr. Carroll recently became a full professor there. She has been involved extensively in the international library scene, particularly in West Germany and Iran. In addition, she is the organizing chairperson of the IFLA Section for School Libraries. She is a member of Beta Phi Mu Honorary Library Science Society.

J. PERIAM DANTON, after education at Oberlin College, U. S. A. , the University of Leipzig, Columbia University School of Library Service, Williams College, and the University of Chicago (Ph. D.), embarked upon careers as an academic librarian and a naval officer. These careers were followed by a period of fifteen years during which he was Dean, School of Librarianship, University of California, Berkeley, and another period of fifteen years in which he taught and researched a variety of topics as a Berkeley faculty member. He has been a Fulbright Professor in Germany and in Austria and has consulted in several other countries. Danton has been President, American Association of Library Schools, and Chairman, IFLA Committee on Library Education. He is on the editorial boards of the Library Quarterly and the International Library Review.

DONALD P. ELY was educated at the State University of New York, Albany, Syracuse University (Ph. D.) and Columbia University, U. S. A. He has served on the faculty of Syracuse University since 1956 and is now a Professor and Director, Center for the Study of Information and Education as well as Director, ERIC Clearinghouse on Information Resources there. He was a Fulbright Lecturer at the University of Chile in 1963 and has recently completed an international assignment which took him to several countries. In 1965 and 1966 he was President, Association for Educational Communication and Technology, and he is a member of the American Library Association and the American

Society for Information Science. With Margaret Chisholm, he has
published several textbooks and research studies in audiovisual communications.

D. J. FOSKETT is a graduate of Queen Mary College, University
of London, U.K. and Birkbeck College, University of London, M.A.
After a period of employment in the municipal libraries of Essex
and the special library of the Metal Box Company, Ltd., London,
he accepted his present position, Librarian, Institute of Education,
University of London, in 1957. In 1964 he was Visiting Professor
at the School of Library Science, University of Michigan. Foskett
has been President of the Library Association in 1976 and President
of the Private Libraries Association, 1960-63. He has written on
classification and indexing, reference work, and international library
science and has contributed to the Times Literary Supplement and
Nature as well as to library science journals.

JOHN F. HARVEY was educated at Dartmouth College, University
of Illinois, and University of Chicago (Ph.D.), U.S.A. His career
has been divided between academic library science and library education. Previously, he was Dean, Graduate School of Library Science, Drexel University, Philadelphia and later Chairman, Department of Library Science, University of Teheran. He lived in Iran
for four years where he was the founder of the Iranian Documentation Centre and the Teheran Book Processing Centre. Recently,
he was Dean of Library Services, Hofstra University, Hempstead,
New York. He founded the Drexel Library Quarterly and the Church
and Synagogue Library Association and is currently on the editorial
board of the International Library Review.

JUDITH A. HOFFBERG is a graduate of Brandeis University and the
University of California at Los Angeles, U.S.A. with Masters degrees in both Italian language and literature and library science.
She has had several academic library positions and was in the special recruitment program, Library of Congress, 1965-66. She was
Fine Arts Librarian at the University of Pennsylvania until she
moved to the Glendale, California, Public Library where she headed
the Brand Library. In 1970 she founded the Art Librarians Society
of North America and is now its Acting Executive Secretary and Editor. She is a member of Phi Beta Kappa Honorary Society and
the Renaissance Society of America.

NORMAN HORROCKS was born in England and graduated from the
University of Western Australia, Manchester University and the University of Pittsburgh Graduate School of Library and Information Sciences (Ph.D.). He has been employed at the Manchester Public Library; British Council, Cyprus; the State Library of Western Australia; and the University of Pittsburgh Graduate School of Library
and Information Sciences. Currently, he is Director, School of Library Service, Dalhousie University, Halifax, Nova Scotia, Canada.
He has been Chairman, International Relations Round Table and International Relations Committee, American Library Association.
Horrocks is a member of the Beta Phi Mu Honorary Library Science
Society and a Fellow of the Library Association.

DAVID KASER is a graduate of Houghton College, University of
Notre Dame, and the University of Michigan (Ph. D.), U. S. A. He
became Assistant Director of Libraries, Washington University, St.
Louis, in 1959. Thereafter he was Director, Joint University Libraries, Nashville, and then Director of Libraries, Cornell University. He is Professor of Library Science, Indiana University,
Bloomington, at the present time. Kaser has been an American Library Association Counselor, Chairman, University Library Section
and President, Association of College and Research Libraries, Executive Board member, Association of Research Libraries, and
Chairman, Association of Southeast Research Libraries. Kaser has
published several books on publishing history as well as international library science. He has been Editor of College and Research Libraries and is a member of Phi Beta Kappa Honorary Fraternity.

JOHN G. LORENZ was Deputy Librarian of Congress, U. S. A. , 1965-
76. During most of the time when he was writing the present paper
he was Acting Librarian of Congress. Lorenz is a graduate of City
College, New York, Columbia University School of Library Service,
and Michigan State University. Recently he became Executive Director, Association of Research Libraries, Washington, D. C. Lorenz
has been an active leader in the International Federation of Library
Associations, the American Library Association, the Association of
Research Libraries, and has been a consultant to UNESCO and other
organizations.

ANNE PELLOWSKI is a graduate of the College of St. Theresa,
U. S. A. , Ludwig Maxmillian University in Munich and Columbia Uni-
versity School of Library Service. After a period as a children's
librarian in New York City and a period as a library school instruc-
tor in Maryland, Wisconsin, and New York, in 1966 she became
Children's Center Director, U. S. Committee for UNICEF, New York
City, her present position. She has been a member of numerous
American Library Association committees and has published The
World of Children's Literature and Folk and Fairy Tales Series.
Her language facility includes English, French, German, Spanish,
Polish, and Russian.

FRANK L. SCHICK was born in Vienna, has a B. A. from Wayne
State University, a B. L. S. and M. A. in Political Science from the
University of Chicago, and an M. L. S. and Ph. D. from the University
of Michigan. He has worked in the Wayne State University Library,
University of Michigan School of Library Science, U. S. Office of Ed-
ucation, School of Library and Information Science, University of
Wisconsin, Milwaukee, and is now Head of the Library Surveys
Branch, National Center for Education Statistics, Washington, D. C.
He has been active in international library standards and statistics
programs.

ANTHONY THOMPSON has Bachelor's and Master's degrees from
Cambridge University, England. His work at Cambridge was mostly
in European languages. After working in the British Museum, the
University of Cape Town, Edinburgh College of Art, and the Science

Museum, London, he was General Secretary, International Federation of Library Associations, 1962-70.   He was a faculty member of the Wales College of Librarianship, Aberystwyth, 1970-75. Thompson has published extensively in the fields of library vocabulary and international library association work.   Currently, he is a freelance author, lecturer and translator.

BRIAN C. VICKERY has an M. A. in Chemistry from Brasenose College, Oxford University.   He had a career as a chemist, was a chemical librarian in industry and spent four years as principal scientific officer of the National Lending Library, Boston Spa.   Later, Vickery was Librarian, University of Manchester Institute of Science and Technology, Head of Research and Development, Aslib, London, and finally and most recently, Director, School of Library, Archive and Information Studies, University College, London.   He has had numerous consultancies in England and Iran and has published several monographs.   Vickery is a Fellow of the Library Association, London.

INDEX

Aman, Mohammed M.   177, 179, 221-256, 275
American Association of School Librarians   115, 129-130
American Library Association   31, 43, 59-61, 95, 104, 129-130,
    146, 149, 163, 165-167, 178, 180, 208, 211, 219-220, 243, 263,
    267, 271, 276, 278
    International Library Education Committee   50-51, 60
    International Relations Committee   5, 49-52, 55, 60, 277
    International Relations Office   5, 46, 48-49, 57
    International Relations Round Table   v, 5, 50-53, 56-57, 275,
        277
American National Standards Institute   31, 34
Amir-Arjomand, Lily   105-106
ARLIS/NA (Art Libraries Society of North America)   271-272, 274,
    277
ARLIS/UK (Art Libraries Society of the United Kingdom)   271-274
Art libraries   270-274
Asheim, Lester   164, 171, 179
Association of International Libraries   39-40, 42-44, 53
Audio-visual media   201-220

Bereday, G. Z. F.   21, 28
Betancourt, Virginia   105-106
Bibliography   221-256
BIREME (Biblioteca Regional de Medicina)   142-144, 147
Boaz, Martha   v, 167-180, 275
Bone, Larry Earl   160, 163-166, 168, 178-180
Bottomore, T. B.   16, 27-28
Bowker, R. R. Company   226-229, 233, 254-256, 266
Brewster, Beverly   59, 178
British Council   24, 48, 156, 159, 277
British Library   69, 71-73, 80
Brodman, Estelle   134, 145
Brown, A. G.   181-200, 275

Campbell, H. C.   6, 13, 91-102, 162, 164, 175, 178-179, 266,
    275-276
Campbell, Joan   133-147, 276
Camputaro, Carolyn   ix
Canadian Library Association   53, 55-56, 59-61, 220
Canadian National Library   65, 73-75, 86-88, 90, 237, 246, 251,
    257-258